East Af   ning

In the world of competitive sport, debate surrounding the predictors of success is intense, and the disproportionate success of east African distance runners has generated much theorising. Within the academic community, research is specialised and has been restricted by isolation inside either the natural science or the social science communities. *East African Running: Towards a Cross Disciplinary Perspective* presents a rare collaboration between leading researchers from both sports sciences and social sciences to offer the fullest yet exploration of the questions raised by the east African running phenomenon. The text covers:

- Socio-economic and cultural perspectives
- Physiological perspectives
- Athleticogenomic perspectives

Presenting a uniquely integrated approach, this book is a fascinating resource for students and researchers interested in the sources of success in endurance sport.

Yannis Pitsiladis is Reader in Exercise Physiology and Director of the International Centre for East African Running Science (ICEARS) at the University of Glasgow. **John Bale** is Emeritus Professor of Sport Studies at Keele University. **Craig Sharp** is Emeritus Professor of Sport Science in the Centre for Sports Medicine and Human Performance at Brunel University, London. **Timothy Noakes** is Discovery Health Professor of Exercise and Sports Science at the University of Cape Town and Director of the UCT/MRC Research Unit for Exercise Science and Sports Medicine, Cape Town.

East African Running

Toward a cross-disciplinary perspective

Edited by Yannis Pitsiladis, John Bale, Craig Sharp and Timothy Noakes

Routledge
Taylor & Francis Group

LONDON AND NEW YORK

First published 2007
by Routledge
2 Park Square, Milton Park, Abingdon, Oxon OX14 4RN

Simultaneously published in the USA and Canada
by Routledge
270 Madison Ave, New York, NY 10016

Routledge is an imprint of the Taylor & Francis Group, an informa business

© 2007 Selection and editorial matter, Yannis Pitsiladis, John Bale,
Craig Sharp and Timothy Noakes; individual chapters, the contributors

Typeset in Goudy by
by Keystroke, 28 High Street, Tettenhall, Wolverhampton
Printed and bound in Great Britain
by The Cromwell Press, Trowbridge, Wiltshire

British Library Cataloguing in Publication Data
A catalogue record for this book is available from the British Library

Library of Congress Cataloging in Publication Data
East African running: toward a cross-disciplinary perspective/edited by
Yannis Pitsiladis . . . [et al.].
    p. cm.
Includes bibliographical references and index.
1. Running–Africa, East. 2. Athletes–Africa, East.
3. Running–Physiological aspects. 4. Human genetics.
I. Pitsiladis, Yannis, 1967–
GV1061.23.A35E37 2006
796.4209676–dc22   2006021399

ISBN10: 0–415–37787–0 (hbk)
ISBN10: 0–415–37788–9 (pbk)
ISBN10: 978–0–203–09934–6 (ebk)

ISBN13: 978–0–415–37787–4 (hbk)
ISBN13: 978–0–415–37788–1 (pbk)
ISBN13: 978–0–203–09934–6 (ebk)

Contents

Figures

We are indebted to the people and archives for permission to reproduce photographs. Every effort has been made to trace copyright holders, but in a few cases this has not been possible. Any ommissions brought to our attention will be remedied in future editions.

Tables

Contributors

John Bale is emeritus professor of Sports Studies at Keele University UK and guest professor at the University of Aarhus. He is also an honorary professor at the University of Queensland. Bale has pioneered the geographical study of sport and among his many publications are *Imagined Olympians* (University of Minnesota Press), (with Joe Sang) *Kenyan Running* (Frank Cass), and *Running Cultures* (Routledge). He has lectured at several universities in north America, Europe and Africa and has been a visiting professor at the University of Jyväskylä (Finland) and the University of Western Ontario.

Mike K. Boit went to St Patrick's High School in Iten, Kenya. He obtained degrees from Eastern New Mexico University, Stanford University, and the University of Oregon. He joined Kenyatta University in 1987 where he is currently the Chairman of Exercise and Sport Science. He teaches human anatomy and research methods (among other subjects) in addition to student advising from undergraduate to Ph.D. levels. In athletics he won a Bronze medal in 800 metres at the Munich Olympics event and a Commonwealth Gold medal in the same event in Edmonton, Canada, 1978.

Dirk L. Christensen is currently doing his Ph.D. on type 2-diabetes among the general population in Kenya, where he has also lectured. He has written extensively on many aspects of the success of Kenyan runners, including a book (in Danish) and a series of scientific papers on their diet intake and performance. These publications have mainly been based on field studies in Kenya. He is a former research assistant at the Copenhagen Muscle Research Centre in Denmark, and is currently with the Department of Epidemiology at the University of Copenhagen in Denmark.

Jim Denison is a lecturer in Coach Education and Sports Development at the University of Bath, United Kingdom. His book, *Moving Writing: Crafting Movement in Sport Research* (Peter Lang), is a co-edited scholarly monograph outlining various ethnographic writing practices in sport studies. He is also the author of, *Bannister and Beyond: The Mystique of the Four-Minute Mile* (Breakaway Books) and *The*

Greatest (Breakaway Books), the authorized biography of the Ethiopian long-distance running legend, Haile Gebrselassie. Denison is also the editor of *The Coach*, a bi-monthly magazine for track and field coaches. He is currently at work on a number of projects related to athletes' and coaches' experiences.

Kyriacos I. Eleftheriou graduated from University College London Medical School, where he also completed his basic surgical training. He is pursuing a career in Orthopaedic and Trauma Surgery and has a keen interest in sports-related injuries. He is part of a research group headed by Dr H. Montgomery and Mr F. Haddad investigating how environmental and genetic factors are involved in the regulation of bone remodelling in health and exercise as well as the processes of osteoporosis, bone healing and failure of joint prostheses.

Barry W. Fudge is in the final year of a Ph.D. at the University of Glasgow. His studies focus on the makings of the elite athlete, with particular emphasis on Kenyan endurance runners. The two chapters presented in this book by Barry Fudge are the culmination of a number of studies conducted at a high altitude training camp in Kenya (Global Sports Training Camp, Kaptagat, Eldoret). These studies provide a unique insight into the preparation of some of the best runners in the world for major competition (i.e. Athens Olympics, Helsinki World Championships) and although these chapters do not provide an explanation for the 'east African running phenomenon', they do challenge traditionally accepted paradigms in sport and exercise science.

William H. Goodwin is a forensic geneticist at the University of Central Lancashire. He has studied polymorphisms in mitochondrial DNA for the purposes of assessing the evolutionary history of modern humans and also as a tool in human identification.

Yolande Harley gained her Ph.D. in exercise physiology from the University of Cape Town (UCT), South Africa, specializing in research investigating the integrative nature of fatigue and the complex relationship between multiple physiological factors and ethnic performance differences. Her work has involved collaboration with many varied research groups, including genetic studies with the Chemical Pathology Department at UCT, muscle biochemistry research with the Exercise Physiology Laboratory of the University of California at Berkeley, neuromuscular work with colleagues from University College Dublin, and CNS research with the Biomedical Engineering Unit at UCT. She currently works as a scientific writer in the United Kingdom.

Grant Jarvie is Chair and Head of the Department of Sports Studies at the University of Stirling. His first book back in 1985 was about Class, Race and Sport in South Africa while his most recent book *Sport, Culture and Society: Can Sport Change the World?* (Routledge, 2006) provides further insights into sport's social role in different parts of the world, including Africa. He is an Honorary Professor with the Academy of Physical Education and Sport, Warsaw, Poland. Grant is a past President of the British Society of Sports History and Convenor of the British Sociological Association Sport Study Group. Born in Motherwell, Scotland he has lectured throughout the world and currently serves as a Panel Member on the 2008 Research Assessment Exercise for Sport-Related Studies.

Bengt Kayser is professor at the Faculty of Medicine of the University of Geneva in Switzerland and director of the Institute of Movement Sciences and Sports Medicine. One of his early research interests concerned the study of the limits to human endurance performance at high altitude. At present his main areas of research concern the limits of endurance exercise, physical activity for health and health promotion.

David Kingsmore graduated from Aberdeen University with a medical degree in 1992. After completing a research degree in pharmacology and a doctorate in surgery, he completed his surgical training in 2005 specializing in renal transplant and vascular surgery. Initially involved in exercise testing of athletes in extreme conditions, he now has applied these techniques to investigating peripheral vascular disease and peri-operative cardiac risk in addition to working as a full time renal transplant and vascular surgeon in the Western Infirmary and Gartnavel Hospitals in Glasgow, Scotland.

Henrik B. Larsen is a researcher at the Copenhagen Muscle Research Centre, University of Copenhagen, where he has studied the physiology of running. He is author of many articles on different aspects of sports physiology. He is a former 400 m runner and has represented Denmark on the junior national team. He is also a former Danish middle- and long-distance running coach (1987–95). Currently he is pursuing a number of scientific investigations attempting to reveal the reasons for the Kenyan superiority in middle- and long-distance running.

Helen M. Luery works at University College London as Head of Cardiopulmonary Exercise Testing at the Institute of Human Health and Performance and conducts research into the role of exercise in the prevention and treatment of disease, the role of Cardiopulmonary Exercise Testing in the evaluation of surgical patients and the interaction between genetics and exercise training. Helen has received certification in Cardiopulmonary Exercise Testing at University of California Los Angeles and is a member of the board of advisors for the International Society for Exercise Intolerance Research and Education.

Daniel G. MacArthur is a Ph.D. student at the Institute for Neuromuscular Research at the Children's Hospital at Westmead in Sydney, Australia. He completed a Bachelor of Medical Science (Honours) degree at the University of Sydney in 2002, receiving the University Medal. His research focuses on the functional consequences and evolutionary history of a common null polymorphism in the *ACTN3* gene, which results in complete deficiency of the skeletal muscle protein α-actinin-3 in more than a billion humans worldwide, and has recently been shown to be associated with athletic performance and skeletal muscle function (MacArthur and North (2004) 'A gene for speed? The function and evolution of α-actinin-3', *Bioessays* 26:786–95).

John Manners is a writer widely recognized as an authority on east African athletes. He spent a year in Kenya as a child accompanying his father, who was doing anthropological field work among the Kalenjin. He returned to the same area ten years later as a teacher and athletics coach, and later still as a journalist. Since the mid-1970s, he has written on east African runners for such publications as *Time*, *Sports Illustrated* and *Runner's World*, and contributed to documentaries for CBS, NBC, BBC 1 and Channel 4. He was the first to attempt a rigorous exploration of the ethnic dimension of east African running.

Hugh E. Montgomery is a consultant in Intensive Care Medicine at UCL Hospitals, and Director of the UCL Institute for Human Health and Performance. He obtained a first class degree in circulatory/respiratory physiology in 1984, and graduated from medical school in 1987. His work has emphasized the development of an approach to studying human disease through the examination of health. In particular, he pioneered the use of gene-environment interaction models to explore human (patho)physiological pathways. He has published more than 150 scientific articles, and has written and edited medical and scientific texts.

Brian Moore has been working in the field of applied sports haematology since 1999. He has haematologically profiled many of the world's leading athletes including World and Olympic Champions and record holders, across a range of disciplines, including athletics, rowing, swimming, sailing and triathlon, through two Olympic Games. He was a global collaborator in the Australian Institute of Sport projects investigating patterns of erythropoietic activity amongst elite athletes and relating them to performance. He completed his Ph.D. under the supervision of Professor Craig Sharp and is currently project leader of the Global Haematological Profiling Initiative supporting the Great Britain Olympic squads in their preparations toward Beijing.

Kathryn H. Myburgh is Head of the Department of Physiological Sciences and Director of the Exercise Science and Muscle Biology Groups at Stellenbosch University, South Africa. She serves as the current President of the Physiological Society of Southern Africa. She learned her trade as a Sport Scientist at the University of Cape Town, followed by further postdoctoral training in Biology at Stanford University and University of California at San Francisco. She is applying her past experience as an international-calibre artistic gymnast, junior national coach and international judge to the sport of athletics, assisting the Centre of Excellence for Youth and Junior athletes in the Boland region of South Africa.

Norman Myers is a Fellow of Oxford University and an Adjunct Professor at Duke University (USA). Norman took up residence in Kenya in mid-1958, where he spent 24 very agreeable years before switching to England in late 1982. Within a month of his first arrival in Kenya he took up coaching of several prominent distance runners in the Kisii highlands and was astonished at the seemingly easy-going attitude to training. Many of the daily work-outs were no more than Myers would have done while a student at Oxford University, even though that training did nothing better than equip him to run against several dozen European and American Universities. He subsequently went on to coach athletes from other Bantu tribes, notably the Kikuyu and Kamba; and, more notably, the Nandi and Kipsigis and other Kalenjin tribes, and also the Maasai tribe. By 1970 he held coaching diplomas from Britain, Kenya and California, though he considers that because those mainstream coaching methods were rather inflexible, they did not offer sufficient creativity for world-class athletes. He likewise applied his training methods to his own preparations for the up-and-down trip on Kilimanjaro, for which he held the record for a number of years.

Timothy D. Noakes is Professor in the Discovery Health Chair of Exercise and Sports Science at the University of Cape Town and Visiting Professor in Exercise Science at the University of Glasgow. He is also director of the MRC/UCT Research Unit for Exercise Science and Sports Medicine. He is author of *Lore of Running* and has run more than 70 marathon and longer foot races including seven 90 km Comrades Marathons with a best time of 6hrs 49min. His research interests are the role of the brain in regulating exercise performance and fluid and thermal balance during exercise. He is rated as an A1 scientist, the highest such rating, by the National Research Foundation of South Africa.

Kathryn N. North is the Douglas Burrows Professor of Paediatrics in the Faculty of Medicine at the University of Sydney. Professor North is trained as a paediatric physician, neurologist and clinical geneticist and has a doctorate from the University of Sydney for Research into Neurogenetics. She completed a postdoctoral fellowship in Boston at Harvard Medical School and returned to Australia in 1995 as the recipient of the Children's Hospital Research Career Development Award. At the Children's Hospital at Westmead, she is Head of the Neurogenetics Research Unit and Deputy Head of the Institute for Neuromuscular Research. Her laboratory research interests focus on the molecular basis of inherited muscle disorders – particularly the muscular dystrophies and congenital myopathies – as well as genes which influence normal skeletal muscle function and elite athletic performance.

William O'Connell, or Brother Colm as he is best known, is Director of Athletic Coaching at St Patricks High School in Iten, Kenya. This school has been credited with producing the greatest number of successful runners among schools in Kenya, if not the entire world. St Patricks-Iten was founded in 1961 by the Irish Patrician Brothers. At the time of his arrival at the school in 1976, there were only *murram* (muddy) roads, the school had no electricity, telephone or even regular water supply. He arrived the week in 1976 that saw the withdrawal of Kenyan and African athletics from the Montreal Olympics. A fellow teacher at the school was Peter Foster who was the brother of Brendan (Big Bren) who was running the 10,000 m. Peter was instrumental in developing Brother Colm's interest in athletics. Brother Colm has helped to produce some of the best runners in the world such as Wilson Kipketer, Mathew Birir, Bernard Barmasai, Susan Chepkemei, Seif Said Shaheen, Isaac Songok and Augustine Choge.

Vincent O. Onywera went to Moi High School Kabarak in Nakuru, Kenya. He obtained his bachelor's and master's degrees from Kenyatta University. He joined Kenyatta University in 1995 as an undergraduate student and was awarded a university scholarship that enabled him to rise through the ranks of graduate assistant, tutorial fellow to lecturer in the Department of Sports and Exercise Science. He is the coordinator of the Human Performance Laboratory at Kenyatta University. He teaches exercise physiology, nutrition for human performance, fitness testing and kinathropometry (among other subjects). He is also an advisor to undergraduate students at the university. Vincent is a founding member of ICEARS (International Centre for East African Running Science). He is in his final year of a Ph.D. focusing on the physiological and genetic determinants of elite Kenyan running success.

Robin Parisotto has had over 20 years' experience in haematology laboratories most recently testing the blood of elite athletes at the Australian Institute of Sport (AIS) for a period of almost 9 years. Parisotto's haematological investigations into elite athlete performance eventually culminated in the ground-breaking development of the first ever blood tests to be used at the Olympic Games for the purposes of detecting recombinant erythropoietin (EPO). He has published some 20 papers in various journals and co-authored a chapter in the American College of Sports Medicine Resources for Clinical Exercise Physiology on the use of haematological markers as indicators of health, illness or to detect blood doping.

Yannis Pitsiladis is a Reader in Exercise Physiology at the Institute of Biomedical and Life Sciences at the University of Glasgow and Director of the 'International Centre for East African Running Science', or ICEARS (<www. icears.org>) set up to investigate the physiological, genetic, psycho-social and economic determinants of the phenomenal success of east African distance runners in international athletics. Recent projects include the study of west African sprinters (including elite sprinters from the USA) and the study of world-class swimmers. He is a Visiting Professor in Exercise Physiology at two Kenyan universities: Kenyatta University (Nairobi) and Moi University (Eldoret).

Robert A. Scott started studying the success of east African runners as part of his undergraduate degree, following his interest in the determinants of human performance. After graduating with a B.Sc. (Hons) in Physiology and Sports Science, he continued to work in this area by undertaking a Ph.D. The perception that the success of African runners is a genetically mediated phenomenon was investigated during Robert's Ph.D. studies, where he undertook the first studies to use genetic techniques to investigate the determinants of east African running success.

Craig Sharp graduated in 1956 in Veterinary Medicine from Glasgow University, joined Veterinary Physiology there under Dr (later Sir) James Black, Nobel Laureate, later transferring to the Department of Experimental Medicine, under W. F. H. Jarrett FRS. Seconded to Kenya in 1964, he joined Birmingham University's Department of Sports Science in 1971. Selected for four Olympic Games as coach or physiologist, but alas not as a runner, he co-founded and directed the British Olympic Medical Centre. He is Emeritus Professor of Sports Science at Brunel University, has honorary chairs at Stirling and Exeter, and an external post at the International Equine Institute, Limerick, Ireland.

Klaas R. Westerterp is a professor in Human Energetics at Maastricht University, the Netherlands. Among his present fields of interest in research are energy metabolism and body composition, with special emphasis on observations in daily living conditions using accelerometers and labeled water. From 1997 to 2003 he was a member of the Editorial Board of the *British Journal of Nutrition*. From 1999 to 2005 he was head of the Department of Human Biology. He is member of the FAO/WHO/UNU Expert group on Human Energy Requirements.

Bezabeh Wolde is a lecturer in Physical Education and Sport at Kotebe College of Teacher Education, Addis Ababa, Ethiopia and during his time as the Secretary General of the Ethiopian Olympic Committee was instrumental in facilitating the first demographic and genetic study to investigate the determinants of Ethiopian running success (see Scott *et al.* (2003) 'Demographic characteristics of elite Ethiopian endurance runners', *Medicine and Science in Sports and Exercise* 35, 1727–32).

Foreword

Shortly after I arrived in Kenya in 1958, I was asked to coach a group of Kisii athletes in the western sector of Kenya overlooking Lake Victoria. These were Bantu people, quite distinct ethnically from the Nilo-Hamitic people next door who included the Kalenjin tribes who have provided the bulk of Kenya's famous distance runners for almost half a century. Kenya is a kind of ethnic crossroads in sub-Saharan Africa, featuring four ethnic groupings who are almost as different from each other as British people are from Eskimos. Not only the Kisii but other Bantu tribes in Kenya such as the Kikuyu and Kamba, also non-Bantu tribes such as the Maasai and Somalis, have supplied runners who could take on the best in the world. Not all of these fundamental ethnic factors have been fully recognized by certain observers who have written about the 'secrets' of what makes Kenya's runners tick, so I am delighted to find a book comprising some of the best analyses by some of the best experts in the field – just as I feel gratified to write this Foreword.

On arrival in Kisii-land I found that two of the local athletes, Nyandika Mayoro and Arere Anentia, had already established themselves as world-class athletes over 5,000 and 10,000 metres. Yet they had accomplished this almost entirely through self-coaching – or, as they themselves agreed, virtually no coaching at all. Their training was a case of 'Just go out and run as you feel like it', with next to nothing in the way of interval training, let alone fartlek and other elaborations. So I told them about the kinds of training I had been put through while a student at Oxford and working with the famous Austrian coach Franz Stampfl who had supervised Bannister, Chataway and Brasher. I had never achieved much as a runner and I had almost blown a gasket to break half an hour for six miles, but I had learned how one could greatly improve through interval running and other forms of systematized training.

The following year I was posted to Maasailand where I encountered a tribe with no experience of athletics at all but with raw talent in astonishing abundance. To cite a single instance: I organized a tribal sports day, the first ever. The Maasai declined to take part: what was the point of running round and round a track in the equatorial sun? The only persons who agreed to take part were young men in the local detention camp who were offered a one-week reduction of sentence.

Running barefoot on a sandy patch of savannah, clad in nothing but the traditional tribal cloak, a group of teenagers broke two minutes for 800 metres while scarcely breaking sweat, and others showed similar talent over 1500 and 5,000 metres. The Maasai subsequently excelled at middle distance rather than long distance, as witness their medals at international level, and for reasons that nobody has researched in depth.

I then took up residence in Nairobi, where I remained for 21 years. I enjoyed coaching various athletes from time to time, including the Kisii man Naftali Temu who won the 1968 Olympics 10,000 metres, and Douglas Wakihuru, a Kikuyu living at sea level in Mombasa and winner of leading marathons (so much for the supposed imperative of living at altitude). I eventually worked with a dozen athletes who gained fame and (eventually) fortune at international level – and they comprised as many non-Kalenjin runners as outright Kalenjins, notwithstanding the popular view that most Kenyan runners are from the Nandi, Kipsigis and other Kalenjin tribes.

The most important point in all this is that I did not coach anyone in a conventional sense, even though I held a Kenyan coaching diploma to go with the one I had gained in Britain and one in California. For one thing I did not have the time to see athletes on a frequent and regular basis. For another and more important thing, the athletes did not particularly want to be coached in usual fashion. They would gladly be advised or guided, but specific coaching instructions were not for them. They ran because they simply enjoyed it and because they felt nobody else could have much idea of what they could do or wanted to do. Only they could figure what was truly quality training or ultimate racing: 'I am the one in charge of my exhaustion point'. This accorded with my own view of coaching, that the only real coach an athlete can trust is the person he sees in the mirror, and only he can really work out what would be the most productive form of training on any particular day. An outsider can offer 'big picture' ideas and supply various other sorts of support, but that is all.

I put these views into personal practice when I took a crack at the record for up and down Kilimanjaro. I had acclimatized to altitude at Nairobi's 5,600 feet for only four years; does one have to be born and bred at altitude in order to gain the full benefit (could it be genetically encoded?). I put in a half year of distance training, culminating in three trial efforts each extending over a weekend. Came the day when I left the Outward Bound School at Loitokitok on the Kenya side of the mountain, heading off just before dawn. I ran up through maize fields and montane forest, then jogged up moorlands and finally maintained a fast stride up the scree to the crater rim and the eventual summit, all of it non-stop for 13,000 feet and taking almost exactly nine hours. Then a speedy descent in four hours and 38 minutes, to take one hour and a half off the previous record. My effort was subsequently cut by 18 minutes by an Outward Bound instructor, the School believing the record should be 'theirs'. To my best knowledge, that is how things stood for decades despite occasional efforts by European athletes spending a few months in Kenya by way of Olympic training. Today we have the spectacle of

Africans taking huge chunks off the record, needing a mere eight hours for the round trip. Stupendous indeed.

My own run in February 1962 proved to be one of the finest days in my whole life. I sensed that I was not running 'against' the mountain, rather I was running with it. I felt I was carrying on a conversation with it the entire way. Fanciful as it may sound, I felt that as long as I was doing it together with the dear mountain, I was drawing strength from it. I never felt totally tired, and at the end of it all I jumped into my car and drove 120 miles back to Nairobi, no sweat. In fact, when I reached the halfway stage in the descent, I felt I did not want to sully a fine day in company with the mountain by using it for a mere record. I broke off my run to go picking mountain flowers, taking 45 minutes for the simple pleasure of it.

I felt I had spent a day running in the spirit of what I had learned from numerous African athletes. 'We run because we like it, through the light bright land'.

Professor Norman Myers, MA, Ph.D.
11 February 2006

Introduction

Craig Sharp and John Bale

'*Semper ex Africa aliquid novi*', wrote Pliny the Elder two millennia ago, and such novelty is still a truism, as is herein demonstrated, regarding modern African endurance running success, whose causes the subsequent chapters vigorously attempt to chart. The Kenyan population of 32 million represents 0.5% of the world. Yet in 2004, 51% of the world top 10 male performances from 800 m to the Marathon, (including the steeplechase) were run by Kenyan athletes, and in the equivalent all-time top 20 IAAF male outdoor lists of June 2005, 55% were Kenyan, whose women athletes are rapidly emulating their menfolk, especially in the longer distances. One might also note that, at about three million or 10% of the population, the Kalenjin group provides an unduly high proportion of those Kenyan runners. Similarly, but not quite so emphatically, Ethiopia has revealed a relative 'overproduction' of elite runners. As athletics fans we both recall the inspiring victories of Abebe Bikila in the 1960 and 1964 Olympic marathons.

Kenya first gained tremendous Olympic success in 1968, with gold from Kipchoge Keino, Amos Biwott and Naftali Temu, in 1500 m, 3,000 m steeple-chase, and 10,000 m respectively. One of us (CS) realized that Kenyan runners were very serious long before, when one day, at the Kabete track in 1964, one of them said to him: 'We won't be seeing you for a while, Craig – we are off to altitude training camp.' 'But, you *are* at altitude,' he said, 'this track is over 1500 m.' 'Ah, that's not altitude for us,' they said, 'we're off to Thomson's Falls!' (in Nyahururu, almost 1,000 m higher).

Craig's interest in east African running stemmed from running cross-country for Scotland and in spending much of the 1960s working as a scientist in Kenya, living on the edge of the Muguga forest, at an altitude of some 2,500 m, 17 miles 'up the hill' from Nairobi, near the edge of the Rift Valley Escarpment. He once won the annual 54-mile race-walk from Nairobi to Naivasha (in 1965), ran the then-fastest ascent of Kilimanjaro (in a time which coincidentally almost exactly equalled Tim Noakes' excellent personal best for the Comrade's Marathon), and used to run the (nine miles) drag for the Limuru Hunt, played squash for Kenya, and timed his pet cheetah over 220 yards (201.2 m) at 7.0 s (mean), i.e. 29 m.s^{-1}, or 64 mph. Thus, Craig's is a triple interest; in running, in east Africa and in Sports Science, as is that of almost all of the authors featured in the following chapters.

The contributors to this book discuss many aspects of the spectacular African running success of recent years. Yet in the 1970 Commonwealth Games, Craig's friend and sometime training partner, Lachie Stewart of Scotland, beat reigning Olympic Champion Naftali Temu to gold in a sprint finish in the 10,000 m. In 1982, David Moorcroft, running alone and unpaced took over five seconds off Henry Rono's great 5,000 m world record, to post 13:00.41. Although beaten by 0.62 s by Wilson Kipketer, Sebastian Coe's 800 m world record of 1:41.73 lasted more than 16 years and today remains the third fastest in history. So, there was a period when Great Britain, never mind the rest of the world, could challenge the best African runners. And in Paula Radcliffe we still can. But among the men, that happens no longer – and this book considers some of the possible reasons why not.

The book breaks new ground in several ways. First and foremost it brings together authors from a wide range of scholarly disciplines. The few existing books on east African running have approached the subject from either 'cultural' (e.g. Bale and Sang (1996) *Kenyan Running*, London: Frank Cass) or 'training' perspectives (e.g. Dave Prokop (ed.) (1975) *The African Running Revolution*, Mountain View: World Publications). The present book, however, has contributions from scholars whose specialisms range from sociology to genetics. Such an approach stresses the limitations of monocausation and the different contributions that varied disciplines can make to the exploration of body-cultural practices. Additionally, the book has contributions from north America, Africa, Australia and Europe, revealing a global interest in the east African 'running phenomenon'.

The text contains 14 chapters: two are sociological and two historical; one relates to fluid balance, and two to nutrition; four deal with physiological aspects; and three cover what Craig has termed 'athleticogenomics'.

The first contribution, John Bale's 'Kenyan Running before the 1968 Mexico Olympics', traces the rise of athletics there from the early local sports meetings in the 1920s, noting the importance of the famous Alliance High School's athletics, under Edward Crittenden and later Carey Francis, who might be termed 'the father of Kenyan running'. The Alliance High School had been founded by the Church of Scotland Mission, and Craig remembers watching their inter-house 4 × 440 yards relay, which was won in a time faster than the then (1965) Scottish Native Record, i.e. by one school house team! In the early 1950s, after the establishment of the Kenya AAA, Kenyan athletes competed at the British AAA championships at London's White City and turned in fine performances in the high jump and javelin as well as in the distance events. Kenya's first major medals came from Seraphino Antao in the 1962 Commonwealth Games, with gold in the 100 and 220 yards. Thus John Bale notes that early Kenyan athletes were at least as competitive in speed and power events as in endurance running! Indeed, he poses the query as to why Kenya has declined in such disciplines.

This is followed by Grant Jarvie's chapter on 'The promise and possibilities of running in and out of east Africa' that fluently discusses the sociology of market forces affecting African runners, whereby relatively large numbers of them 'defect', mainly to Europe. The reasons for this 'trade in muscle' are almost entirely financial; for example, Commonwealth and two-time world champion as well as world-record holder Stephen Cherono (running for Qatar as Said Saaeed Shaheen) reputedly has some 50 dependents living on his earnings. Jarvie applies a revealing 'location quotient' to highlight running 'hot-spots' by country, gained by relating a country's number of runners in the world top three (at events from 800 m to Marathon) to that country's population, expressed as a percentage of the global population. Unsurprisingly, Kenya heads the world list.

John Manners in 'Raiders from the Rift Valley: cattle raiding and distance running in east Africa' attempts to bridge history, ethnography and genetics in an imaginative and entertaining hypothesis. His idea is that traditional practices of Kenya's Kalenjin and other east African pastoral peoples may have functioned indirectly as selection mechanisms offering significant reproductive advantages to strong runners. After briefly examining the extraordinary success of the Kalenjin and the likelihood that it may in some degree be attributable to collective genetic factors, Manners cites ancient practices of east African pastoralists, ranging from cattle raiding to female circumcision, to suggest that these peoples were deliberately 'breeding for bravery' to strengthen their military forces, and that in doing so they may also have been selectively favouring hereditary traits that have proven instrumental in successful competitive distance running.

Jim Denison in 'The Haile Gebrselassie story: a biography of difference' relates his experiences in trying to research and write Haile's biography, and he succeeds in providing an insightful account of the local citizen, family man and role model inside the athlete; a reminder that the public face of such celebrities may be very different from their private persona. This acts as a reminder that great sportspersons from poorer countries play a different, and probably far more influential, social role than their equivalents in more affluent regions. Denison also reminds us of the problematic nature of European representations of 'the African'.

On the vital and controversial aspect of fluid intake, Barry Fudge, Yannis Pitsiladis, David Kingsmore, Timothy Noakes and Bengt Kayser, in 'Outstanding performances despite low fluid intake: the Kenyan running experience', note the striking finding of remarkably low daily fluid intakes in senior and junior runners of the highest elite status. These amount to about 1.1 litres and 1.2 litres respectively of water and tea, per day, much less than, for example, American College of Sports Medicine (ACSM) recommendations. The authors pose an intriguing and important question, as an aside, on whether the Africans drink too little – or are the ACSM recommendations too high? Are results from the hot and humid laboratory experiments genuinely transferable to the track and road, or are they unrepresentative of race conditions? The authors pursue the possibility that there may exist a 'tolerable range of dehydration' which not only will *not* decrease performance, but which may advantage the runner by decreasing body mass. But they note that this needs to be investigated experimentally.

Appropriately following fluid, come two contributions on nutritional aspects. The first, by Barry Fudge, Bengt Kayser, Klaas Westerterp and Yannis Pitsiladis on 'Energy balance and body composition of elite endurance runners: a hunter-gatherer phenotype?' provides an eloquent discussion on the implications for health and performance of short-term negative energy balance, practised as a form of body mass-cycling, such that the elite Kenyan endurance runners may start their races several kilograms, or 5–10%, lighter than their routine body mass. In this, they are similar to some other sports (e.g. martial arts, boxing and light-weight rowing) in which competitors have to 'make the weight'. Fudge and colleagues provide data on Kenyan runners, and on the effects of reducing body mass on endurance running performance, and on the effects of experimental variation on the distribution of body mass. They look to road-cycling and migratory birds for comparisons, and speculate on what is tantamount to an evolutionary origin of the practice, via a hunter-gatherer culture, which involved seasonally variable food-store (and body-mass) cycling, with lowering of body mass providing a possible ergogenic effect on endurance running ability. They end their chapter with the splendid conjecture that the rationale for their hypothesis: 'is reflected by the hegemony in world endurance running for the last several decades' of east African competitors.

Dirk Christensen, in 'Diet and endurance performance of Kenyan runners; a physiological perspective', then provides a detailed field study, concluding that the Kenyans' 'simple, and in some aspects sub-optimal, diet' cannot explain their great performances. Indeed, if anything, they perform well in spite of their diet. Hence, either their diet is sub-optimal – in which case they would perform even better if they improved it; or, Kenyans in general, and their runners in particular, have adapted physiologically to sub-optimal intakes, in which case their performance would not necessarily be improved by dietary changes. Nevertheless, they are forced into dietary changes when they live or compete abroad. This may affect or be affected by the lipid-oxidation marker enzyme 3-hydroxyl-coA-dehydrogenase (HAD), which is up to 50% higher in Kenyans compared to Scandinavian elite runners, and the author discusses the significance of this.

Henrik Larsen, in 'Dominance of Kenyan Kalenjins in middle- and long-distance running', presents the first of the physiology chapters. His is an in-depth report on $\dot{V}O_2$ max, fractional utilization of $\dot{V}O_2$ max, leg muscle oxidative enzymes, HAD, muscle capillaries, plasma lactate response, NH_3 response, and running economy in terms of $O_2.kg^{-1}.km^{-1}$, $O_2.kg^{0.67}.km^{-1}$ or $O_2.kg^{-0.75}.km^{-1}$. Of these parameters, Larsen notes that the main two differences are shown in the percentage utilization of $\dot{V}O_2$ max during racing and the better running economy, both of which he believes to be crucial, especially the latter.

But, he also cautions that the presence of Western managers, Western coaches, and the socio-cultural environment of 'Western' Kenya are also very important, as shown by Kalenjin, and specifically Nandi, success.

Kathryn Myburgh, in 'Understanding the dominance of African endurance runners: exercise biology and an integrative model', aims to understand the dominance of the African runners through a very ambitious integrative model of exercise biology. Here, she comprehensively and holistically considers the contribution of multiple biological systems, but with a major focus on running economy which many consider to be a factor of paramount importance in east African running ability. The holistic approach of this chapter covers almost the entire exercise physiology syllabus and emphasizes the interplay between biology and sport science disciplines and the importance of an in-depth understanding.

Yolande Harley and Timothy Noakes, in 'Studies of physiological and neuromuscular function of black South African distance runners', begin by reiterating Dr Myburgh's point that inter-individual differences in performance are the product of many different mechanisms, none of which is the exclusive 'limiting factor'. As befits one of the world's great sports physiologists and his colleague, they authoritatively and clearly discuss relevant anthropometric cardio-respiratory, biomechanical, metabolic, neuromuscular and central nervous system (CNS) factors in their integration, noting pertinently that 'fatigue during exercise involves both descending signals from the CNS to the periphery, as well as ascending signals to the CNS from the periphery'. They hypothesize that a 'central governor', involving the integrated function of multiple interrelated biological factors, might provide a higher final CNS motor output in black African runners, causing them to maintain a higher mean running speed over the course of a race than their Caucasian colleagues. Harley and Noakes specifically comment that they do not include genetic, nutritional, psychological, social or environmental factors in this particular chapter brief.

The physiology side is completed by Brian Moore, Robin Parisotto, Craig Sharp, Yannis Pitsiladis and Bengt Kayser in 'Erythropoietic indices in elite Kenyan runners training at altitude: effects of descent to sea level', who have, in the person of Dr Moore, researched (in conjunction with the Australian Institute of Sport) changes in a variety of blood parameters in Kenyan athletes in terms of their altitude training camps. In addition they provide important information regarding the 'OFF-hr' detection model of EPO use, and examine a variety of (independent) haematological parameter changes on descent from altitude camp. The data provide a very strong argument that the high haemoglobin values recorded at altitude among the Kenyan athletes are certainly not due to any form of 'blood doping', and indicate the significantly improved discriminatory power of these parameters relative to standard haemoglobin and haematocrit detection protocols.

Daniel MacArthur and Kathryn North in their 'Genes and human elite athletic performance' provide the first of three chapters about the topic, which Craig has termed 'athleticogenomics'. This is a rapidly burgeoning area in sports science, partly due to the vast increase in publicly available data on the location of many human genes, and partly to an increase in the understanding of the physiological and biochemical function of many such genes and of their possible relation to training and sport. They note that most associations have been made on Caucasians, but believe that there are suggestions that genetic factors influencing human performance 'may differ substantially between ethnic groups', and give examples of two polymorphisms strongly associated with Caucasian elite athletes, but which failed to show an association with equivalent east African cohorts. However, as they say, very many more linkage analyses, and more carefully targeted association studies need to be done.

Helen Luery, Kyriacos Eleftheriou and Hugh Montgomery in 'Genetics and endurance performance' critically view genetic markers associated particularly with: $\dot{V}O_2$ max; with oxygen delivery and utilization (involving ventilation, cardiac output, oxygen extraction, skeletal muscle mass and running economy); and with elite long-distance running. They note that there are over 100 gene variants related to human performance, but that there are 'virtually none to explain the physiological differences between elite African endurance athletes and their Caucasian counterparts'. In the case of Dr Montgomery's pioneering ACE I-allele, associated with fatigue resistance and enhanced endurance performance, a study by Pitsiladis and colleagues has attempted to identify an association of the ACE I/D genotype with endurance performance in east African runners, but neither genotype seemed associated with elite endurance status.

Robert Scott, William Goodwin, Bezabeh Wolde, Vincent Onywera, Mike Boit, William O'Connell and Yannis Pitsiladis review the 'Evidence for the "natural" east African athlete', partly via a clever look at the unique maternal and paternal genetic contributions. They begin by reminding the reader that all human populations are composed of subsets of African genetic variation. Thence they discuss nuclear variants and polymorphisms in mitochondrial DNA (mt-DNA), which are subject to a matrilinear pattern of inheritance (mitochondria not being transmitted by spermatozoa: and mtEVE being there at the beginning). In particular they have looked at mtDNA variation in elite Ethiopian athletes, but their data did not support a role for mtDNA polymorphisms in their running success. Switching their attention to the patrilinear Y-chromosome – the male equivalent of mtDNA, whose haploid nature implies that Y-haplotypes pass on undisturbed in their non-recombining state (apart from mutation) from one generation to the next – they have found three Y-chromosome haplogroups which are associated with elite athletic status in Ethiopians – possibly modulating their response to altitude? However, they are careful to note that such candidate genes may well not be unique to east Africa, but may confer advantage on any population, and their conclusion is that any single gene may simply 'fine-tune' performance, and that it is 'unjustified at present to identify the phenomenon of east African running success as genetically mediated'. But, note the words 'at present', although the authors are very careful to distance themselves from perpetuating a myth of genetic distance running superiority in terms of its presenting 'stereotype threat' to non-African runners.

In a book such as this there are inevitable omissions. There is little in it that deals with issues of gender though as women gradually come to match the performance of men in athletics, work on this subject will inevitably increase. Likewise, almost all of the book deals with two countries of eastern Africa rather than east Africa per se. It would be instructive in subsequent studies to examine the factors influencing running success (or relative lack of) in, say, Tanzania and Uganda. The former, in particular, may reveal the significance of political ideology in the history of African running.

In conclusion, the holistic view of east African endurance running success provided in the current text makes for a very interesting, challenging, and at times provocative set of possible explanations. Doubtless there are more to come, especially on the athleticogenomics side of the athletes, and probably also on aspects of their running biomechanics, as well as in terms of their psychology and training regimens. However, in their eclectic mix, the current chapters provide a highly authoritative, comprehensive and stimulating introduction to one of the most fascinating topics in world sport. Collectively, the contributors validate Pliny's prophetic view that there is indeed always something new coming out of Africa.

Part 1

Socio-economic and cultural perspectives

Chapter 1

Kenyan running before the 1968 Mexico Olympics

John Bale

Introduction

The 1968 Olympic Games are often regarded as the point of 'take-off' for the east African domination of middle- and long-distance running. At these Games athletes from Ethiopia and Kenya dominated most of the races that had traditionally been the preserve of European runners. The relative dominance of Kenyan running, in particular, is referred to in several of the chapters in this book but little work has been done to explore the antecedents and genesis of this cultural phenomenon. In this chapter I stress the cultural character of Kenyan running – the making of it by colonial policies and prejudices – and I seek to deny the existence of what are sometimes termed 'natural athletes'. In a sense, therefore, this chapter blurs the distinction explicit in the binary of nature–culture (or nature–nurture). In my exploration of pre- and early modern Kenyan running my approach is to explore the ways in which (mainly) colonial writers represented this body culture.

It is commonly assumed that those African runners who appeared on the Olympic stage in the late 1960s were, in some way, 'natural' athletes with 'raw talent'. This kind of rhetoric clashed with another, one that represented 'the African' as an 'idle savage' made listless from the African heat and humidity. It was also widely felt that if Africans were runners they would be sprinters – in the words of David Wiggins (1989: 158) they would have 'great speed but little stamina'. Today, however, east Africans are primarily admired for their long-distance running performances. Three problems present themselves in these sentences. As I noted, the concept of the 'natural athlete' presumes the utility of the binary of natural-cultural. It is today widely recognized that no person can be purely natural or purely cultural. Nature may be culture's other but there is much traffic between them (Watts 2005). Second, east Africa is not Africa; and east Africa is not Kenya. Within the broad region known as east Africa some countries are seen to 'produce' a disproportionate number of elite runners while others produce hardly any. As is shown in other chapters (e.g. Chapter 14 by Scott and colleagues), even within countries like Kenya and Ethiopia, there are marked regional variations in running 'productivity' (I make no excuses here for using metaphors from Economics for, after all, these athletes are produced). Additionally, it should be stressed that the word 'running' is far from transparent. As Brett St Louis (2003: 84) has noted, running may appear close to being a 'natural' activity and 'as a set of universalized physical activities', endowing it with 'intrinsic and naturalized properties that ignore the given and interested social contexts [and] their particular rules and regulations'. Running assumes a variety of 'configurations' that include, for example 'folk' running in pre-colonial Africa and 'achievement' (or 'sportized') running in the modern Olympic Games.

For purposes of convenience I will arrange this chapter around four broad chronological periods. The first is the germinal phase, dating from the early twentieth century to about 1920. The second is the incipient phase lasting from the 1920s until the 1930s; the third is the struggle for hegemony phase from the 1930s to the 1950s; the fourth is the take-off phase from the 1950s to 1968. This model was conceptualized by Robertson (1990) who included a fifth phase, that of uncertainty. This final stage is not included here, but if space permitted it would take the story of Kenyan running up to the present day, a topic dealt with by Grant Jarvie in the following chapter (Chapter 2).

Running in pre- and early-colonial Kenya

The anthropologists, travellers, missionaries and explorers who charted east Africa from the end of the nineteenth century onward made frequent allusions to the body cultural practices of indigenous peoples. To suggest that such practices were the 'germs' of modern sportized running is, I suggest, erroneous. There is little evidence in colonial writing to indicate that individuals who performed well in indigenous forms of athleticism could seamlessly convert those skills into superficially similar western forms. Here is a familiar historical problem, that of continuity or change. Of course, 'running' had existed in Africa from time immemorial but the Swedish traveller Gerhard Lindblom (1920), who in 1910–12 was studying the Kamba south of Mount Kenya, confirmed that 'no real sports' were found there. By this he meant no western sports – body-cultural activities that were characterized by markers of western norms. Most significant, perhaps, is that modern sport is structured by rules and regulations that are global in their application and acceptance (Stovkis 1992). In this sense, the rules and results of modern running form a kind of global 'currency', understood and adhered to in most nations of the modern world.

Lindblom's way of seeing, of course, reflected a European sensibility. The kinds of running which existed in the region that he was visiting were different from what he had experienced in his native Sweden. Running in east Africa was required for hunting and fighting. Additionally, running formed parts of certain games and also elements of rites of passage. In some cases running in pre- and early-colonial times had elements of competition. The colonial way of seeing east African running can be exemplified in several allusions to Maasai running. The nineteenth-century French geographer Elisée Reclus (1876: 364) observed that 'the men of pure Masai blood average six feet high, and generally have slim, wiry figures, admirable for running'. Others commented that 'the whole race (sic) is proficient in speedy and long-distance running' (Hinde and Hinde 1901: 38), while in a description of a Maasai shepherd it was noted that 'his gait, as he strides, is an example of what human carriage can be at its best' (Ross 1927: 130). Additionally, it was stated that the Maasai 'are extraordinarily fleet of foot, and can run without tiring for incredible distances. Their usual pace is a long, sloping trot' (Hinde and Hinde 1901). The 'incredible distances' noted above were sometimes quantified as part of the imperial project of measuring as much as possible when it came to describing native peoples. For example, John Boyes (1912: 61) believed that 'the Masai runner thinks no more of carrying a message sixty miles a day than we should a three mile stroll'. The American writer–explorer Ernest Hemingway (1954: 214), recalling his travels in Kenya, witnessed Maasai running 'smoothly, loosely and with pride. They were running too, at the pace of a fast miler'.

In their descriptions of indigenous body cultures, the European colonizers did not only use words and idealized language. More important for the history of African athletics was the introduction of western forms of running (i.e. racing) that were recorded by the scientific certainty of the stopwatch. As early as 1902, the year in which the regiment of the King's African Rifles was founded, the Harrow-educated soldier, ornithologist and racist, Captain Richard Meinertzhagen, organized a cross-country race for his soldiers at Muranga. He recorded that the winner took 'exactly 14 minutes' to complete the 3,600 metres course. Here we have two qualities of the European foot race that differed from the indigenous running of the native people. Time and distance were measured and recorded.

The Christian missions held sports days at least as early as 1906. Although the earliest of these events were more like junior school sports with events like obstacle and sack racing it did not take long for them to adopt the more conventional norms of achievement-oriented sport. By the early 1920s boys and girls were taking part in well-organized sports days at various mission stations throughout British East Africa. Pith-helmeted colonials were in charge but a large spectatorship of Africans showed these events to be popular (Bale and Sang 1996).

Missionaries and military had ideological agenda in encouraging the adoption of western sports among young African men. John W. Arthur who arrived at the Church of Scotland Mission at Thogoto, Kenya, to take care of physical education and sport, felt that the values of the English public schools should be disseminated among native peoples. Games and sports would be played for 'moral benefit as much as recreational relief'. Athletics and football would 'stiffen the backbone of these boys by teaching them manliness, good temper and unselfishness – qualities amongst others which have done so much to make a Britisher' (quoted in Murray-Brown 1972: 47). Baron Pierre de Coubertin (2000: 704) felt that if 'one wishes to extend to natives in colonized countries what we boldly call the benefits of "athletic civilization", they must be made to enter into the broad athletic system with codified regulations and comparative results, which is the necessary basis of that civilization'. He also argued that the time had come 'for sport to advance to the conquest of Africa [. . .] and to bring to the people the enjoyment of disciplined muscular effort' (ibid: 702). Additionally, it was felt that the introduction of competitive running (amongst other British sports) would serve as an alternative to the native dancing which was deemed sexually explicit and lascivious, and hence undesirable. Western running, therefore, was seen as a form of social control but for decades it was practised alongside the indigenous forms of running noted earlier.

Incipient sportization

Western running, with its characteristic of record(ing) rather than ritual (Guttmann 1978) was established in east Africa by missionaries, the military and other European agencies such as schools, plantation owners, police, and prison officers. However, in the early days a bureaucracy – one of the principal characteristics of modern sport – to organize sports events was missing. Running was disorganized and facilities (such as they were) varied in quality from place to place. Running 'tracks' were little more than uncut grassy spaces.

The bureaucratization of Kenya was initiated by the colony's first Director of Education, James Orr. In early 1924 he suggested that an African native sports association be formed. Following a meeting of prominent European members of the police, army, schools and church, the Arab and African Sports Association (AASA) was formed. Although the east Africa Protectorate had become the Kenya Colony, a national athletics federation, in the form assumed by many European nations by the mid-1920s, was not deemed appropriate. The AASA was not intended to cater for white settlers and the customary unofficial 'colour bar' remained in place. A hierarchical structure was built around local events from which athletes would be drawn for a national meeting.

By the 1920s the missionaries were organizing more formal athletics events. Such events were first held in the early 1900s but they blurred the distinction between playfulness and seriousness. During the 1920s Kenyan running could be described as hybrid in character. It was not yet fully westernized and retained much local tradition. To be sure, the formation of the AASA reflected modernity but in the composition of athletic events, the pre-modern co-existed with the modern. The flavour of local sports meetings in Kenya at the time was well caught in the words of Daphne Moore, later the wife of the Governor of Kenya, who attended a Maasai sports event in 1929:

> We trooped off to the sports ground after lunch and spent the afternoon there, till dark, watching the Maasai doing the high and long jumps, 100 yards, bolster bar, etc. For each event there was a junior and an open entry, the junior competitors being the boys of the Maasai Government School

[. . .] and the senior warriors from every part of the Maasai reserve. [. . .] The audience watched the proceedings with enormous interest and much display of partisanship, but mishaps on the part of competitors raised far more applause than exhibitions of athletic skill. The two most popular and most interesting events were the spear-throwing and the tug-of-war. [. . .] The target was a lion skin stretched out on sticks and the men had to throw from a distance of thirty yards.

(Watkins 1993: 57)

This description illuminates two aspects of Kenyan athletics in the late 1920s. First, recognisably modern events such as the 100 yards were contested alongside spear throwing, not for distance but for accuracy. The modern and the pre-modern took part alongside each other. Second, applause appeared to be greatest for the mishaps, performed by those who might be termed fools, clowns or grotesques. There was a place for fun and laughter that contrasted with the deadly seriousness of modern competitive sport. Also missing from the description are quantified results of the various events. Additionally, it could be added that the site on which the events took place was an open expanse of grassland edged by bushes with the athletes competing barefoot in native clothing.

The first formal athletics meeting held in Kenya under the auspices of the AASA for non-Europeans, was in early 1925 at the race course in Nairobi. Teams from the various districts competed against each other but it was not until the 1930s that competition took place between the provinces. The language used to describe these events reflected a European mind-set, the 'African Olympics' imposing the Coubertinian ethic on the African peoples. By 1929 Maasai sports days became important enough to attract officials from Nairobi, including the governor or his representative (Watkins 1993).

In 1926 Alliance High School ('the Eton of Kenyan schools') was founded in Kikuyu. The school was to leave an indelible mark on the history of Kenyan athletics. A master at the school, which was for native Africans only, Edward Crittenden, had been educated at Whitgift School in London and Oriel College, Oxford. He had been a sprinter at school and was able to renew his acquaintance with sport when he arrived at Alliance. Despite his educational background he favoured the fascistic trait of brawn over brain and asserted that to develop sport among native peoples a teacher should 'be prepared to throw himself vigorously into out-of-class activities, valuable lines such as games' (Kenya National Archives). The ethos that was established at Alliance was later to attract the headmastership of Carey Francis (see below), regarded by many as the 'father' of Kenyan running (Greaves 1969). Schools such as the Government African School (GAS) at Kapsabet that had been established in 1926 were also to become major agents in the sportization of Kenyan running.

The establishment of the AASA and the significance of growing competitive sports reflect the growth of western sport in Kenya. But it was not yet the

dominant form of body-cultural practice, and modern and pre-modern characteristics of running co-existed. Even so, the number of agencies promoting
athletics was going far beyond the schools, the missionaries and the army.
The arrival of R.G.B. Spicer as Commissioner of Police in 1925 stimulated the
growth of athletics among police recruits. But Spicer's racism could not be
hidden. He thought it necessary to push the mainly Kikuyu athletes 'hard', in
order that 'the comatose mind of the raw native may be awakened' (Spicer 1925:
7). Plantation owners were other major agents who used running to assist
in social control, to keep the locals busy and out of mischief. In 1933 Kipchoge
Keino's father won a six miles race organized by the tea plantation on which he
worked. His prize was a valuable four gallons of oil (Noronha 1970).

The hegemony of achievement sport

The breakthrough of achievement running dominating the traditional modes
was finally established in 1951 when the Kenyan AAA was formed. This bureaucracy symbolized a national unit that demarcated itself from the folk and
tribal traditions and while the flavour of early colonial sports meetings in Kenya
continued into the 1950s, the 1930s displayed signs of sporting modernity. One
of the basic characteristics of achievement sport is its quest for records and
recordings. The notion of a 'Kenyan record' barely existed in the 1920s. Nor did
international competitions. However, by 1934 the two were clearly recognized
when an inter-territorial athletics contest between Kenya and Uganda took
place at Kampala, Uganda. It was recorded that at the meeting the Kenyan
half-mile 'record' was reduced to 1 minute 59.3 seconds. In 1936 a Kenyan 'mile
record' of 4 minutes 38.5 seconds was recorded for Kamunya (Abmayr and
Pinaud 1994: 141). There was also a growing tendency to see Kenyan results
through the mind-set of the European – in other words, the use of statistics as a
basis for comparisons. In the early 1950s Carey Francis, the dynamic new
headmaster of Alliance High School, commented on a half mile performance of
1 minute 57.8 seconds by Luka Njeru. A two-minute half-mile in the conditions
prevailing in Kenya 'is in some sense comparable to a 4-minute mile in the great
world outside', he observed (Greaves 1969: 140).

The number of agencies encouraging serious sport had included the missions,
schools, military, plantation owners, and the prison service. However, these
agencies masked the contribution of individuals who had a disproportionate
impact on the changing ideology of Kenyan running. The aforementioned Carey
Francis exemplified the sporting-missionary–schoolmaster, commonly regarded
as a bearer of 'muscular Christianity'. He had been educated at Trinity College,
Cambridge where he was an able player of football. In the late 1920s he became
a lecturer in Mathematics at Peterhouse College. However, he resigned the
academic life and, in the spirit of Baden-Powellism, went to Kenya where he
'thought educating Africans would be something like running Christian scouts'
(Greaves 1969: 17). He nurtured sport at Alliance School and is regarded by

many as the father of Kenyan sport. He was prescient enough to predict that the African schoolboy would bear comparison with English boys 'in athletic prowess' (ibid.).

Internationalization of Kenyan running resulted from discussions held between Kenyan and Ugandan representatives in 1934 when it was agreed that an inter-territorial athletics competition would be held between the two colonies. The first of these was held at Kampala in the same year. The success of this meeting stimulated the governing bodies of both colonies to affiliate to the Amateur Athletic Association (AAA) of England in 1936.

The Kenyan AAA was founded in 1951, a sure sign that the status of athletics had become formalized. The international nature of Kenyan running, and the role of the army in its development, was reinforced in 1952 when a Kenyan member of the Kings African Rifles named Kipsang competed in the Malayan Championships and won the three miles event in 15 minutes 3.4 seconds. Another Kenyan won the javelin throw. Later in the year a multi-ethnic Kenyan team took part in the Indian Ocean Games in Madagascar, an event that attracted a team of French Olympic athletes. This event was significant in that it signalled the emergence of Nyandika Maiyoro in the 3,000 metres. It is recorded that he only started the race when the rest of the field was 100 metres down the track. Although still wearing his clothes he stripped as he ran and proceeded to win the race by 50 metres. Maiyoro was to become a major figure in the promotion of Kenyan running to a global audience. In 1953 a Kenyan team took part in an international meet in Zambia (then Northern Rhodesia) and dominated the event, the best performance being by a javelin thrower who threw nearly 200 feet (61 metres).

Disorganization featured in some of the early championships. The measurements of the tracks or, more likely, the distance run, were sometimes inaccurate. The number of laps each runner had completed could be confused if large numbers of athletes were taking part. For example, in the 'African Olympics' of 1947 the winners of the three miles and six miles were respectively timed as being much faster than the exiting world records. The excited spectators thought that a sensation had occurred until it was discovered that the races had been run over incorrect distances. Similar dubious performances were also recorded at the national championships of 1948 and 1949 (Bale and Sang 1996: 88–9).

In the 1940s and 1950s ambiguity could still be seen in the character of running in Kenya. While national championships could be held in stadia that would be recognized as specialized sports facilities by Europeans, the Africanist, Joy Adamson, included in her book *The Peoples of Kenya* an image of a 'six miles race' held on an open expanse of grassland, carrying a club and in native garb (Figure 1.1).

Figure 1.1 A Maasai runner taking part in a 'long distance race' held in Kenya in the 1940s or 1950s.

Racing in a global system

The formation of the Kenya AAA enabled it to prepare for participation in more major competitions, notably the Empire Games, a colonial mimic of the Olympics. The 1954 Empire Games were held in Vancouver and the Kenyan team, a diversified group of athletes made up of sprinters, distance runners, jumpers and throwers, were selected to compete. En route to Canada the team took part in the English AAA Championships at the White City Stadium in London. This was arguably the key moment in the history of Kenyan running – the first visit of a Kenyan athletics team to Europe. Competitions with neighbouring African nations had been replaced by entry into the global sports system.

It is worth noting, I believe, the way in which the British sporting press reacted to the presence of Africans at the English championships. The most likely Kenyan threat to British competitors (and the best of the generally unknown Kenyans) was thought to be the Maasai high jumper Jonathan Lenemuria. It was also possible, thought the broadsheet journalists, that another threat could come from a Kenyan javelin thrower. No mention was made of middle- or long-distance runners. On the eve of the 1954 championships, therefore, Kenya did not present an image of a nation of natural runners and potential champions. The two track events that are relevant to this discussion were the six miles and the three miles, run in that order on different days. In the six miles' championship the spectators were surprised to see a barefooted black athlete from Kenya, Lazaro Chepkwoney, lining up with some of the luminaries of the British track scene, notably Gordon Pirie. Chepkwoney's strategy was to rush into the lead and run at an uneven pace that, to an extent, upset his British antagonists (Figure 1.2). However, after 15 laps he dropped out, confirming the stereotype of the stamina-lacking African. Nevertheless, he was the first Kenyan competitor to contest a major European Championship event.

The following day the three miles' event took place and again a Kenyan faced the best that Britain could offer. The field included the well-known British runner Chris Chataway. The Kenyan was Nyandika Maiyoro from the Kissii district. Like his compatriot he set off at a fast pace that, if sustained, would produce a world record. He led the field for much of the race. In the final stages he was overtaken by the British runners, Chataway and Fred Green, who went on to break the world record. Maiyoro faded but still finished in third place, ahead of many of Britain's best distance runners. Following the meeting, it was recorded in *Athletics World* that two 15-year-old Kenyan boys had run under 15 minutes 30 seconds for the three miles, suggesting that the distance running potential was even greater than the presence of Chepkwony and Maiyoro might suggest.

Kenyans did not win any medals in Vancouver. They were noted by dedicated track fans but not by the world's sporting public. Kenyan athletes, therefore, did not appear to be natural athletic marvels who could emerge from Africa and defeat the best the West could offer. Indeed, Kenya was not the most successful African nation in the Vancouver Games. Nigerian and Ugandan athletes took the first three places in the high jump and Kenya was absent from the medal table. Maiyoro ran in the three miles and broke the Kenyan record but failed to gain a top placing.

Two years later the Kenyans made their first Olympic appearance at Melbourne. Maiyoro was again a dominant presence. Although meeting with no success in the heats of the 1500 metres he placed seventh in the 5,000 metres and beat Chataway by over 10 seconds. It was an impressive performance at the highest level of competition. Two years later Maiyoro and another Kenyan team returned to the White City on their way to the Empire Games in Cardiff. Maiyoro gained a silver medal in the three miles and a number of other Kenyans enhanced the nation's reputation. Arere Anentia won another three miles race, Kiptalem Keter was seventh in the half-mile and Bartonjo Rotich qualified for the final of the 440 yards hurdles. At the Cardiff Games the Kenyan team improved significantly on their Vancouver performance. Maiyoro was disappointing, but in the six miles Anentia and Kanuti Sum finished third and sixth respectively, while Rotich was third in the 440 yards hurdles. Leresae finished fourth in the high jump. The bronze medals of Anentia and Rotich signalled a landmark in Kenyan sports history – the first medals won by Kenyan athletes in major athletic competition.

The 1960 Rome Olympics are generally regarded as a major moment in the emergence of African running. It is associated with the marathon victory of the Ethiopian, Abebe Bikila. However, the performances of the Kenyans should

Figure 1.2 Lazaro Chepkwony running against Gordon Pirie during the AAA six miles championship in London, Friday evening, 9 July 1954 – the first occasion that a Kenyan distance runner had raced in Europe.

not be overlooked. If progress can be measured by Olympic performance Kenya was certainly on an upward trend. Maiyoro climaxed his career with an impressive sixth place in the 5,000 metres in an 'African record' time of 13 minutes 52.8 seconds. Other Kenyan successes were Seraphino Antao who reached the semi-finals of the 100 metres, and Rotich did likewise in the 400 metres hurdles.

By now Kenyan teams were regularly competing in the major international athletics festivals. In the 1962 (now) Commonwealth Games in Perth, athletes from a wider range of events than ever before took part. They ranged from the 100 yards to the six miles and from the 440 yards hurdles to the triple jump. Given the present day identification of long-distance running with Kenya, it is worth noting that the first major international gold medals came not from a distance runner but from a sprinter. In Perth, Antao won the 100 and 220 yards while Kimaru Songok won a silver medal in the 440 yards hurdles. The profile presented by the team was not one of 'stamina' but of speed.

Maiyoro's distinguished career had come to an end but waiting to replace him was a young Nandi, Kipchoge Keino. His role models had been Maiyoro and Keter. He was to a large degree self-trained but had marked out his own running track and trained methodically, keeping a record of his training times. He was ambitious and monitored his results in training and racing. In Perth he was buried in the results of the heats of the mile, and in the three miles finished well down the field. However, a few years later he would be described as the 'world's most exciting athlete' (Watman 1965: 16).

Even so, Kenya could not yet be unambiguously described as a nation of distance runners. The first Olympic medal won by a Kenyan runner was by Wilson Kiprugut in 1964 when, at Tokyo, he gained a bronze medal in the 800 metres – an event that balances aerobic with anaerobic capabilities. And at the next Olympics, the notorious altitude Games at Mexico City, Kenyan track athletes won 11 medals in 6 events, ranging from the 4 × 400 metres relay and the 800 metres, to the steeplechase and the 10,000 metres. Although Kenya was no longer able to offer field event athletes to contest the best in the world, sprinters and long-distance runners continued to co-exist in the national Olympic team. In 'explaining' the Kenyans' successes many of the most experienced journalists in world track and field labelled altitude as the key explanatory factor. And the Kenyan victory in the steeplechase was described as 'humiliating to a lover of distance running' (Bank 1969: 18). Kenyan runners were seen as aberrations and it was implied that things would return to 'normal' when the next Olympics would be sited at sea level.

Rightly or wrongly Mexico City was widely regarded as the breakthrough for east African running. However, such a breakthrough did not simply 'happen'. Colonialization and its various agents sowed the seeds of achievement sport. In 1949 the governing bodies of sport in Kenya requested the appointment of a Colony Sports Officer. The successful appointee was A. E. (Archie) Evans who developed a well-organized hierarchical system of athletic competition in the country. It was Evans who was to initiate the formation of the Kenya AAA in 1951, and inter-ethnic competitions could now commence. Schools for Africans grew rapidly in the 1950s and these too continued the earlier tradition of athleticism. These included Cardinal Otunga High School in Kisii and St Patrick's High School at Iten, built by Dutch and Irish Christian groups respectively.

Concluding comments

For over half a century before Kenyan athletes achieved global significance, running had been practised in Africa in various forms. In its modern configuration – that of achievement orientation – it was not of world significance until the mid-1950s, though from the 1900s onwards Kenyans were being trained in the culture of modern western sport. Before the early 1970s Kenyan athletics was not synonymous with middle- and long-distance running. Nor was it synonymous with any particular group within Kenya. It was the Maasai that had been heralded as great runners by colonialist observers, and the first great Kenyan athletes, Maiyoro and Antao, were of Kisii and Indian origin. The national teams competed in international events with diversified teams with (as far as comparison is possible) sprinters and hurdlers being as good as middle-and long-distance runners, and javelin throwers and high jumpers being as good as both.

Modern running in Kenya has become a regional rather than a Kenyan phenomenon. Most regions of the country supply few, if any, athletes to the Kenyan elite. Modern athletics has become much more specialized than the early modern versions with its displays of a wide range of skills including jumping and throwing. The precise social dynamics that produced a decline in Kenyan high jumping and javelin throwing have yet to be explored but this could be as interesting as the current concern for 'explaining' Kenyan running.

Bibliography

Abmayr, W. and Pinaud, Y. (eds) (1994) *L'Athlétisme Africain '94*, Paris: Editions Polymédias.

Adamson, J. (1967) *The Peoples of Kenya*, London: Collins & Harvill.

Bale, J. and Sang, J. (1996) *Kenyan Running*, London: Frank Cass.

Bank, D. (1969) 'Dick Bank's Mexico Reflections', *Athletics Weekly* 1, 18–23.

Boyes, J. (1912) *King Of The Wa-Kikuyu*, London: Methuen.

Coubertin, Pierre de (2000) *Olympism: Selected Writings*, ed. Müller, N., Lausanne: IOC.

Eichberg, H. (1998) *Body Cultures*, ed. Bale, J. and Philo, P., London: Routledge.

Greaves, L. B. (1969) *Carey Francis of Kenya*, London: Rex Collings.

Guttmann, A. (1978) *From Ritual to Record*, New York: Columbia University Press.

Hemingway, E. (1954) *Green Hills of Africa*, London: Cape.

Hinde, S. and Hinde, H. (1901) *The Last of the Masai*, London: Heinemann.

Lindblom, G. (1920) *The Akamba of British East Africa*, Uppsala: Appelberg.

Murray-Brown, J. (1972) *Kenyatta*, London: Allen & Unwin.

Noronha, F. (1970) *Kipchoge of Kenya*, Nakuru: Elimu Publishers.

Reclus, E. (1876) *The Universal Geography* (vol. 13), London: Virtue

Robertson, R. (1990) 'Mapping the global condition: globalisation as the central concept', *Global Cultures*, ed. Featherstone, M., London: Sage, pp. 15–30.

Ross, W. M. (1927) *Kenya from Within*, London: Allen & Unwin.

Spicer, R. G. B. (1925) *Annual Reports*, Nairobi: Police Department.

St Louis, Brett (2003) 'Sport, genetics and the "natural athlete": the resurgence of racial science', *Body and Society* 9, 75–95.

Stovkis, R. (1992) 'Sports and civilization: is violence the central problem', in *Sport and Leisure in the Civilising Process: Critique and Counter Critique*, ed. Dunning, E. and Rojek, C., Basingstoke: Macmillan, pp. 121–36.

Watkins, E. (1993) *Jomo's Jailer: the Life of Leslie Whitehouse*, Calais: Mulberry Books.

Watman, M. (1965) 'Keino: the world's most exciting athlete', *Athletics Weekly* 19, 16.

Watts, M. (2005) 'Nature-Culture', *Spaces of Geographical Thought*, ed. Cloke, P. and Johnston, R., London: Sage, pp. 142–74.

Wiggins, D. (1989) ' "Great speed but little stamina": the historical debate over black athletic superiority', *Journal of Sport History* 16, 158–85.

Chapter 2

The promise and possibilities of running in and out of east Africa

Grant Jarvie

Introduction

In addressing the promise and possibilities of running in and out of Africa this contribution begins by making a number of introductory remarks. First, that while it draws evidence from specific parts of Africa, notably Kenya and Ethiopia, many of the themes in this chapter could relate to other parts of Africa in the twenty-first century. With a population of about 690 million people living in 53 countries and one disputed territory, covering a total area of 11.7 million square miles, Africa is the world's second-largest continent (Meredith 2005). The Sahara covers 3.3 million square miles, almost 25 per cent of land mass. Cairo is the biggest city in Africa, home to 9.2 million people. Sudan is the largest country covering 968,000 square miles but the most populated country in Africa is Nigeria, which, with more than 125 million people, is also the tenth most populated country in the world. Liberia has not only the highest un-employment rate in Africa (85%) but the highest in the world. Angola has the highest infant mortality rate, 192.5 deaths per 1,000 live births, while 18 of the top 20 countries worldwide with the highest infant mortality rates are in Africa. The richest country in Africa per capita is Mauritius, with US$11,400 of GDP per head. Somalia and Nigeria are amongst the world's poorest countries with Somalia, the second poorest in the world, at $500 of GDP per capita. Sixteen African countries are in the top 20 poorest in the world, with 70% of Africa's population surviving on less than $2 a day. To put this in some comparative context, for the season 2003–4 the wage and transfer bill of the four English football divisions stood at £1,049 billion, a figure which eclipses the gross domestic product of some small African nations such as Lesotho and Mauritania, and could wipe out most of the debt of many countries both within and outside of Africa. The first point then is that the relational position of Africa in the world and the relations that make-up Africa itself are complex and uneven in the same way that the social and economic resources that flow in and out of parts of Africa are also complex, uneven, differentiated and in some cases unjust.

While running and athletics provide the focus for this collection of essays, this is only part, albeit a significant part, of the history and explanation of sport in Africa. Athletics itself is part of a larger complex history of sport in Africa which has highlighted some of the promise and possibilities of sport to unite, divide, reconcile and produce social change. The development, background and symbolism of sports in 'other' communities, the All-African Games, the African Nations Cup, the past Rugby World Cup in South Africa (1995) and the future World Football Cup in South Africa (2010) has made parts of Africa a particularly fertile soil for thinking more internationally about sport, culture and society in places other than Europe or the West. Attempts had been made to hold African Games in Algiers as early as 1925 and Alexandria in 1928, but they failed owing to, amongst other reasons, colonial politics and economic difficulties. The impact of colonialism was such that in the early 1960s the Friendship Games were held amongst French-speaking countries in Africa. At the conference of African Ministers for Youth and Sport held in Paris in 1962, it was decided that the Games would thereafter be called the Pan-African Games, as they would include countries other than those colonized by the French. The African Games eventually emerged in 1965 as a force for African solidarity and a means of uniting the continent against South Africa's apartheid regime. That same year the Games were granted official recognition by the International Olympic Committee (IOC). Some 2,500 athletes from 30 independent African States attended the 1965 All-Africa Games held in Brazzaville, Congo. The sixth African Games were held in 1995 with the inclusion of (post-apartheid) South Africa for the first time (Levinson and Christensen 1996).

The 2003 Eighth African Games were hosted in Abuja, Nigeria with the specific mission to act 'as a wake-up call for an African continent threatened by war, disease, hunger and poverty and to respond positively to the challenge by using sports as a strong weapon' in this struggle (Jarvie 2006: 187). The world has recently viewed the images and pleas for help highlighted by the international singer and songwriter Bob Geldof in parts of Africa such as Ethiopia. It is often forgotten that humanitarian political leaders, such as Nelson Mandela, the former South African President, have repeatedly stated that sport is a force that mobilises the sentiments of a people in a way that nothing else can (*The Observer*, 13 July 2003). The second point then is this – that perhaps the promise and possibilities of running, in and out of east Africa, lie in the potential of running and other sports to make a difference to *some* people's lives in certain parts of Africa.

Many analysts have attempted to highlight and isolate particular aspects of the Kenyan, Tanzanian or Ethiopian running success, or the emergence of the Cameroon or Nigerian football teams or South Africa's Rugby 1995 World Cup victory in an effort to explain or analyse the state of sport in Africa. Throughout the 1970s Julius Nyerere of Tanzania often remarked that in developing nations sport helped bridge the gap between national and global recognition. Immanuel Wallerstein suggested that African citizens could feel affection for the victorious athlete and the nation (Jarvie 1993). In the first match of the 2002 World Football Cup in Japan and South Korea, Senegal defeated their former colonial rulers and the then world champions France. The country's President praised the success of the team in terms of defending the honour of *Africa* (*The Times Higher Educational Supplement*, 14 June 2002).

With particular reference to the success of runners from Kenya, Ethiopia, Algeria, Sudan and Tanzania, particularly middle- and long-distance running, varied and complex explanations have been offered to date. This book reflects and develops some if not all of the common explanations. These include (i) physiological explanations relating to diet, energy balance, neuromuscular functioning, anatomy, genetic make-up and body composition; (ii) anthropological explanations relating to ways of life, the place, traditions, customs and rituals in African life and the meaning of running to different groups of people; (iii) historical explanations concerning colonialism, imperialism, racism and the way in which different African nations have responded to independence and the part that sport has historically played in nation building; and (iv) sociological and political economic explanations highlighting a division of labour, power and corruption in both world and local athletics, the struggle for recognition and respect by both men and women runners from different parts of Africa, the development of sport in Africa and the role of sport in the development of Africa.

Finally by means of introduction it is perhaps insightful to consider just one example and suggest that the explanation of Kenyan or Ethiopian running success principally lies in local explanations. While the G8 political leaders of some of the world's leading nations met in 2005 in Gleneagles, Scotland – the same Gleneagles that gave name to the 1977 Gleneagles Agreement which banned South Africa from world sport – to evaluate how best to intervene in Africa, is it perhaps too much to suggest that much of the promise and possibilities of athletics, sport, governance and social change principally lie in African hands and that any policies or explanations about sport in Africa must first and foremost take into account what Africa is saying?

The 3,000 m steeplechase at the 2005 World Athletic Championships held in Helsinki was won by Saif Saaeed Shaheen in a time of 8 minutes 13.31 seconds. The official world championship records will show that the gold medal went to Qatar, a country in which Saif Saaeed Shaheen is viewed as an athletic icon. The athlete's successful defence of this world championship 3,000 m steeplechase gold medal was his 21st successive victory since 2002 (*The Herald*, 10 August 2005). His elder brother Chris Kosgei won the gold for Kenya in 1999 but unlike Shaheen did not defect to Qatar. Saif Saaeed Shaheen, born Stephen Cherono, won his first world steeplechase title in 2003, 17 days after defecting to the oil rich state which had granted him a passport (*The Herald*, 15 January 2005: 10). In that same race Shaheen's brother Abraham ran for Kenya, refused to call him anything other than Stephen and did not congratulate him after the race. Kenyan athletic officials, writes Gillon, were so upset at losing this steeplechase world title for the first time since 1987, that they stopped Shaheen running for Qatar at the 2004 Athens Olympics (*The Herald*, 15 January 2005).

Kenya won gold, silver and bronze medals in the men's 3,000 m steeplechase at the 2004 Athens Olympic Games.

Athletes such as Shaheen are single minded and mono-causal when it comes to explaining both personal and Kenyan athletic success. It is important here not to be confused by simple western stereotypes about non-western cultures. The context is such that as a boy Shaheen's family 'had 60 cows and 30 goats until a drought . . . left the family with 7 cattle and 3 goats . . . and it cost him his education', since the animals would have been sold to pay for his school fees (*The Herald*, 15 January 2005). As Stephen Cherono he was raised in Kamelilo a village in Keyo in which there was no water-tap and every day after school, he walked three kilometres to collect 10 litres of water, which cost two dollars for three days. The move to Qatar was allegedly based upon an offer of a least $1,000 dollars a month for life (*The Herald*, 15 January 2005). About 50 people now depend upon that athlete's success for their livelihoods. He puts eight children through school with two at college in America and, when asked to explain Kenyan running success said that the answer is simple 'an athlete in Kenya runs to escape poverty' and 'I fight to survive' (*The Herald*, 10 August 2005).

Stories of war, famine, disease, corruption and other western stereotypes should not blind academics and analysts to the many success stories that sport in Africa provides, but nor should the fact that sport provides many resources of hope and self-help stop us from listening to and understanding what Africa has to say. Can Kenyan and Ethiopian athletic success be recognized as an international sporting force on its own terms or is there a price to pay for buying into the contemporary global commercial world of sport? In attempting to provide a brief insight into the promise and possibilities of running in and out of east Africa the remainder of this chapter provides a substantive comment on the environmental context that has contributed to an exodus of running talent from Africa; an examination of the motivations behind running for Kenyan woman and a reflection upon the relationship between poverty and running in Ethiopia. These social and historical explanations will hopefully compliment other explanations provided in this book while also providing additional and original substantive material upon which to base the above.

The environment, capitalism and African athletic migration

Despite colonialism, Africa remains a place that is powerfully moulded by its harsh environment. Environmental determinism as an explanation for east African running success tends to appear in *at least* two different forms of narrative which are illustrated in the following: (i) *The Sunday Times* of April 2004, commenting upon a sedentary western way of life, noted 'that Kenyans have been running while the developed world has been using cars, trains and planes', and (ii) *The Toronto Star* of March 2004, again in reference to Kenyan running success, talks of 'the physics of running as good genes, impeccable form and bodies built to run as the only real secrets of the long-distance runner'. But if environmental determinism is the answer to the production of a long line of athletic talent emerging out of Africa, east Africa in particular, then why does this not happen in other places such as Peru and Lesotho? Furthermore, rarely in such discussions is the environment taken to mean the workings of international capitalism which have historically influenced Africa's stocks of mineral wealth but also levels and rates of athletic migration in and out of parts of Africa. The tension between athletic dreams, income and education, and why parents are willing to send their children away while they are still too young in the hope that they might make the family rich through athletic success is also partially an outcome forged by an environment in which the flow of capital is increasingly international, but rarely fair or just (Fulcher 2004).

The reasons for athletic export and import are multi-faceted and often need to be analysed on a case-by-case basis. The most common explanations for the migration of athletic labour tend to include some or all of the following: (i) that athletic labour is drawn by economic forces to where the core sources of economic wealth tended to be located, a process that leads to a relational situation whereby those countries on the periphery are influenced by those at the core. In such instances the migration of athletic labour can lead to the de-skilling of talent in donor countries; (ii) that specific historical relations between certain places often leads to athletes migrating for cultural and historical reasons to certain other places; (iii) that different categories or typologies of migrants can be identified and thus migration groups and patterns may be seen to be as different as they are similar (the work on sports labour migration pioneered by Maguire identifies pioneers, mercenaries, settlers, returnees and nomadic cosmopolitans as specific types of nomadic sports groups; Maguire 1999, 2005); or (iv) political reasons for migration which might include lack of government support for the athlete or the withholding of training grants or, alternatively, the decision by some countries to offer forms of citizenship to some athletes in return for switching nationalities. The reasons for labour migration are complex with motivations being interdependent upon a number of factors including all of the aforementioned. Multi-faceted accounts provide a more comprehensive and complex picture of athletic labour migration between and within places, in the same way that multi-faceted accounts of east African running success are more satisfactory than those that tend to highlight mono-causal explanations. It may be useful at this point to think about where African athletes move to and what are some of the reasons given by the runners themselves for moving to and from certain places.

African sports labour migration has been commented upon extensively and existing research has been keen to note the complex economic, political, cultural and emotional processes that have contoured labour migration amongst athletes (Armstrong and Giulianotti 2004; Bale and Sang 1996; Bale and Maguire 1994). Issues of dependency, de-skilling, employment rights, child

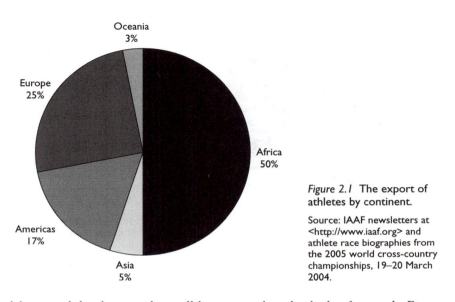

Figure 2.1 The export of athletes by continent.

Source: IAAF newsletters at <http://www.iaaf.org> and athlete race biographies from the 2005 world cross-country championships, 19–20 March 2004.

labour, and development have all been central to this body of research. Figure 2.1 provides a substantive insight into the number of athletes exported from different continents – Africa, Asia, the Americas, Europe and Oceania. This specific data set allows one to note that 50% (n = 56) or more of migrating athletes, in the cases highlighted, come out of Africa.

Figure 2.2 breaks down the export of athletes country by country, and again illustrates that Morocco, Kenya, Ethiopia and Nigeria are high exporters of athletic talent in comparison with other countries. Of the 50 countries affected by the export of athletes, 21 were from Africa. As shown in Figure 2.3, Europe is the main importer of defecting athletes with 68 out of 111 (61%) of athletes moving to Europe. Asian countries, which were less of a significant exporter of athletes, feature more prominently in terms of importing athletes, with 20% of defecting athletes moving to Asia. Africa, the main exporter of athletic labour in 2005 remains, with 3%, the continent with the lowest levels of imported athletic labour. This partially confirms that even in terms of the migration rates associated with athletic labour, the de-skilling of certain continents and countries and the unequal flow of athletic talent in and out of Africa is highly differentiated when compared to other more developed parts of the world.

The international flow of athletes from Kenya has recently been referred to as 'a global trade in muscle' in which Kenyan athletes have switched allegiance from the country of their birth to the oil-rich states of Qatar and Bahrain (Simms and Rendell 2004). This scramble for African talent, write Simms and Rendell (2004), may be equated with the exploitation of Africa's mineral wealth during different periods of colonial rule. The assertion is that those living in poverty provide the muscle while the rich countries of the world capture the

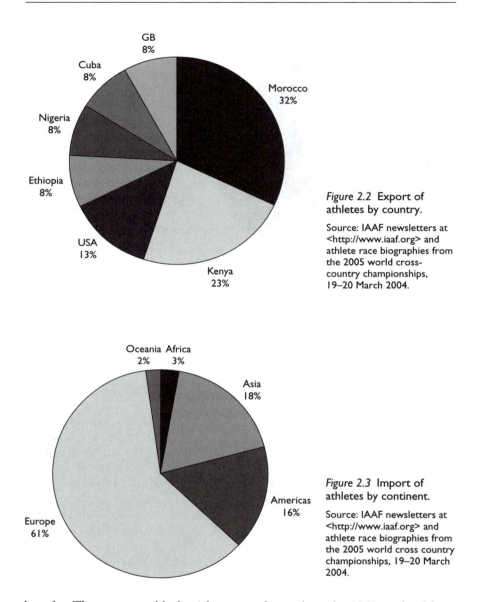

Figure 2.2 Export of athletes by country.

Source: IAAF newsletters at <http://www.iaaf.org> and athlete race biographies from the 2005 world cross-country championships, 19–20 March 2004.

Figure 2.3 Import of athletes by continent.

Source: IAAF newsletters at <http://www.iaaf.org> and athlete race biographies from the 2005 world cross country championships, 19–20 March 2004.

benefits. The new scramble for Africa started as early as the 1960s with athletes being lured to American colleges, but now the oil-rich countries of the world simply buy athletic talent that is then lost to Africa. Gyulai (2003) recognizes that the freedom of movement of athletes may give rise to conflicting interests between different member federations of the International Athletic Federation (IAAF), but believes that there should be no exception to the increased mobility of individuals within the rules of free-market trade and global sporting capitalism. The IAAF notes that the rules with regard to the movement of athletes should not be to the detriment of the member federations (Gyulai 2003). Kenya has recently moved to try to stem the flow of athletes out of Kenya by tightening up on the circumstances and conditions under which athletes may be granted visas to leave the country.

In the same way that the all too easily accepted truths about globalization have ignored the uneven and differentiated forms of capitalism emerging in the twenty-first century, so too it is crucial not to ignore the injustices and uneven patterns of sports labour migration. It is essential that any contemporary understanding of global sport must actively listen to and engage with other sporting communities, places and voices. Perhaps it is impossible for humanity or global sport to arrive at an understanding of the values that unite it, but if the leading capitalist nations ceased to impose their own ideas on the rest of the sporting world and start to take cognizance of 'other' sporting cultures, then the aspiration of global sport might become more just and less charitable. It is not charity which Africa or African runners want but the tools by which Africans can determine their own well-being and life chances in a more equable sporting world (Jarvie 2006; McAlpine 2005). If large parts of Africa are kept poor as a result of unfair trade arrangements, which facilitate cheap European and American imports that keep parts of Africa poor and dependent, then why should the resources afforded by running not be viewed as a viable route out of poverty for those who can make it?

Running in and out of Kenya

What exactly are the motivations and barriers that some Kenyan runners have to overcome to maintain a presence on the international athletic circuit today? Since the Kenyan National Team first participated in an inter-continental event in 1954, the emergence of what some have called 'the Kenyan running phenomenon' has both progressed and regressed at different rates and at different times. Between 1980 and 2003, 48% of the top male middle-distance performances were attributed to Kenyan runners, they were unbeatable in the 3,000 m steeplechase throughout the 1990s with 100% of the top performances in the world and 87% of the top three performances. Morocco temporarily broke the Kenyan dominance in 2001 and 2002 before the title returned to a Kenyan in 2003, although Stephen Cherono as previously mentioned had switched his allegiances to Qatar for financial incentives by this time. To put this in a comparative context, we can use the location quotient utilized by Bale and Sang (Bale and Sang 1996). To calculate the location quotient the percentage number of elite runners from a certain country (in this case athletes in the world top three) is divided by the population of the country expressed as a percentage of the total world population. A quotient of above unity indicates that the country is producing runners at more than the average rate. In 2002 there were

18 male and female Kenyan athletes in the world top three at all distances between 800 m and the marathon, which amounts to 37.5% of the total. As the Kenyan population is 32.4 million, 0.5% of the world population, this gives a 'location quotient' of 75. However this number disguises the gendered output of athletic talent from the country. When genders are calculated separately, Kenya is seen to produce elite males at 134 times the predicted rate, while females have a location quotient of 16.

The common factors produced by the conventional wisdom when answering the question how do we explain the success of Kenyan runners include variables such as altitude, physiology, genetics, diet, culture and psychology, all of which are admirably covered in this book, yet an audit of property in the Eldoret Central Business District owned by athletes reveals a remarkable departure from the past when athletes only had their medals to show for the years of jet-setting and scaling heights of sporting success (*East African Standard*, 17 November 2003). Nowadays money is arguably the most important motivation for athletes. While Kenya is better off than many other African countries, people are still poor and unemployment is high. To a European athlete, an Olympic gold medal may be the pinnacle of their career however for most Kenyan athletes it is simply a gateway to earn money which could transform their own lives and that of their communities. That running can also be a fundamental escape from poverty for some girls and women in Kenya is supported by the findings from a survey of 250 elite female Kenyan athletes between the ages of 12 and 50 carried out during 2003. All 80% of the respondents could be classified as being elite in the sense that they were either Olympian, International or Junior athletes who had shown major potential. Participants had been involved in running for an average of 7.9 years. The following hierarchy of reasons was given as the key factors that influenced the women's decisions to run (Figure 2.4).

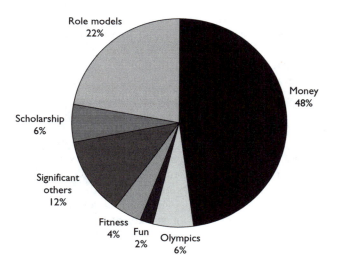

Figure 2.4
Motivations for running amongst elite female Kenyan runners.

An overwhelming majority of the female athletes admitted their primary motivation for taking up athletics was money (49.2%). In contrast only 6% were motivated by the Olympics. From these results it is quite clear that athletic success is viewed as a gateway to money and an improved life. Money could also be seen as providing a means for women to gain independence when they have traditionally been reliant on and answerable to the men in their lives. Athletes from the entire age range cited money as their primary motivation, even before the amount of money available reached the epic proportions of today. Only a small minority of the athletes were driven by fun (1.5%) or fitness (3.5%). Those who did cite fun or fitness as a motivation tended to be younger men or women (average ages 22.0 and 16.4 years, respectively). Almost 6% of the female athletes questioned were driven by the thought of winning an athletics scholarship (average age 16.2 years).

Kenyan women are not afraid to set their sights outside Kenya and are keen to travel across continents to further their education and improve their quality of life. Significant others were an important motivation for Kenyan female athletes (12.1%). This is noteworthy as it shows the importance of family support as young girls embark on their athletic careers. Clearly, if more families were supportive of their daughters, one could expect a lot more of them to emerge as successful athletes. Those who did cite significant others as a motivation tended to be relatively young (average age 17.5 years). Similarly, the influence of role models is quite significant – 22.1% of those questioned cited this as their primary motivation. This goes a long way to explaining the time it has taken for Kenyan female athletes to make an impact on the world stage. The oldest athlete who reported being motivated by a role model was only 30 years old (average age 17.1 years). Athletes of older generations had no visible role models to emulate. It took time before young Kenyan women were able to view the impact of successful athletes such as Tegla Louroupe, Joyce Chepchumba, Lornah Kiplagat, Sally Barsosio and others.

In a country where the average wage is less than a euro or a dollar a day, the lucrative European and American road race circuits are attractive career options for Kenyan athletes. When Catherine Ndereba broke the world record in the Chicago marathon in October 2001, she received a $75,000 prize purse, $100,000 for breaking the world record and a Volkswagen Jetta worth $26,125. This was in addition to a not insignificant appearance fee merely for turning up (Schontz 2002). A world championship gold medal has been estimated to be worth $60,000, as well as opening other lucrative avenues in terms of qualification for appearance fees in big races (*East African Standard*, 17 November 2003). Money is perhaps more of a motivation to women due to the independence it buys them. 'Once a woman begins to earn her own money, she is valued immediately by her family and her community' (Schontz 2002). The barriers for women acquiring wealth in Kenya are inherently unequal: for instance, women cannot inherit land and they often invariably live on land as a guest of their male relatives, but athletic wealth in some cases can help buy land. Therefore as Kenyan women win road races and track meets, they can acquire control of substantial amounts of money allowing them to invest in their own land – a once unlikely prospect for women not born into wealthy families.

African promises, sport and poverty

Nelson Mandela has described child poverty as the modern slavery; thousands have demonstrated against it; New Labour on coming to power in Britain in 1999 vowed to eliminate child poverty within a generation; eradicating it has been viewed as one of the most successful strategies to halt terrorism and it has been the object of fundraising campaigns by some of the world's top musicians and sportsmen and women. James Wolfensohn, head of the World Bank noted in July 2004 that, in terms of expenditure, the priorities were roughly $900 billion on defence, $350 billion on agriculture, and $60 billion on aid of which about half gets there in cash (Settle 2004: 16). Oxfam recently noted that it would cost £3.2 billion to send all the world's children to school. Poverty may be one of the few truly global phenomena in that in relative and absolute terms it exists worldwide and while governments and policies change, the needs of the world's poor invariably remain the same (Jarvie 2006).

The notion of poverty is not new but it is often suppressed, not just in the literature and research about sport, culture and society, but in this case it is highlighted as a fundamental reason and motivation for why some athletes run. Historically, sport used to be a possible route out of poverty in the western world. Many NGOs have been at the forefront of initiatives involving sport as a facet of humanitarian aid in attacking the social and economic consequences of poverty. The Tiger Club Project in Kampala, Uganda is one of many such initiatives using sport. The objectives of the Tiger Club include: (i) helping street children and young people in need; (ii) providing children with food, clothing and other physical needs; (iii) help with education and development; (iv) enabling children to realize their potential so that they can gain employment; (v) providing assistance to the natural families or foster carers of children and young adults; and (vi) providing medical and welfare assistance (Tiger Club Project Annual Report 2003). The 2003 Annual Report stated that in 2002, 263 children had been offered a permanent alternative to the street; a further 116 street children and young people were in the START programme which meant full-time schooling; and 161 young people resettled in their village of origin and were provided with the means for income generation. Of those resettled children 76% have remained in their villages (Tiger Club Project Annual Report 2003).

Every year about 200 million people move in search of employment – about 3% of the world's population (Seabrook 2003). Legal migrants who leave their homes in poor countries to provide labour or entertainment in other parts of the world are generally regarded as privileged. Many African runners have provided an exhilarating spectacle for global sports audiences but what is often forgotten is that the money raised from these performances often provides pathways of hope for other people. Sociologists such as Maguire (1999, 2005) have helped to pave the way for an extensive body of research into the causes of sports labour migration across different parts of the world yet very little has been written about the part played by some athletes in earning money to support whole families and even villages in their country of origin. When the career of a leading world athlete from a developing country is brought to a premature end, the consequences often extend far beyond the track. Maria Mutola the Mozambican, former Olympic and five-time world indoor 800 m champion and world-record holder routinely sends track winnings back to her country of origin. Chamanchulo, the suburb of Maputo in which Mutola grew up, is ravaged by HIV, passed on in childbirth or breast milk to 40% of the children (Gillon 2004). In 2003 when Mutola became the first athlete to collect $1 million for outright victory on the Golden League Athletic Grand Prix Circuit, part of the cash went to the foundation she endowed to help provide scholarships, kit, education and coaching for young athletes (Gillon 2004). Farms and small businesses have often been sustained by her winnings on the circuit, which have provided for the purchasing of tractors, fertilizers and the facilities to drill small wells.

Perhaps one of the last words in this chapter prior to concluding should be left to the Ethiopian athlete and politician, once Olympic champion and former world-record holder, Haile Gebrselassie who has left us in no doubt about both the social and political responsibility of the athlete and the limits and possibilities of sport in relation to poverty in his country (see Chapter 4 in this book). In an interview reported in *The Times* of March 2003 Haile Gebrselassie drew attention to the context and circumstances that were his early life. Talking of his life aged 15 he said: 'This was all at a time when my father was cross with me because I was doing athletics and my country was going through famine in which millions died and all I had was running – I just ran and ran all the time and I got better and better.' Talking of the necessity to run: 'I only started running because I had to – we were six miles from school and there was so much to be done on the farm that I ran to school and back again to have enough time to do farming as well as school work.' Finally his views on the political responsibility of the athlete left one in no doubt about the priorities – 'eradicating poverty is all that matters in my country. When I am training I think about this a lot; when I am running it is going over in my mind – as a country we cannot move forward until we eradicate poverty and whereas sport can help – the real problems will not be overcome just by helping Ethiopians to run fast.' In reality sport can only make a small contribution, but small contributions can sometimes make a difference. How sport can help in the fight against poverty should not be shelved as a historical question until much more has been done to fight both relative and absolute experiences of poverty worldwide and to note what sport can or cannot do to help.

The truth about global sport as a universal creed is that it is also a ruthless engine of injustice. The social dimension and possibilities of global sport remain as empty slogans and constant historical reminders proclaiming the principles of equality, justice and the eradication of poverty have not sufficed to make a reality of it. There is just one thing that many corporate lobbyists and social movements understand and that is that the real issue is not trade, whether it is the plundering of athletic talent or mineral wealth from Africa, but power. A fundamental gap continues to exist both within sport and capitalism between the outcome of universal, often western prescriptions, and local realities. Sport including athletics needs to be more just and less charitable, however it continues to provide a pathway for hope for some in different parts of the world. It continues to hold both a promise and possibilities for some in different parts of Africa.

Concluding remarks

Increased aid, combined with debt reduction is supposed to make it easier for African countries to invest in health, education and infrastructure. The idea behind this is to allow the continent to achieve a level playing field whereby it can compete with the rest of the world, emulating Asia by selling quality products and providing skilled labour. It is ironic that while the G8 leaders in Scotland were meeting to discuss Africa's future, the African Union involving the leaders of 53 African Countries met in Libya. This organization is important because it provides a potential forum for Africa to speak with one voice.

Africa is excluded from so much global decision making – no permanent seat on the UN Security Council and poor representation in the World Bank and International Monetary Fund. African leaders of course attended the Gleneagles summit but only at the invitation of the eight real world powerbrokers. In contrast, Africans were in charge of the meeting in Libya and with one voice they made it clear that the efforts of the G8 summit to write off African debt fell far short of what was needed. The G8 plan aimed ultimately to write off £32 billion debt for 38 poor countries, not all of them in Africa. Africa's total debt burden in 2002 was estimated to be in the region of £168 billion. The United States of America remains resistant to moves to alleviate world poverty and, in particular, the stipulated Millennium Goal Target that the wealthy countries of the world should donate 0.7% of national income to the developing world. The African Union did pass a resolution expressing gratitude for the progress that was being made on aid but above all asking for a fair and equitable trading system in the world and not charity. Trade justice is what many African anti-poverty campaigners have been asking for. To save Africa those outside of Africa must first of all listen to it, and this applies as much to explanations for athletic running success as it does to explanations of poverty and the workings of capitalism. Africa will make its own future, running cannot free people from poverty but in some cases poverty and the need for money can be a powerful motivation to run in and out of Africa. This is as powerful an explanation for running success as many of the other reasons highlighted in this book.

George Weah (Liberia's greatest ever footballer) ran for President in the General Election of 2005 in Liberia. One of 13 siblings, Weah was raised in a Monrovian slum, played as many as three football games a day until in 1987 a Cameroonian club bought him for $5,000. Stops in France, Italy and England followed. In 1995, he was voted world footballer of the year and he ended up in New York commuting to training sessions in Europe on Concorde. Weah's playing career coincided with Liberia's civil war. Weah tried to help: he gave money, urged child soldiers to go to school and ran the national football team almost as a private charity. He provided the team kit, hotels and goals although rarely quite enough of those. Increasingly athletes such as George Weah, Haile Gebrselassie, and others have realized that African countries are increasingly electing their leaders, and as athletes on the world stage they command a degree of visibility, loyalty and in some cases increased credibility because they have become rich honestly, by their own efforts and have not forgotten the local context. Sport in these cases has helped to fashion resources of hope in many different ways.

Finally, while it is important to explain and understand economic, social, historical, physiological and many other explanations of what sport can do for society, the more important intellectual and practical questions often emanate from questions relating to social change. Historically, the potential of sport lies not with the values promoted by global sport or particular forms of capitalism, for as we have shown in this chapter these are invariably unjust and uneven. The possibilities that exist within sport are those that can help with radically different views of the world perhaps based upon opportunities to foster trust, obligations, redistribution and respect for sport in a more socially orientated humane world. Sport's transformative capacity must not be overstated, it is limited and it needs to get its own house in order, but possibilities do exist within sport to provide some resources of hope within a world that is left wanting on so many fronts. To ignore the capacity of sport to assist with social change is not an option, particularly for students, teachers and researchers of sport. This has to be near the top of any research agenda for those working in this and related fields for the foreseeable future.

Acknowledgements

The research for this chapter would not have been possible without the help and assistance of a number of people, most notably those at Kenyatta University and in particular Vincent O. Onywera who helped with the survey of Kenyan athletes, and Toni Macintosh and Jane Dunlop who assisted with the collection of some of the research presented in this chapter.

Bibliography

Armstrong, G. (2004) 'The lords of misrule: football and the rights of the child in Liberia, West Africa', *Sport in Society* 7, 473–502.

Armstrong, G. and Giulianotti, R. (eds) (2004) *Football in Africa: Conflict, Conciliation and Community*, Basingstoke: Palgrave.

Bale, J. (2004) *Running Cultures: Racing in Time and Space*, London: Routledge.

Bale, J. and Maguire, J. (eds) (1994) *The Global Sports Arena: Athletic Talent Migration in an Interdependent World*, London: Frank Cass.

Bale, J. and Sang, J. (1996) *Kenyan Running: Movement Culture, Geography and Global Change*, London: Frank Cass.

Dowden, R. (2005) 'To save Africa we must listen to it', *New Statesman* 14 March, 18–21.

Fabian Society (2005) 'Fabian review', *African Promise* 116, 1–28.

Fulcher, J. (2004) *Capitalism: A Very Short Introduction*, Oxford: Oxford University Press.

Gebrselassie, H. (2003) 'Triumph and despair', *The Times* 10 March, 12.

Gillon, D. (2004) 'Candle who brings a ray of hope', *The Herald* 24 November, 12.

Gillon, D. (2005) 'No barriers to Shaheen's success', *The Herald* 10 August, 34.

Gillon, D. (2005) 'View from man who races to escape poverty', *The Herald* 15 January, 10.

Gyulai, I. (2003) 'Transfers of nationality', *IAAF News* 64, 2–4.

Jarvie, G. (1993) 'Sport, nationalism and cultural identity', in *The Changing Politics of Sport*, ed. Allison, L., Manchester: Manchester University Press, pp. 54–84.

Jarvie, G. (2006) *Sport, Culture and Society; Can Sport Change the World?* Routledge: London.

Kuper, S. (2005) 'Football messiah who plays politics at home', *Financial Times* 11 September, 10.

Leseth, A. (2003) 'Michezmo: dance, sport and politics in Dar-es-Salaam, Tanzania', in *Sport, Dance and Embodied Identities*, ed. Dyck, N. and Archetti, E., Oxford: Berg, pp. 231–48.

Levinson, D. and Christensen, K. (1996) *Encyclopedia of World Sport*, Oxford: ABC-CLIO.

McAlpine, J. (2005) 'Africa has spoken, but did any of us bother to listen?' *The Herald* 7 July, 20.

Maguire, J. (1999) *Global Sport: Identities. Societies, Civilizations*, Cambridge: Polity Press.

Maguire, J. (2005) *Power and Global Sport: Zones of Prestige, Emulation and Resistance*, London: Routledge.

Maguire, J. A. (2004) 'Sport labour migration research revisited', *Journal of Sport and Social Issues* 28, 477–82.

Maguire, J., Jarvie, G., Bradley, J. and Mansfield, J. (2002) *Sport Worlds: A Sociological Perspective*, Champaign, IL: Human Kinetics.

Meredith, M. (2005) *The State of Africa: A History of Fifty Years of Independence*, London: Free Press.

The Nation (2003) 'Athletics: Kenya still has the best record from Africa', *East Africa News* 23 August, 2–4.

Seabrook, J. (2003) 'Don't punish the poor for being poor', *New Statesman* 23 September, 6–7.

Settle, D. (2004) *Fighting Poverty: The Facts*, Swindon: Economic and Social Research Council.

Shontz, L. (2002) 'Fast forward: the rise of Kenya's women runners', *post-gazette.com sports* 22 October, Pittsburgh.

Simms, A. and Rendell, M. (2004) 'The global trade in muscle', *New Statesman* 9 August, 24–5.

Tiger Club Project (2003) *Annual Report 2003*, Uganda: Kampala.

Chapter 3

Raiders from the Rift Valley

Cattle raiding and distance running in east Africa

John Manners

In 1997, I wrote a paper discussing factors that might account for the extraordinary competitive running success of the Kenyan ethnic group known as the Kalenjin (Manners 1997: 14–27). One hypothesis advanced briefly in that paper had to do with the possible connection between running success and the traditional practice of cattle raiding, i.e. stealing cattle from people outside one's own group. This chapter will explore that connection further.

While both running success and a tradition of cattle raiding can be found in a number of east African tribes, both have been most dramatically in evidence among the Kalenjin. So most of what follows deals directly with the Kalenjin, and largely by extension, with other groups.

The Kalenjin number about 3 million, some 10% of Kenya's population. Yet over the years, members of this group have collected about 75% of the country's top athletic prizes, and an even more disproportionate share of the world's highest honours (Manners 1997: 14–18).

In 2004, for example, in a four-week span in March and April, the height of the spring road racing season, Kalenjin men won marathons in London, Boston, Rotterdam, Turin, and Xiamen (Fujian, China); half-marathons in Lisbon, Milan, Berlin, Prague and Prato; 10 km races in Brunssum, Vancouver, Charleston, New Orleans, Paderborn, Dongio, Gualtieri, Barcelona and Hilversum; and a big 10-mile race in Washington, DC – 20 major road races on three continents, all with significant prize money and large international fields. Kalenjin women, who lag somewhat behind the men for reasons there is no space to discuss here, won the women's division in 11 of those 20 races.

In 1997, Kalenjin runners were comparative strangers to road racing. They concentrated on track and cross country. But the global athletics marketplace has exerted its influence, and the Kalenjin have gone to where the money is, road racing, the only discipline in men's athletics that has grown in the past decade. Unfortunately for Kenya, the supply of Kalenjin talent is not inexhaustible, and road racing's gain has been to some extent track and cross country's loss, as reflected in medal tallies in recent global championships. Perhaps most significantly, in 2004, for the first time in 19 years, Kenya lost the men's team title at the World Cross Country Championships – to their Rift Valley rivals, Ethiopia.

Nevertheless, time-based world rankings in various distance events show that Kalenjin runners have more than held their own. Table 3.1 shows the percentages of Kalenjin men among the top 10 and top 20 performers worldwide in the six Olympic endurance events, for the year 2003 and for 'all-time' (performance data from Matthews 2004: 286–96, 374–97).

As the averages at the bottom of the table show, men from this single ethnic group, 1/2000th of the world's population, make-up half the top performers in the history of one of the world's most widely practised sports.

What accounts for these extraordinary numbers? The explanations most commonly advanced point to two principal factors, altitude and role models. Since the 1968 Olympics in Mexico City, where Kenyans and Ethiopians won 10 medals on a track that was 2,200 m above sea level, altitude has tended to be the first thought of those trying to account for the east African running phenomenon – and with good reason. Almost all world class east African runners come from highland areas (see Chapter 14 for details), and the thin air at the 2,000 m elevations common in such places has been shown to boost aerobic capacity in several ways. Living at altitude alone is not enough, as the dearth of Nepalese and Peruvians among the world's running elite might suggest, but it seems to help, over the course of a runner's lifetime, or down through the generations.

Table 3.1 Kalenjin percentage of world's top performers, men – end 2003

Event	Time period	% Top 10	% Top 20
800 m	2003	40	25
	All time	30	20
1500 m	2003	60	55
	All time	40	35
5,000 m	2003	70	50
	All time	30	45
10,000 m	2003	50	45
	All time	60	55
3,000 m SC	2003	60	50
	All time	90	85
Marathon	2003	70	60
	All time	50	55
Average	2003	58	48
	All time	50	49

Key: Steeplechase (SC).

What about role models? In 2003, the general secretary of the Kenyan athletics federation estimated that as many as 2,000 Kenyans were running professionally in various parts of the world (Okeyo 2003). That figure may be a little high, but it gives a sense of how common professional-calibre athletes are in Kenya, especially in certain tribal areas. There is probably nowhere in Kalenjin country that is further than 10 miles from the birthplace of a professional runner. It is true that many of these professionals are second- and third-rank road runners living very modestly for months or years at a time in western countries, sending home what they can to pay relatives' school fees, and struggling to accumulate a little capital to buy some land back home. Yet even the modest $10,000 or $20,000 that one of these journeymen might make in a year (Buster 1998; Gaskell 1998; Templeton 2003) is well worth striving for in the eyes of a young man with no job and no prospects in a country with a *per capita* GDP of about $1,000 a year (World Almanac 2005: 792). So, such a young man might reason, if a runner from the next village can make that kind of money, why can't I? And he starts training, with a vengeance.

This is a common scenario, and it stands to reason that such neighbourhood and national role models are indeed significant contributors, augmented by the strong motivator of poverty and the essential precondition of a functioning athletics infrastructure. But role models, even taken together with altitude, are scarcely sufficient to account for the phenomenon. For one thing, these factors don't explain what gave rise to the earliest role models, or why there are three times more of them in Kalenjin country than in the rest of Kenya combined. For another, there are the sheer numbers – a thousand or more Kalenjin making a living in the very small world of professional running.

Earning even a modest income as a runner requires a lot more than simply deciding that's what you want to be when you grow up. Consider the poor Americans. Thousands of trained, disciplined distance runners emerge each year from US colleges, and some of the best devote themselves to professional running careers. But since the mid-1990s, when the east African influx began on the US road racing circuit, all but a handful of the Americans have shown themselves quite unable to compete. US race directors even put together an American-only circuit of races for their floundering compatriots to enable them to win some prize money. But lately even on that circuit, the top men's money has most often gone to two naturalized citizens born, respectively, in Eritrea and Somalia (USA Running Circuit 2005).

Thus it seems that for most people, wishing and striving in emulation of even the most inspirational of role models isn't enough to get a runner to even the lowest rung of the professional ladder. For east Africans, however, and for the Kalenjin in particular, wishing and striving very often seem to do the job.

Most interesting are instances when such wishing and striving have not been a lifelong preoccupation – when running has been taken up more or less by chance, comparatively late in life, by young men who had never before thought of themselves as runners. Over the years I have assembled a dozen informal case studies of Kalenjin who have found themselves in such circumstances. Most were young men in their twenties when, by mistake or by deception, they received offers of US college athletic scholarships to which they were not in the least entitled. Below are three examples.

Amos Korir arrived at Allegheny Community College in Pennsylvania in 1977 ostensibly as a pole-vaulter. But on his first day at track practice, he saw his teammates warming up at a height that was about 30 cm (12 in.) above his personal best, and he quickly informed the coach that he was actually not a pole-vaulter but a middle-distance runner, although he had never competed at such a distance. By 1981 he ranked third in the world in the steeplechase (Korir 1994).

Julius Randich was 25 when in 1990 he was offered a scholarship to Lubbock Christian University in Texas because his childhood friend, James Bungei, was a runner there, and the coach had asked Bungei for a recommendation. Randich had never competed and smoked as much as he could afford, but he accepted the scholarship and by the end of his first year he was the national small-college (NAIA) champion at 10,000 m (Randich 1998).

Paul Rotich, in 1988 at the age of 22, was sent off to South Plains Junior College in Texas by his wealthy father with enough money to cover tuition and living expenses for two years. Unfortunately, he spent nearly all the money in his first year, but rather than return home in disgrace, Paul, who had been comfortably sedentary all his life, decided to train in hopes of earning a track scholarship. He was significantly overweight when he started, but by the end of his first season he had qualified for the National Junior College Cross Country Championships, and he went on to secure a full scholarship to complete his BA, and to be named 'All American' 10 times in various events (Rotich 1994).

There are more such stories, but these three make the point: altitude and role models notwithstanding, there appears to be, widely dispersed among the Kalenjin, a capacity for competitive distance running that seems to enable almost any random member of the group, with training, to reach a degree of proficiency that would rank him, at minimum, at a level approaching national class in most Western countries. If that is indeed the case, where does that capacity come from? And why do the Kalenjin appear to be particularly blessed?

These questions bring us back to the original topic, the possible connection between running success and cattle raiding, or, more broadly, between running and what anthropologists call the 'cattle complex', the set of customs common to many pastoral, or cattle-herding, societies. Throughout east Africa, the ethnic groups that have turned out the majority of their countries' international runners are all historically pastoralist peoples. These include the Oromo of Ethiopia, the Iraqw and Barabaig of Tanzania, the Sebei of Uganda, and the Tutsi of Burundi, as well as the Kalenjin. It may be worth noting that all these groups except the Tutsi are linguistically related in varying degrees; the Sebei are actually a Kalenjin group, living just across the border from Kenya, and the Barabaig speak a language that shares about half its basic vocabulary with Kalenjin (Ehret 1971: 94).

Why is running success so concentrated among these groups? The history and customs of the Kalenjin and these related peoples may provide clues.

In the nineteenth and early twentieth century, travellers, colonial officials and even anthropologists romanticized these pastoral groups, not for their running but for their fierceness. For whatever reason – perhaps to defend and augment their herds – these peoples were highly aggressive toward outsiders. Such aggressiveness was reinforced in most of the groups by two ancient customs: ritual circumcision as initiation into adulthood, and a system of age-grades that determined social roles. Circumcision, and the recovery and training period that followed, were explicitly devoted to preparing young men for the rigours of combat; while the age-grade system designated the role of 'warrior' for all new initiates and required them to spend their time defending the group's herds and capturing animals from others.

When European colonists arrived early in the last century, they placed a high premium on quelling these unruly peoples. The British in Kenya were particularly concerned about the Maasai, another pastoral group who were already celebrated as the conquerors of the east African plains. But partly as a result of earlier European incursions, the Maasai had been depleted by disease and internal wars, and they quickly accepted *Pax Britannica*. The most significant resistance to the British came from the Kalenjin, in particular from the Nandi subgroup. The Nandi fought the British for 10 years and significantly delayed the construction of the hugely expensive Uganda Railway, which passed along the southern flank of their territory. Eventually they were subdued in what was by far the biggest military operation of British east Africa's entire 'pacification' period (Matson 1974: 5–6; Lonsdale 1989: 19–21).

Interestingly, that very act of resistance appeared to endear the Kalenjin to their conquerors. After one particularly bloody engagement, in which his troops mowed down more than 100 Nandi warriors with a Maxim gun, a Major C.C. Cunningham wrote to the colony's chief administrator: 'The Nandi proved themselves a sporting lot. They charged quite like understudies of the dervishes' (quoted in Matson 1972: 155). The British quickly classed the Kalenjin as a 'martial race' or 'warrior tribe', like many of their fellow pastoralists elsewhere in east Africa (Kirk-Greene 1980: 401–2), and that designation had some possibly interesting consequences.

Once the Kalenjin resistance had been put down, the British still had to deal with the restive members of the tribe's warrior age set, the *murenik*, who continued to raid other tribes for cattle. There are many references in colonial reports about the *murenik*'s refusal to give up what they regarded as both occupation and sport (Matson 1970: 66; Matson 1972: 12; Ng'eny 1970: 113). The British responded with vigorous police activity to interdict and punish stock theft, and they expropriated land on the Kalenjin borders and gave it over to European settlement as buffer zones (Lonsdale 1989: 26).

In addition, the colonial authorities occasionally promoted athletics as a surrogate for raiding. I have a letter from a former colonial officer, Arthur

Walford, who recalls one such campaign in the 1930s among the Kalenjin sub-group, the Kipsigis, using the slogan 'Ongechurge eng' uroriet ne ma luget', which Walford translates as 'Show your valor in sport and games, not in war'. He then adds, 'Unfortunately, the Second World War began shortly after this laudable precept had begun to take hold, and it had to be put into reverse in order to recruit for the Kings African Rifles' (Walford 1973).

The first part of Walford's account is particularly intriguing. If the Kalenjin propensity for cattle raiding earned them extra encouragement from the British to take up athletics instead, that might help to explain where the first running role models came from and why they were disproportionately Kalenjin. I also learned from other 'old colonials' that those arrested for stock theft had some-times been put to work building sports stadiums and running tracks. There seemed to be a strange kind of symbiosis between rustling and running.

Unfortunately, I have been unable to find any evidence of a general policy of encouraging sport as a surrogate for cattle raiding among the Kalenjin, and records show that convict labour built sports stadiums all over the country. The most concerted use of sport as an instrument of social control seems to have been among the Kikuyu in the late 1950s, after the Mau Mau rebellion (Askwith 1995: 146–57).

The second part of Walford's statement, about recruiting Kalenjin warriors into the military, also raised an interesting possibility – that it was in the uniformed services, the army and the police, that the Kalenjin got their early encouragement in athletics. With traditional raiding activities effectively curtailed, and a growing need for cash to pay hut taxes and school fees, the murenik found themselves obliged to find paying jobs, and the most honourable form of employment for a warrior was as a soldier.

Most of Kenya's early Olympic medalists – e.g. Kipchoge Keino, Kiprugut Chumo, Benjamin Kogo, Naftali Temu – were soldiers or policemen, and it was in those services that they had received the coaching that had developed their talent. It is also true that the Kalenjin, being viewed as a 'martial race', were recruited into the uniformed services in numbers greatly out of proportion to their population (Kirk-Greene 1980: 402), and that such recruitment often took place at local athletics meetings, where ambitious officers enlisted top athletes to boost their units' fortunes in inter-service competitions (Harris 1993).

These rather indirect effects of the traditional cattle complex go some way to explaining where the early role models came from, and their concentration among the Kalenjin. However, what is most intriguing are indirect effects that the traditional practices may have had in an entirely different context. Cattle raiding, and other elements of the cattle complex, may have functioned as genetic selection mechanisms, ultimately favouring strong runners.

Cattle raiding was common to most of east Africa's pastoral peoples, but in Kenya, the Kalenjin were arguably its foremost practitioners (Matson 1970: 63). This was particularly true after the decline of the Maasai in the nineteenth century. However, it was the distinctive nature of Kalenjin raids, as well as their frequency, that may be significant here. Maasai raids typically involved large armies marching in broad daylight into another tribe's territory and effectively intimidating their victims into yielding up their livestock (Chumba 2004). Kalenjin raids, by contrast, usually relied on stealth and speed. Most were small, ad hoc operations carried out by 20 men or fewer, moving at night. They might trek more than 100 miles to capture a herd that had previously been scouted and found vulnerable. The aim was to silently round up the cattle and drive them out of range of pursuers before an alarm was raised (Matson 1970: 63–7; Ng'eny 1970: 113).

The returning warriors were greeted by their jubilant villagers, songs of praise having already begun while the raid was still underway. Further singing would celebrate the deeds of the raiding party's *kiptaiyat*, or leader, and those who had distinguished themselves in the action. The spoils were divided evenly among surviving members of the party, with the *kiptaiyat* and the distinguished warriors getting first choice (Huntingford 1953: 85).

A young man who distinguished himself on a raid could expect to receive more than his share of invitations to participate in future raids, and if he survived, he might accumulate a considerable herd and a considerable reputation for valour. Cattle were needed to pay bride price, a common feature of pastoral societies. The more cattle a young man had, the brighter his marriage prospects, especially if he acquired them in raids on which he earned favourable repute – the other prerequisite for marriage (Chumba 2004). Thus the better a man was at cattle raiding, the more wives he would be able to marry and the more children he was likely to father.

What did it take for a warrior to distinguish himself? Courage certainly, coolness under fire, and perhaps leadership or tactical cleverness. But in view of the need to move unruly cattle quickly and quietly over long distances, it also required fleetness of foot and endurance. In a society that confers such a significant reproductive advantage on men who possess these attributes, it seems reasonable to suggest that whatever genetic configuration might underlie them could well spread through the group.

Of course this is hardly a verifiable hypothesis, but it is worth exploring further. The Kalenjin are highly conscious of heredity, perhaps as an outgrowth of their experience in breeding cattle. The tribe as a whole, and each of the major subgroups, are strongly endogamous (they marry within the group), but each of the couple of dozen hereditary clans within the subgroups are strictly exogamous (must marry outside the clan) – explicitly as a precaution against inbreeding. When a marriage is contemplated, the first question that the prospective bride's parents ask of the representatives of the prospective groom is what his clan is (Hollis 1909: 61; Oboler 1985: 102–4). And they also ask for examples of successful alliances between the groom's clan and the bride's – that is, marriages that have produced healthy children (Chumba 2004).

When a man is already married and seeking a second or third wife, additional criteria apply. 'Polygamy', I was told by one of my Kalenjin informants, 'is not for just anyone. The man has to be upright and courageous. If he has a reputation for courage, men with daughters ready to marry will seek him out' (Chumba 2004).

Before marriage, every Kalenjin adolescent had to undergo ritual circumcision as initiation into adulthood. The slow and painful operation was observed by watchful elders looking for the slightest flinch by a young initiate, which would cause him to fail this very public test and to be permanently labeled *kibitet*, or coward, and be consigned for life to a kind of internal exile (Hollis 1909: 54–5). A *kibitet* would, understandably, not be invited on cattle raids, and he would not be permitted to speak in tribal councils. Perhaps most significantly, he would generally not be able to marry (Chumba 2004). The ostensible reason for the operation, and for the consequences of failure, were to test a boy's ability to stand up to pressure and pain, and to prepare him for the rigours of a warrior's life. But the marriage prohibition was explicitly intended to keep a *kibitet* from propagating.

Female circumcision, or clitoridectomy, was once universal among the Kalenjin, as it was among most east African pastoralists. On the Horn of Africa, where the practice may have originated, the explicit aim of the operation was to reduce a young woman's pleasure in sex and thus help to ensure her chastity. A Kalenjin man, if asked the reason for this operation among his people, will often say the same thing. Interestingly, however, Kalenjin girls were expected to bear their excruciating operation as stoically as the boys, thus demonstrating a quality that would seem altogether irrelevant to chastity (Hollis 1909: 59). In addition, like many of the peoples of their Nilotic language family, the Kalenjin were not known for their chaste sexual behaviour (Goldschmidt 1976: 299). The early colonial literature, for example, is full of disapproving references to the practice of free love between warriors and unmarried girls (Eliot 1905: 132–3), and Kalenjin tradition also required that men routinely offer their wives to visiting age-mates. At the time of initiation, girls were examined to determine if they were virgins, and any found to be intact would be given a cow as a reward by her family and would be expected to earn a higher bride price. My informants tell me that they know of very few girls who were thus rewarded (Chumba 2004; Oboler 1985: 94–5).

So, if chastity was relatively unimportant to the Kalenjin, what was the real purpose of the operation? On the other hand, if it really was about chastity, why did it make any difference whether a girl bore the operation stoically or screamed hysterically? She was not going to be a warrior; there was no need for her to be courageous. Why bother to label a girl *chebitet* – the female equivalent of *kibitet* – if she winced or cried out, and thus effectively keep her from marrying? When I asked Kalenjin informants these questions, they responded as though the answer should have been self-evident. A *chebitet* had to be identified because, if she married, she might bear cowardly sons (Chepsiror 1994; Serem 1994).

What all this suggests is simply this: the Kalenjin were deliberately breeding for bravery. Men who had demonstrated particular valour were effectively encouraged by the society to have a lot of children, and men and women who had shown an absence of courage were generally kept from having any.

Of course, while the Kalenjin appear to think of courage as hereditary, it is probably fair to say that most Westerners do not. Yet an increasing number of behavioural traits are being found to have genetically-determined neuro-chemical bases. For example, the variable dopamine-receptor D_4DR gene on chromosome 11, appears to be associated with gradations of human thrill-seeking (Hamer and Copeland 1998). Possibly some forms of courage may have a comparable genetic component.

What does courage have to do with distance running? Quite a lot, especially in the closing stages of a tough race. But, more to the point here, because of the way the Kalenjin were assessing it, what they were actually breeding for was more than bravery. Their circumcision ritual tests not only the ability to withstand physical pain, but also to hold up under intense public pressure in a long-anticipated trial – perhaps not unlike a major athletic competition. And to distinguish himself on a Kalenjin cattle raid a warrior had to exhibit not just physical courage, but also stamina, speed and the ability to respond effectively in a crisis.

Finally, if we assume the constellation of traits the Kalenjin were actually breeding for are not unconnected with what makes a successful competitive distance runner, and if we assume further that those traits are in some degree heritable – two large assumptions, admittedly – was there time for the group's selective mating practices to have spread those traits throughout the population?

Natural selection is commonly thought to be a glacial process. But when a hereditary trait confers significant reproductive advantage, the process may move much faster. The population geneticist Luca Cavalli-Sforza has calculated, for example, that in societies in which adults drink fresh milk, an individual's ability to digest lactose confers approximately a 10% selection advantage over an individual unable to digest lactose. He has further calculated that a selection advantage of that magnitude can result in the advantaged trait becoming nearly universal in an affected population in little more than 1,000 years (Cavalli-Sforza 1996: 12–13).

With such a variety of attributes, heritable and otherwise, involved in being esteemed courageous in Kalenjin society, it is impossible to calculate the overall magnitude of the selection advantage, but clearly a significant reproductive edge was conferred on possessors of those attributes, and it seems reasonable to suggest that the traits, in so far as they are heritable, could have pervaded the population over the course of the 2,000 or more years since the Kalenjin and their ancestors adopted the cattle complex. The same may be true of east Africa's other pastoral peoples, although possibly to a lesser degree because of different customs regarding reproductive choices.

In a sense, all these societies – with their repeated tests of courage and their rewards, in terms of reproductive opportunity, for those who passed the tests – were, like the Kalenjin, trying to strengthen their military forces, but in so doing they may have fostered the development of traits that have made their modern heirs conquerors in an entirely different realm.

Bibliography

Askwith, T. (1995) *From Mau Mau to Harambee*, Cambridge: Cambridge African Monographs.

Buster, L. (1998) Athletes' agent, personal communication, 31 August.

Cavalli-Sforza, L. L., Menozzi, P. and Piazza, A. (1996) *The History and Geography of Human Genes*, Princeton, NJ: Princeton University Press.

Chepsiror, K. (1994) Nandi elder, personal communication, 12 December.

Chumba, J. (2004) Nandi elder, personal communication, 28 April.

Gaskell, D. (1998) Athletes' agent, personal communication, 31 August.

Ehret, C. (1971) *Southern Nilotic History*, Evanston, IL: Northwestern University Press.

Eliot, C. (1905) *The East Africa Protectorate*, London: Edward Arnold.

Goldschmidt, W. (1976) *Culture and Behavior of the Sebei*. Berkeley, CA: University of California Press.

Hamer, D. and Copeland, D. (1998) *Living With Our Genes*, New York: Doubleday.

Harris, T. (1993) Former colonial officer, personal communication, 22 August.

Hollis, A. C. (1909) *The Nandi: Their Language and Folklore*, Oxford: Oxford University Press.

Huntingford, G. W. B. (1953) *The Nandi of Kenya*, London: Routledge & Kegan Paul.

Kirk-Greene, A. H. M. (1980) '"Damnosa Hereditas": ethnic ranking and the martial races imperative in Africa', *Ethnic and Racial Studies* 3, 393–414.

Korir, A. (1994) Personal communication, 12 December.

Lonsdale, J. (1989) 'The Conquest State, 1895–904', in *A Modern History of Kenya 1895–1980*, ed. Ochieng, W. R., Nairobi: Evans Brothers Limited, pp. 6–34.

Manners, J. (1997) 'Kenya's running tribe', *The Sports Historian* 17 (2), 14–27.

Matson, A. T. (1970) 'Nandi traditions on raiding', in *Hadith*, ed. Ogot, B. A., Nairobi: East African Publishing House, pp. 61–78.

Matson, A. T. (1972) *Nandi Resistance to British Rule*, Nairobi: East African Publishing House.

Matson, A. T. (1974) *The Nandi Campaign against the British 1895–1906*, Nairobi: Transafrica Publishers.

Matthews, P., ed. (2004) *Athletics 2004: The International Track and Field Annual*, Cheltenham: SportsBooks Ltd.

Ng'eny, S. K. A. (1970) 'Nandi resistance to the establishment of British Administration 1893–1906', in *Hadith*, ed. Ogot, B. A., Nairobi: East African Publishing House, pp. 104–29.

Oboler, R. S. (1985) *Women, Power, and Economic Change: The Nandi of Kenya*, Stanford, CA: Stanford University Press.

Okeyo, D. (2003) quoted in O. Okoth 'Why runners burn out fast', *East African Standard*, 10 November, Nairobi.

Randich, J. (1998) Personal communication, 14 June.

Rotich, P. (1994) Personal communication, 26 August.

Serem, D. K. (1994) Nandi elder, personal communication, 12 December.

Templeton, J. (2003) Athletes' agent, personal communication, 29 May.

USA Running Circuit (2005) <http://www.usatf.org/events/2005/USARunningCircuit/champions.asp>.

Walford, A. (1973) Personal communication, 19 March.

World Almanac and Book of Facts (2005) New York: World Almanac Books.

Chapter 4

The Haile Gebrselassie story

A biography of difference

Jim Denison

Introduction

The Ethiopian long-distance runner, Haile Gebrselassie, is recognized across the world as one of the greatest distance runners of all time. Over the course of his decade-long international track career (he has now moved onto road running), he won two Olympic gold medals at 10,000 metres, four world championships at 10,000 metres and set 17 world records over five different distances. In January 2003 I was approached by Gebrselassie's Dutch manager, Jos Hermens, and asked to write Gebrselassie's official biography (Denison 2004). This invitation came about because I was leading (and I still do) a double life as an academic and a sports journalist. More specifically, as a former middle-distance runner I was writing regular feature stories for a number of popular running magazines in the USA and England such as *Runner's World* and *Athletics Weekly*. And my networks within international track and field put me in regular contact with a wide range of athletes, managers, promoters and members of the media.

My reaction to Hermens's invitation was mixed. Of course I was excited by the prospect of entering Gebrselassie's life and documenting his extraordinary career. But at the same time I was worried about whether I would be able to write 'authoritatively' and 'convincingly' about someone so different from me. I had never been to Ethiopia, and what little I did know about Ethiopia was limited to the stories of famine, drought and disease that dominated the world's headlines in the early 1980s. To understand Gebrselassie's life I knew I had to confront the obvious differences he and I shared – white, black, American, Ethiopian. I knew I had to visit him at home. I had to travel to Ethiopia. And in this paper I reflect on my first visit to Ethiopia, my experiences there and my concerns over the biographical writing process.

Being Haile Gebrselassie

Born on 18 April 1973, Haile Gebrselassie is a grown man with a deep sense of his own humanity and responsibility. He is married and he has three beautiful girls; he is a homeowner and he operates multiple businesses; he also sits on the

Figure 4.1 Haile and his collection of Mercedes cars, prizes from his World Championship victories.

board of numerous international aid organizations, travels the world, speaks English fluently, and has met dignitaries, presidents and prime ministers from over a dozen countries.

Nevertheless there is still a part of us that does not want to allow him to grow-up and become anything more than a stereotype. For example, as a boy Gebrselassie ran six miles to and from school six days a week carrying his books in one hand while hopping barefoot over stones and wading through waist-high rushing river water – a common stereotype ascribed to African runners. He also came from a family of 10 who shared a single room with a mud floor and sticks and leaves for walls. And Gebrselassie's size – 5 feet 4 inches (163 cm) and 121 lbs (55 kg) – his appearance – patient, content – and his accomplishments – physical and sporting – satisfy our desire to believe in something intuitive and complete: the natural athlete Bale (2001, 2004) might say. In this way, Gebrselassie remains the object of our western gaze where Africa, or more specifically, Ethiopia, symbolizes some outer, exotic land.

For the most part, western representations of African distance runners tend to emphasize their running ability as 'natural'. For Gebrselassie this has taken the form of newspaper articles that include romantic descriptions of the open, altitude-induced Ethiopian countryside – the site of Gebrselassie's workouts –

Figure 4.2 Haile at work as CEO of his own construction company.

and imaginative portrayals of his 'perfect' running body. This excerpt from an article in the *Daily Telegraph* is emblematic of this approach to try to understand Gebrselassie's remarkable achievements.

> His wrists are tiny. You notice that. More like struts than bones. In fact, his whole construction, especially on high-speed moves through gasping, trailing Olympic fields, seems based on materials not quite normal in regular human specimens. Kevlar and helium, maybe? Flesh and blood, skin and bones, shouldn't move that smoothly, airily, rhythmically, endlessly.
>
> (Mott 2002: 35)

According to Bale (2001, 2004), and Bale and Sang (1996), Africans are widely considered by many to develop into champion runners because of their 'natural way of life'. No one imagines young Africans running purposefully on confined measured spaces like tracks but instead running for fun or to meet their transport needs. Thus, we come to believe that running for Africans is something they take to easily, without thought or consideration. Their running is done without intention, we think, and certainly without government funding, coaching or the help of scientifically derived training programmes. Such stereotypes, however, can be harmful because as hooks comments:

stereotypes, like fictions, are created to serve as substitutions, standing in for what is real. . . . They are a fantasy, a projection onto the Other that makes them less threatening. Stereotypes abound when there is distance. They are an invention, a pretence that one knows when the steps that would make real knowing possible cannot be taken – are not allowed.

(hooks 1992: 341)

Over the course of his long career Gebrselassie has been framed in the West by the natural runner stereotype. Such misperceptions Bale (2001) argues, makes it easier for the western runner to rationalize his or her failure and contextualize defeat. The western athlete, as a consequence, Bale says, hides behind the pretence of the 'natural African runner', and denies the African athlete ambition and zeal, qualities that could pose a real threat to western runners' perceptions of their ability and potential. For if African distance runners are just thought of as natural athletes it becomes impossible for white athletes to succeed, and hence much easier to accept defeat. However, if African runners are credited with the ability to train and compete intelligently, what explanation does the white athlete have to explain his or her failure except to admit that they must not be training and competing as intelligently as their African counterpart? Being exposed in such a way, of course, poses a real threat to the long-standing stereotype of westerners as more intelligent than Africans.

Indeed, from our western perspective Gebrselassie's Ethiopianess – our stereotypes – seem to be on constant display whenever he comes to our shores to run. His skin is dark, and although he is fluent in English, we can't help but notice his 'mysterious' native language – Amharic. We question his religious identity in the wake of 11 September and wonder if he poses a security risk. When actually, like most Ethiopians he is Christian. Throughout English literature Africa has stood as the antithesis of civilization: a non-rational place where charms, spells, incantations, and magic spark fire and rain, save lives and tame wild animals. Africa is seen as the periphery to our core, the outside to our inside, the back to our front. A place, the Nigerian scholar, Chinua Achebe, says, 'where man's vaunted intelligence and refinement are finally mocked by triumphant bestiality' (1989: 34).

In the wake of such an interpretation, Africa has been reduced by many to a prop: African humanity and the African people exist to help the European examine his or her own troubled psyche. The early Europeans to arrive in Africa – Dr David Livingstone, Sir Henry Morton Stanley – described what they saw in crude, ethnocentric forms: 'The African is ugly and mysterious', they wrote in their journals, 'just limbs or rolling eyes, and in this way subhuman'. These travellers were what the anthropologist Clifford Geertz (1973) might call, 'disrespectful guests'. By their presence, they made the life of their hosts more difficult, when, actually, the ethical and careful visitor should prove an illuminating guest as he or she honestly tries to discover the 'truth' of where they are.

Throughout the 200-year history of African exploration and colonization – the great African land grab – accounts from white men in sun helmets trekking through the bush have dominated our perceptions. Views that actually acknowledge Africans' full and complex humanity are sorely missing. Although recently a number of post-colonial scholars (e.g. Kirshenblatt-Gimblett 1998; Lindfors 2003; Pieterse 1992) have awakened us to the fact that 'others' are indeed flesh and blood subjects, not museum pieces posing for our benefit. In this way, Ethiopian people have come to be seen not as half-made and naïve but as independent and self-determining. They have seen problems in the past and dealt with them adequately – drought, famine, disease. Despite what Joseph Conrad (1995) might have wanted us to think, the African soul is not rudimentary. Ethiopians, after all, have learned to live between various worlds and languages – their own, ours. Ethiopia has its own culture and history that doesn't begin with us (Pankhurst 1982, 1990).

However, as Gebrselassie runs around the tracks of Europe or America he is still confined by the four sides of a television picture and in the process he becomes the symbolic 'native' we are allowed to possess. He does not need to speak (or read and think), but just smile. We only expect him to act . . . to run. Isn't he just performing what is natural for him anyway? Moreover, we rarely see

Figure 4.3 Haile stretching following one of his training sessions at Entoto, 11,000 feet above sea level.

Gebrselassie at home. We do not understand his language, his myths, his customs. The Ethiopian landscape is generally unknown to us. As a result, we struggle to read and interpret its socio-cultural and historical subtleties. We have no sense of the ordinary, that which is wholly unexotic: Gebrselassie pumping gas into his car, or shopping for groceries, or watching the television news, or enjoying some time with his friends or reading a bedtime story to one of his girls. Do Ethiopian people do these things? Do African runners do these things? That is how distanced African life is from our lives, and how excluded it is from our imagination. So we might fashion stories of Africanness that originate from somewhere 'Once Upon a Time'. Stories that no longer exist – stories that quite possibly never existed in the first place. And so it was with all of this 'racial folklore' (Hoberman, personal conversation) occupying my mind, that I travelled to Ethiopia with my notebook and pen in hand to try and figure out how to write Gebrselassie's biography.

A trip to Ethiopia

Departure: 30 April 2003

Shaving this morning I could not help but notice how white I am. Not white as in pale, as in, *I need to get some sun.* But white as in a white man, a Caucasian. Of all the amazing and spectacular events I expect to experience in Ethiopia, one of them will certainly be standing out as such an obvious minority. Surprisingly, my Lufthansa flight to Addis Ababa is filled mostly with other white people: German businessmen, American missionaries, intrepid New Zealanders on their one year overseas' experience. There does not seem to be a single Ethiopian aboard?

A visit to the countryside: 3 May 2003

It is an early start to the day, 6:30 in the morning. I am met outside my hotel by Haile's driver, Getaneh. We are heading out of Addis Ababa for the day on the road to Asela; we will collect Haile 13 miles into our journey, the point where he will complete his morning run. Asela is where Haile was born and we are going there to visit his father and some of his brothers and sisters. The three-hour drive over broken roads takes us through various-sized towns and villages. And for each place Haile has a story or something interesting to point out: a hotel owned by a friend, a military base or a new irrigation system being put in. The traffic is immense and hazardous: walkers, cyclists, animals, cars, trucks. We stop for juice in an area renowned for its sugar cane, mango and pineapple – what a lush place off the banks of Ethiopia's largest internal river. The locals are ecstatic to see Haile, and as usual he charms them and remembers to pass out some money before we leave. We arrive into Asela and drive past Haile's high school and primary school. We stop at a small hotel for lunch before going on to meet Haile's family. They are overjoyed to see Haile, and to welcome the man they have read about in the Addis Ababa *Tribune*, Haile's 'white shadow'.

City walk: 6 May 2003

This is my first outing alone through Addis Ababa, and how different it feels to be separated from Haile and the security and fanfare his company brings. It is early in the morning, just past sunrise, but Addis is wide awake. The buses are already full, every shop along Haile Gebrselassie Avenue is open for business. I feel somewhat precarious in my position; a gaze surrounds me: I am so obviously different, so obviously the other. It is like I am a swimmer in strange and unfamiliar waters. And I can't help but watch my back as I slowly paddle on. If I go under will I be lost forever?

Reflections

To undertake biographical research into an 'other' – a person unrepresentative of your own background and experience – your initial steps tend to come from what you can find in texts: quotes, pictures, descriptions. And because you can't really 'feel' or 'be' the life you are studying you run the risk of giving more importance to that which may in truth be spurious – a statement in a newspaper article, an expression in a photograph. And you do this while the actual life of your subject carries on in unrelated trajectories.

However, the test for a successful biography, I believe, is the same as the test for any successful narrative: integrity in motion. It is not the facts gleamed from texts that make a biography come alive, it is the story, the facts run by the eye at the correct speed. Unlike a novelist, however, who can invent a character, put that character in a situation, and then sit back and neatly watch what happens, a biographer, or any other type of social scientist or non-fiction writer has to do with his or her main character what that person has really done or is doing. And quite often that is something messy, or unrelated to building a coherent tale. But what a marvellous condition of the human mind it is that even non-fiction plots take on the illusion of clean continuity. As John Updike said, 'The "Marx" that the historian has imagined keeps behaving, in every new set of conditions, like his Marx' (2003: 76).

To a large degree, this was how I worked with my material from Gebrselassie's life. Despite going past the textual evidence I collected at the beginning of the project, and actually spending some real time with Gebrselassie in Ethiopia, I still found it difficult to move beyond the initial bits of information about his life that first floated to the surface – his upbringing, his sporting achievements, his race. It is in this way, apparently, that the intuition of the whole seems to precede the accumulation of the parts. In other words, I always felt that my relationship with Gebrselassie was largely defined and informed by our differences – white, black, American, Ethiopian – and our understandings of those differences. Try as we might, or more likely try as I might – the well-intentioned writer – difference is something very difficult to transcend.

Every day during the writing of Gebrselassie's biography when I sat down in front of my computer to describe the look and feel of Addis Ababa, for example, or the dynamics of Gebrselassie's relationship with his friends and family, or the intricacies of Ethiopia's tribal distinctions – an aspect of Ethiopian culture so complex that Gebrselassie even refused to try to explain it to me – I felt incredibly restrained. It was also hard for me to understand Gebrselassie's 'true' motivations as a runner and those factors that might explain his incredible success: Is it the biological or the biographical? Along the way I formed my own theories, and of course I can be open to understanding differences in people, but clearly I can never get inside those differences and offer an authoritative explanation on anything.

My concerns regarding the efficacy of understanding others' lives has led me to speculate, What do people read biographies for in the first place? And sport biographies, in particular. Most people probably read biographies for simple information. And in the case of the many running enthusiasts who bought my book, that probably means finding out the types of workouts Gebrselassie does, what he eats before races and the behind-the-scenes details of his Olympic victories in Atlanta in 1996 and Sydney in 2000. But don't people also collect information – factual or fictional – in order to acquire the ability to understand that information? In other words, to break down the wall of print, pictures and statistics – records, times, measures of blood and bone – to find out what it is really like inside a person's life and how best to explain and account for that life in some definitive manner? I thought that by travelling to Ethiopia I would be able to supplant my previous textual interpretations of Gebrselassie's life and his achievements, and develop a more honest rendering of 'Haile Gebrselassie the man'. But that did not seem to happen. Rather, I believe now that my initial intuitions born through our differences and sustained through various discourses made what 'realities' I saw and felt in person with Gebrselassie in Ethiopia just that much more sensible. Does this then define biography as the simple transfer of intuitive knowledge into a story that at best can only claim to be authentic? Moreover, is that such a bad thing? Maybe it is a more honest approach to writing, whereby in the case of my biography of Gebrselassie, I remain the writer, me, and he remains the runner, him. In other words, we both remain different.

Gayatri Spivak (in Sharpe and Spivak 2002) would probably agree with my assessment of biographies as unauthentic representations, even adding that I have not extended my relationship with Gebrselassie because I did not practise my craft under the best model of fieldwork. But that is because I had a commercial understanding with Gebrselassie, not an educational one. My role was clearly spelled out in my contract: 'to produce the life story of Haile Gebrselassie, the runner, for immediate release following the 2004 Athens Olympics'. My goal, therefore, could not be the patient effort to learn without necessarily transmitting that learning to others, what Spivak says should be every researcher's goal because that is what enables the fieldworker or the scientist to learn without having to focus on digesting his or her findings and material for production. If one's energies as a researcher or a writer are towards production, she says, 'you are constantly processing, and you are processing your work into what you already know. You're not learning something' (2002: 620).

With respect to writing about others and difference, Spivak's comments are especially relevant (see Sharpe and Spivak 2002). It is difficult to learn something, particularly in my case when what I was writing had to abide by a number of commercial forces: price points, serialization, suitability to a white-adult-male readership. But surely my biography of Gebrselassie says something insightful about Africanness in general, and Ethiopia in particular? Or maybe my contribution is to help explain the politics of whiteness, and how white subjectivities are also created and performed historically through a series of complex and shifting discourses and interactions. And come to think of it, more than anything else it might enable us to better understand what we already know about African runners.

Bibliography

Achebe, C. (1989) *Hopes and Impediments: Selected Essays*, London: Doubleday.

Bale, J. (2001) 'Nyandika Maiyoro and Kipchoge Keino: transgression, colonial rhetoric and the postcolonial athlete', in *Sports Stars: The Cultural Politics of Sporting Celebrity*, ed. Andrews, D. L. and Jackson, S. J., London: Routledge, pp. 218–23.

Bale, J. (2004) *Running Cultures: Racing in Time and Ace*, London: Routledge.

Bale, J. and Sang, J. (1996) *Kenyan Running: Movement Culture, Geography and Global Change*, London: Frank Cass.

Conrad, J. (1995) *Heart of Darkness*, London: Penguin.

Denison, J. (2004) *The Greatest*, New York: Breakaway Books.

Geertz, C. (1973) *The Interpretation of Culture*, New York: Basic Books.

hooks, b. (1992) 'Representing whiteness in the black imagination', in *Cultural Studies*, ed. Grossberg, L., Nelson, C. and Treichler, P., London: Routledge, pp. 338–46.

Kirshenblatt-Gimblett, B. (1998) *Destination Culture: Tourism, Museums, and Heritage*. Berkeley, CA: University of California Press.

Lindfors, B. (2003) 'Ethnological show business: footlighting the dark continent', in *Performance Studies*, ed. Striff, E., MacMillian: London, pp. 29–40.

Mott, S. (2002) 'Ethiopian demi-god runs first marathon since days of childhood poverty', *The Daily Telegraph* 12 April, 35–6.

Pankhurst, R. (1982) 'The history of an Ethiopian icon', *African Affairs* 81, 117–25.

Pankhurst, R. (1990) *A Social History of Ethiopia*, Addis Ababa: University of Addis Ababa.

Pieterse, J. N. (1992) *White on Black: Images of Africa and Blacks in Western Popular Culture*, New Haven, CT: Yale University Press.

Sharpe, J. and Spivak, G. C. (2002) 'A conversation with Gayatri Spivak: politics and the imagination', *Signs* 28, 609–24.

Updike, J. (2003) 'The conditions of biography', *The New Yorker* 25 February, 74–8.

Part 2

Physiological perspectives

Chapter 5

Outstanding performance despite low fluid intake

The Kenyan running experience

Barry W. Fudge, Yannis Pitsiladis, David Kingsmore, Timothy D. Noakes and Bengt Kayser

Introduction

Kenya has been increasingly successful in international racing over the last four decades since its emergence in world athletics in the 1960s (Table 5.1). Despite being a comparatively small country comprising just 0.5% of the total population of the world, the majority (51%) of top ten yearly performances from 800 m to marathon in 2004 were from Kenyan athletes. Two recent investigations reported the nutritional and lifestyle practices of elite Kenyan endurance runners preparing for major national competition – the National Championships 2003 and the 2004 Athens Olympic national trials (Onywera *et al.* 2004; Fudge *et al.* 2006). The athletes studied were training at a high altitude training camp in Kenya (Global Sports Training Camp, Kaptagat, Eldoret, Kenya) and included world and junior champions. The most striking finding was the remarkably low daily fluid intake of these senior and junior endurance runners, primarily water (1.1 ± 0.3 and 0.9 ± 0.5 L·d^{-1}, respectively)

Table 5.1 Percentage of Kenyan athletes in IAAF top ten yearly rankings in events ranging from 800 m to marathon

Year	% Top 10
2004	51
2000	49
1996	47
1992	40
1988	16
1984	7
1980	*
1976	*
1972	7
1968	9
1964	1

Note: * Kenyan withdrawal from International Competition due to a boycott.

and milky tea (1.2 ± 0.3 and 0.9 ± 0.3 L·d⁻¹, respectively). Furthermore, these elite athletes did not consume liquids before or during training, rarely consumed liquids after training, and only consumed modest amounts when they did drink. This finding is remarkable given that such fluid intake is substantially less than the current recommendations of various organizations such as the American College of Sports Medicine (ACSM) (ACSM 1996a, 1996b), the National Association of Athletic Trainers (NAAT) (Casa *et al.* 2000; Binkley *et al.* 2002), and the US Army (Montain *et al.* 1999). The ACSM suggests 0.4 to 0.6 L of fluid 2 to 3 hours before exercise, 0.6 to 1.2 L·hr⁻¹ while exercising and total replacement of all fluid lost during exercise afterwards (ACSM 1996a, 1996b), a pattern and volume of fluid replacement similar to that of NAAT, and the US Army (Casa *et al.* 2000; Binkley *et al.* 2002; and Montain *et al.* 1999, respectively).

This chapter therefore addresses the question: how can the outstanding performances of elite Kenyan endurance runners be explained despite an *ad libitum* fluid intake that is well below the prevailing recommendations? In an attempt to answer this question, the rationale, the limitations, and the progression of hydration research over the last several decades is reviewed, particularly in the context of actual race-performance evidence versus laboratory investigations.

Evolution of fluid intake guidelines

During the first half of the twentieth century it was typically believed by many sportsmen that consuming fluid, or indeed eating during an endurance event, was not necessary, but was in fact, a sign of weakness (Noakes 1993). For example, Arthur Newton, an ultra-marathon runner holding several world records in events ranging from 50 to 130 miles in the early part of the twentieth century, commented: 'Even in the warmest English weather, a twenty-six mile run ought to be manageable with no more than a single drink, or at most two' (Newton 1948; referenced in Noakes 1993). During the 1930s and 1940s the first data on the effects of working in the heat on fluid and electrolyte requirements were reported in the scientific literature. Early studies reported observations of the effects of climatic conditions on people working outside, for example workers building the Hoover Dam in Nevada (see e.g. Adolph and Dill 1938), and non-combatant experimental subjects, particularly relevant to desert warfare in the Second World War (see e.g. Adolph 1947). However it was almost two decades later before a study was performed in athletes which reported a linear relationship ($r = 0.67$) between core temperature (T_c) and dehydration (0–5% body mass loss) in runners following two 32 km field tests (Wyndham and Strydom 1969). This finding prompted the suggestion that those exercising for prolonged periods of time would need to consume fluids. Interestingly, better performance was accompanied by higher T_c and greater body mass losses, a finding confirmed in other reports (Pugh *et al.* 1967; Muir *et al.* 1970). Although the report by Wyndham and Strydom is often credited as the original work on hydration and exercise performance (ACSM 1975, 1987), it was not the first; Buskirk and Beetham (1960) reported a linear relationship between dehydration and T_c in marathon runners ($r = 0.58$; improved to $r = 0.66$ after controlling for rate of work). Nevertheless Wyndham and Strydoms' study was the major stimulus for further work on hydration and exercise performance, and was the initial evidence used in guidelines by the ACSM for suggesting specific fluid intake (ACSM 1975, 1987, 1996a, 1996b). These ACSM guidelines and Position Statements/Stands have been significantly revised and amended over the last three decades (ACSM 1975, 1987, 1996a, 1996b; Table 5.2).

However, there has been a recent challenge to prevailing fluid intake guidelines. A major comparative review concluded that the main points and rationale are 'not evidence-based, since none of the Position Statements/Stands refers to specific, prospective, interventional studies from which such definite conclusions can be drawn' (Noakes 2004). For example, an addition to the Position Stand made in 1987 was 'such dehydration will subsequently reduce sweating and predispose the runner to hyperthermia, heat stroke, heat exhaustion, and muscle cramps' (ACSM 1987: 530) and referenced Wyndham and Strydom (1969), despite this study not actually investigating the incidence of hyperthermia, heat stroke, heat exhaustion or muscle cramps. Similarly, the subsequent Position Stand in 1996 (ACSM 1996a: ii) suggested 'Adequate fluid consumption before and during race can reduce the risk of heat illness, including disorientation and irrational behaviour, particularly in longer events such as the marathon' and cited Wyndham and Strydom (1969), Costill et al. (1970) and Gisolfi and Copping (1974), again despite none of these studies actually investigating any of these conditions in a controlled intervention trial with varying rates of fluid ingestion. The fluid intake guidelines suggested by the ACSM have been questioned as being based on an extrapolation of a few observational studies whose aims were not to investigate differing rates of fluid intake in controlled prospective trials (Noakes 2004, 2006 a and b; Noakes et al. 2006; Noakes and Speedy 2006). The guidelines from other bodies producing recommendations can be similarly criticized, such as those of the NAAT (Casa et al. 2000; Binkley et al. 2002) and of the US Army (Montain et al. 1999).

The current debate on adequate fluid intake during endurance exercise has turned vociferous and shows little sign of being resolved without further experimental and observational evidence (Noakes 2000, 2001). Despite the paucity of evidence, recommendations have been continuously evolving. An alternative approach has been taken in guidelines proposed by the International Marathon Medical Directors Association (Noakes and Martin 2002; Noakes 2003) that suggests a radically different hypothesis, namely that athletes should consume fluid as dictated by thirst, and not drink to their tolerable limit (ACSM 1996a, 1996b). These guidelines have also been adopted by other organizations such as USA Track and Field (Casa 2003). Similarly, the International Consensus Guidelines for the prevention of exercise-associated hyponatraemia invoke the

Table 5.2 Summary of main additions to ACSM Position Statements/Stands for fluid intake recommendations since 1975 to present

Position Stand	Additions/main points	Cited authors
1975 (ACSM 1975)	• Athletes should 'be encouraged to frequently ingest fluids during competition' • Rationale: 'reduce rectal temperature and prevent dehydration'	
1987 (ACSM 1987)	• 'Fluid consumption before and during the race will reduce the risk of heat injury, particularly in longer runs such as the marathon' • 'Such dehydration will subsequently reduce sweating and predispose the runner to hyperthermia, heat stroke, heat exhaustion, and muscle cramps'	• Wyndham and Strydom 1969; Costill et al. 1970; Gisolfi and Copping 1974 • Wyndham and Strydom 1969
1996 (ACSM 1996a, 1996b)	• 'Adequate fluid consumption before and during race can reduce the risk of heat illness, including disorientation and irrational behaviour, particularly in longer events such as the marathon' • Dehydration can 'predispose the runner to heat exhaustion or the more dangerous hyperthermia and exertional heat stroke' • 'Intravenous (IV) fluid therapy facilitates rapid recovery (in runners with heat exhaustion)' • Athletes should 'replace their sweat losses or consume 150–300 ml every 15 minutes (600–1200 ml)'	• Wyndham and Strydom 1969; Costill et al. 1970; Gisolfi and Copping 1974 • Hubbard and Armstrong1988; Pearlmutter 1986 • Hubbard and Armstrong 1988; Nash 1985

Note: Present authors' additions in italics.

Source: Adapted from Noakes 2004.

same advice (Hew-Butler et al. 2005). In the following paragraphs the evidence behind these opposing guidelines will be briefly reviewed.

Rationale and limitations of fluid intake guidelines

Dehydration: critique of traditional concepts

Athletes exercising in the heat can achieve sweat rates up to 2.5 L·hr^{-1} (Sawka and Montain 2000). The traditional view of the cardiovascular response to this is that dehydration causes a progressive decline in stroke volume with a subsequent increase in heart rate, to ensure that cardiac output is maintained (Ekelund 1967). This decrease in stroke volume is attributed to a decrease in plasma volume due to water loss in sweat (Sawka et al. 1984; Sawka et al. 1985; Montain and Coyle 1992a). There is ultimately a limiting maximum heart rate and, with failure to accommodate the ongoing reduction in stroke volume, a reduction in cardiac output. Furthermore, circulating blood volume, available for the muscle mass engaged in the exercise, may be further decreased by cutaneous vasodilatation to allow heat dissipation, with consequent decreased venous return, reduced stroke volume, reduced end-diastolic filling pressure and resultant further cardiovascular stress (Rowell 1986). Thus the rationale given to explain an ergogenic effect of ingesting copious volumes of fluid during exercise is threefold: the fluid ingested would: 1. maintain plasma (blood) volume and reduce cardiovascular strain; 2. improve heat dissipation via convection; and 3. allow sufficient body water for sweat production and optimum evaporative cooling. Thus, it was proposed that water intake during exercise reduces cardiovascular and thermoregulatory strain and should ultimately improve exercise performance, especially in the heat (ACSM 1996a, 1996b).

However, the scientific evidence for the above reasoning is weak at best. First, the hypothesis that increased cutaneous blood flow reduces stroke volume has been seriously challenged. Gonzalez-Alonso et al. (1995) demonstrated that a combination of heat stress and dehydration results in a marked reduction of cutaneous blood flow as skin and systemic vascular resistance increase while the cardiovascular system attempts to cope with the challenge of reductions in cardiac output. Furthermore, two similar studies showed that despite marked reductions in muscle blood flow as a result of dehydration after 2 hours of exercise, substrate (glucose and free fatty acids) and oxygen delivery, oxygen consumption and lactate removal did not change (Gonzalez-Alonso et al. 1998, 1999). More recently, Gonzalez-Alonso et al. (2000) found that stroke volume was similar while exercising at moderate intensity in hot (35°C) vs. cold (8°C) conditions, both in the euhydrated and dehydrated condition even though cutaneous blood flow varied. It follows that an increase in cutaneous blood flow does not explain the reduction in stroke volume, nor the progressive increase in heart rate (cardiac drift) observed during prolonged exercise, both of which are exacerbated in the heat. By contrast, Fritzsche et al. (1999) demonstrated that cardiac drift is completely prevented with a β_1-adrenoceptor blocker ingested immediately before exercise, suggesting that the decrease in stroke volume during prolonged exercise is more likely to be the result of an increase in heart rate (Coyle and Gonzalez-Alonso 2001) leading to a reduction in diastolic filling time (Sheriff *et al.* 1993). The latter authors found that exercising in the lying position negated these effects, suggesting that there is also a postural component leading to a reduction in central blood volume and diastolic cardiac filling.

Second, modest dehydration (up to 3 L) does not alter sweat rate (Ladell 1955; Costill *et al.* 1970; Armstrong and Maresh 1998; Daries *et al.* 2000; Cheuvront and Haymes 2001a; Saunders *et al.* 2005). Costill *et al.* (1970: 523), for example, reported similar sweat rates in subjects consuming fluids and subjects consuming no fluids: 'each runner's skin was sufficiently wetted by sweating to permit maximal evaporation in all test conditions'. If modest dehydration does not impair sweat rates, consuming fluid cannot therefore improve the sweating rate further. This is particularly relevant, as 70–90% of heat loss during running is achieved through sweating (Sawka and Montain 2000). However, the exact relationships between air velocity, temperature and humidity, sweat evaporation and sweat rates remain to be experimentally established.

Finally, there is some confusion in the literature between haemoconcentration (net capillary filtration and a loss of plasma volume) and haemodilution (net absorption and expansion of plasma volume) of the blood volume in response to exercise (Pivarnik *et al.* 1984; Senay *et al.* 1980; reviewed by Harrison 1985). The effect on plasma volume varies with exercise mode and it is important to clarify the type of exercise being considered. For example, Gore *et al.* (1992) demonstrated that the effects on plasma volume of cycling were not the same as running because of differences in posture. Indeed even at rest, rising from a seated to an upright position results in haemoconcentration. Contradictory findings and thus confusion potentially may be caused by failure to differentiate between exercise-induced changes and postural changes in plasma volume (Harrison 1985). For the purpose of the rest of this chapter, only the literature on running will be considered.

A number of studies have shown that plasma volume during running exercise is maintained, despite water losses between 1–3 L (Costill *et al.* 1970; Edwards and Harrison 1984; Galbo *et al.* 1975; Rocker *et al.* 1976; Whiting *et al.* 1984; Myhre *et al.* 1985; Maughan *et al.* 1985; Daries *et al.* 2000; Cheuvront and Haymes 2001a). Thus, in conditions of moderate dehydration, plasma volume is maintained with water from other body-water compartments. The corollary has also been well demonstrated: Watt *et al.* (2000) demonstrated that plasma volume expansion did not alter heart rate, T_c, skin blood flow and ultimately exercise performance in the heat. Similarly, Grant *et al.* (1997) demonstrated that acute expansion of plasma volume served only to alter cardiac function at the onset of exercise, and did not attenuate the classic cardiac drift during prolonged exercise. Thus there appears to be a stabilization of plasma volume during running exercise. Indeed Edwards and Harrison (1984) suggest that no further reduction in plasma volume occurs despite a clear reduction in total body water, at least during levels of water loss up to 1–3 L (Gore *et al.* 1992). This might be explained by a shift of protein into the vascular compartment via the lymphatic system, thus contributing to the maintenance of plasma volume (Senay 1970). Such a protein shift during exercise has been reported in the literature (Senay 1975; Edwards *et al.* 1983; Pivarnik *et al.* 1984; Edwards and Harrison 1984).

In conclusion, in conditions of modest dehydration such as encountered during typical endurance exercise activities, fluid intake does not alter plasma volume, sweat rate or cardiovascular function. While fluid ingestion does improve performance compared to no fluid ingestion, the key aspect remains on the volume of fluid ingested: is there any benefit to drinking more fluid than *ad libitum*?

Body fluid balance during running exercise

Exercise induces sweating, and the loss of water will affect body-fluid distribution (Sawka *et al.* 2001). Sweat is hypotonic relative to plasma, hence relatively more fluid is lost compared to electrolytes, and the resulting elevation of extracellular tonicity will result in water diffusion from the intracellular to the extracellular fluid compartment along hydrostatic and osmotic-oncotic pressure gradients (Costill *et al.* 1976; Durkot *et al.* 1986; Morimoto *et al.* 1998; Sawka and Coyle 1999). For example, Nose *et al.* (1983) demonstrated that a large quantity of the total body water deficit due to thermal dehydration in the rat was intracellular from muscle and skin. The authors concluded that all fluid compartments compensate for fluid lost in sweating in order to maintain adequate circulation to the brain, or more probably, to maintain serum osmolality. The overall picture is further complicated by other mechanisms that may also be contributing to total body water balance during exercise, and the lack of clarification in studies between mass lost from water versus other causes of loss of body mass (Olson and Saltin 1970; Pivarnik *et al.* 1984; Pastene *et al.* 1996; Cheuvront and Haymes 2001b). For example, Noakes (2003) noted that any body mass lost during exercise includes oxidized metabolic fuel (Pastene *et al.* 1996). In addition, loss of body mass versus water loss may be complicated by metabolic water production and glycogen water decomplexing that potentially could provide a reservoir of additional water for the maintenance of plasma volume (Olson and Saltin 1970). The potential relevance of this effect was demonstrated by Pastene *et al.* (1996) who calculated that, despite athletes losing 2 kg of body mass during a marathon, they may be dehydrated by a mere 242 g when allowance is made for those sources, whereas plasma volume would be unchanged after consideration of postural induced alterations. Thus water losses are distributed throughout body fluid compartments while plasma volume is defended for effective circulation and osmotic regulation; similarly, any addition of water via fluid intake, metabolic water production or water decomplexing helps compensate for total water losses throughout the body fluid compartments.

The importance of metabolic rate as a factor in determining rectal temperature response to exercise

An alternative theory to the degree of dehydration as the cause of the rise in T_c has been proposed (Noakes *et al.* 1991). Noakes *et al.* (1991) propose that the primary factor in determining T_c is the rate of energy expenditure, or the metabolic rate (see also Wyndham *et al.* 1970; Saltin and Hermansen 1966; Greenhaff 1989). Early studies already clearly demonstrated that relative exercise intensity (i.e. percentage maximal oxygen consumption ($\dot{V}O_2$ max)) correlates well with rectal temperature during exercise (Saltin and Hermansen 1966). Furthermore, the highest placed finishers in a marathon typically have the highest post-race rectal temperatures (Maron *et al.* 1975; Noakes *et al.* 1991; Pugh *et al.* 1967), a finding consistent with observations of elite athletes completing a marathon at a higher percentage of $\dot{V}O_2$ max than non-elite runners (Maughan and Leiper 1983; Fox and Costill 1972). Pugh *et al.* (1967) measured rectal temperatures, sweat rates and body mass loss during a marathon run in warm conditions. They reported that the winner's compared to average race finisher's mean speed was higher (16 vs. 13 km·hr⁻¹), their estimated $\dot{V}O_2$ was higher (54 vs. 44 mL·kg⁻¹·min⁻¹), their body mass loss was double (5.23 vs. 2.85 kg) and their post-race rectal temperature was higher (41.1 vs. 39.0°C). Collectively these data indicate that faster runners work at higher metabolic rates, and therefore become hotter and more dehydrated, but win the race.

Environmental influences on the development of hyperthermia and the impact on performance

Whether at rest or exercising, in temperate or hot environments, the body attempts to homeostatically maintain internal body temperature within a narrow range. It does so in a complex interaction between the central nervous system (CNS), the cardiovascular system and the skin. The thermoregulatory centre in the hypothalamus receives information regarding core and skin temperatures from circulating blood and skin receptors, respectively. Body temperature is dependent on the balance between metabolic heat production and heat loss to the environment. Heat exchange between the body and the surrounding environment is determined by the following heat-storage equation:

$$S = M \pm R \pm K \pm C - E$$

Where S denotes the amount of stored heat, M is the metabolic heat produced, R, K and C are the heat lost or gained via radiation, conduction and convection, respectively, and E is the evaporative heat loss. When ambient temperature is lower than skin temperature and heat loss is favoured due to a thermal gradient, heat is transferred to the skin by conductive blood flow where it is dissipated via convection, radiation and sweat evaporation. When ambient temperature rises and reduces the effectiveness of convection and radiation, sweat evaporation becomes the most effective means of heat loss. Snellen *et al.* (1970) experimentally determined that for 1 L of evaporated sweat, 600 kcal of heat is removed. However, when humidity increases (i.e. ambient water vapour pressure increases) heat loss through sweat evaporation can be severely limited even resulting in net heat gain by the body. A common method to assess the potential thermal load is by Wet Bulb Globe Temperature (WBGT) which provides information regarding humidity, radiation, and dry bulb (air) temperature. At a humidity of 100%, the wet bulb temperature equals the dry bulb temperature; otherwise the wet bulb temperature is lower than that of the dry bulb. The ACSM (ACSM 1987) suggests a WBGT not higher than 28°C for competition.

There is no doubt that an increasing thermal load decreases exercise performance (Adams *et al.* 1975; Nielsen *et al.* 1993; Galloway and Maughan 1997). For example, Galloway and Maughan (1997) exercised eight male volunteers to exhaustion at four different ambient temperatures. The authors demonstrated that time to exhaustion was influenced by ambient temperature: exercise duration was shortest at 31°C (51.6 ± 3.7 min) and longest at 11°C (93.5 ± 6.2 min). Evidence supporting heat accumulation as a factor limiting performance can also be found outside the laboratory (Suping *et al.* 1992; McCann and Adams 1997; Cheuvront and Haymes 2001a). Indeed, Figure 5.1 shows the relationship between marathon performance and air temperature for the top ten all-time marathon times and the summer Olympic results since 1972. The top ten marathons of all time were run in conditions significantly

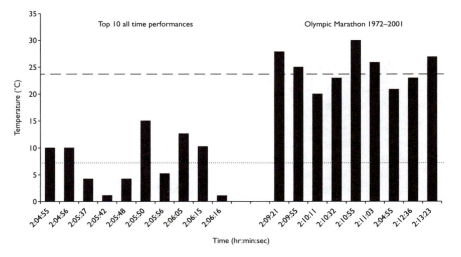

Figure 5.1 Top ten marathon performances of all-time compared to Olympic marathons from 1972 to 2004.

Note: Dotted line represents the average temperature (7.3°C) for all-time best marathons; dashed line represents average temperature (24.8°C) for Olympic marathons.

cooler (7.3 ± 4.9°C) than the summer Olympic games (24.8 ± 3.3°C) of the past four decades. This strongly suggests an effect of ambient temperature on marathon performance, in agreement with the laboratory results of Galloway and Maughan (1997). Interestingly, none of the winning times presented in Figure 5.1 for the Olympic marathon is sufficiently fast to be included in the top 200 all-time performances. There is a similar deterioration in performance with increasing thermal load for track races such as the 3,000 m steeplechase and the 10,000 m (McCann and Adams 1997).

Given the importance of the environment in determining thermal load and running performance, hydration research must take environmental conditions into account. However, many studies have not done so: Table 5.3 (adapted from Noakes 2004), presents the environmental conditions and prevailing wind speed used in each of the four classic studies on the effects of dehydration on T_c (Wyndham and Strydom 1969; Costill et al. 1970; Gisolfi and Copping 1974; Montain and Coyle 1992b). At least two of the studies (Gisolfi and Copping 1974; 33°C, 38% humidity; Montain and Coyle 1992b; 33°C, 50% humidity) stand out as being performed in 'weather' conditions that would be in the 'High Risk' zone for thermal injury as suggested by the ACSM (ACSM 1987). Furthermore, the facing wind speed (i.e. the main route for heat loss via convection) in three out of the four studies was well below typical outdoor conditions during competition (di Prampero et al. 1979). Adams et al. (1992) found that the rate of whole body cooling may be different when exercising in the laboratory compared to outdoors. The authors reported that subjects had higher whole body temperatures (i.e. rectal and oesophageal) when exercising in wind-still conditions (0.75 km·hr^{-1}) compared to a facing wind velocity of 11.25 km·hr^{-1}. Similarly, a previous study that compared wind-still conditions

Table 5.3 Ambient temperature (T_a), humidity and wind speed in each of the four classic studies on the effects of dehydration on temperature regulation

Reference	Exercise	T_a (°C)	Humidity (%)	Wind speed (km·hr^{-1})
Wyndham and Strydom (1969)	Running	9–17	29–96	*
Costill et al. (1970)	Running	25–26	49–55	5.7
Gisolfi and Copping (1974)	Running	33	38	2.1
Montain and Coyle (1992)	Cycling	33	50	8.6

Note: *Field test: in contrast to others that were on an indoor treadmill.

(0.75 km·hr^{-1}) to an air velocity of 15.5 km·hr^{-1} found rectal and skin temperatures to be significantly higher in the wind-still conditions (Shaffrath and Adamas 1984).

More recently, Saunders *et al.* (2005), compared the temperature of subjects cycling at 33.0 ± 0.4°C in four different wind velocities: 0.2 km·hr^{-1} (wind-still conditions), 10 km·hr^{-1} (to replicate many laboratory studies), and 100% and 150% of calculated road speed facing wind velocities based on the equation of di Prampero *et al.* (1979). At the same time, 58.8 ± 6.8% of sweat losses were replaced with oral liquids (Saunders *et al.* 2005). The authors reported that in wind-still or low facing wind velocities, excessive heat storage occurs while exercising at moderate and high intensities, due to a failure of the environment to absorb and dissipate heat as evidenced by higher sweat rates during wind-still conditions.

Thus the interpretation of the results of classic studies used as evidence to support specific fluid intake guidelines is incorrect for athletes exercising outdoors (ACSM 1975, 1987, 1996a, 1996b; NAAT, Casa *et al.* 2000; Binkley *et al.* 2002; and the US Army, Montain *et al.* 1999). Indeed, these studies (Wyndham and Strydom 1969; Costill *et al.* 1970; Gisolfi and Copping 1974) may have underestimated the body's ability to adapt to mild dehydration since they were performed on subjects exercising in unnaturally low facing wind speeds and 'High Risk' thermal loads. This may perhaps in part explain the subsequently published excessive fluid intake guidelines (Saunders *et al.* 2005).

Consideration of the artificial environmental conditions imposed on subjects during experimental conditions may also explain why several recent studies have reported no benefit of drinking high rates of fluid compared to *ad libitum* (McConnell *et al.* 1997; Daries *et al.* 2000; Cheuvront and Haymes 2001a; Kay and Marino 2003; Saunders *et al.* 2005). The practical limitation of the early laboratory experiments is confirmed in observations of elite athletes who do not consume substantial volumes of fluid during exercise despite competing extremely well, even at the later stages of the effort (Wyndham and Strydom 1969; Pugh *et al.* 1967; Noakes 1993; Onywera *et al.* 2004; Fudge *et al.* 2006).

Furthermore, there appears to be no direct evidence that a high rate of fluid intake has an impact on the incidence of heat illness (Epstein *et al.* 1999; Noakes 1995, 1998; Sharwood *et al.* 2002, 2004). Noakes (2004) has proposed that a major consideration leading to the ACSM recommendation of drinking 1.2 L·hr^{-1} (ACSM 1996a, 1996b), was the finding of Montain and Coyle that there was a thermal advantage of 0.2°C when consuming fluid that equalled sweat loss; compared to what can be described as *ad libitum* fluid intake (38.4°C when consuming 712 mL·hr^{-1} vs. 38.6°C when consuming 1190 mL·hr^{-1}; see Montain and Coyle 1992b; Coyle 1994). It seems highly unlikely that such modest increases in core temperatures could have had any significant impact on racing performance. Moreover, the subject consuming the higher forced volumes of fluid might have incurred a weight disadvantage of around 800 g (the weight difference between the lower and higher rates of ingestion).

The above reasoning poses the interesting possibility that there may exist a tolerable range for dehydration that will not impact negatively on running performance, but which may even confer an advantage by preventing the increases in body mass due to consumption of large volumes of fluid (Armstrong *et al.* 1985; Sawka and Montain 2000; Coyle 2004). Indeed, the simple concept of reducing body mass while keeping power constant, and thereby reducing the energy cost of running, is certainly valid. In fact, Wyndham and Strydom (1969) reported no correlation with percentage dehydration and T_c until a 3% weight deficit had occurred. Similarly, Ladell (1955) found a linear correlation between percent dehydration and an increase in T_c only beyond 2.5 kg of body mass loss. A recent review (Cheuvront and Haymes 2001b) of the endurance running literature reported no effect of dehydration on core temperature for losses of body mass up to 3.1% (mean < 2.5%), whereas a positive relationship was found between the level of dehydration and rise in core temperature when losses were greater than 3% body mass. Coyle (2004) suggests that a range of 1–2% may be tolerable in temperate conditions and that > 2% may be tolerated in colder environments.

Figure 5.2 depicts a theoretical model to highlight the potential effects of no fluid intake, *ad libitum* intake, and total fluid replacement on performance. Here *ad libitum* fluid intake may present a balance between drinking enough fluid to maintain an optimal zone of tolerable dehydration and reducing the

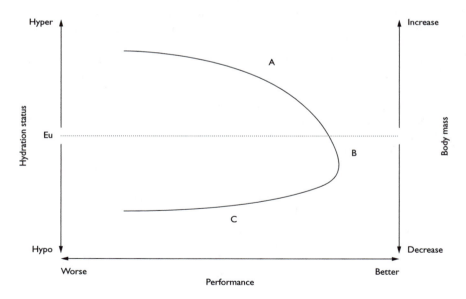

Figure 5.2 Theoretical model illustrating effect of varying rates of fluid ingestion on running performance.

Note: A an excess fluid intake; B an *ad libitum* fluid intake; and C no fluid intake.

absolute energy cost of movement by reducing the athlete's body mass. Once beyond a tolerable range of dehydration or due to extreme thirst, the gradient of the curve flattens; in this situation there may be a more progressive decline in performance. While an attractive oversimplification, this cannot be the full explanation, as up to 10% dehydration has been found in winning athletes. To our knowledge, only one study has attempted to investigate the advantages of a reduced body mass due to dehydration (Armstrong et al. 1985). In this study, dehydration was induced via diuretic administration leading to a significantly reduced plasma volume. However, diuretic-induced dehydration may be an ineffective method for replicating exercise-induced dehydration, as it typically produces an iso-osmotic hypovolaemia, resulting in a much greater ratio of plasma to body water loss (Sawka and Montain 2000). In addition, the direct effect of the diuretic on the brain was not considered. Thus, further well-controlled studies are required to test the validity, the performance, and the health implications of runners completing the last part of a race mildly dehydrated, but with a reduced energy cost of running.

Hydration, hyperthermia and performance

In summary, there is no evidence that fluid intake during exercise increases sweat rates, increases stroke volume or reduces overall cardiovascular strain. Nor does it alter skin and muscle blood flow, increase the oxygen and substrate delivery to the working muscle, nor does it enhance the transport of muscle and blood lactate. It may, however, improve performance when consumed *ad libitum*, i.e. when a state of modest dehydration has developed.

Sceptics may reason that consuming enough fluid to satisfy the ACSM guidelines (e.g. 'replace all of the water lost through sweating'), or at least consuming 'the maximal amount that can be tolerated' will not do any harm. This is incorrect: first, because it now seems clear that these guidelines lack solid scientific basis, since based upon four studies that investigated the effects of high ambient temperature conditions on performance using uncharacteristically low facing wind speeds and therefore unnaturally high thermal loads that cannot be extrapolated to out-of-doors exercise. Second, although not within the scope of the present paper, over-consumption of fluid leading to water intoxication can result in the life-threatening consequence of hyponatreamia (Ayus et al. 2000; Davis et al. 2001; Hsiesh et al. 2002; Hew et al. 2003; Roberts 2000; Noakes 2003; Noakes et al. 1990, 2004; Irving et al. 1991; Frizzell et al. 1986; Speedy et al. 1999; Sharwood et al. 2002, 2004; Almond et al. 2005; Hew-Butler et al. 2005). This condition is more likely to develop in slower runners rather than the elite athletes considered in this chapter, as they take longer to complete the course, and thus consume substantial volumes of fluid, possibly resulting in dangerously low serum sodium concentrations of < 130 mmol·L^{-1} (Almond et al. 2005). Third, the low fluid intake by elite athletes reported by this laboratory (Onywera et al. 2004; Fudge et al. 2006) supports previous anecdotal and scientific observations that elite athletes may typically consume only 200–500 mL·hr^{-1} during racing, irrespective of ethnicity or challenging environmental conditions (see Noakes 1993 for review) – a pattern of fluid consumption not unique to Kenyan athletes. It is possible that this is due to the difficulty of ingesting large volumes of fluid during high intensity exercise, and also to the time cost of slowing to collect a water bottle and consuming the liquid. Indeed, Costill *et al.* (1970) reported that abdominal discomfort was evident at ingestion rates of 1.0 L·hr^{-1}. Finally, *ad libitum* fluid intake appears sufficient to maintain performance despite not replacing all losses, and allows the athlete to be somewhat lighter, thus minimizing the energy cost of running (see next chapter for more discussion on this). Hence, any dehydration-related potential hyperthermia may be offset by *ad libitum* fluid intake, not as a result of maintenance or increases in blood (plasma) volume, but rather for a presently unknown aspect of whole body water maintenance. For example Kay and Marino (2000) hypothesized that ingested fluid below body temperature may act as a 'heat sink' slowing the increase in body temperature. The authors proposed the following equation to estimate the effect of ingested fluid on T_c:

$$\Delta T_c \times 3.49 \times m = \Delta T_w \times 4.18 \times W_w$$

Where ΔT_c denotes change in body temperature, 3.49 and 41.18 are the specific heat of body tissue and water (respectively) in kJ·kg^{-1}·°C^{-1}, ΔT_w is the change in water temperature of the ingested fluid (assuming that the fluid will equilibrate with internal temperature), m is body mass (kg) and finally W_w is the volume of the ingested fluid. Kay and Marino (2000) showed that this equation could explain thermoregulatory changes for exercise durations of 1–4 hours both in moderate and hot environments. However, the same authors (Kay and Marino 2003) reported a significant limitation during self-paced exercise. An alternative hypothesis may be that ingestion of fluids, which increase or compensate for body mass loss, may attenuate increases in whole body temperature since it takes 0.83 kcal of heat production per kg of body mass to raise the T_c by 1°C. Thus an expansion of body water may lead to greater heat dissipation throughout the body beyond the heat capacity of the water itself (Kay and Marino 2000). Therefore athletes commencing exercise in a hypohydrated state will be at an immediate disadvantage as T_c will rise quicker (Sawka *et al.* 1992; Buono and Wall 2000). Buono and Wall (2000) reported that subjects entering exercise in a hypohydrated state terminated exercise 60 min earlier and with a higher rectal temperature than euhydrated subjects. Furthermore, several studies investigating the effects of high ambient temperature on T_c found no elevations in T_c for exercise duration below 1 hour (Montain and Coyle 1992b; Cheuvront and Haymes 2001; Kay and Marino 2003; Saunders *et al.* 2005). The significance of reaching a high T_c, and indeed the rate of whole body temperature elevation, has been highlighted by Nielsen *et al.* (1993), who reported that high body temperature per se seems closely associated with exhaustion.

Furthermore, Tatterson *et al.* (2000) hypothesized that the rate of rise in temperature may determine CNS pace-setting mechanisms so that the individual can complete the exercise below their own critical whole body temperature. Tucker *et al.* (2004) reported lower power output and reduced integrated electromyographic activity (iEMG) during a self-paced cycling time trial in the heat (35°C), compared to the cold (15°C), before T_c reached high values. This corroborates the earlier results of Tatterson *et al.* (2000) which suggest an anticipatory response that adjusts muscle recruitment to avoid reaching a critically high body temperature.

Thus it would appear that commencing exercise in a euhydrated state is more important than remaining in a euhydrated state during exercise. Commencing exercise with a 'normal' body mass may result in an attenuation of T_c compared to commencing exercise in a dehydrated state. The implication of the rate of rise in T_c may be evident through pacing strategies employed by the CNS and ultimately through performance outcome. Fluid intake strategies could be individually tailored to enable an athlete to remain within a tolerable range of dehydration that will maintain body mass in a pre-determined zone whilst maintaining optimum performance. Anticipating the hydration required is subject to many inputs, not just the degree of dehydration.

Conclusion

In conclusion, elite Kenyan endurance runners and also elite runners of other ethnicity, consume less fluid than is recommended by current fluid intake guidelines, but nevertheless perform exceptionally well. The current fluid intake recommendations thus do not reflect the practice of the best performers in the world, possibly because they are based on laboratory studies that are not representative of actual race situations. It is clear that replacing all water lost via sweating does not have a greater benefit on cardiovascular function or thermoregulation than drinking *ad libitum*, but might actually confer a disadvantage due to an increase in body mass and an increase in the energy cost of running. Conversely, it is possible that elite runners are capable, by only consuming water as dictated by thirst, to avoid carrying excess body mass that may increase their energy cost. It seems highly unlikely that this minimum water intake during exercise can increase the total heat capacity of the body or maintain whole body water just enough to protect plasma volume. A better but more difficult explanation may centre on central neurological control which responds to a variety of stimuli, with thirst being the most obvious and direct measure of hydration. Elite runners of any ethnicity seem naturally capable of choosing the optimal compromise between the potential effects of dehydration, the thermoregulatory effects of fluid intake, and a minimal energy cost of running.

Bibliography

Adams, W. C., Fox, R. H., Fry, A. J. and Macdonald, I. C. (1975) 'Thermoregulation during marathon running in cool, moderate, and hot environments', *Journal of Applied Physiology* 38, 1030–37.

Adams, W. C., Mack, G. W., Langhans, G. W. and Nadel, E. R. (1992) 'Effects of varied air velocity on sweating and evaporative rates during exercise', *Journal of Applied Physiology* 73, 2668–74.

Adolph, E. F. (1947) *Physiology of Man in the Desert*, New York: Interscience Publishers.

Adolph, E. F. and Dill, D. B. (1938) 'Observations on water metabolism in the desert', *American Journal of Physiology* 123, 369–78.

Almond, C. S., Shin, A. Y., Fortescue, E. B., Mannix, R. C., Wypij, D., Binstadt, B. A., Duncan, C. N., Olson, D. P., Salerno, A. E., Newburger, J. W. and Greenes, D. S. (2005) 'Hyponatremia among runners in the Boston Marathon', *New England Journal of Medicine* 352, 1550–6.

American College of Sports Medicine (1975) 'Position statement on prevention of heat injuries during distance running', *Medicine and Science in Sports and Exercise* 7, vii–ix.

American College of Sports Medicine (1987) 'Position stand on the prevention of thermal injuries during distance running', *Medicine and Science in Sports and Exercise* 19, 529–33.

American College of Sports Medicine (1996a) 'Position stand: heat and cold illnesses during distance running', *Medicine and Science in Sports and Exercise* 28, i–x.

American College of Sports Medicine (1996b) 'Position stand: exercise and fluid replacement', *Medicine and Science in Sports and Exercise* 28, i–vii.

Armstrong, L. E. and Maresh, C. M. (1998) 'Effects of training, environment, and host factors on the sweating response to exercise', *International Journal of Sports Medicine*, 19, S103–S105.

Armstrong, L. E., Costill, D. L. and Fink, W. J. (1985) 'Influence of diuretic-induced dehydration on competitive running performance', *Medicine and Science in Sports and Exercise* 17, 456–61.

Ayus, J. C., Varon, J. and Arieff, A. I. (2000) 'Hyponatremia, cerebral edema, and non-cardiogenic pulmonary edema in marathon runners', *Annals of Internal Medicine* 132, 711–14.

Binkley, H. M., Beckett, J., Casa, D. J., Kleiner, D. M. and Plummer, P. E. (2002) 'National Athletic Trainers' Association position statement: exertional heat illnesses', *Journal of Athletic Training* 37, 329–43.

Buono, M. J. and Wall, A. J. (2000) 'Effect of hypohydration on core temperature during exercise in temperate and hot environments', *Pflüügers Archiv European Journal of Physiology* 440, 476–80.

Buskirk, E. R. and Beetham, W. P. (1960) 'Dehydration and body temperature as a result of marathon running', *Med. Sport* 14, 493–506.

Casa, D. J. (2003) 'Proper hydration for distance running – Identifying individual fluid needs. A USA Track and Field Advisory', Available online at: <http://www.usatf.org/groups/Coaches/library/hydration/ProperHydrationForDistanceRunning.pdf>.

Casa, D. J., Armstrong, L. E., Hillman, S. K., Montain, S. J., Reiff, R. V., Rich, B. S. E., Roberts, W. O. and Stone, J. A. (2000) 'National Athletic Trainers' Association position statement: fluid replacement for athletes', *Journal of Athletic Training* 35, 212–24.

Cheuvront, S. N. and Haymes, E. M. (2001a) 'Ad libitum fluid intakes and thermoregulatory responses of female distance runners in three environments', *Journal of Sports Sciences* 19, 845–54.

Cheuvront, S. N. and Haymes, E. M. (2001b) 'Thermoregulation and marathon running: biological and environmental influences', *Sports Medicine* 31, 743–62.

Costill, D. L., Cote, R. and Fink, W. (1976) 'Muscle water and electrolytes following varied levels of dehydration in man', *Journal of Applied Physiology* 40, 6–11.

Costill, D. L., Kammer, W. F. and Fisher, A. (1970) 'Fluid ingestion during distance running', *Archives of Environmental Health* 21, 520–5.

Coyle, E. F. (1994) 'Fluid and carbohydrate replacement during exercise: how much and why?', Available online at: <http://www.gssiweb.com>.

Coyle, E. F. (2004) 'Fluid and fuel intake during exercise', *Journal of Sports Sciences* 22, 39–55.

Coyle, E. F. and Gonzalez-Alonso, J. (2001) 'Cardiovascular drift during prolonged exercise: new perspectives', *Exercise and Sport Sciences Reviews* 29, 88–92.

Daries, H. N., Noakes, T. D. and Dennis, S. C. (2000) 'Effect of fluid intake volume on 2-h running performances in a 25 degrees C environment', *Medicine and Science in Sports and Exercise* 32, 1783–9.

Davis, D. P., Videen, J. S., Marino, A., Vilke, G. M., Dunford, J. V., Van Camp, S. P. and Maharam, L. G. (2001) 'Exercise-associated hyponatremia in marathon runners: a two-year experience', *Journal of Emergency Medicine* 21, 47–57.

Di Prampero, P. E., Cortili, G., Mognoni, P. and Saibene, F. (1979) 'Equation of motion of a cyclist', *Journal of Applied Physiology* 47, 201–6.

Durkot, M. J., Martinez, O., Brooksmcquade, D. and Francesconi, R. (1986) 'Simultaneous determination of fluid shifts during thermal-stress in a small-animal model', *Journal of Applied Physiology* 61, 1031–1034.

Edwards, R. J. and Harrison, M. H. (1984) 'Intravascular volume and protein responses to running exercise', *Medicine and Science in Sports and Exercise* 16, 247–55.

Edwards, R. J., Harrison, M. H., Cochrane, L. A. and Mills, F. J. (1983) 'Blood-volume and protein responses to skin cooling and warming during cycling exercise', *European Journal of Applied Physiology and Occupational Physiology* 50, 195–206.

Ekelund, L. G. (1967) 'Circulatory and respiratory adaptation during prolonged exercise', *Acta Physiologica Scandinavica* S292, 1–38.

Epstein, Y., Moran, D. S., Shapiro, Y., Sohar, E. and Shemer, J. (1999) 'Exertional heat stroke: a case series', *Medicine and Science in Sports and Exercise* 31, 224–8.

Fox, E. L. and Costill, D. L. (1972) 'Estimated cardiorespiratory responses during marathon running', *Archives of Environmental Health* 24, 316–24.

Fritzsche, R. G., Switzer, T. W., Hodgkinson, B. J. and Coyle, E. F. (1999) 'Stroke volume decline during prolonged exercise is influenced by the increase in heart rate', *Journal of Applied Physiology* 86, 799–805.

Frizzell, R. T., Lang, G. H., Lowance, D. C. and Lathan, S. R. (1986) 'Hyponatremia and ultramarathon running', *JAMA* 255, 772–4.

Fudge, B. W., Westerterp, K. R., Kiplamai, F. K., Onywera, V. O., Boit, M. K., Kayser, B. and Pitsiladis, Y. P. (2006) 'Evidence of negative energy balance using doubly labelled water in elite Kenyan endurance runners prior to competition', *British Journal of Nutrition* 95, 59–66.

Galbo, H., Holst, J. J. and Christensen, N. J. (1975) 'Glucagon and plasma catecholamine responses to graded and prolonged exercise in man', *Journal of Applied Physiology* 38, 70–6.

Galloway, S. D. and Maughan, R. J. (1997) 'Effects of ambient temperature on the capacity to perform prolonged cycle exercise in man', *Medicine and Science in Sports and Exercise* 29, 1240–9.

Gisolfi, C. V. and Copping, J. R. (1974) 'Thermal effects of prolonged treadmill exercise in heat', *Medicine and Science in Sports and Exercise* 6, 108–13.

Gonzalez-Alonso, J., Calbet, J. A. L. and Nielsen, B. (1998) 'Muscle blood flow is reduced with dehydration during prolonged exercise in humans', *Journal of Physiology (Lon.)* 513, 895–905.

Gonzalez-Alonso, J., Calbet, J. A. L. and Nielsen, B. (1999) 'Metabolic and thermodynamic responses to dehydration-induced reductions in muscle blood flow in exercising humans', *Journal of Physiology (Lon.)* 520, 577–89.

Gonzalez-Alonso, J., Mora-Rodriguez, R. and Coyle, E. F. (2000) 'Stroke volume during exercise: interaction of environment and hydration', *American Journal of Physiology Heart and Circulatory Physiology* 278, H321–H330.

Gonzalez-Alonso, J., Mora-Rodriguez, R., Below, P. R. and Coyle, E. F. (1995) 'Dehydration reduces cardiac output and increases systemic and cutaneous vascular resistance during exercise', *Journal of Applied Physiology* 79, 1487–96.

Gore, C. J., Scroop, G. C., Marker, J. D. and Catcheside, P. G. (1992) 'Plasma volume, osmolarity, total protein and electrolytes during treadmill running and cycle ergometer exercise', *European Journal of Applied Physiology and Occupational Physiology* 65, 302–10.

Grant, S. M., Green, H. J., Phillips, S. M. and Sutton, J. R. (1997) 'Effects of acute expansion of plasma volume on cardiovascular and thermal function during prolonged exercise', *European Journal of Applied Physiology and Occupational Physiology* 76, 356–62.

Greenhaff, P. L. (1989) 'Cardiovascular fitness and thermoregulation during prolonged exercise in man', *British Journal of Sports Medicine* 23, 109–14.

Harrison M. H. (1985) 'Effects on thermal stress and exercise on blood volume in humans', *Physiological Review* 65, 149–209.

Harrison, M. H., Edwards, R. J. and Leitch, D. R. (1975) 'Effect of exercise and thermal-stress on plasma-volume', *Journal of Applied Physiology* 39, 925–31.

Hew, T. D., Chorley, J. N., Cianca, J. C. and Divine, J. G. (2003) 'The incidence, risk factors, and clinical manifestations of hyponatremia in marathon runners', *Clinical Journal of Sports Medicine* 13, 41–7.

Hew-Butler, T., Almond, C., Ayus, J. C., Dugas, J., Meeuwisse, W., Noakes, T., Reid, S., Siegel, A., Speedy, D., Stuempfle, K., Verbalis, J. and Weschler, L. (2005) 'Consensus statement of the 1st International Exercise-associated Hyponatremia, Consensus Development Conference, Cape Town, South Aftica, 2005', *Clinical Journal of Sports Medicine* 15, 402.

Hsieh, M., Roth, R., Davis, D. L., Larrabee, H. and Callaway, C. W. (2002) 'Hyponatremia in runners requiring on-site medical treatment at a single marathon', *Medicine and Science in Sports and Exercise* 34, 185–9.

Hubbard, R. W. and Armstrong, L. E. (1998) 'The heat illnesses: biochemical, ultrastructural, and fluid-electrolyte considerations', in *Human Performance Physiology and Environmental Medicine at Terrestrial Extremes*, ed. Pandolf, K. B., Sawka, M. N. and Gonzalez, R. R., Indianapolis, IN: Benchmark Press, pp. 305–59.

Irving, R. A., Noakes, T. D., Buck, R., van Zyl, S. R., Raine, E., Godlonton, J. and Norman, R. J. (1991) 'Evaluation of renal function and fluid homeostasis during recovery from exercise-induced hyponatremia', *Journal of Applied Physiology* 70, 342–8.

Kay, D. and Marino, F. E. (2000) 'Fluid ingestion and exercise hyperthermia: implications for performance, thermoregulation, metabolism and the development of fatigue', *Journal of Sports Sciences* 18, 71–82.

Kay, D. and Marino, F. E. (2003) 'Failure of fluid ingestion to improve self-paced exercise performance in moderate-to-warm humid environments', *Journal of Thermal Biology* 28, 29–34.

Ladell, W. S. S. (1955) 'The effects of water and salt intake upon the performance of men working in hot and humid environments', *Journal of Physiology* (Lon.) 127, 11–46.

Maron, M. B., Horvath, S. M. and Wilkerson, J. E. (1975) 'Acute blood biochemical alterations in response to marathon running', *European Journal of Applied Physiology and Occupational Physiology* 34, 173–81.

Maughan, R. J. and Leiper, J. B. (1983) 'Aerobic capacity and fractional utilisation of aerobic capacity in elite and non-elite male and female marathon runners', *European Journal of Applied Physiology and Occupational Physiology* 52, 80–7.

Maughan, R. J., Whiting, P. H. and Davidson, R. J. (1985) 'Estimation of plasma volume changes during marathon running', *British Journal of Sports Medicine* 19, 138–41.

McCann, D. J. and Adams, W. C. (1997) 'Wet bulb globe temperature index and performance in competitive distance runners', *Medicine and Science in Sports and Exercise* 29, 955–61.

McConell, G. K., Burge, C. M., Skinner, S. L. and Hargreaves, M. (1997) 'Influence of ingested fluid volume on physiological responses during prolonged exercise', *Acta Physiologica Scandinavica* 160, 149–156.

Montain, S. J. and Coyle, E. F. (1992a) 'Fluid ingestion during exercise increases skin blood-flow independent of increases in blood-volume', *Journal of Applied Physiology* 73, 903–10.

Montain, S. J. and Coyle, E. F. (1992b) 'Influence of graded dehydration on hyperthermia and cardiovascular drift during exercise', *Journal of Applied Physiology* 73, 1340–50.

Montain, S. J., Latzka, W. A. and Sawka, M. N. (1999) 'Fluid replacement recommendations for training in hot weather', *Military Medicine* 164, 502–8.

Morimoto, T., Itoh, T. and Takamata, A. (1998) 'Thermoregulation and body fluid in hot environment', *Brain Function in Hot Environment* 115, 499–508.

Muir, A. L., Percyrob, I. W., Davidson, I. A. and Walsh, E. G. (1970) 'Physiological aspects of Edinburgh Commonwealth Games, *Lancet* 2, 1125–8.

Myhre, L. G., Hartung, G. H., Nunneley, S. A. and Tucker, D. M. (1985) 'Plasma-volume changes in middle-aged male and female subjects during marathon running', *Journal of Applied Physiology* 59, 559–63.

Nash, H. L. (1985) 'Treating thermal-injury –disagreement heats up', *Physician and Sports Medicine* 13, 134–44.

Newton, A. F. H. (1948) 'Drinks and the marathon', *Athletic Review* July, 14–16.

Nielsen, B., Hales, J. R. S., Strange, S., Christensen, N. J., Warberg, J. and Saltin, B. (1993) 'Human circulatory and thermoregulatory adaptations with heat acclimation and exercise in a hot, dry environment', *Journal of Physiology* (Lon.) 460, 467–85.

Noakes, T. D. (1993) 'Fluid replacement during exercise', *Exercise and Sport Sciences Reviews* 21, 297–330.

Noakes, T. D. (1995) 'Dehydration during exercise: what are the real dangers?', *Clinical Journal of Sports Medicine* 5, 123–8.

Noakes, T. D. (1998) 'Fluid and electrolyte disturbances in heat illness.' *International Journal of Sports Medicine* 19, S146–S149.

Noakes, T. D. (2000) 'Hyponatraemia in distance athletes. Pulling the IV on the dehydration myth', *Physician and Sports Medicine* 28, 71–6.

Noakes, T. D. (2001) 'Hyponatraemia or hype?' *Physician and Sports Medicine* 29, 22–40.

Noakes, T. D. (2003) 'Overconsumption of fluids by athletes', *BMJ* 327, 113–14.

Noakes, T. D. (2004) 'Can we trust rehydration research?' in *Philosophy and Science of Exercise, Sports and Health*, ed. McNamee, M., Abingdon, Oxfordshire, UK: Taylor & Francis, pp. 144–68.

Noakes, T. D. (in press, 2006a) 'Drinking guidelines for exercise: What is the evidence that athletes should either drink "as much as tolerable" or "to replace all the weight lost during exercise" or "ad libitum"?' *Journal of Sports Sciences*.

Noakes, T. D. (in press, 2006b) 'Laboratory research, commercial interests and advice to the public on fluid ingestion during exercise. Who is accountable when deaths occur?' *European Journal of Sports Sciences*.

Noakes, T. D. and Martin, D. E. (2002) 'IMMDA-AIMS Advisory statement on guidelines for fluid replacement during marathon running', *New Studies in Athletics* 17, 13–24.

Noakes, T. D. and Speedy, D. B. (in press, 2006) 'Case proven: exercise-associated hyponatraemia is due to overdrinking. So why did it take 20 years and at least 10 avoidable deaths before original evidence was accepted?', *British Journal of Nutrition*.

Noakes, T. D., Myburgh, K. H., du, P. J., Lang, L., Lambert, M., van der, R. C. and Schall, R. (1991) 'Metabolic rate, not percent dehydration, predicts rectal temperature in marathon runners', *Medicine and Science in Sports and Exercise* 23, 443–9.

Noakes, T. D., Norman, R. J., Buck, R. H., Godlonton, J., Stevenson, K. and Pittaway, D. (1990) 'The incidence of hyponatremia during prolonged ultraendurance exercise', *Medicine and Science in Sports and Exercise* 22, 165–70.

Noakes, T. D., Sharwood, K. A., Collins, M. and Perkins, D. R. (in press, 2006) 'Three independent mechanisms cause exercise-associated hyponatraemia. Evidence from 2135 weighed competitive athletic performances', *Proceedings of the National Academy of Sciences*

Noakes, T. D., Sharwood, K., Collins, M. and Perkins, D. R. (2004b) 'The dipsomania of great distance: water intoxication in an Iron-man tri-athlete', *British Journal of Sports Medicine* 38, E16.

Nose, H., Morimoto, T. and Ogura, K. (1983) 'Distribution of water losses among fluid compartments of tissues under thermal dehydration in the rat', *Japanese Journal of Physiology* 33, 1019–29.

Olsson, K. E. and Saltin, B. (1970) 'Variation in total body water with muscle glycogen changes in man', *Acta Physiologica Scandinavica* 80, 11–18.

Onywera, V. O., Kiplamai, F. K., Boit, M. K. and Pitsiladis, Y. P. (2004) 'Food and macronutrient intake of elite Kenyan distance runners', *International Journal of Sport Nutrition and Exercise Metabolism* 14, 709–19.

Pastene, J., Germain, M., Allevard, A. M., Gharib, C. and Lacour, J. R. (1996) 'Water balance during and after marathon running', *European Journal of Applied Physiology and Occupational Physiology* 73, 49–55.

Pearlmutter, E. M. (1986) 'The Pittsburgh Marathon: playing weather roulette', *Physician and Sports Medicine* 14, 132–8.

Pivarnik, J. M., Leeds, E. M. and Wilkerson, J. E. (1984) 'Effects of endurance exercise on metabolic water production and plasma-volume', *Journal of Applied Physiology* 56, 613–18.

Pugh, L. G. C., Corbett, J. L. and Johnson, R. H. (1967) 'Rectal temperatures weight losses and sweat rates in marathon running', *Journal of Applied Physiology* 23, 347–52.

Roberts, W. O. (2000) 'A 12-yr profile of medical injury and illness for the Twin Cities Marathon', *Medicine and Science in Sports and Exercise* 32, 1549–55.

Rocker, L., Kirsch, K., Wicke, J. and Stoboy, H. (1976) 'Role of proteins in regulation of plasma-volume during heat-stress and exercise', *Israel Journal of Medical Sciences* 12, 840–3.

Rowell, L. B. (1986) *Human Circulation: Regulation during Physical Stress*, New York: Oxford University Press, pp. 363–406.

Saltin, B. and Hermansen, L. (1966) 'Esophageal rectal and muscle temperature during exercise', *Journal of Applied Physiology* 21, 1757–62.

Saunders, A. G., Dugas, J. P., Tucker, R., Lambert, M. I. and Noakes, T. D. (2005) 'The effects of different air velocities on heat storage and body temperature in humans cycling in a hot, humid environment', *Acta Physiologica Scandinavica* 183, 241–55.

Sawka, M. N. and Coyle, E. F. (1999) 'Influence of body water and blood volume on thermoregulation and exercise performance in the heat', *Exercise and Sport Sciences Reviews* 27, 167–218.

Sawka, M. N. and Montain, S. J. (2000) 'Fluid and electrolyte supplementation for exercise heat stress', *American Journal of Clinical Nutrition* 72, 564S–572S.

Sawka, M. N. and Montain, S. J. (2001) 'Hydration effects on thermoregulation and performance in the heat', *Comparative Biochemistry and Physiology: Part A, Molecular and Integrative Physiology* 128, 679–90.

Sawka, M. N., Francesconi, R. P., Pimental, N. A. and Pandolf, K. B. (1984) 'Hydration and vascular fluid shifts during exercise in the heat', *Journal of Applied Physiology* 56, 91–6.

Sawka, M. N., Young, A. J., Francesconi, R. P., Muza, S. R. and Pandolf, K. B. (1985) 'Thermoregulatory and blood responses during exercise at graded hypohydration levels', *Journal of Applied Physiology* 59, 1394–401.

Sawka, M. N., Young, A. J., Latzka, W. A., Neufer, P. D., Quigley, M. D. and Pandolf, K. B. (1992) 'Human tolerance to heat strain during exercise – influence of hydration', *Journal of Applied Physiology* 73, 368–75.

Senay, L. C. (1970) 'Movement of water, protein and crystalloids between vascular and extravascular compartments in heat-exposed men during dehydration and following limited relief of dehydration', *Journal of Physiology* (Lon.) 210, 617–35.

Senay, L. C., Jr (1975) 'Plasma volumes and constituents of heat-exposed men before and after acclimatization', *Journal of Applied Physiology* 38, 570–5.

Senay, L. C., Jr, Rogers, G. and Jooste, P. (1980) 'Changes in blood plasma during progressive treadmill and cycle exercise', *Journal of Applied Physiology* 49, 59–65.

Shaffrath, J. D. and Adams, W. C. (1984) 'Effects of air-flow and work load on cardiovascular drift and skin blood-flow', *Journal of Applied Physiology* 56, 1411–17.

Sharwood, K. A., Collins, M., Goedecke, J. H., Wilson, G. and Noakes, T. D. (2004) 'Weight changes, medical complications, and performance during an Ironman triathlon', *British Journal of Sports Medicine* 38, 718–24.

Sharwood, K., Collins, M., Goedecke, J., Wilson, G. and Noakes, T. (2002) 'Weight changes, sodium levels, and performance in the South African Ironman Triathlon', *Clinical Journal of Sports Medicine* 12, 391–9.

Sheriff, D. D., Zhou, X. P., Scher, A. M. and Rowell, L. B. (1993) 'Dependence of cardiac filling pressure on cardiac-output during rest and dynamic exercise in dogs', *American Journal of Physiology* 265, H316–H322.

Snellen, J. W., Mitchell, D. and Wyndham, C. H. (1970) 'Heat of evaporation of sweat', *Journal of Applied Physiology* 29, 40–4.

Speedy, D. B., Noakes, T. D., Rogers, I. R., Thompson, J. M., Campbell, R. G., Kuttner, J. A., Boswell, D. R., Wright, S. and Hamlin, M. (1999) 'Hyponatremia in ultradistance triathletes', *Medicine and Science in Sports and Exercise* 31, 809–15.

Suping, Z., Guanglin, M., Yanwen, W. and Li, J. (1992) 'Study of the relationships between weather conditions and the marathon race, and of meteorotropic effects on distance runners', *International Journal of Biometeorology* 36, 63–8.

Tatterson, A. J., Hahn, A. G., Martin, D. T. and Febbraio, M. A. (2000) 'Effects of heat stress on physiological responses and exercise performance in elite cyclists', *Journal of Science and Medicine in Sport* 3, 186–93.

Tucker, R., Rauch, L., Harley, Y. X. and Noakes, T. D. (2004) 'Impaired exercise performance in the heat is associated with an anticipatory reduction in skeletal muscle recruitment', *Pflüügers Archiv European Journal of Physiology* 448, 422–30.

Watt, M. J., Garnham, A. P., Febbraio, M. A. and Hargreaves, M. (2000) 'Effect of acute plasma volume expansion on thermoregulation and exercise performance in the heat', *Medicine and Science in Sports and Exercise* 32, 958–62.

Whiting, P. H., Maughan, R. J. and Miller, J. D. (1984) 'Dehydration and serum biochemical changes in marathon runners', *European Journal of Applied Physiology and Occupational Physiology* 52, 183–7.

Wyndham, C. H. and Strydom, N. B. (1969) 'The danger of an inadequate water intake during marathon running', *South African Medical Journal* 43, 893–6.

Wyndham, C. H., Strydom, N. B., van Rensburg, A. J., Benade, A. J. and Heyns, A. J. (1970) 'Relation between $\dot{V}O_2$ max and body temperature in hot humid air conditions', *Journal of Applied Physiology* 29, 45–50.

Chapter 6

Energy balance and body composition of elite endurance runners

A hunter-gatherer phenotype

Barry W. Fudge, Bengt Kayser, Klaas R. Westerterp and Yannis Pitsiladis

Introduction

Optimal athletic performance depends upon sports-specific body build and body composition (Tittel and Wutscherk 1992). For example, 100 m runners are more muscular than endurance athletes who are typically slender and lean (Weyand and Davis 2005). Athletes use training and diet manipulation to achieve body size and body composition judged optimal for an athletic discipline (Loucks 2004). Noakes (2000) suggests that endurance runners aim to be as light as possible before competition since achieving a lighter body mass for endurance running may improve performance by reducing the energy cost of running per unit distance. In support of this, two studies on elite Kenyan endurance runners (Onywera *et al.* 2004; Fudge *et al.* 2006) reported that these athletes were in negative energy balance prior to major competition (National Championships 2003 and Athens Olympic Games 2004 national trials, respectively). Considering the repeated competitive success of east African runners in the last several decades (Pitsiladis *et al.* 2004), the lifestyle and nutritional practices of these runners may possibly represent an optimal pattern for elite endurance running even though not conforming to current official fluid and nutritional intake guidelines (see Chapter 5 for more on this). These observations raise several interesting questions: what are the limits of gaining advantage from lowering body mass for endurance performance? Are top athletes, who are typically lean, close to this limit? Considering endurance running ability as a key development in human evolution (Bramble and Lieberman 2004), and today's athletes as the closest equivalent of early *Homo* in terms of daily physical activity levels (Cordain *et al.* 1998), it is of interest to compare the bioenergetics and dietary patterns of modern athletes to those thought to be of our early ancestors. Therefore, the aim of the present chapter is to discuss the implications for health and racing performance of a short-term negative energy balance and consequent reduction in body mass as found in elite Kenyan endurance runners prior to major competition. The lifestyle and nutritional practices of elite Kenyan endurance runners are described elsewhere in this book by Christensen (see Chapter 7).

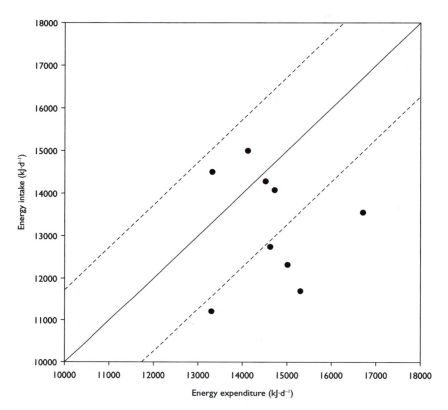

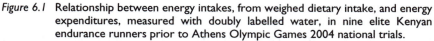

Figure 6.1 Relationship between energy intakes, from weighed dietary intake, and energy expenditures, measured with doubly labelled water, in nine elite Kenyan endurance runners prior to Athens Olympic Games 2004 national trials.

Note: Solid line: line of identity, dashed lines, +/– 2SD.

Source: Fudge et al. 2006.

Observations of elite Kenyan endurance runners

A number of studies have reported the energy balance status of Kenyan runners (Mukeshi and Thairu 1993; Christensen et al. 2002; Onywera et al. 2004; Fudge et al. 2006). Onywera et al. (2004) estimated energy intake by weighed dietary record and found this to be significantly lower than the energy expenditure as assessed by Physical Activity Ratio (Ainsworth et al. 2000) (EI: 12.5 ± 1.2 MJ·d⁻¹ vs. EE: 15.1 ± 0.5 MJ·d⁻¹), suggesting that the athletes were in negative energy balance prior to competition. These results corroborated those of an earlier study that evaluated the nutrient intake of Kenyan runners (Mukeshi and Thairu 1993). The reported energy intake in the latter study was very low (EI: 9.8 MJ·d⁻¹) and, considering that the athletes were training intensely, the validity of these results were questioned by the authors of another study which assessed the dietary intake of Kenyan runners (Christensen *et al.* 2002). Christensen and colleagues studied 12 adolescent (15–20 y) male Kenyan runners during a two-week period and found them to be in energy balance (EI: 13.2 ± 2.7 MJ·d^{-1} vs. EE: 13.2 ± 2.8 MJ·d^{-1}). However, those athletes were regarded as promising junior athletes competing at regional level and were studied during a period of regular training. The most recent study (Fudge *et al.* 2006) used the gold-standard double labelled water method to measure energy expenditure and found that the athletes were, on average, in negative energy balance (EI: 13.2 ± 1.3 MJ·d^{-1} vs. EE: 14.6 ± 1.0 MJ·d^{-1}; $p < 0.005$) prior to the Athens Olympic trials (Figure 6.1). Anecdotal evidence corroborates these observations (Mukeshi and Thairu 1993; Onywera *et al.* 2004; Fudge *et al.* 2006) in elite Kenyan endurance athletes. For example, the Kenyan winner of the women's 2004 London Marathon, former marathon world-record holder Margaret Okayo weighed only 39 kg at the time of the race although her usual body mass is 43 kg. Similarly, the winner of the 2005 Chicago marathon, Felix Limo also from Kenya (current 15 km world-record holder), had a starting weight of 59 kg but has a typical body mass of 64 kg. Concerns have been raised however with regard to the health and future performance implications of over-frequent body mass cycles in elite athletes before and after competition (Onywera *et al.* 2004). The American College of Sports Medicine (ACSM) and the American Dietetic Association and the Dieticians of Canada (ACSM 2000) state that periods of negative energy balance can promote lethargy, increase risk of injury and illness, prolong recovery from strenuous exercise, and reduce exercise performance. Onywera *et al.* (2004) suggested that this mechanism might explain the high incidence of world class athletes in Kenya who initially do well on the international racing scene but then disappear from athletics prematurely, presumably through injury or 'burn-out'. This reasoning lacks solid experimental data and remains speculative. At present there is a lack of well-controlled investigations on the effect of negative energy balance on long-term health of elite runners; mainly because of the difficulty involved in designing and conducting such studies.

In the short term, body mass reduction induced by a hypo-caloric diet in training athletes does not seem to reduce performance, maximal oxygen consumption ($\dot{V}O_2$ max), strength, or endurance as long as dietary intake provides sufficient carbohydrate and protein to maintain glycogen stores and muscle mass, respectively (McMurray *et al.* 1985; Fogelholm 1990; Horswill *et al.* 1990). McMurray *et al.* (1985) reported that seven days of 1,000 kcal·d^{-1} dietary deficit induced by exercise did not reduce exercise capacity in six endurance-trained males consuming a diet sufficient in carbohydrate and protein. Furthermore, it was found that subjects were not as glycogen-depleted due to the negative energy balance as may have been expected. These authors suggested this was due to the subjects utilizing twice as much fat during submaximal exercise compared to the controls as evidenced by indirect calorimetry. Therefore, in the short term, it may be that the benefits of being as light as possible before racing outweigh the potential negative consequences providing that athletes are consuming a diet high in carbohydrate (e.g. 67.3 ± 7.8%, 9.8 g·kg⁻¹ body mass·d⁻¹) with sufficient protein (e.g. 15.3 ± 4.0%, 2.2 g·kg⁻¹ body mass·d⁻¹) as is typically the case in Kenya (Fudge *et al.* 2006). This is in contrast to what appears to be the case in athletes from industrialized countries where carbohydrate intake can be at the lower end of the range recommended for endurance athletes (e.g. 6.1 g·kg⁻¹ body mass·d⁻¹, Moses *et al.* 1991), especially when a typically western diet of 55–58% carbohydrate (ACSM 2000) is consumed. Costill and Miller (1980) reported that runners consuming a diet high in carbohydrate (70%) training two hours per day for three days compared to runners consuming a normal diet (40–60%) were better able to maintain muscle glycogen. In addition to the favourable diet composition of the Kenyan elite runners (Onywera *et al.* 2004; Fudge *et al.* 2006), the timing of their post-training meal was always within 60 minutes of exercise, i.e. in line with current recommendations for maximizing glycogen re-synthesis rates after exercise (ACSM 2000). The ability

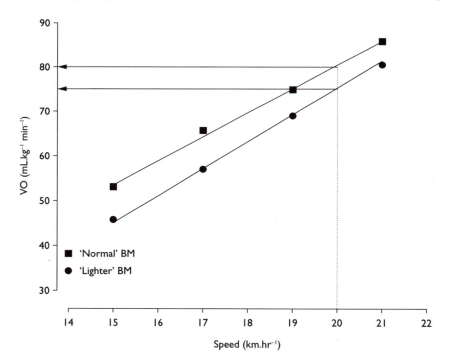

Figure 6.2 Theoretical graph highlighting the effect of a reduction in body mass on energy cost while running at about marathon world record pace (about 20 km·hr⁻¹).

Note: The oxygen cost expressed per kg of body mass for a hypothetical 60 kg athlete, with an oxygen consumption of 4.5 L·min⁻¹, is 80.4 mL·kg⁻¹·min⁻¹. A reduction in body mass of 4 kg (i.e. fat mass) would equate to an oxygen cost of 75.0 mL·kg⁻¹·min⁻¹ to run at the same speed.

of the Kenyan athletes to apparently spontaneously: (1) consume the correct amount of carbohydrate; and (2) do this at the right moment, is striking since they are not exposed to nutritional guidelines and advice compared to elite athletes in western countries. As a result, considering the success of these athletes on the international racing circuit, it is conceivable that their diet and lifestyle is conducive to elite performance and that the reported loss in body mass prior to competition may be beneficial for performance.

Effects of body mass on endurance running performance

The concept of reducing body mass to improve endurance running performance by way of reducing the energy cost of locomotion at a submaximal velocity is not new (Buskirk and Taylor 1957; Cureton et al. 1978; Cureton and Sparling 1980; Taylor et al. 1980; Williams and Cavanagh 1987; Myers and Steudel 1985; Jones and Knapik 1986; Taylor 1994; Noakes 2000). Taylor et al. (1980) reported that when a human or animal carries extra mass while walking and running, the energy cost per unit distance increases in direct proportion to the added load expressed as a percentage of body mass. For example, when a 60 kg subject carries an extra 5 kg (i.e. about 8% of body mass), metabolic rate, at a given speed of locomotion, increases by about 8%. Cureton et al. (1978) demonstrated that the addition of 5, 10 and 15% respectively of body mass: (1) increased the energy requirement of running at submaximal speeds, without affecting absolute $\dot{V}O_2$max; (2) lowered the work rate at $\dot{V}O_2$ max; and (3) lowered the pace that could be maintained for a given period of time. Any excess body fat carried by an endurance runner can thus be expected to reduce performance because it increases the energy required to work at any given level of exercise without contributing to energy-producing capacity (Buskirk and Taylor 1957; Cureton and Sparling 1980). Conversely, reducing body fat mass should enhance running performance by reducing the energy required to run at the same submaximal speed. For example, the oxygen cost for a hypothetical 60 kg athlete, running at marathon world-record pace (about 20 km·hr^{-1}), with an oxygen uptake of 4.5 L·min^{-1}, would be 80.4 mL·kg^{-1}·min^{-1}. It follows that a reduction in body fat mass of 4 kg would lower the oxygen cost to 75.0 mL·kg^{-1}·min^{-1} to run at the same speed (Figure 6.2). If the difference in oxygen cost (6.7%) translates into a performance gain of similar magnitude, this would reduce the time of a world-record pace marathon by 8 minutes 32 seconds! This is of course a gross over-simplification of a complex system; nevertheless it does highlight the potential benefits of a reduction in body fat mass for racing performance. Interestingly, although an example from road cycling rather than running, Coyle (2005a) reported that the seven times Tour de France winner (1999–2005), Lance Armstrong, improved his power-to-body-mass ratio (W·kg^{-1}) when cycling at a given percentage of $\dot{V}O_2$ max (e.g. 83%) by 18% between 1992 and 1999 (i.e. 4.74 vs. 5.60 W·kg^{-1} at a $\dot{V}O_2$ of 5.0 L·min^{-1}). A major feature of the Tour de

France compared to other professional road cycling races is the four to six high mountain stages which can comprise three or more long (>10 km) climbs (5–10% mean gradient) that require competitors to work against gravity (Lucia et al. 2003). As a result, a high power-to-body-mass ratio at maximal or near to maximal intensities is an important determinant of success for uphill cycling (Lucia et al. 2003). The reduction in body mass by Lance Armstrong from 78.9 kg in 1992 to ~72.0 kg during his victories in the Tour has been suggested to account for around one-half (8–9%) of his improved power to body mass ratio with the remainder accounted for by improved mechanical efficiency (Coyle 2005a). In a reply to this view, Martin et al. (2005) suggested that the timing of testing may have been a limitation of this study (i.e. tested five times over a seven-year period with only the first and last test conducted in the same month of a given year). As a result these authors suggested that a reduction in body mass and training 'may be equally, if not more, important to Armstrong's performance than the 9% improvements in cycling efficiency' (Martin et al. 2005: 1628). Indeed, in his book, Coyle (2005b: 67) quotes Lance Armstrong as saying 'Losing weight is the single most important thing you can do. You have to train. You have to be strong, of course. But if you're too heavy, it's all over'. The book details some of his training goals leading up to his 2004 Tour de France victory and corroborates this statement. Six months prior to the race Armstrong weighed 79.5 kg and his goal was to be 5.5 kg lighter for racing; by the time of the race he weighed 74.0 kg, increased his power-to-body-mass ratio to 6.6 $W \cdot kg^{-1}$ from 5.9 $W \cdot kg^{-1}$ and went on to win the Tour.

Both professional road cyclists and elite endurance runners may benefit from a reduction in body mass prior to major competition, but due to the differing nature of the respective sports (i.e. uphill cyclists must overcome gravity in a body-mass-supported sport) the effect on performance may be dissimilar due to mass distribution within the body. For example, a limitation in some of the energy cost of locomotion studies (e.g. Cureton et al. 1978) is that the extra mass was added only to the trunk and not distributed between trunk and limbs, as would be expected when gaining weight. Indeed, the handicap effect is larger on running when extra mass is added distally; Myers and Steudel (1985) compared adding weight proximally to the centre of mass (i.e. the waist) and distally on the limbs (i.e. foot/ankle) during running and reported that the energy cost was increased by a factor of 1.5–5.5 by the latter. Similarly, Jones et al. (1986) measured the energy cost of wearing shoes of varying weight during running and walking and reported an average increment in oxygen cost of 1% per 100 g of weight added. In his 2003 review, Larsen (2003) has postulated that the superior running economy of Kenyan runners could partly be explained by their low body mass index combined with the fact that the majority of their body mass is distributed proximally, with the mass of the lower limbs being kept to a minimum, especially in the calf and thigh area (Figure 6.3). Evidence favouring superior running economy in Kenyan endurance runners compared to Caucasian athletes was first presented by Saltin et al. (1995). In that study, Kenyan runners

Figure 6.3 Photographs illustrating very low mass of the thigh and calf area in elite Kenyan endurance runners.

Photographs courtesy of Dr Y. P. Pitsiladis.

exhibited better running economy compared to their Scandinavian counterparts whilst running at submaximal running speeds even though their absolute $\dot{V}O_2$ max was not different. This finding has been corroborated by Weston *et al.* (2000) who reported that African runners were 5% more economical than Caucasians running at 16.1 km·hr^{-1} (47.3 ± 3.2 vs. 49.9 ± 2.4 mL·kg^{-1}·min^{-1}). Whether these anthropometric factors are indeed typical of Kenyans and responsible, in part at least, for their outstanding running performances remains to be determined.

Further evidence for a possible ergogenic effect on endurance running as a result of reducing body mass may be found by considering the evolution of human dietary patterns and bioenergetics (see Leonard and Ulijaszek 2002 for review). Around 2.5 million years ago there was a dramatic change in climate that reduced the amount of tropical forests and led to a dramatic increase in open, drier grassland in central Africa (Foley 1987). This increased high quality food availability and led to grazing animals becoming a more attractive choice for energy provision. The change from a shaded environment, which required low levels of physical activity to obtain food, to an open environment exposed to oppressive solar radiation, necessitated hard physical exertion to run prey to thermoregulatory exhaustion or compete with other scavengers, such as wild dogs and hyenas, for carcasses containing marrow, brain and other tissues (Carrier 1984; Bramble and Lieberman 2004). Bramble and Lieberman have proposed that endurance running over extended time periods is a distinct and unique characteristic of humans. Such running prowess allowed our early human ancestors in the savannah environment to exploit protein-rich resources and was a key step in evolution of *Homo*. The genetic make-up of contemporary humans has not changed since the emergence of the anatomically modern human, *Homo sapiens sapiens*, despite radical changes in living conditions and lifestyle over approximately 50,000 years since then (Vigilant *et al.* 1991; Wilson and Cann 1992). Consequently, men and women today have genes that evolved in a hunting gathering era lasting several millions of years. Cordain *et al.* (1998) suggest that today's endurance runners may be the closest humans to our ancestors in terms of daily physical exertion. Although not a perfect model, hunter-gatherer societies are the best available gauge for assessing the physical activity levels of early *Homo*. Societies such as the Ache, !Kung, Agta, Hazda, Hiwi, Efe, San, and Inuit (Figure 6.4) may provide the best available snapshot of physical activity and eating patterns for which we are genetically engineered (Cordain *et al.* 1998) and allow a good comparison with today's elite athletes. For example, Table 6.1 presents physical activity levels and daily ranges for selected species and groups which highlight the distinct similarity between estimated physical activity levels of our early ancestors, recent hunter-gatherer societies and elite Kenyan endurance runners. The contrast with the physical activity levels of a typically non-active person from the United Kingdom (Table 6.1) is corroborated by a study which reveals that traditional societies have around 50% greater aerobic power than age-matched affluent westerners

Figure 6.4 Two G/wi hunters track a red hartebeest they've just shot with poisoned arrows in Ghanzi District, Botswana.

Image: © Peter Johnson/CORBIS.

(Cordain *et al.* 1998). Interestingly, Saltin *et al.* (1995) reported that Kenyan boys who walked and ran a long distance to school each day, but did not formally train for athletics, had $\dot{V}O_2$ max values some 30% higher than those who did not. This is also corroborated by two studies that implicate childhood endurance activity as a key selection process in the determination of Ethiopian (Scott *et al.* 2003) and Kenyan (Onywera *et al.* 2006) endurance success. Therefore, although chronic endurance training as a result of running from a young age may be an important determinant of success for future athletic performance, this remains to be scientifically proven (see Chapter 15).

Endurance running was a key step in human evolution, and traditional hunter-gatherer societies provide a window into the physical activity and eating patterns of early *Homo*. Jenike (2001: 216) has suggested that seasonal variation in energy intake may have been 'a near-universal characteristic of hunter-gatherer societies'. Indeed, Table 6.2 presents the variation in energy intake of various hunter-gatherer societies. Seasonal variation seen here is due to availability of plant foods and animals and is probably exacerbated in individuals who rely on a high protein diet because of the high metabolic demands in capturing prey (Speth and Spielmann 1983). Cordain *et al.* (2000) have suggested that this may have accounted for most hunter-gatherers (73% of worldwide hunter-gatherer societies) with the majority of their dietary energy being consumed as animal food (56–65%). The difference in energy intake between low and high

Table 6.1 Body mass (BM), physical activity level (PAL) (i.e. ratio of total energy expenditure/basal metabolic rate), and daily range for selected species and groups

Species/group	Sex	BM (kg)	PAL	Day range (km)
Fossil hominids[†]				
A. afarensis	M/F	37.1	1.6	–
A. africanis	M/F	35.3	1.6	–
A. robustus	M/F	44.4	1.6	–
H. habilis	M/F	48	1.7	–
H. erectus	M/F	53	1.8	–
H. sapiens (early)	M/F	57	1.8	–
Human foragers[†]				
!Kung	M	46	1.7	14.9
Ache	M	59.6	2.2	19.2
Elite athlete[‡]				
Kenyan endurance runners	M	56.0	2.3	16.4
UK population[§]				
Non-active	M	70	1.4	–

Notes: [†]From Leonard and Robertson 1992.
[‡]From Fudge *et al.* 2006.
[§]From Department of Health 1991.

Source: Adapted from Leonard and Robertson 1992; Cordain *et al.* 1998.

Table 6.2 Seasonal variation in energy intake of specific hunter-gatherer societies

Group	High season (MJ·person^{-1}·d^{-1})	Low season (MJ·person^{-1}·d^{-1})	% of High season
[†]Ache	21.28	11.95	56
[‡]Efe	11.98	8.86	74
[§]Hazda	15.48	7.95	51
[*]Hiwi	11.53	5.65	49

Notes: [†]From Hill *et al.* 1984.
[‡]From Bailey and Peacock, 1988.
[§]From Cohen, 1989.
[*]From Hurtado and Hill, 1990.

Source: Adapted from Jenike 2001.

season can be large. For example, the Ache (Hill *et al.* 1984), the Hazda (Cohen 1989) and the Hiwi (Hurtado and Hill 1990) all consume about half the energy intake during the low season as compared to the high season. Archaeological data corroborate seasonal food shortage and significant fluctuations in body mass

(Sobolik 1994a,b; Jenike 2001). Periods when food was plentiful followed by times when food was sparse throughout human evolution has undoubtedly resulted in the modern-day human's ability to fluctuate body mass, in particular fat mass, in order to cope with nutritional stress. This is reflected in the growing number of obese individuals in affluent western societies (Prentice and Jebb 1995; Ebbeling *et al.* 2002) and is the basis of the 'thrifty genotype' hypothesis proposed by Neel (1962). Chakravarthy and Booth (2004: 4) proposed that 'cycling of food stores, blood insulin, insulin sensitivity, and metabolic regulatory proteins, driven by cycles of feast–famine and physical activity–rest, have moulded the selection of "thrifty" genes and genotype, some with functions that are predominately for glycogen conservation and replenishment, as the speculation is made that our ancestors were more likely to survive with these adaptations than without them'. Considering the importance of endurance running in hunting and scavenging (Bramble and Lieberman 2004), this invites the intriguing possibility that *Homo* may have evolved to be able to run when faced with a reduction in body mass as a result of food shortage and possibly explains why humans as a result of training adapt to conserve glycogen and use fat as an energy source during endurance exercise (Mole *et al.* 1971). However, it is also clear that there must have been a limit to how much body mass *Homo* could lose before this would affect their ability to hunt and compete for food.

Recurring reductions in body mass due to food shortage may have indirectly been a key step in the evolution of *Homo*. However, could a reduction in body mass (for a variety of different reasons) prior to competition in the modern endurance runner also be an important determinant of performance success? Heinrich (2001: 202) proposed that 'when we need food, having the speed and mobility to chase it down is obviously advantageous'. This implies that smallness and lightness may have benefited *Homo* in capturing prey. Recent investigations carried out on endurance runners corroborate this statement (Marino *et al.* 2000; 2003). For example, two studies by Marino *et al.* (2000, 2003) reported that heavier runners display a greater degree of heat retention than lighter individuals and that this may be a major factor limiting the performance of physically larger and heavier athletes in distance running events. Furthermore, it was reported that heavier runners self-selected a slower running speed than lighter runners when running in the heat and that this speed was inversely related to body mass (reviewed by Harley and Noakes Chapter 10). This suggests that excess body mass would not be advantageous for endurance running in the savannah environment, nor equally in an Olympic marathon due to thermoregulatory limitations (see Chapter 5). Figure 6.5 presents a schematic model of this; it follows that a reduction in body mass as a consequence of a food shortage or hard physical work/exercise, results in increased mobility and speed for the hunter-gatherer, and similarly optimal endurance running performance for the modern athlete. Indeed, the anthropomorphic features of current world-record holders in endurance events do seem to corroborate this

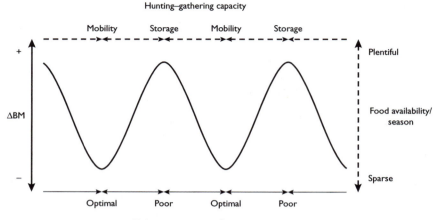

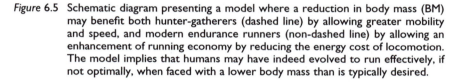

Figure 6.5   Schematic diagram presenting a model where a reduction in body mass (BM) may benefit both hunter-gatherers (dashed line) by allowing greater mobility and speed, and modern endurance runners (non-dashed line) by allowing an enhancement of running economy by reducing the energy cost of locomotion. The model implies that humans may have indeed evolved to run effectively, if not optimally, when faced with a lower body mass than is typically desired.

statement with the east African endurance runners being typically very slender (Weyand and Davis 2005). Another example in nature of a similar body mass 'trade-off' can be seen in small birds in which studies of flight mechanics (Hedenström 1992; Blem 1975) suggested that extra body mass would decrease flight performance and hence increase predation risk (Witter and Cuthil 1993). However, these birds must build up large fat stores in order to support migration. Hence body mass is a good indicator of the balance between starvation and predation risk and presumably this will greatly reflect the species vulnerability. Indeed, MacLeod *et al.* (2005) suggested that the decline of the house sparrow by 60% between 1970 and 2000 in the UK (Crick *et al.* 2002; Gregary *et al.* 2002) may be due to mass-dependant predation as the birds are unable to increase body mass in an attempt to reduce their high starvation risk; house sparrows are the most frequent prey for cats and sparrow hawk predation (MacLeod *et al.* 2005). Furthermore, Westerterp and Drent (1985) reported that starlings reduce body mass for flying (i.e. feeding nestlings) compared to sitting (i.e. incubating) since this results in a reduction in the energy cost of flight. Hence, the quantity of 'extra' body mass that is acceptable is intrinsically linked to the extent of mobility required for either hunting or risk aversion in order to survive in most animals and a reduction in energy cost of movement. Elite endurance running performance today may be regarded as the equivalent of hunting, competing, and/or scavenging for food that has occupied most human existence on the planet (Åstrand and Rodahl 1986). Therefore, it is not surprising that elite endurance runners, such as Margaret Okayo, Felix Limo and other athletes studied (Onywera *et al.* 2004; Fudge *et al.* 2006), 'instinctively' reduce body mass prior to racing.

Conclusion

Given the fact that east African endurance athletes dominate global competition, it is reasonable to consider their training habits and lifestyle as being close to optimal for athletic performance. Body-mass-cycling, with a negative energy balance prior to competition, appears to be a frequent finding in these athletes. Although it is unclear what constitutes an optimal loss in body mass prior to competition, the performance implications for the modern athlete of a reduction in body mass were very likely evident when *Homo* was chasing its prey on the savannah grasslands in central Africa. However, athletes and coaches should be cautious in deliberately trying to lose excess body mass; rather a sensible diet and training that aims to optimize an adequate mix of metabolic fuel stores for racing and a body size that enables a reduced oxygen cost of movement is paramount. For example, in Kenya, where a set of standard weighing scales is rare, even in the camp where the elite athletes are based during training (e.g. Global Sports Training Camp, Kaptagat, Eldoret, Kenya), athletes rely on instinct alone. The rationale for the suggestions presented here is reflected by the hegemony of east African athletes in world endurance running for the last several decades.

Bibliography

Ainsworth, B. E., Haskell, W. L., Whitt, M. C., Irwin, M. L., Swartz, A. M., Strath, S. J., O'Brien, W. L., Bassett, D. R., Jr, Schmitz, K. H., Emplaincourt, P. O., Jacobs, D. R., Jr and Leon, A. S. (2000) 'Compendium of physical activities: an update of activity codes and MET intensities', *Medicine and Science in Sports and Exercise* 32, S498–S504.

American College of Sports Medicine (2000) 'Joint Position Statement: nutrition and athletic performance. American College of Sports Medicine, American Dietetic Association, and Dietitians of Canada', *Medicine and Science in Sports and Exercise* 32, 2130–45.

Åstrand, P. O. and Rodahl, K. (1986) *Textbook of Work Physiology*, New York: McGraw Hill, pp. 1–11.

Bailey, R. C. and Peacock, N. R. (1988) 'Efe Pygmies of northeast Zaïre: subsistence strategies in the Ituri forest', in *Coping with Uncertainty in Food Supply*, ed. de Garine, I. and Harrison, G. A., Oxford: Claredon Press, pp. 88–117.

Blem, C. R. (1975) 'Geographic variation in wing loading of the house sparrow', *Wilson Bulletin* 87, 543–9.

Bramble, D. M. and Lieberman, D. E. (2004) 'Endurance running and the evolution of *Homo*', *Nature* 432, 345–52.

Buskirk, E. and Taylor, H. L. (1957) 'Maximal oxygen intake and its relation to body composition, with special reference to chronic physical activity and obesity', *Journal of Applied Physiology* 11, 72–8.

Carrier, D. R. (1984) 'The energetic paradox of human running and hominid evolution', *Current Anthropology* 25, 483–95.

Chakravarthy, M. V. and Booth, F. W. (2004) 'Eating, exercise, and "thrifty" genotypes: connecting the dots toward an evolutionary understanding of modern chronic diseases', *Journal of Applied Physiology* 96, 3–10.

Christensen, D. L., Van Hall, G. and Hambraeus, L. (2002) 'Food and macronutrient intake of male adolescent Kalenjin runners in Kenya', *British Journal of Nutrition* 88, 711–17.

Cohen, M. N. (1989) *Health and the Rise of Civilisation*, New Haven, CT: Yale University Press.

Cordain, L., Gotshall, R. W., Eaton, S. B. and Eaton, S. B. (1998) 'Physical activity, energy expenditure and fitness: an evolutionary perspective', *International Journal of Sports Medicine* 19, 328–35.

Cordain, L., Miller, J. B., Eaton, S. B., Mann, N., Holt, S. H. and Speth, J. D. (2000) 'Plant-animal subsistence ratios and macronutrient energy estimations in worldwide hunter-gatherer diets', *American Journal of Clinical Nutrition* 71, 682–92.

Costill, D. L. and Miller, J. M. (1980) 'Nutrition for endurance sport: carbohydrate and fluid balance', *International Journal of Sports Medicine* 1, 2–14.

Coyle, E. F. (2005a) 'Improved muscular efficiency displayed as Tour de France champion matures', *Journal of Applied Physiology* 98, 2191–6.

Coyle, D. (2005b) *Lance Armstrong: Tour de Force*, New York: HarperCollins.

Crick, H. Q. P., Robinson, R. A., Appleton, G. F., Clark, N. A. and Rickard, A. D. (2002) *Investigation into the Causes of the Decline of Starlings and House Sparrows in Great Britain: BTO Research Report No. 290*, London: Department of Environment, Food and Rural Affairs.

Cureton, K. J. and Sparling, P. B. (1980) 'Distance running performance and metabolic responses to running in men and women with excess weight experimentally equated', *Medicine and Science in Sports and Exercise* 12, 288–94.

Cureton, K. J., Sparling, P. B., Evans, B. W., Johnson, S. M., Kong, U. D. and Purvis, J. W. (1978) 'Effect of experimental alterations in excess weight on aerobic capacity and distance running performance', *Medicine and Science in Sports* 10, 194–9.

Department for Health (1991) *Dietary Reference Values for Food Energy and Nutrients for the United Kingdom*, London: HMSO.

Ebbeling, C. B., Pawlak, D. B. and Ludwig, D. S. (2002) 'Childhood obesity: public-health crisis, common sense cure', *Lancet* 360, 473–82.

Fogelholm, M. (1990) 'Effects of bodyweight reduction on sports performance', *Sports Medicine* 18, 249–67.

Foley, R. (1987) *Another Unique Species: Patterns in Evolutionary Ecology*, Harlow: Longman Scientific and Technical.

Fudge, B. W., Westerterp, K. R., Kiplamai, F. K., Onywera, V. O., Boit, M. K., Kayser, B., Pitsiladis, Y. P. (2006) 'Evidence of negative energy balance using doubly labelled water in elite Kenyan endurance runners prior to competition', *British Journal of Nutrition* 95, 59–66.

Gregary, R. D., Wilkinson, N. I., Noble, D. G., Robinson, J. A., Brown, J. A., Hughes, J., Proctor, D., Gibbons, D. W. and Galbraith C. A. (2002) 'The population status of birds in the United Kingdom, Channel Islands, and the Isle of Man: an analysis of conservation concern', *British Birds* 95, 410–48.

Hedenström, A. (1992) 'Flight performance in relation to fuel load in birds', *Journal of Theoretical Biology* 158, 535–7.

Heinrich, B. (2001) *Why We Run: A Natural History*, New York: HarperCollins.

Hill, K. R., Hawkes, K., Hurtado, M. and Kaplan, H. (1984) 'Seasonal variance in the diet of Ache hunter-gatherers in Eastern Paraguay', *Human Ecology* 12, 101–35.

Horswill, C. A., Hickner, R. C., Scott, J. R., Costill, D. L. and Gould, D. (1990) 'Weight loss, dietary carbohydrate modifications, and high intensity, physical performance', *Medicine and Science in Sports and Exercise* 22, 470–6.

Hurtado, A. M. and Hill, K. R. (1990) 'Seasonality in a foraging society: variation in diet, work effort, fertility, and sexual division of labour among the Hiwi of Venezuela', *Journal of Anthropological Research* 46, 293–346.

Jenike, M. (2001) 'Nutritional ecology: diet, physical activity and body size', in *Hunter-Gatherers: an Interdisciplinary Perspective*, ed. Panter-Brick, C., Layton, R. and Rowley-Conwy, P., Cambridge: Cambridge University Press, pp. 205–38.

Jones, B. H., Knapik, J. J., Daniels, W. L. and Toner, M. M. (1986) 'The energy cost of women walking and running in shoes and boots', *Ergonomics* 29, 439–43.

Larsen, H. B. (2003) 'Kenyan dominance in distance running', *Comparative Biochemistry and Physiology: Part A, Molecular and Integrative Physiology* 136, 161–70.

Leonard, W. R., Robertson, M. L. (1992) 'Nutritional requirements and human evolution: a bioenergetics model', *American Journal of Human Biology* 4, 179–95.

Leonard, W. R. and Ulijaszek, S. J. (2002) 'Energetics and evolution: an emerging research domain', *American Journal of Human Biology* 14, 547–50.

Loucks, A. B. (2004) 'Energy balance and body composition in sports and exercise', *Journal of Sports Sciences* 22, 1–14.

Lucia, A., Earnest, C. and Arribas, C. (2003) 'The Tour de France: a physiological review', *Scandinavian Journal of Medicine and Science in Sports* 13, 275–83.

MacLeod, R., Barnett, P., Clark, J. and Cresswell, W. (2005) 'Mass-dependant predation risk as a mechanism for house sparrow decline?' *Biology Letters*. Available online at: <http://www.journals.royalsoc.ac.uk/link.asp?id=ph68364 r85288n32>.

Marino, F. E., Lambert, M. L. and Noakes, T. D. (2003) 'Superior running performance of African runners in warm humid but not in cool environments', *Journal of Applied Physiology* 96, 124–30.

Marino, F. E., Mbambo, Z., Kortekaas, E., Wilson, G., Lambert, M. I., Noakes, T. D. and Dennis, S. C. (2000) 'Advantages of smaller body mass during distance running in warm, humid environments', *Pflüügers Archiv European Journal of Physiology* 441, 359–67.

Martin, D. T., Quod, M. J., Gore, C. J. and Coyle, E. F. (2005) 'Has Armstrong's cycle efficiency improved?' *Journal of Applied Physiology* 99, 1628–9 (author reply 1629).

McMurray, R. G., Ben-Ezra, V., Forsythe, W. A. and Smith, A. T. (1985) 'Responses of endurance-trained subjects to caloric deficits induced by diet or exercise', *Medicine and Science in Sports and Exercise* 17, 574–9.

Mole, P. A., Oscai, L. B. and Holloszy, J. O. (1971) 'Adaption of muscle to exercise. Increase in levels of palmityl CoA synthetase, carnitine palmityltransferase, and palmityl CoA dehydrogenase, and in the capacity to oxidize fatty acids', *Journal of Clinical Investigation* 50, 2323–30.

Moses, K. and Manore, M. M. (1991) 'Development and testing of a carbohydrate monitoring tool for athletes', *Journal of the American Dietetic Association* 91, 962–65.

Mukeshi, M. and Thairu, K. (1993) 'Nutrition and body build: a Kenyan review', *World Review of Nutrition and Dietetics* 72, 218–26.

Myers, M. J. and Steudel, K. (1985) 'Effect of limb mass and its distribution on the energetic cost of running', *Journal of Experimental Biology* 116, 363–73.

Neel, J. V. (1962) 'Diabetes mellitus a "thrifty" genotype rendered detrimental by "progress"?' *American Journal of Human Genetics* 14, 352–3.

Noakes, T. D. (2000) 'Physiological models to understand exercise fatigue and the adaptations that predict or enhance athletic performance', *Scandinavian Journal of Medicine and Science in Sports* 10, 123–45.

Onywera, V. O., Kiplamai, F. K., Tuitoek, P. J., Boit, M. K. and Pitsiladis, Y. P. (2004) 'Food and macronutrient intake of elite Kenyan distance runners', *International Journal of Sports Nutrition* 14, 709–19.

Onywera, V. O., Scott, R. A., Boit, M. K. and Pitsiladis, Y. P. (2006) 'Demographic characteristics of elite Kenyan runners', *Journal of Sports Sciences* 24 (4), 415–22.

Pitsiladis, Y. P., Scott, R. A., Moran, C., Wilson, R. H. and Goodwin, W. H. (2004) 'The dominance of Kenyans in distance running', *Equine and Comparative Exercise Physiology* 1, 285–91.

Prentice, A. M. and Jebb, S. A. (1995) 'Obesity in Britain: gluttony or sloth?' *BMJ* 311, 437–9.

Saltin, B., Larsen, H., Terrados, N., Bangsbo, J., Bak, T., Kim, C. K., Svedenhag, J. and Rolf, C. J. (1995) 'Aerobic exercise capacity at sea level and at altitude in Kenyan boys, junior and senior runners compared with Scandinavian runners', *Scandinavian Journal of Medicine and Science in Sports* 5, 209–21.

Scott, R. A., Georgiades, E., Wilson, R. H., Goodwin, W. H., Wolde, B. and Pitsiladis, Y. P. (2003) 'Demographic characteristics of elite Ethiopian endurance runners', *Medicine and Science in Sports and Exercise* 35, 1727–32.

Sobolik, K. D. (1994a) 'Introduction', in *Paleonutrition: The Diet and Health of Prehistoric Americans*, ed. Sobolik, K. D., Carbondale IL: Centre for Archeoligical Investigations, Southern Illinois University, pp. 1–20.

Sobolik, K. D. (1994b) 'Paleonutrition of the Lower Pecos Region of the Chihuahuan Desert', in *Paleonutrition: The Diet and Health of Prehistoric Americans*, ed. Sobolik, K. D., Carbondale IL: Centre for Archeoligical Investigations, Southern Illinois University, pp. 247–64.

Speth, J. D. and Spielmann, K. A. (1983) 'Energy source, protein metabolism, and hunter-gatherer subsistence strategies', *Journal of Anthropological Archaeology* 2, 1–31.

Taylor, C. R. (1994) 'Relating mechanics and energetics during exercise', *Advances in Veterinary Science and Comparative Medicine* 38, 181–215.

Taylor, C. R., Heglund, N. C., McMahon, T. A. and Looney, T. R. (1980) 'Energetic cost of generating muscular force during running. A comparison of large and small animals', *Journal of Experimental Biology* 86, 9–18.

Terjung, R. L., Baldwin, K. M., Winder, W. W. and Holloszy, J. O. (1974) 'Glycogen repletion in different types of muscle and in liver after exhausting exercise', *American Journal of Physiology* 226, 1387–91.

Tittel, K. and Wutscherk, H. (1992) 'Anatomical and anthropometric fundamentals of endurance', in *Endurance in Sport*, ed. Shepard, R. J. and Åstrand, P. O., Oxford: Blackwell Scientific Publications, pp. 35–45.

Vigilant, L., Stoneking, M., Harpending, H., Hawkes, K. and Wilson, A. C. (1991) 'African populations and the evolution of human mitochondrial DNA', *Science* 253, 1503–7.

Westerterp, K. R., Drent, R. (1985) 'Energetic costs and energy-saving mechanisms in parental care of free-living passerine birds as determined by the D2O18 method', Proceedings of the XVIIIth Ornithological Conference, Moscow, 392–8.

Weston, A. R., Mbambo, Z. and Myburgh, K. H. (2000) 'Running economy of African and Caucasian distance runners', *Medicine and Science in Sports and Exercise* 32, 1130–4.

Weyand, P. G. and Davis, J. A. (2005) 'Running performance has a structural basis', *Journal of Experimental Biology* 208, 2625–31.

Williams, K. R. and Cavanagh, P. R. (1987) 'Relationship between distance running mechanics, running economy, and performance', *Journal of Applied Physiology* 63, 1236–45.

Wilson, A. C. and Cann, R. L. (1992) 'The recent African genesis of humans', *Scientific American* 266, 68–73.

Witter, M. S. and Cuthil, I. C. (1993) 'The ecological costs of fat storage', *Philosophical Transactions of the Royal Society of London* B340, 73–92.

Chapter 7

Diet and endurance performance of Kenyan runners

A physiological perspective

Dirk L. Christensen

Introduction

A nutritionally adequate diet is essential to an optimal functioning of the body in general and to performance in sports in particular. In other words, the elite athlete relies on a diet providing sufficient energy, as well as an adequate content of macro- and micronutrients. It is important to emphasize two aspects in this context. First of all, there is no precise answer to an adequate content of macro- and micronutrients in a diet. It depends on many different aspects such as physiological bioavailability, short- and long-term physiological adaptability as well as training volume and intensity. Furthermore, all national and international recommendations are based on consensus decisions of scientific boards. Second, the majority of the recommendations of these scientific boards are based on investigations carried out in Caucasians living in Europe, north America or Australia. Hence, they might not reflect the African reality, and physiological response to life-style including diet often differs between different ethnic groups. Taking these aspects into consideration is important when discussing diet intake and performance of the Kenyan runners.

It is interesting that only a handful of nutritional studies including Kenyan runners have been carried out over the past 10–15 years in spite of a bulk of general knowledge based on scientific investigations within the area of diet and performance among athletes. Even though the interest in east African and especially Kenyan running performance is enormous, this lack of scientific evidence when it comes to diet intake among these athletes is hardly surprising given the high occurrence of under- and malnutrition on the African continent. Especially, evidence of protein-energy and micronutrient malnutrition has been shown several times over the past ~80 years in Kenya (Jansen *et al.* 1987; Ngare and Muttunga 1999; Leenstra *et al.* 2004). This indicates potential performance problems for Kenya-based athletes in training and competition. For the reasons described above, studies focusing on public health in general with great emphasis on children have therefore been dominating nutritional studies in Kenya as well as the rest of east Africa. In the latter, however, not a single study on athletes and nutrition has been carried out.

Food consumption and availability

Most of the Kenyan runners are of Nilotic descent belonging to the Kalenjin sub-group, also known as highland Nilotes. As all other Nilotic sub-groups the Kalenjin have historically been pastoralists and therefore relied on milk and blood as well as meat as their staple foods. However, it is a misconception to regard all Nilotes as pure pastoralists since most of them have supplemented their diet with grain foods, especially during the dry season when the milk production is low (Sutton 1974; Nestel 1989). The Kalenjin in particular have a tradition for a mixed diet relying much more on grain foods than especially the Maasai and the Samburu, both of whom prefer to live as pure pastoralists and only consume grain foods when low on staple foods.

Most of the foods consumed by the Kalenjin runners are traditional but not indigenous to their diet. Present-day Kalenjin and their food habits are a 'product' of the mixed culture from migration waves and inter-marriage initiated approximately 3,000 years ago by Cushitic agriculturists and Nilotic herdsmen from present-day Ethiopia and the Sudan, respectively, as well as hunter-gatherer groups in present-day Kenya. The grains first cultivated and consumed among the Kalenjin were sorghum and finger millet (eleusine). The staple foods of today, maize and kidney beans, are relative newcomers to the Kenyan diet: so is the relatively small amount of cultivated vegetables eaten by the Kenyan runners. Green vegetables used to be more common in the Kenyan diet, but intensive cultivation of the land that started with the European settlement of the fertile highlands has contributed to the diminishment of formerly popular indigenous green vegetables (Phillip 1943). Nevertheless, the fertility of the so-called Kenyan highlands stretching from Nairobi and westwards almost all the way to the border of Uganda, has secured the Kalenjin and other peoples of the same region reliable food availability albeit based on a small selection of food items of mainly plant foods (i.e. maize, kidney beans, cabbage, curly kale, bread – wheat, meat – beef, milk, coffee and tea). The domination of plant foods is clearly demonstrated in all the modern studies including Kenyan runners, as carbohydrate intake was very high (>70% of total energy intake) and fat intake proportionally low (~13–15% of total energy intake). Protein intake was high even though intakes of some essential amino acids were borderline to low.

The study we carried out among Kalenjin sub-elite adolescent runners (Christensen et al. 2002) showed that milk was not as important a diet item as we had expected. Milk was served on a daily basis, both as a pure drink and mixed with coffee (it is commonly mixed with tea as well) but made up only 6% of the total energy intake. We were somewhat surprised by this low milk intake, but we were told that extra milk (the amount was not specified) was consumed prior to important competitions. Our study was carried out early in the athletics season with only minor competitions scheduled in the region where the runners trained and competed. However, in a later study, Onywera et al. (2004) did document a much higher milk intake among elite male runners (13%

of daily energy intake) while in training camp prior to major competition. Still, this was far from the average milk intake of Nilotes (Maasai) living as pure pastoralists, as it amounted to between 2–6 $L \cdot d^{-1}$ (Biss *et al.* 1971). This shows that there is a substantial difference in macronutrient distribution of the diets of Kenyan (Kalenjin) runners and traditional pastoralists, most notably in the carbohydrate to fat intake ratio. The physiological response and performance implications of the macronutrient intake of the runners will be discussed later in this chapter (see Table 7.1 for an overview of the macronutrient intake of Kenyan runners).

Methodological considerations

The few investigations involving Kenyan athletes give us some basic knowledge of the nutritional intake of some of the best distance runners in the world, at least while they live and train in Kenya (e.g. Onywera *et al.* 2004; Fudge *et al.* 2006). All of these studies have been carried out in the field, and they therefore lack the sophistication of laboratory-based studies. In spite of this lack of quality seen from a basic physiological point of view, the results of these studies have certain advantages. They have been carried out where the athletes live and train while in Kenya, which gives us an excellent view into the dietary practice of 'free-living' runners. Laboratory-based studies inevitably create artificial environments thereby limiting the 'environmental physiological' information. In the field study that we carried out among male sub-elite student-athletes at a boarding school in the heart of the Kenyan highlands, food samples were collected and subsequently analysed in the laboratory thus providing in-depth knowledge of the local foods consumed by the runners.

In the few field studies put together on Kenyan runners the following methods have been applied:

- Study periods up to two consecutive weeks
- Daily interviews (24-hour recall)
- Collection of food samples
- Laboratory and food table analysis of macro- and micro-nutrient content
- Doubly labelled water method.

Doubly labelled water is the best method available for in-the-field assessment of energy balance and one such study in elite Kenyan runners has recently been conducted (Fudge *et al.* 2006) and confirmed the findings previously reported by these authors (Onywera *et al.* 2004) (see Chapters 5 and 6 in this book for details). Apart from the sub-elite student-athletes, adult male elite runners have taken part in the Kenyan diet studies, which give us good data on food consumption prior to, as well as during, exposure to running at world-class elite level (Figure 7.1). Unfortunately, no female athletes from Kenya have so far participated in any diet studies.

Figure 7.1 Rose the cook preparing lunch for elite Kenyan athletes living and training at the high altitude training camp (Global Sports Training Camp, Kaptagat, Eldoret, Kenya) situated in the North Rift Valley (altitude: 2400 m a.s.l.). These athletes in the studies by Onywera *et al.* (2004) and Fudge *et al.* (2006) were highly trained and included World, Olympic and Junior Champions frequently competing in major national and international middle- and long-distance running events.

Carbohydrate intake and glycogen resynthesis

An abundance of evidence has appeared in the literature over a span of several decades showing that a high daily intake of carbohydrate is advantageous in performance as well as in post-exercise recovery (Burke *et al.* 2001 and Burke *et al.* 2004 have made excellent reviews). The official guidelines recommend high carbohydrate intakes of 60–70% of total energy intake (Devlin and Williams 1991), and are believed to be necessary for optimal glycogen replenishment and performance (Sherman 1983; Costill 1985). However, these guidelines have been questioned by Noakes (1997) on the grounds that athletes in training do not consume such high amounts of carbohydrate, and that the carbohydrate intake of athletes has not increased over the past 50 years. This statement is true for athletes in industrialized countries, but when it comes to at least the former part of the statement, it is certainly not true for athletes residing in developing countries. The studies on Kenyan runners already cited in this chapter have clearly shown very high carbohydrate intakes at different levels of talent development (sub-elite and elite) and training intensity (different periods of in-season).

It is important to emphasize that a high intake of carbohydrate, expressed as a percentage of total energy intake, is crucial only when the diet is low in energy (such as shown in many studies on female endurance athletes) in order for the athlete to replenish his/her liver and skeletal muscle glycogen stores (for a review see Burke 1995). A high carbohydrate intake in relation to body mass is more important. There are guidelines for short-term/single events as well as long-term or routine situations (Burke et al. 1995).

In our study of adolescent Kalenjin runners, they had a daily carbohydrate intake of 8.7 g·kg⁻¹ body mass, which is well above the 6–7 g·kg⁻¹ body mass thought necessary for replenishment of liver and skeletal muscle glycogen stores after an hour's daily training at 75% $\dot{V}O_2$ max (Pascoe et al. 1990). The Kalenjin student-athletes only ran an average of 10 km/day, but intensity was high and probably above 75% $\dot{V}O_2$ max as training included distance as well as interval running during the early athletics season. The high intensity is indicated in the classic study by Saltin et al. (1995a) including, among others, Kalenjin adolescent male runners from the same boarding school in Marakwet as we used for our diet study. Off-season they trained at intensities between 72% and 98% in 9 out of 10 training sessions. The assumption is made that the very high training intensity elicits glycogen depletion to the same extent as exercise of longer and lower intensity.

In a study on elite Kenyan (all Kalenjin) runners, Onywera et al. (2004) reported a very high relative carbohydrate intake of 10.4 g·kg⁻¹ body mass. These results were later confirmed in a follow-up study by the same group (Fudge et al. 2006) (see Chapters 5 and 6). The training intensity was relatively high and the volume more than twice the amount observed among the adolescent student-athletes. This combination clearly shows the need for the very high relative carbohydrate intake.

It has been shown that the optimal glycogen replenishment is obtained within the first 30–60 minutes after cessation of exercise (Ivy et al. 1988). This is due to initial post-exercise synthesis of skeletal muscle glycogen that does not require the presence of insulin (Price et al. 1994). In our study of Kalenjin runners we observed that they were fed breakfast and dinner immediately after their early morning run and late afternoon training session, respectively, indicating optimal conditions for skeletal muscle glycogen replenishment. In addition, the staple food maize (64% of total energy intake) has a high glycaemic index (Ayuo and Ettyang 1996), which further indicates glycogen resynthesis conditions close to perfect for the adolescent runners while based at the boarding school.

Fat intake

It is not surprising that the fat intake of the Kenyan runners was very low (~13 to 15%) with a daily intake of only 46 g (Christensen *et al.* 2002; Onywera *et al.* 2004; Fudge *et al.* 2006). Based on reported food intake, similar low fat intakes have been observed previously in the general population in Kenya (van Steenbergen *et al.* 1984) as well as among other distance runners in developing countries, for instance in Mexico as studied by Cerqueira *et al.* (1979).

In spite of the fact that carbohydrate is the most essential energy substrate in prolonged, intensive physical exercise (>60% $\dot{V}O_2$ max), it is a fact that glycogen stores are limited, and during prolonged, intensive exercise they can be considerably reduced (Costill *et al.* 1973; Sherman 1983). It has been known for many decades that fat contributes to the energy substrate to a larger extent as muscular work increases over time (Ahlborg *et al.* 1974). Furthermore, it is almost seven decades since Christensen and Hansen (1939) showed that fat oxidation improves with training. The improved fat-oxidation is most probably caused by improved muscular oxidative capacity (Henriksson 1977; Gollnick and Saltin 1982; Kiens *et al.* 1993). Furthermore, an increased fat intake at the expense of carbohydrate has been shown to significantly affect substrate oxidation during exercise (Helge *et al.* 1996). This may indicate that the training-induced enzymatic adaptation in skeletal muscle is dependent on diet intake – and thereby access to each of the substrates during training (Helge and Kiens 1997).

Saltin *et al.* (1995b) measured the hydroxyacyl-CoA-dehydrogenase (HAD) enzyme activity in thigh (*m. vastus lateralis*) and calf (*m. gastrocnemius*) muscles. The HAD enzyme activity is regarded as a marker for lipid oxidation. Amazingly, the HAD enzyme activity was 20% and 50% higher in the thigh and calf muscles, respectively, in the Kenyan runners as compared to Scandinavian elite runners. When considering the very high carbohydrate intake of the Kenyan runners and the indication that diet intake affects training-induced enzymatic adaptation in skeletal muscle, it is intriguing that their fat oxidation seems to be so efficient. Could it be that they have physiologically adapted to their dietary past of high intakes of fat (primarily milk)? Considering that the shift in diet towards a high carbohydrate intake has existed for some generations and given the almost immediate enzymatic response to diet change as shown by Helge *et al.* (1996), it would seem unlikely that this is the case. Furthermore, high glycogen reduces and low glycogen increases the effect of training on a number of proteins in lipid metabolism. Therefore, fat oxidation and enzymatic activity of skeletal muscle in Kenyan athletes, and how it affects performance, must be investigated in future studies.

Protein and essential amino acid intake

To this day, there is vigorous scientific debate in the literature on the protein intake needed for athletes, including endurance runners. The methodological approaches have been different and this may be part of the reason why the results and conclusions have been equivocal. For example, in a study using strict energy balance control Forslund et al. (1999) showed that an increased energy turnover after aerobic exercise was not due to increased rates of urea production and/or protein synthesis. Thus, the authors were in line with the daily protein intake recommendations of the World Health Organization, which is 0.8 g·kg^{-1} (body mass) (FAO/WHO/UNU 1985). On the other hand, Lemon et al. (1997) show increased urea and total nitrogen excretion, i.e. increased protein metabolism, during and after exercise, but this study was not controlled by a strict energy balance.

As for the Kenyan runners, they had a high daily total protein intake ranging from 1.3 to 1.6 g·kg^{-1} and even a relatively good intake of quality protein (essential amino acids) despite their grain-based diet (Christensen et al. 2002; Onywera et al. 2004; Fudge et al. 2006). This clearly indicates that the total protein intake of the Kenyan runners was sufficient, even when compared to those investigations that have shown an increased need for protein intake (1.2–1.4 g·kg^{-1}) in individuals engaged in endurance exercise (for a review, see Lemon 2000). High intake of total protein was also found in the study of the ultra-distance Mexican Tarahumara runners (Cerqueira et al. 1979), whose diet was indeed very similar to the diet of the Kenyan runners at the macronutrient level. Interestingly, there was no malnutrition at the total protein level for runners based in developing countries, despite the fact that several studies on the general population in Kenya have shown the opposite, as mentioned earlier in this chapter. Also, it has been known for many years that a low daily energy intake requires an elevated protein intake (Munro 1951; Walberg et al. 1988). The Kalenjin student-athletes in our study had an adequate amount of energy, while the elite runners in the studies of Onywera et al. (2004) and Fudge et al. (2006) were reportedly in energy deficit. For a comprehensive discussion on energy balance and performance (see Chapter 6 in this book).

The essential amino acid intake of Kenyan runners has only been investigated in our study of boarding school runners, and it showed a low-to-borderline intake especially of isoleucine and histidine (partly essential only) because these runners were still physically growing, which may result in increased need for essential amino acid intake (Sinclair 1985). The deficit of some essential amino acids could be a limiting factor in performance, but it is also possible that a physiological adaptation to low essential amino acid intake has taken place, in which a high protein turnover has resulted in an enhanced re-utilization of essential amino acids (Christensen et al. 2002).

As noted earlier, the runners supplement with extra milk prior to important competition, and the study on elite Kenyan runners while in training camp did

Table 7.1 Daily macronutrient intake of Kenyan runners

	Total intake (g)	Relative intake $(g \cdot kg^{-1})$	Recommended $(g, g \cdot kg^{-1})$
Carbohydrate	465–600	8.7–10.4	500–600/6–10
Protein	75–88	1.3–1.6	0.8–1.4
Fat	46	0.8	N/A

indeed show a higher intake compared to the student-athletes studied in early athletics season. This higher milk intake will add isoleucine and histidine as well as other essential amino acids to their diet; thus a potential physiological adaptation to low amino acid intake would probably have only been necessary for limited periods of time (Christensen *et al.* 2002; Christensen 2004; Onywera *et al.* 2004; Fudge *et al.* 2006).

Overall macronutrient intake

For an interesting comparison an overview of total macronutrient intake of Kenyan runners as compared to other distance runners in the world is shown in Figure 7.2. Not surprisingly, the Kenyan (Kalenjin) runners along with the Mexican runners show a typical low-income country diet intake with the exception of a sufficient intake of total protein. However, it is interesting to observe

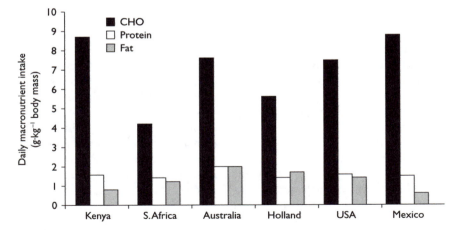

Figure 7.2 Daily macronutrient intake of male Kenyan distance runners as compared to other distance runners in the world.

Source: Data from Christensen *et al.* (2002), Peters and Goetzsche (1997), Burke *et al.* (1991), van Erp-Baart *et al.* (1989), Niekamp and Baer (1995), Cerqueira *et al.* (1979).

that only the Dutch and especially the South African runners have carbohydrate intakes below recommended values for endurance athletes (van Erp-Baart *et al.* 1989; Peters and Goetzsche 1997). It should be noted that the South African runners had a much higher carbohydrate intake prior to competition, while the figures chosen for this chapter show the more common training diet.

Micronutrient intake

Most of the literature on micronutrient intake and exercise has dealt with vitamin and mineral supply and performance enhancement (for a review, see Lukaski 2004) for athletes on an adequate diet. This reflects the reality for athletes in Europe, north America and Australia except for special groups such as female vegetarian runners, who may experience anaemia among other problems (Snyder *et al.* 1989). However, in an African context the picture is quite different. Micronutrient deficiency is widespread, even though clinical signs reflecting the deficiency may not always be apparent. This could be due to a physiological adaptation to low intake, but it is also possible that many studies have not succeeded in telling the whole story. 'Hidden' supplements, such as gathering of wild plants rich in vitamins or the inclusion of drinking water as a source of calcium, may not be accounted for. For example, Muskat and Keller (1968) showed that rural Kenyans did supplement their diet with wild vegetables, after the authors had wondered why their subjects did not show any clinical signs of vitamin deficiency as their 'normal' diet was reportedly low in key vitamins. Whether or not such supplements are important for Kenyan runners, who often live isolated in training camps or boarding schools, remains to be determined.

The only study to date to have comprehensively investigated the micronutrient intake of Kenyan runners was carried out among student-athletes at a boarding school in Marakwet (Christensen *et al.* 2005). The results reflect the classical low overall micronutrient intake among African populations, even though vitamin C intake was surprisingly high (95% of WHO recommendations) when considering the low green-vegetable intake. Here the results from this study have been compared to recommendations of the Food and Agriculture Organization of the United Nations/World Health Organization (FAO/WHO 2001). For the sake of clarity, and because of the complexity of micronutrient function and interaction, only a selected few will be discussed here, namely those that stand out because of low intakes (i.e. vitamins A, E, B_{12}, C, folic acid and calcium), or extremely high intake (i.e. iron).

Vitamins A, E and C are important anti-oxidants and all were consumed at levels of 17%, 65% and 95% of the FAO/WHO recommendations, respectively. When looking at the staple foods of the Kenyan runners combined with low intake of green vegetables and meat (both rich in vitamins) the low anti-oxidant vitamin intake is not a surprise. Especially a deficiency of vitamin E can lead to a reduced cell respiration due to disturbances of electron transport, i.e.

oxidative stress (Carabello 1974; Sen *et al.* 1994), which would be especially apparent in hypoxia (Simon-Schnass and Pabst 1988), thus reflecting the physical environment of the Kenyan athletes. Oxidative stress may also lead to free-radical-mediated fat peroxidation (Dillard *et al.* 1978; Davies *et al.* 1982).

Another interesting feature of the Kenyan diet was the extremely high intake of iron of 152 mg/day. The reason why this has not been reported in other studies on Kenyan athletes based exclusively on questionnaires (Mukeshi and Thairu 1993) may be due to the extremely long cooking time (4–6 hours) in iron containers that contaminates the food with iron. Since the majority of this high iron intake was of the non-haem type, haemochromatosis (i.e. damage to the liver) is unlikely to occur. It is important to emphasize that very high iron intakes due to contamination from either containers or iron-rich soil is not un-common in Africa as shown by studies in Ethiopia and South Africa (Hofvander 1968; Charlton *et al.* 1973). Does the high iron intake in combination with living at medium altitude (between 2,000 and 3,000 m) result in extremely high haemoglobin levels in Kenyan runners? (See Chapter 11.) This is not the case and there are several reasons for this. First of all, non-haem iron is poorly absorbed compared to haem iron from meat. Second, two other vitamins essential for the formation of haemoglobin, folic acid and vitamin B_{12}, were both consumed at low levels of just 56% and 55%, respectively, of FAO/WHO recommendations (2001). Third, Kenyans are plagued by malaria parasites and infestations such as hook-worm, both negatively affecting haemoglobin levels. Two studies measuring haematocrit (Mukeshi and Thairu 1993) and haemoglobin (Larsen *et al.* 2004), did show levels of just 43.5% and 8.6–8.8 g·100mL^{-1} (results for two groups of untrained Kalenjin boys), respectively, which is not surprising given the above-mentioned negative factors. Figure 7.3 shows the selected vitamin intake of Kalenjin runners as compared to other runners from different continents.

The last micronutrient to be considered in this chapter is the intake of calcium, which was low at just ~600 g·day^{-1} or 47% of FAO/WHO recommendations. It seems as if calcium absorption and intake are inversely related (Fairweather-Tait and Teucher 2002), and physical activity may be more critical to skeletal development of adolescents – to which group the Kenyan individuals in our study belonged – than calcium intake (Welten *et al.* 1994). Even though stress fractures are more likely to occur in athletes with low calcium intake (Myburgh *et al.* 1990), the bone strength of Kenyan runners is unlikely to be compromised to any serious degree. In 1990–1 when carrying out the major study on Kenyan vs. Scandinavian runners, the international research team headed by world-renowned Swedish physiologist Bengt Saltin handed out questionnaires asking for information on sport injuries *inter alia*. As it turned out, only 3 in 18 adolescent Kalenjin runners had a history of injuries even though they typically ran ~80 km·wk^{-1} at 75–85% of $\dot{V}O^2$ max (unpublished data). The intake of selected minerals in the Kenyans is compared to other runners from different continents in Figure 7.4.

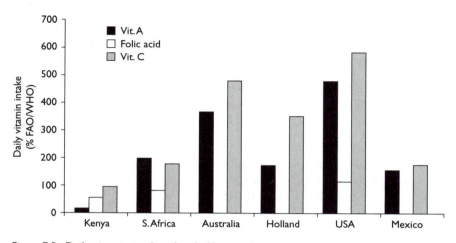

Figure 7.3 Daily vitamin intake of male Kenyan distance runners as compared to other distance runners in the world.

Source: Data from Christensen *et al.* (unpublished data), Peters and Goetzsche (1997), Burke *et al.* (1991), van Erp-Baart *et al.* (1989), Niekamp and Baer (1995), Cerqueira *et al.* (1979).

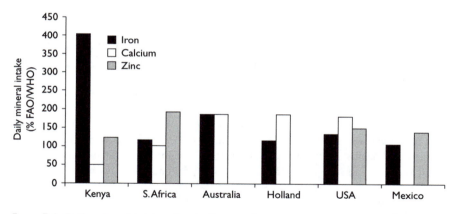

Figure 7.4 Daily mineral intake of male Kenyan distance runners as compared to other distance runners in the world.

Source: Data from Christensen *et al.* (unpublished data), Peters and Goetzsche (1997), Burke *et al.* (1991), van Erp-Baart *et al.* (1989), Niekamp and Baer (1995), Cerqueira *et al.* (1979).

Conclusion and perspectives for the future

In conclusion, when all aspects of the Kenyan diet are considered, it becomes clear that the runners' simple and in some aspects sub-optimal diet cannot explain their great performances. If anything, they perform very well despite their diet. A considered analysis of the current literature reveals two contrasting views:

- The diet is sub-optimal, and the runners therefore need a change of diet including micronutrient supplements. There is room for performance improvement.
- The diet intake is sufficient from a qualitative point of view because Kenyan runners have adapted physiologically to the sub-optimal intakes. There is no room for performance improvement.

Only carefully designed investigations carried out in the laboratory can identify the correct view. Furthermore, some runners may respond positively to a diet change, some may not. As the diet most likely changes when Kenyan runners are training and competing out of Kenya, it would be worth looking into physiological changes associated with this dietary change, especially into skeletal muscle enzymes with emphasis on the HAD enzymatic activity, given the intriguing results by Saltin *et al.* (1995a and b). Furthermore, the study of physiological adaptation to low (by Caucasian standards) micronutrient intake through bioavailability would add to our understanding of Kenyan running performance, as well as the performance of other athletes residing in low-income countries.

Acknowledgements

The author would like to thank the helpful staff at Marakwet High School in Kenya, and especially former athletics coach at Marakwet High School, Samson Kimobwa, as well as the student-athletes who volunteered as subjects. The author is also grateful and indebted to his following colleagues and co-authors (in alphabetical order): Professor Henrik Friis, Dr Gerrit van Hall, Professor Leif Hambraeus, Dr Jette Jakobsen, Dr Henrik B. Larsen and Professor Bengt Saltin.

Bibliography

Ahlborg, G., Felig, P., Hagenfeldt L., Hendler, R. and Wahren, J. (1974) 'Substrate turnover during prolonged exercise in man', *Journal of Clinical Investigation* 53, 1080–90.

Ayuo, P. O. and Ettyang, G. A. (1996) 'Glycaemic responses after ingestion of some local foods by non-insulin dependent diabetic subjects', *East African Medical Journal* 73, 782–5.

Biss, K., Taylor, C. B., Lewis, L. A., Mikkelson, B. and Ho K.-J. (1971) 'Atherosclerosis and lipid metabolism in the Masai of East Africa', *African Journal of Medical Science 2*, 249–57.

Burke, L. M. (1995) 'Nutrition for the female athlete', in Krummel, D. and Kris-Etherton, P. (eds) *Nutrition in Women's Health*, Gaithersburg, MD: Aspen Publishers, pp. 263–98.

Burke L. M., Gollan, R. A. and Read, A. S. (1991) 'Dietary intakes and food use of groups of elite Australian male athletes', *International Journal of Sport Nutrition* 1, 378–94.

Burke, L. M., Collier, G. R., Beasley, S. K., Davis, P. G., Fricker, P. A., Heeley, P., Walder, K. and Hargreaves, M. (1995) 'Effect of coingestion of fat and protein with carbohydrate feedings on muscle glycogen storage', *Journal of Applied Physiology* 78, 2187–92.

Burke, L. M., Cox, G. R., Cummings, N. K. and Desbrow, B. (2001) 'Guidelines for daily carbohydrate intake – do athletes achieve them?' *Sports Medicine* 31, 267–99.

Burke, L. M., Kiens, B. and Ivy, J. L. (2004) 'Carbohydrates and fat for training and recovery', *Journal of Sports Sciences* 22, 15–30.

Carabello, F. B. (1974) 'Role of tocopherol in the reduction of mitochondrial NAD', *Canadian Journal of Biochemistry* 52, 679–88.

Cerqueira, M. T., Fry, M. M. and Connor, W. E. (1979) 'The food and nutrient intakes of the Tarahumara Indians of Mexico', *American Journal of Clinical Nutrition* 32, 905–15.

Charlton, R. W., Bothwell, T. H. and Seftel, H. C. (1973) 'Dietary iron overload', in Callender, S. (ed.) *Clinics in Hematology* vol. 2, London: W. B. Saunders & Co., pp. 383–404.

Christensen, D. L. (2004) 'Diet intake and endurance performance in Kenyan runners', *Equine and Comparative Exercise Physiology* 1, 249–53.

Christensen, D. L., van Hall, G. and Hambraeus, L. (2002) 'Food and macronutrient intake of male adolescent Kalenjin runners in Kenya', *British Journal of Nutrition* 88, 711–17.

Christensen, D. L., Jakobsen, J. and Friis, H. (2005) 'Vitamin and mineral intake of twelve adolescent male Kalenjin runners in western Kenya', *East African Medical Journal* 82, 637–42.

Christensen, E. H. and Hansen, O. (1939) 'Respiratorischer Quotient und O_2-Aufnahme', *Skandinavisches Archiv füür Physiologie* 81, 180–9.

Costill, D. L. (1985) 'Carbohydrate nutrition before, during, and after exercise', *Federation Proceedings* 44, 364–8.

Costill, D. L., Bennett, A., Branam, G. and Eddy, D. (1973) 'Glucose ingestion at rest and during prolonged exercise', *Journal of Applied Physiology* 34, 764–9.

Davies, K. J. A., Quintanilha, A. T., Brooks, G. A. and Parker, L. (1982) 'Free radicals and tissue damage produced by exercise', *Archives of Biochemistry and Biophysics* 209, 539–54.

Devlin, J. T. and Williams, C. (1991) 'Final consensus statement: foods, nutrition and sports performance', *Journal of Sports Sciences* 9 (Suppl.), iii.

Dillard, C. J., Litov, R. E., Savin, W. M., Dumelin, E. E. and Tappel, A. I. L. (1978) 'Effects of exercise, vitamin E and ozone on pulmonary function and lipid peroxidation', *Journal of Applied Physiology* 45, 927–32.

Fairweather-Tait, S. J., Teucher, B. (2002) 'Iron and calcium bioavailability of fortified foods and dietary supplements', *Nutrition Reviews* 60, 360–7.

Food and Agriculture Organization/World Health Organization/United Nations University (1985) *Energy and Protein Requirements Report of a Joint Expert Consultation*, Technical Report Series, No. 724, Geneva: WHO.

Food and Agriculture Organization of the United Nations/World Health Organization (2001) *Human Vitamin and Mineral Requirements*, Report of a Joint FAO/WHO Expert Consultation, Bangkok, Thailand: Food and Nutrition Division; Rome: FAO.

Forslund, A. H., El-Khoury, A. E., Olsson, R. M., Sjödin, A. M. and Hambraeus, L. (1999) 'Effect of protein intake and physical activity on 24-h pattern and rate of macronutrient utilization', *American Journal of Physiology* 276, E964–E976.

Fudge, B. W., Westerterp, K. R., Kiplamai, F. K., Onywera, V. O., Boit, M. K., Kayser, B. and Pitsiladis, Y. P. (2006) 'Evidence of negative energy balance using doubly labelled water in elite Kenyan runners prior to competition', *British Journal of Nutrition* 95, 59–66.

Gollnick, P. D. and Saltin, B. (1982) 'Significance of skeletal muscle oxidative enzyme enhancement with endurance training', *Clinical Physiology* 2, 1–12.

Grandjean, A. C. (1989) 'Macronutrient intake of US athletes compared with the general population and recommendations made for athletes', *American Journal of Clinical Nutrition* 49, 1070–6.

Helge, J. W. and Kiens, B. (1997) 'Muscle enzyme activity in humans: role of substrate availability and training', *American Journal of Physiology* 41, R1620–R1624.

Helge, J. W., Richter, E. A. and Kiens, B. (1996) 'Interaction of training and diet on metabolism and endurance during exercise in man', *Journal of Physiology* 492, 293–306.

Henriksson, J. (1977) 'Training induced adaptations of skeletal muscle and metabolism during sub-maximal exercise', *Journal of Physiology* 270, 661–75.

Hofvander, Y. (1968) 'Hematological investigations in Ethiopia, with special reference to high iron intake', *Acta Medica Scandinavica* 11 (74) (Suppl.), 494.

Ivy, J. L., Katz, A. L., Cutler, C. L., Sherman, W. M. and Coyle, E. F. (1988) 'Muscle glycogen synthesis after exercise: effects of time of carbohydrate ingestion', *Journal of Applied Physiology* 64, 1480–5.

Jansen, A. A. J., Horelli, H. T. and Quinn, V. J. (1987) 'Food and nutrition in Kenya: a historical review', Kenya: University of Nairobi.

Kiens, B., Éssen-Gustavsson, B., Christensen, N. J., and Saltin, B. (1993) 'Skeletal muscle substrate utilization during submaximal exercise in man: effect of endurance training', *Journal of Physiology* 469, 459–78.

Larsen, H. B., Christensen, D. L., Nolan, T. and Søndergaard, H. (2004) 'Body dimensions, exercise capacity and physical activity level in adolescent Nandi boys in western Kenya', *Annals of Human Biology* 31, 159–73.

Leenstra, T., Kariuki, S. K., Kurtis, J. D., Aloo, A. J., Kager, P. A. and ter Kuile (2004) 'Prevalence and severity of anemia and iron deficiency: cross-sectional studies in adolescent school-girls in western Kenya', *European Journal of Clinical Nutrition* 58, 681–91.

Lemon, P. W. R. (2000) 'Beyond the zone: protein needs of active individuals', *Journal of the American College of Nutrition* 19, S513–S521.

Lemon, P. W. R., Dolny, D. G. and Yarasheski, K. E. (1997) 'Moderate physical activity can increase dietary protein needs', *Canadian Journal of Applied Physiology* 22, 494–503.

Lukaski, H. C. (2004) 'Vitamin and mineral status: effects on physical performance', *Nutrition* 20, 632–44.

Miller, M. J. and Munroe, E. (1951) 'Schistosome dermatitis in Quebec', *Canadian Medical Association Journal* 65, 571–5.

Mukeshi, M. and Thairu, K. (1993) 'Nutrition and body build: a Kenyan review', *World Review of Nutrition and Dietetics* 72, 218–26.

Munro, H. N. (1951) 'Carbohydrate and fat as factors in protein utilization and metabolism' *Physiological Reviews* 31, 449–88.

Muskat, E. and Keller, W. (1968) 'Nutzung von Wildpflanzen als zusätzliche Vitaminquelle bei der Ernährung der Bevölkerung Kenias', *Internationale Zeitschrift für Vitaminforschung* 38, 538–44.

Myburgh, K. H., Hutchins, J., Fataar, A. B., Hough, S. F. and Noakes, T. D. (1990) 'Low bone density is an etiologic factor for stress fractures in athletes', *Annals of Internal Medicine* 113, 754–9.

Nestel, P. S. (1989) 'Food intake and growth in the Maasai', *Ecology of Food and Nutrition* 23, 17–30.

Ngare, D. K. and Muttunga, J. N. (1999) 'Prevalence of malnutrition in Kenya', *East African Medical Journal* 76, 376–80.

Noakes, T. D. (1997) 'Challenging beliefs: *ex Africa semper aliquid novi*', *Medicine and Science in Sports and Exercise* 29, 571–90.

Onywera, V.O., Kiplamai, F. K., Tuitoek, P. J., Boit, M. K. and Pitsiladis, Y. P. (2004) 'Food and macronutrient intake of elite Kenyan distance runners', *International Journal of Sport Nutrition and Exercise Metabolism* 14, 709–19.

Pasoce, D. D., Costill, D. L., Robergs, R. A., Davis, J. A., Fink, W. J. and Pearson, D. R. (1990) 'Effects of exercise mode on muscle glycogen restorage during repeated days of exercise', *Medicine and Science in Sports and Exercise* 22, 593–8.

Peters, E. M. and Goetzsche, J. M. (1997) 'Dietary practices of South African ultra-distance runners', *International Journal of Sports Nutrition* 7, 80–103.

Philip, C. R. (1943) 'Nutrition in Kenya', Ref. no. 38/1276/9, vol. X (mimeographed) Nairobi, Medical headquarters.

Price, T. B., Rothman, D. L., Taylor, R., Avison, M. J., Shulman, G. I. and Shulman, R. G. (1994) 'Human muscle glycogen resynthesis after exercise: insulin-dependent and -independent phases', *Journal of Applied Physiology* 76, 104–11.

Saltin, B., Larsen, H., Terrados, N., Bangsbo, J., Bak, T., Kim, C. K., Svedenhag, J. and Rolf, C. J. (1995a) 'Aerobic exercise capacity at sea level and at altitude in Kenyan boys, junior and senior runners compared with Scandinavian runners', *Scandinavian Journal of Medicine and Science in Sports* 5, 209–21.

Saltin, B., Kim, C. K., Terrados, N., Larsen, H., Svedenhag, J. and Rolf, C. J. (1995b) 'Morphology, enzyme activities and buffer capacity in leg muscles of Kenyan and Scandinavian runners', *Scandinavian Journal of Medicine and Science in Sports* 5, 222–30.

Sen, C. K., Packer, L. and Hanninen, O. (eds) (1994) *Exercise and Oxygen Toxicity*, Amsterdam: Elsevier Science.

Sherman, W. M. (1983) 'Carbohydrates, glycogen and muscle glycogen super-compensation', in Williams, M. H. (ed.) *Ergogenic Aids in Sport*, Champaign, IL: Human Kinetics, pp. 3–26.

Simon-Schnass, I. and Pabst, H. (1988) 'Influence of Vitamin E on physical performance', *International Journal for Vitamin and Nutrition Research* 58, 49–54.

Sinclair, D. (1985) *Human Growth After Birth*, Oxford: Oxford Medical Publications.

Snyder, A. C., Dvorak, L. L. and Roepke, J. B. (1989) 'Influence of dietary iron source on measures of iron status among female runners', *Medicine and Science in Sports and Exercise* 21, 7–10.

Sutton, J. E. G. (1974) 'The settlement of East Africa', in Ogot, B. A. (ed.) *Zamani: A Survey of East African History*, Nairobi: East African Publishing House/Longman, pp. 70–97.

van Erp-Baart, A. M. J., Saris, W. H. M., Binkhorst, R. A., Vos, J. A. and Elvers, J. W. (1989) 'Nationwide survey on nutritional habits in elite athletes. Part I. Energy, carbohydrate, protein, and fat intake', *International Journal of Sports Medicine* 10 (Suppl. 1), S3–S10.

van Steenbergen, W. M., Kusin, J. A., Nordbeck, H. J. and Jansen, A. A. (1984) 'Food consumption of different household members in Machakos, Kenya', *Ecology of Food and Nutrition* 14, 1–9.

Welten, D. C., Kemper, H. C., Post, G. B., Van Mechelen, W., Twisk, J., Lips, P., Teule, G. J. (1994) 'Weight-bearing activity during youth is a more important factor for peak bone mass than calcium intake', *Journal of Bone and Mineral Research* 9, 1089–96.

Walberg, J. L., Ruiz, V. K., Talton, S. L., Hinkle, D. E. and Thye, F. W. (1988) 'Exercise capacity and nitrogen loss during a high or low carbohydrate diet', *Medicine and Science in Sports and Exercise* 20, 34–43.

Chapter 8

Dominance of Kenyan Kalenjins in middle- and long-distance running

Henrik B. Larsen

Introduction

Today the Kenyan dominance in middle- and long-distance running is so profound that it has no equivalence to in other sport in the world. Thus, the average proportion of Kenyan runners in the six all-time top 20 lists for men in the distances from 800 m to marathon including steeplechase is 55.0% (Figure 8.1).

The Kenyan dominance has been even more profound at the world cross-country championships, at which the Kenyan senior men won the team title in the long distance every year from 1986 to 2003. At ten of these championships, the Kenyan dominance was so marked that the Kenyan team was able to beat

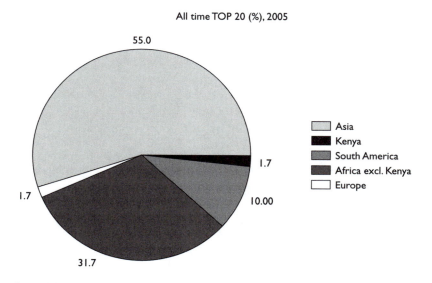

All time TOP 20 (%), 2005

55.0

1.7

1.7

10.00

31.7

Asia
Kenya
South America
Africa excl. Kenya
Europe

Figure 8.1 The average proportion of Kenyan runners in the six all-time top 20 lists for men in the distances from 800 m to marathon including steeplechase is 55%.

Source: IAAF, All Time Outdoor Lists, June 2005 <http://www.iaaf.org>.

a team chosen from the best finishers from the rest of the world. Furthermore, the performances of Kenyan men in middle- and long-distance events at the Olympic games and world championships on track have shown the Kenyan superiority. Even more remarkable is the fact that the majority of Kenyan achievements have been produced by a group of eight small tribes, the Kalenjin, which number only about three and a half million people. Among the Kalenjin tribes, the Nandi has shown the most profound results. Even though the Nandi tribe constitutes only approximately 2% of the Kenyan population it is the most successful single tribe in Kenya to date with respect to performance in running. Therefore, one question that arises is what makes Kenyan runners perform so well? Factors to consider are genetic endowment, upbringing, training and the fact that most of the runners live and train at an altitude of around 2,000 metres above sea level.

Middle- and long-distance running performance depends on several factors, including physical, physiological, metabolic, biomechanical, psychological, social and behavioural characteristics. Outstanding performance in long-distance running requires an optimal combination of high capacity for aerobic energy output, a high fractional $\dot{V}O_2$ max utilization during competition and good running economy. Thus, high correlations have been demonstrated between $\dot{V}O_2$ max and running performance in groups of runners of quite different abilities (Costill et al. 1971, 1973b; Farrell 1979; Maughan and Leiper 1983; Sjödin and Svedenhag 1985). However, when groups of athletes with very similar running performances or athletes with a relatively narrow range of $\dot{V}O_2$ max are studied, the $\dot{V}O_2$ max becomes a less sensitive predictor of performance (Conley and Krahenbuhl 1980; Sjödin and Svedenhag 1985). In addition, a moderate relationship has been shown between running economy and performance in groups of runners heterogeneous with respect to running ability (Sjödin and Svedenhag 1985), whereas no significant correlation has been found between oxygen cost of running and performance in groups of runners with a narrow performance range (Davies and Thompson 1979). However, for athletes with a relatively narrow $\dot{V}O_2$ max range the running economy has been shown to be a better predictor of performance than $\dot{V}O_2$ max (Conley and Krahenbuhl 1980). Finally, several investigations have demonstrated that the $\dot{V}O_2$ max fraction actually exploited throughout the race is crucial for performance in distance running (Costill et al. 1971; Davies and Thompson 1979; Maughan and Leiper 1983). Although the significance of each of the above factors may be difficult to identify in specific groups of runners, di Pramprero et al. (1986) have demonstrated that when taking all three factors into consideration, a relationship between performance and $\dot{V}O_2$ max, fractional $\dot{V}O_2$ max utilization, and running economy emerges. Therefore, when studying performance in endurance running one should consider all three factors. Consequently, differences between Kenyans and non-Kenyans with respect to $\dot{V}O_2$ max, fractional $\dot{V}O_2$ max utilization and running economy and physiological variables that may be of importance for these factors as well as their trainability will be highlighted in the following.

Maximal oxygen uptake

Since the early work of Hill and Lupton (1923), exercise physiologists have associated the limits of human endurance with the ability to consume oxygen maximally (i.e. $\dot{V}O_2$ max). A high $\dot{V}O_2$ max is a function of training effort and natural endowment, and it is commonly accepted that $\dot{V}O_2$ max – determined by a combination of central factors (e.g. cardiac output) and peripheral factors (e.g. muscle capillary density) – is one of the factors limiting endurance performance. Comparing Kenyan athletes with athletes of non-African descent Saltin *et al.* (1995b) revealed that Kenyan elite long-distance runners have a very high $\dot{V}O_2$ max (79.9 ml·kg^{-1}·min^{-1}), but it was not higher than the level observed in Scandinavian elite runners (79.2 ml·kg^{-1}·min^{-1}) (Table 8.1). In this comparison, body dimension was accounted for by dividing max $\dot{V}O_2$ in l·min^{-1} with body mass in kilograms. However, when comparing various species of different sizes in the animal kingdom scaling has proved useful. Also, when comparing humans with differences in body mass the same approach has successfully been applied. Since Svedenhag (1995), who has been studying runners, their $\dot{V}O_2$ max and their running economy, preferred to express $\dot{V}O_2$ max per kg of body mass raised to an exponent of 0.75, we decided to use this exponent in order to compare Scandinavian and Kenyan elite runners. This normalization revealed a trend for a higher $\dot{V}O_2$ max of the Scandinavian runners compared to the Kenyan runners (226.1 vs. 218.7 ml·kg$^{-0.75}$·min^{-1}) (Table 8.1). In the study of Kenyan elite runners, only few of the very best participated or were in top shape. Therefore, the possibility exists that the very best, when top trained, have values higher than the mean of 79.9 ml·kg^{-1}·min^{-1}. This was true for one of the Kenyan runners (J. Machuka) who reached 84.8 ml·kg^{-1}·min^{-1}, which is higher than the $\dot{V}O_2$ max observed in any of the Scandinavian runners. This observation is in line with previous findings on the two former Kenyan world-record holders, Kipchoge Keino who had a $\dot{V}O_2$ max value of 82.0 (Saltin and Åstrand 1967) and Henry Rono who had 84.3 ml·kg^{-1}·min^{-1} (see Saltin *et al.* 1995b; Henry Rono was studied by Philip Gollnick). Several studies of Caucasian elite runners have revealed $\dot{V}O_2$ max values similar to these highest values of Kenyan runners. Thus, the former world-record holder Dave Bedford had a $\dot{V}O_2$ max value of 85.0 ml·kg^{-1}·min^{-1} (Bergh 1982) while Steven Prefontaine had a $\dot{V}O_2$max value of 84.4 ml·kg^{-1}·min^{-1} (Pollock 1977) (Table 8.1). Such high $\dot{V}O_2$ max values are not mandatory to be successful. Kenyan elite runners as well as American elite middle- and long-distance runners may have a $\dot{V}O_2$ max value just below 80 ml·kg^{-1}·min^{-1} as reported by Pollock (1977). In this respect, the studies by Coetzer *et al.* (1993) of black South African elite distance runners are interesting. These runners could run a half marathon in 62/63 minutes with a relatively low mean $\dot{V}O_2$ max value of 71.5 ml·kg^{-1}·min^{-1} (Table 8.1). This is about 11% lower than Kenyan elite runners. Thus, a relatively low $\dot{V}O_2$ max of black South African runners seems to be a common feature at a given performance level compared to Caucasian runners. Weston *et al.* (2000) have

Table 8.1 Summary of published values of maximal oxygen uptake in populations of different ethnic origin

	n	$\dot{V}O_2$ max		
		$l \cdot min^{-1}$	$ml \cdot kg^{-0.75} \cdot min^{-1}$	$ml \cdot kg^{-1} \cdot min^{-1}$
Bosch et al. 1990	9 black South African marathon runners	3.59	60.4	167.8
	10 white South African marathon runners	4.49	63.2	183.5
Coetzer et al. 1993	11 black South African elite distance runners	3.90	71.5	189.5
	9 white South African elite middle-distance runners	5.00	71.0	206.8
Weston et al. 2000	8 black South African distance runners	3.80	60.7	173.2
	8 white South African distance runners	4.60	69.9	201.2
Saltin et al. 1995b	6 Kenyan elite distance runners	4.48	79.9	218.7
	6 Scandinavian elite distance runners	5.25	79.2	226.1
	3 Scandinavian elite middle-distance runners	5.08	75.5	216.1
Saltin et al. 1995b	16 Kenyan junior runners	3.55	63.3	173.3
	6 untrained Kenyan boys	2.19	47.1	122.9
Larsen et al. 2004	11 untrained adolescent Kenyan town boys	2.71	50.2	135.9
	19 untrained adolescent Kenyan village boys	2.94	55.1	148.9
Pollock 1977	11 white US elite middle- and long-distance runners	4.97	78.8	222.1

shown that black South African runners, with similar mean 10 km race times as white South African runners, had the lowest $\dot{V}O_2$ max. Likewise, black South African marathon runners with the same race time as white South African marathon runners, have a lower $\dot{V}O_2$ max than the white runners when the data are normalized for differences in body mass (164 vs. 184 ml $O_2 \cdot kg^{-0.75} \cdot min^{-1}$, Bosch et al. 1990) (Table 8.1).

A key question is whether untrained Africans have a high $\dot{V}O_2$ max already at a young age. To answer this question untrained adolescent Nandi town boys were studied (Larsen et al. 2004; Saltin et al. 1995b). When studied at an altitude of 2,000 metres these boys had $\dot{V}O_2$ max values in the same range as untrained Danish teenagers studied at sea level (Andersen et al. 1987). It can be argued that the $\dot{V}O_2$ max of the Kenyan boys would be higher if they were tested at sea level. However, a study by Favier et al. (1995) revealed that they do not gain much in $\dot{V}O_2$ max when tested at sea level. Although there may be a small difference, one also has to consider that the body mass of the Nandi boys was only ~54 kg (Larsen et al. 2004) which is ~12 kg less than that of Caucasian boys of the same age (Andersen 1994). If $\dot{V}O_2$ max is normalized with the exponent of 0.75, the Kenyan boys will actually have a lower $\dot{V}O_2$ max than the Caucasian boys. The fact that no difference was observed with respect to $\dot{V}O_2$ max between untrained Kenyan and Danish boys is in line with findings by Boulay et al. (1988), who have reviewed the literature about racial variation in work capacities and concluded that there is no valid or reliable evidence of clear racial difference in $\dot{V}O_2$ max. However, findings by Trowbridge et al. (1997) revealed that the $\dot{V}O_2$ max level of African-American (primarily of west African origin) prepubertal children aged 5–10 years is about 15% lower compared to Caucasian children of the same age. This is consistent with findings by Skinner et al. (2001) who demonstrated that $\dot{V}O_2$ max of untrained black north American men was ~10% lower than in untrained white north American men. In addition, Suminski et al. (2000) found that arm-max of untrained African-American men was ~17% lower when compared to arm-$\dot{V}O_2$ max of untrained Caucasian American men.

The Kenyan world elite runners are not fostered in towns but in small villages and rural areas. Therefore, Nandi village boys have been compared to Nandi town boys by Larsen et al. (2004). The village boys had a mean $\dot{V}O_2$ max approximately 10% higher than the $\dot{V}O_2$ max of the town boys and the higher $\dot{V}O_2$ max was related to a higher daily physical activity level of the village boys. Although the $\dot{V}O_2$ max of the village boys is quite high, it is far from being at a level required to become an elite runner. However, since several of the Nandi village boys had a good $\dot{V}O_2$ max despite limited training background, this has led to the speculation that the trainability of Kenyans (the Nandis) is larger than might be observed in Caucasians. Indeed, anecdotal evidence suggests that Kenyan runners are able to abstain from regular intense training for months, but nevertheless within months and, with surprisingly little training, they can be back among the best runners in the world. In addition, several physiological studies indicate that the trainability of $\dot{V}O_2$ max includes a significant genetic component (Bouchard et al. 1992, 1999: Prudhomme et al. 1984). However, two studies (Larsen et al. 2005; Larsen and Søndergaard in press) investigating the response to training of untrained Kenyan and Danish boys with similar initial $\dot{V}O_2$ max, revealed no difference in trainability of Kenyans compared to Caucasians with respect to $\dot{V}O_2$ max. This is in line with findings by Skinner et al. (2001), who compared the response to training between large groups of black and white north Americans and demonstrated similar elevation of aerobic capacity in these two groups.

Fractional utilization of $\dot{V}O_2$ max

Since the early 1970s, there has been growing interest in how to best utilize $\dot{V}O_2$ max in endurance events, and the ability to sustain a high percentage of $\dot{V}O_2$ max has been a recognized predictor of endurance performance for more than three decades (Costill et al. 1971; Davies and Thompson 1979; Maughan and Leiper 1983). In addition, the running velocity at which blood lactate begins to accumulate (V_{OBLA}) has been a helpful prognostic tool in this research where Sjödin and Jacobs (1981) have demonstrated its value to predict endurance performance. Only a few scientific investigations have compared the $\dot{V}O_2$ max fraction sustained throughout competition when studying people of different ethnic origin. Two studies comparing well-trained black and white South African runners have shown that black South African runners are able to run at a higher fractional $\dot{V}O_2$ max utilization during competition than the white South African runners in the 10 km and marathon distances (Bosch et al. 1990; Weston et al. 2000) (also see Chapter 10 in this book). In addition, Coetzer and colleagues (1993) have demonstrated that while black and white South African elite athletes were able to run at a similar percentage of $\dot{V}O_2$ max over distances from 1.65 to 5 km, the percentage of $\dot{V}O_2$ max sustained by black athletes was greater than that of whites in distances longer than 5 km. Furthermore, the difference between black and white athletes became larger with increased running distance. Part of the explanation of this could be that the black athletes were predominantly long-distance runners whereas the Caucasian athletes, were predominantly middle-distance track athletes. It is of note however that Weston et al. (1999) also found that well-trained black South African runners have a greater ability to sustain high-intensity endurance exercise compared to well-trained white South African runners. To date, the information about which percentage of $\dot{V}O_2$ max Kenyan runners are able to sustain during competition is scarce. It was shown in one runner, Kipchoge Keino, that he utilized his whole $\dot{V}O_2$ max when running 5,000 m and above 97–8% $\dot{V}O_2$ max in a 10-km race (Karlsson et al. 1968). Two studies investigating the average heart rate during a 5,000 m competition in Kenyan Nandi boys and Caucasian boys revealed that the two groups of boys were competing at the same mean percentage of maximal heart rate indicating similar ability for

Kenyans and Caucasians to utilize $\dot{V}O_2$ max during running for about 20 minutes (Larsen *et al.* 2005; Larsen and Søndergaard in press).

Many physiological factors may be crucial for the percentage of $\dot{V}O_2$ max sustained during competition and for the endurance. It appears that the majority of these factors are related to the feature of the muscles involved in the action during running. Moderate to strong relationships between distance running performance and the proportion of type I muscle fibres have been demonstrated (Costill *et al.* 1973a; Sjödin and Jacobs 1981), further supported by findings in well-trained cyclists (Coyle *et al.* 1988). In addition, Sjödin *et al.* (1982) have suggested that the percentage of type I muscle fibres may be an indicator of the potential 'trainability' of the musculature. However, extreme endurance training has been demonstrated to induce a similarly high mitochondrial activity of type I and type II muscle fibres, in line with the fact that the contractile character-istics of a fibre and transformation of the main fibre types are not easily affected by training, whereas the metabolic capacity is; as is the case in the type II fibres (Jansson and Kaijser 1977). Both Kenyan and Scandinavian elite runners have a high proportion of type I muscle fibres (Saltin *et al.* 1995a) (Table 8.2). Similarly, a study comparing untrained Kenyan Nandi boys and Danish boys revealed no difference in the (quite low) percentage of slow-twitch muscle fibres (Larsen *et al.* in press). However, previous findings by Saltin *et al.* (1995a) indi-cate that Kenyan junior runners have a higher proportion of type I muscle fibres than the untrained Kenyan and Danish boys, but this is probably due to selec-tion (Table 8.2). South African distance runners appear to differ from Kenyan runners, having less type I fibres (Coetzer *et al.* 1993; Weston *et al.* 1999) (Table 8.2). Indeed, the proportion of type I muscle fibres in the black distance runners was consistent with findings in sedentary Caucasians (Simoneau and Bouchard 1989). Thus, Kenyan elite distance runners may have a higher proportion of type I muscle fibres than black South African distance runners. This may be one factor explaining the difference in running performance. Major variations in muscle fibre type composition in various ethnic groups in Africa may be a reality. Thus, Ama *et al.* (1986) have demonstrated a very low percentage of type I muscle fibres in west Africans. In contrast, Duey *et al.* (1997) found no differ-ence in the proportion of type I muscle fibres when comparing sedentary black and white north Americans; a finding that may be confounded by the fact that some genetic admixture with Caucasian genes probably exists in the former (Chakraborty *et al.* 1992).

Leg muscle oxidative enzymes

The activity of oxidative enzymes has been shown to be essential for the respiratory capacity of muscle (Henriksson 1977). This has in turn been shown to be significantly related to the level of blood lactate at given work rates (Ivy *et al.* 1980). Thus, a direct link exists between the oxidative potential of the muscles engaged in running and the performance level, as a running speed has to

Table 8.2 Summary of published values of fiber type distribution in the vastus lateralis muscle in populations of different ethnic origin

Study	n	Subject population	Percentage fibre type		
			I	IIa	IIb
Ama et al. 1986	23	sedentary black West Africans	32.6	48.6	19.7
	23	sedentary white Canadians	40.9	41.9	17.1
Duey et al. 1997	14	untrained US blacks	39.5	40.0	22.8
	14	untrained US whites	44.9	36.6	18.3
Coetzer et al. 1993	6	black South African elite distance runners	53.3	46.7	
	5	white South African elite middle-distance runners	63.4	36.6	
Weston et al. 1999	5	black South African distance runners	49.0	51.0	
	7	white South African distance runners	67.1	32.9	
Saltin et al. 1995a	4	Kenyan elite runners	72.5	24.5	3.0
	9	Kenyan junior runners	64.9	30.7	4.4
	6	Scandinavian elite runners	67.7	29.5	2.7
Larsen et al. 2000	10	untrained adolescent Kenyan town boys	44.9	55.1	
	14	untrained adolescent Kenyan village boys	52.5	47.5	

be high before lactate starts to become elevated (Farrell *et al.* 1979; Sjödin and Jacobs 1981; Sjödin and Svedenhag 1985). Indeed, Evertsen *et al.* (1999) have shown positive correlations between the activity of three oxidative enzymes, citrate synthase (CS), succinate dehydrogenase (SDH) and glycerol-3 phosphate dehydrogenase (GPDH) and performance in running. In addition, Weston *et al.* (1999) have shown a positive correlation between the CS activity and performance when running at a standardized percentage of peak treadmill velocity. When comparing the CS activity of Kenyan and Scandinavian elite runners, no differences were found regardless of whether the comparisons were made between the *vastus lateralis* or the *gastrocnemius* muscle in the two groups of runners (Saltin *et al.* 1995a). However, a study comparing untrained Kenyan town and village boys with untrained Danish boys revealed that the CS activity of the Danish boys was ~30% higher compared to the Kenyan boys (Larsen *et al.* in press). The low CS activity of the village boys is somewhat surprising, since the $\dot{V}O_2$ max of these boys and the Danish boys was similar. The fact that Kenyan and Scandinavian elite runners have similar CS activities, while 'untrained' Kenyan boys have a lower activity compared to Danish boys indicates a higher response to training of the Kenyans with respect to CS. However, when comparing the response of CS activity to 12 weeks of standardized training, no difference was observed between Kenyan and Danish boys (Larsen *et al.* in press). These findings are in contrast to observations by Weston *et al.* (1999) who compared the CS activity of black and white South African elite runners as well as black and white sedentary boys. While no difference was observed between the sedentary boys, the CS activity of the black South African elite runners was ~50% higher compared to the white South African elite runners. This indicates a higher response to training of the black South Africans, which may be part of the explanation for the superior performance level of these runners. Finally, it is of note that, when comparing untrained black Africans of west and central African origin with untrained Caucasians, Ama *et al.* (1986) found no difference in the activity of oxidative enzymes, despite the fact that these Africans had a low percentage of type I fibres in their muscle.

HAD (3-hydroxyacyl-CoA-dehydrogenase)

In the early studies of Kenyan runners it was shown that they possessed a higher activity of the β-oxidative enzyme HAD (3-hydroxyacyl-CoA-dehydrogenase activity) in their muscles (Saltin *et al.* 1995a). In line with this, Weston *et al.* (1999) observed that black South African athletes have a higher HAD activity than Caucasian South African athletes. In contrast however, when comparing untrained Kenyan town, village and Danish boys, no differences in HAD activity could be observed (Larsen *et al.* in press). This indicates a higher response to training of the Kenyans. However, when comparing the response to 12 weeks of endurance running in Kenyan and Danish boys, the HAD activity increased only slightly or not at all. Finally, in line with the findings on untrained Kenyan and Danish boys Ama *et al.* (1986) found no difference in HAD activity between sedentary black west Africans and Caucasians.

Capillaries

Capillarization is one of the factors determining the oxidative profile of the musculature and it is closely related to 3-hydroxyacyl-CoA-dehydrogenase. The capillary density has also been shown to correlate positively with the running velocity at which blood lactate begins to accumulate (Sjödin and Jacobs 1981). In addition, a moderate correlation ($r = 0.63$) has been demonstrated between the number of capillaries per mm^2 and the mean marathon running velocity during competition (Sjödin and Jacobs 1981). When comparing the capillarization of Kenyan and Danish elite runners, Saltin *et al.* (1995a) observed a tendency for a higher capillarization of the Kenyan elite runners. Larsen *et al.* (in press) also found that untrained Kenyan boys from a rural area and Danish boys with the same $\dot{V}O_2$ max had similar capillarization. However, Kenyan boys from a town had about 10% fewer capillaries per mm^2 compared to the afore-mentioned two groups of boys, but this is probably due to a significantly lower $\dot{V}O_2$ max of the town boys. Thus, both Kenyans and Caucasians seem to adhere to the general finding of a close coupling between muscle capillaries and $\dot{V}O_2$ max.

Plasma lactate and ammonia response

As discussed above, the blood lactate response to submaximal running is a good predictor of endurance running performance and primarily reflects the local metabolic response in the 'running muscles'. Kenyan elite runners have lower blood lactate levels, both at altitude and at sea level, when running at given exercise intensities compared to Scandinavian elite runners. The difference is most profound at high exercise intensities. When comparing well-trained black and white South African distance runners, Weston *et al.* (1999) have demonstrated that the level of blood lactate was significantly lower in the black African athletes compared to the Caucasians, when running at 88% of peak treadmill velocity. Furthermore, the study revealed that the black South African runners accumulated lactate at a slower rate with increasing exercise intensity.

With the accumulation of lactate in the blood, the ammonia concentration usually also increases. However, a previous investigation revealed that Kenyan elite runners behaved differently. The Kenyans did increase their blood ammonia concentration with increased running speed, but the ammonia levels during higher exercise intensities were markedly lower compared to Scandinavian runners (Saltin *et al.* 1995b). In addition, the peak ammonia concentration following a maximal test on the treadmill was only half to one third in the Kenyan runners compared to the concentration observed in the Scandinavian runners. In line with the findings on elite runners, Larsen *et al.* (2005) and

Larsen and Søndergaard (in press) have found a trend for lower blood ammonia concentrations in untrained Kenyan town and village boys compared to untrained Danish boys at submaximal running velocities. These studies also revealed that the peak ammonia concentration was ~50% higher in the Danish boys as compared to the Kenyan boys. Furthermore, the investigations revealed significant reductions in the blood ammonia levels at submaximal running velocities in Kenyan town and village boys following 12 weeks of endurance running, whereas no change was noted in Danish boys after completing the same standardized training programme. Moreover, the ammonia level after peak exercise was enhanced significantly in the Kenyan village boys after 12 weeks of training, while no change was observed as a result of training in the Kenyan town boys or the Danish boys. In contrast to the findings by Saltin *et al.* (1995b) on Kenyan runners, Weston *et al.* (2000) found that the ammonia level in the blood was significantly higher at race pace in well-trained black South African 10 km runners compared to white South African 10 km runners.

Running economy

Running economy is expressed as the steady-state submaximal oxygen uptake at a given running velocity. The lower the max at a given submaximal running speed, the better the running economy. Dill *et al.* (1930) were probably the first to suggest differences in the amount of oxygen that different athletes actually require when running at the same speed. Indeed, at a given running speed, the submaximal oxygen requirement (in $ml \cdot kg^{-1} \cdot min^{-1}$) has been shown to vary considerably between subjects (Svedenhag and Sjödin 1984).

A previous study by Saltin *et al.* (1995b) revealed that the oxygen cost of running at a given running velocity, normalized for difference in body mass, is lower in Kenyan elite runners than in Scandinavian elite runners. This is consistent with findings in black South African runners. Thus, when comparing well-trained black and white South African runners with similar mean 10 km race times, Weston *et al.* (2000) demonstrated that the blacks had a lower oxygen cost when running, regardless of whether this was expressed per kg or per $kg^{0.67}$ of body mass. Bosch *et al.* (1990) found no difference in running economy when the oxygen uptake was expressed per kg of body mass when comparing black and white South African marathon runners with varying performance levels. However, when normalizing the values for differences in body mass, the running economy of the black South African marathon runners was better (519 vs. 555 $ml \cdot kg^{-0.75} \cdot km^{-1}$). Low oxygen cost of running seems to be a common feature of Kenyans at least for the tribes belonging to the Kalenjin. Thus, the study by Larsen *et al.* (2004) on untrained adolescent Kenyan Nandi boys indicates that their running economy is better than that found in untrained Danish boys of similar age (Larsen and Søndergaard in press). In addition, the study of Nandi boys revealed a similar running economy of town and village boys, although the village boys had a higher $\dot{V}O_2$ max and a higher physical activity level than the town boys. Furthermore, two studies investigating the response to training on the oxygen cost of running of Kenyan and Danish boys (Larsen *et al.* 2005; Larsen and Søndergaard in press) have shown a similar and quite small trainability of running economy of the two groups of boys.

Some studies have demonstrated that a higher proportion of slow-twitch fibres is associated with better running economy (Bosco *et al.* 1987; Kaneko 1990; Williams and Cavanagh 1987). This indicates that changes in metabolic profiles within muscles due to training may be a contributing factor to improvements in running economy. This leads to speculation on whether the superior running economy of Kenyan runners may partially be due to different physiological properties of the muscles involved in running. However, since no general differences have been found with respect to muscular characteristics between Kenyan elite runners and untrained Kenyan boys compared to their Scandinavian counterparts (Saltin *et al.* 1995a; Larsen *et al.* in press) this indicates that these factors do not contribute to the observed difference in running economy. A more likely explanation is differences in body shape and mass of the lower leg. Thus, Kenyan elite distance runners have a more slender body shape compared to Scandinavian elite distance runners (Saltin *et al.* 1995b). In addition, a study of untrained adolescent Kenyan boys indicated that they also have a low body mass and a very low body mass index compared to the majority of boys of similar age from other continents (Larsen *et al.* 2004). This study also indicated that the lower leg circumference of the Kenyan boys is smaller compared to Caucasian boys. Classical studies of human locomotion (Cavagna *et al.* 1964; Fenn 1930) indicate that the work of moving the limbs comprises a substantial part of the metabolic cost of running, just as load-carrying experiments (e.g. Myers and Steudal 1985) have shown that carrying a few grams of mass on the feet/ankle evokes an increase in the metabolic cost of running. Therefore, it can be hypothesized that the superior running economy of the Kenyan runners is primarily due to the fact that they have slender limbs of low mass allowing them to run with a minimal use of energy for swinging the limbs (also see Chapter 6).

Conclusion

Maximal oxygen uptake, fractional max utilization and running economy are crucial factors for performance in running. Investigations of these key factors indicate that the Kenyan superiority in distance running is to a large extent due to a unique combination of these factors. Especially, the running economy of the Kenyans has been shown to be proficient, where body shape appears to be critical. However, since, for example, Ethiopians, black South Africans and Indians seem to have almost the same body shape as the Kenyan Kalenjins (Larsen *et al.* 2004), it may be speculated why these peoples have far from reached the same level in distance running as the Kenyans. Black South African elite runners have been shown to have a running economy similar to the Kenyans. However, these runners do not have the same $\dot{V}O_2$max as the Kenyans.

After realizing the talent for running of the Kalenjins, western managers and coaches have brought financial resources and knowledge about running to Kenya, thereby developing the Kenyan potential and contributing to the Kenyan success in distance running. Whether this could happen in other parts of the world is an intriguing question. In other words, is there any other place in the world, where the people possess physiological properties crucial for running similar to the Kalenjins and where these properties can interact with the socio-economic and cultural environment, in a similar manner as in western Kenya?

References

Ama, P. F. M., Simoneau, J. A., Boulay, M. R., Serresse, O., Thériault, G. and Bouchard, C. (1986) 'Skeletal muscle characteristics in sedentary Black and Caucasian males', *Journal of Applied Physiology* 61, 1758–61.

Andersen, L. B. (1994) 'Blood pressure, physical fitness and physical activity in 17-year-old Danish adolescents', *Journal of Internal Medicine* 236, 323–30.

Andersen, L. B., Henckel, P. and Saltin, B. (1987) 'Maximal oxygen uptake in Danish adolescents 16–19 years of age', *European Journal of Applied Physiology* 56, 74–82.

Bergh, U. (1982) *Physiology of Cross-Country Ski-racing*, Champaign, IL: Human Kinetics.

Bosch, A. N., Goslin, B. R., Noakes, T. D. and Dennis, S. C. (1990) 'Physiological differences between black and white runners during a treadmill marathon', *European Journal of Applied Physiology* 61, 68–72.

Bosco, C., Montanari, G., Ribacchi, R., Giovinali, P., Latteri, F., Iachelli, G., Faina, M., Colli, R., Dal Monte, A., La Rosa, M., Cortili, G. and Saibene, F. (1987) 'Relationship between the efficiency of muscular work during jumping and the energetics of running', *European Journal of Applied Physiology* 56, 138–43.

Bouchard, C., An, P., Rice, T., Skinner, J. S., Wilmore, J. H., Gagnon, J., Pérusse, L., Leon, A. S. and Rao, D. C. (1999) 'Familial aggregation of max response to exercise training: results from the HERITAGE Family Study', *Journal of Applied Physiology* 87, 1003–8.

Bouchard, C., Dionne, F. T., Simoneau, J. A. and Boulay, M. R. (1992) 'Genetics of aerobic and anaerobic performances', *Exercise and Sport Sciences Reviews* 20, 27–58.

Boulay, M. R., Ama, P. F. and Bouchard, C. (1988) 'Racial variation in work capacities and powers', *Canadian Journal of Sport Science* 13, 127–35.

Cavagna, G. A., Saibene, F. P. and Margaria, R. (1964) 'Mechanical work in running', *Journal of Applied Physiology* 19, 249–56.

Chakraborty, R., Kamboh, M. I., Nwankwo, M. and Ferrell, R. E. (1992) 'Caucasian genes in American blacks: new data', *American Journal of Human Genetics* 50, 145–55.

Coetzer, P., Noakes, T. D., Sanders, B., Lambert, M. I., Bosch, A. N., Wiggins, T. and Dennis, S. C. (1993) 'Superior fatigue resistance of elite black South African distance runners', *Journal of Applied Physiology* 75, 1822–27.

Conley, D. L. and Krahenbuhl, G. S. (1980) 'Running economy and distance running performance of highly trained athletes', *Medicine and Science in Sports and Exercise* 12, 357–60.

Costill, D. L., Branam, G., Eddy, D. and Sparks, K. (1971) 'Determinants of marathon running success', *Internationale Zeitschrift füür angewandte Physiologie* 29, 249–54.

Costill, D. L., Gollnick, P. D., Jansson, E. D., Saltin, B. and Stein, E. M. (1973a) 'Glycogen depletion pattern in human muscle fibres during distance running', *Acta Physiologica Scandinavica* 89, 374–83.

Costill, D. L., Thomason, H. and Roberts, E. (1973b) 'Fractional utilization of the aerobic capacity during distance running', *Medicine and Science in Sports and Exercise* 5, 248–52.

Coyle, E. F., Coggan, A. R., Hopper, M. K. and Walters, T. J. (1988) 'Determinants of endurance in well-trained cyclists', *Journal of Applied Physiology* 64, 2622–30.

Davies, C. T. M. and Thompson, M. W. (1979) 'Aerobic performance of female marathon and male ultramarathon athletes', *European Journal of Applied Physiology* 41, 233–45.

di Prampero, P. E., Atchou, G., Brückner, J.-C. and Moia, C. (1986) 'The energetics of endurance running', *European Journal of Applied Physiology: Occupational Physiology* 55, 259–66.

Dill, D. B., Talbert J. H. and Edwards, H. T. (1930) 'Studies in muscular activity. VI: Response of several individuals to a fixed task', *Journal of Physiology* 69, 267–305.

Duey, W. J., Bassett, Jr, D. R., Torok, D. J., Howley, E. T., Bond, V., Mancuso, P. and Trudell, R. (1997) 'Skeletal muscle fibre type and capillary density in college-aged blacks and whites', *Annals of Human Biology* 24, 323–31.

Evertsen, F., Medbø, J. I., Jebens, E., Gjøvaag, T. F. (1999) 'Effect of training on the activity of five muscle enzymes studied on elite cross-country skiers', *Acta Physiologica Scandinavica* 167, 247–57.

Farrell, P. A., Wilmore, J. H., Coyle, E. F., Billing, J. E. and Costill, D. L. (1979) 'Plasma lactate accumulation and distance running performance', *Medicine and Science in Sports* 11, 338–44.

Favier, R., Spielvogel, H., Desplanches, D., Ferretti, G., Kayser, B., and Hoppeler, H. (1995) 'Maximal exercise performance in chronic hypoxia and acute normoxia in high-altitude natives', *Journal of Applied Physiology* 78, 1868–74.

Fenn, W. O. (1930) 'Frictional and kinetic factors in the work of sprint running', *American Journal of Physiology* 92, 583–611.

Henriksson, J. (1977) 'Training induced adaptation of skeletal muscle and metabolism during submaximal exercise', *Journal of Physiology* (*Lond*) 270, 661–75.

Hill, A. V. and Lupton, H. (1923) 'Muscular exercise, lactic acid, and the supply and utilization of oxygen', *Quarterly Journal of Medicine* 16, 135–71.

Ivy, J. L., Withers, R. T., van Handel, P. J., Elger, D. H. and Costill, D. L. (1980) 'Muscle respiratory capacity and fiber type as determinants of the lactate threshold', *Journal of Applied Physiology* 48, 523–27.

Jansson, E. and Kaijser, L. (1977) 'Muscle adaptation to extreme endurance training in man', *Acta Physiologica Scandinavica* 100, 315–24.

Kaneko, M. (1990) 'Mechanics and energetics in running with special reference to efficiency', *Journal of Biomechanics* 23, 57–63.

Karlsson, J., Hermansen, L., Agnevik, G. and Saltin, B. (1968) *Running* (in Swedish) *Framtiden*, Stockholm, Sweden.

Larsen, H. B., Christensen, D. L., Nolan, T. and Søndergaard, H. (2004) 'Body dimensions, exercise capacity and physical activity level of adolescent Nandi boys in western Kenya', *Annals of Human Biology* 31, 159–73.

Larsen, H. B., Nolan, T., Borch, C. and Søndergaard, H. (2005) 'Training response of adolescent Kenyan town and village boys to endurance running', *Scandinavian Journal of Medicine and Science in Sports* 15, 48–57.

Larsen, H. B. and Søndergaard, H. (in press) 'Training response of adolescent Caucasian boys to endurance running',

Larsen, H. B., Søndergaard, H., Asp, S., Calbet, J. A. L. and Saltin, B. (in press) 'Skeletal muscle adaptation to endurance running in adolescent Kenyan town and village boys and in Danish boys',

Larsen, H. B., Søndergaard, H., Nolan, T., Asp, S., Christensen, D. L. and Saltin, B. (2000) 'Trainability of Kenyan village boys compared to Kenyan town boys', *Journal of Physiology (Lond)* 528P, 42P–43P.

Maughan, R. J. and Leiper, J. B. (1983) 'Aerobic capacity and fractional utilisation of aerobic capacity in elite and non-elite male and female marathon runners', *European Journal of Applied Physiology: Occupational Physiology* 52, 80–7.

Myers, M. J. and Steudel, K. (1985) 'Effect of limb mass and its distribution on the energetic cost of running', *Journal of Experimental Biology* 116, 363–73.

Pollock, M. L. (1977) 'Submaximal and maximal working capacity of elite distance runners. Part I: Cardiorespiratory aspects', *Annals of the New York Academy of Sciences* 301, 310–27.

Prud'homme, D., Bouchard, C., Leblanc, C., Landry, F. and Fontaine, E. (1984) 'Sensitivity of maximal aerobic power to training is genotype-dependent', *Medicine and Science in Sports and Exercise* 16, 489–93.

Saltin, B. and Åstrand, P-O. (1967) 'Maximal oxygen uptake in athletes', *Journal of Applied Physiology* 23, 353–8.

Saltin, B., Kim, C. K., Terrados, N., Larsen, H., Svedenhag, S. and Rolf, C. J. (1995a) 'Morphology, enzyme activities and buffer capacity in leg muscles of Kenyan and Scandinavian Runners', *Scandinavian Journal of Medicine and Science in Sports* 5, 222–30.

Saltin, B., Larsen, H., Terrados, N., Bangsbo, J., Bak, T., Kim, C. K., Svedenhag, J. and Rolf, C. J. (1995b) 'Aerobic exercise capacity at sea level and at altitude in Kenyan boys, junior and senior runners compared with Scandinavian runners', *Scandinavian Journal of Medicine and Science in Sports* 5, 209–21.

Simoneau, J.-A. and Bouchard, C. (1989) 'Human variation in skeletal muscle fiber-type proportion and enzyme activities', *American Journal of Physiology* 257 (*Endocrinol. Metab.* 20), E567–E572.

Sjödin, B. and Jacobs, B. (1981) 'Onset of blood lactate accumulation and marathon running performance', *International Journal of Sports Medicine* 2, 23–6.

Sjödin, B., Jacobs, I. and Svedenhag, J. (1982) 'Changes in onset of blood lactate accumulation (OBLA) and muscle enzymes after training at OBLA', *European Journal of Applied Physiology* 49, 45–57.

Sjödin, B. and Svedenhag, J. (1985) 'Applied physiology of marathon running', *Sports Medicine* 2, 83–99.

Skinner, J. S., Jaskólski, A., Jaskólska, A., Krasnoff, J., Gagnon, J., Leon, A. S., Rao, D. C., Wilmore, J. H. and Bouchard, C. (2001) 'Age, sex, race, initial fitness, and response to training: the HERITAGE Family Study', *Journal of Applied Physiology* 90, 1770–6.

Suminski, R. R., Robertson, R. J., Goss, F. L. and Arslanian, S. (2000) 'Peak oxygen consumption and skeletal muscle bioenergetics in African-American and Caucasian men', *Medicine and Science in Sports and Exercise* 32, 2059–66.

Svedenhag, J. (1995) 'Maximal and submaximal oxygen uptake during running: how should body mass be accounted for?' *Scandinavian Journal of Medicine and Science in Sports* 5, 175–80.

Svedenhag, J. and Sjödin, B. (1984) 'Maximal and submaximal oxygen uptakes and blood lactate levels in elite male middle- and long-distance runners', *International Journal of Sports Medicine* 5, 255–61.

Trowbridge, C. A., Gower, B. A., Nagy, T. R., Hunter, G. R., Treuth, M. S. and Goran, M. I. (1997) 'Maximal aerobic capacity in African-American and Caucasian prepubertal children', *American Journal of Physiology* 273, E809–E814.

Weston, A. R., Karamizrak, O., Smith, A., Noakes, T. D. and Myburgh, K. H. (1999) 'African runners exhibit greater fatigue resistance, lower lactate accumulation, and higher oxidative enzyme activity', *Journal of Applied Physiology* 86, 915–23.

Weston, A. R., Mbambo, Z. and Myburgh, K. H. (2000) 'Running economy of African and Caucasian distance runners', *Medicine and Science in Sports and Exercise* 32, 1130–4.

Williams, K. R. and Cavanagh, P. R. (1987) 'Relationship between distance running mechanics, running economy, and performance', *Journal of Applied Physiology* 63, 1236–45.

Chapter 9

Understanding the dominance of African endurance runners

Exercise biology and an integrative model

Kathryn H. Myburgh

Introduction

A comprehensive review of the biology of endurance running is not possible here, and the reader is directed to other publications (Bangsbo and Larsen 2000), or review articles, some of which attempt to be comprehensive (Myburgh 2003) whilst others focus on specific aspects ranging from a possible genetic foundation (Rupert 2003), to physiological (Brandon 1995; Coyle 1999; Sjödin and Svedenhag 1985), training (Billat 2001a and b; Mujika and Padilla 2003) and biochemical aspects (Hawley 2002; Holloszy and Coyle 1984; Irrcher *et al.* 2003). The focus for this chapter will be on providing a schematic framework in which to organize the existing knowledge and predict the scope of future research in answer to the question: 'What makes African endurance athletes so successful?' This chapter will encourage a multidisciplinary rather than a combative approach between disciplines. For example, in this chapter I will place some emphasis on the importance of knowing the best method for collecting phenotypic data against which the search for relevant gene polymorphisms will be evaluated. This is usually only achieved with an in-depth understanding of the phenotype in question and possible controversies surrounding it and the methods to assess it. Within the multi-disciplinary context, it is also important that the findings of sport science research in athletes (e.g. their performance, training habits or psychological traits) are integrated with findings gained from studying the underlying biology. Such studies may uncover aspects outside of the biological factors that contribute to the biological phenotypes.

Finally, it must be kept in mind that most complex research is not done on world-class or even elite athletes. A further extension of this dilemma is that only one athlete out of the world-class group will win the coveted gold medal at the major championship event. Is this simply a matter of competition strategy? Or is a successful competition strategy just one, albeit the final, requirement to ensure that all the other essential factors come to fruition? These ideas are presented in Figure 9.1.

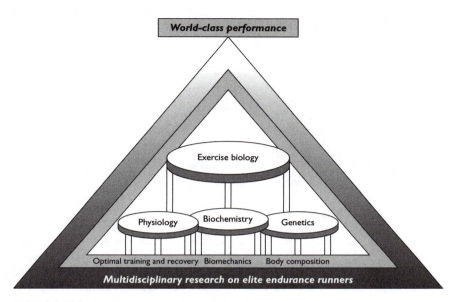

Figure 9.1 Multidisciplinary research on elite endurance runners.

Note: The inner triangle represents a framework for the branches of Exercise Science concerned with the biological mechanisms behind world-class performance. The framework is analogous to a series of three-legged stools. If any one discipline is not used to consider the problem, the multidisciplinary approach may yield an unsatisfactory understanding that could easily be toppled by new hypotheses. Within our context, this is analogous to the sub-elite athlete who is missing an essential component of the repertoire required for elite endurance performance. The middle triangle reflects the acknowledgement that world-class endurance performance (as opposed to elite-level performance) requires *optimal* training, *optimal* biomechanics, *optimal* body composition, and ultimately *optimal* competition strategies. However, athletes the world over attempt to implement these factors and yet the east African endurance athletes remain the most successful. Perhaps there are elements in their social context or their psychological approach that are unique? The challenge that lies ahead is to investigate the interplay between these branches of Sport Science and the branches of Exercise Biology which on the one hand may influence them, or which on the other hand are influenced by them. This will require a multidisciplinary research effort.

Source: Adapted from Myburgh 2003.

Exercise biology

Physiology

No discussion of the physiology of endurance running can neglect the fact that maximal oxygen consumption (VO_2 max) is a good predictor of endurance running performance (e.g. Costill 1967; Foster *et al.* 1978; Sjödin and Svedenhag 1985). However, even though an association between this physiological factor and endurance performance was found when the subjects investigated represented a broad range of performance capabilities, the relationship does not hold true amongst a more homogenous group of highly trained athletes (Conley and Krahenbuhl 1980). This is illustrated by the data on sub-elite endurance runners tested in our laboratory and presented in Figure 9.2. When 53 subjects with personal best times for 10 km between 29 and 42 min were assessed, there was a good correlation between $\dot{V}O_2$ max and performance (see Figure 9.2a), but when the top 50% of athletes were assessed, with personal best times for 10 km below 34 min, the correlation was no longer significant (r = –0.09) (see Figure 9.2b). Half of these athletes clustered between 33 and 34 min for 10 km with greatly varying $\dot{V}O_2$ max. However, even considering only the top quartile (with PB for 10 km falling < 33 min), there was no relationship between running performance and $\dot{V}O_2$ max. This is also an important concept to remember when considering any correlation, or lack of correlation, between a variable and sports performance. In our cohort (runners of indigenous South African descent, with Xhosa as first language for athlete and purportedly also both parents – hereafter Xhosa; and runners of European Caucasian descent hereafter Caucasian), $\dot{V}O_2$ max did not distinguish between sub-elite Xhosa distance runners (see Figure 9.2c closed squares) and their Caucasian counterparts (open squares), as has been shown in several other studies (Bosch *et al.* 1990; Coetzer *et al.* 1993; Marino *et al.* 2004; Weston *et al.* 1999). Neither did Scandinavian elite runners and their Kenyan counterparts differ for $\dot{V}O_2$ max (Saltin *et al.* 1995b). These and other related studies are discussed in depth in a subsequent Chapter 10 in this book by Harley and Noakes.

Undoubtedly, elite endurance performance does require a reasonably high $\dot{V}O_2$ max and Sjödin and Svedenhag (1985) have suggested a cut-off value of 63 ml·kg^{-1}·min^{-1}. This value may be rather specific, especially when taking into account the variety of methods used to assess $\dot{V}O_2$ max (protocols to induce exhaustion differ, as well as equipment to determine oxygen consumption and the duration that the 'maximum' was sustained has ranged from single breaths to 15 s to 1 min). However, when we inserted their cut-off value into Figure 9.2d, it can be seen that it does indeed underpin all the subjects in our cohort who could run 10 km in under 34 min. However, there were many athletes with performances as slow as ~40 min who also exceeded this proposed cut-off value (see Figure 9.2d). To cut off those runners who could not run the 10 km in less than 35 min, we would need to raise the $\dot{V}O_2$ max cut-off to ~72 mml·kg^{-1}·min^{-1} for our cohort. However, since this would now exclude approximately half of our top quartile of athletes who perform very well despite lower $\dot{V}O_2$ max, one might be tempted to assume that a case for the importance of $\dot{V}O_2$ max is closed. Is $\dot{V}O_2$ max assessment simply needed to determine if the athlete can be categorized into the fairly large group of *elite and sub-elite* endurance athletes? If this is the case, is the search for the genotypes that co-exist with the high-$\dot{V}O_2$ max phenotype relevant only for such broad classification rather than for identifying future world champions? Despite many years of research, I believe that these questions still remain to be properly answered. Nevertheless, much progress has already been made, albeit mainly in the arena of sub-elite athletes.

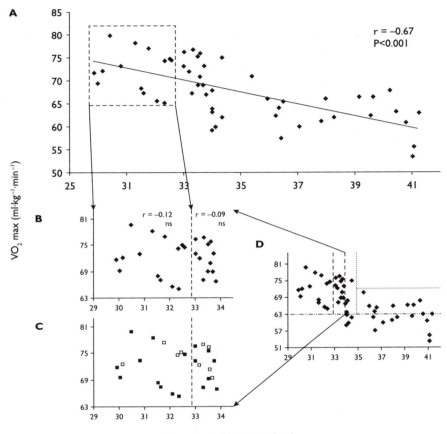

Figure 9.2 10 km personal best (PB) performance (achieved within 6 months of laboratory testing) and $\dot{V}O_2$ max in sub-elite and average endurance runners with preferred distance for road racing of 8 to 21.1 km.

Note: The full cohort of 53 runners is presented in Panels A and D (unpublished data, T. A. Kohn and A. Eksteen, Stellenbosch University). Pearson's correlation analysis was done for data presented in Panel A and for the top 50% of runners presented in Panel B (r = − 0.09) and the top 25% of runners who could achieve a PB of less than 33 min for 10 km. To place these times into perspective the top 25% of the cohort raced at a pace of 3:15 (min:s) or less per km, whereas the top 50% could race at a pace of 3:23 or less per km. In Panel C the Xhosa athletes are depicted by closed squares whereas the Caucasian athletes are depicted by open squares. Panel D illustrates different ways in which the data can be categorized: using the 63 ml·kg⁻¹·min⁻¹ cut-off for $\dot{V}O_2$ max (suggested by Sjödin and Svedenhag (1985)): ----; indicating those runners capable of running 10 km in less than 33 or 34 min: ┊ ; indicating that $\dot{V}O_2$ max would need to be cut-off at ~ 72 ml·kg⁻¹·min⁻¹ to prevent fairly average performers (PB > 35 min), from being counted as sub-elite: ⋯⋯.

For example, if we were to further sub-categorize the elite group of endurance runners as having either a higher $\dot{V}O_2$ max (e.g. > 72 ml·kg^{-1}·min^{-1}), or a relatively 'lower' $\dot{V}O_2$ max (e.g. 63–71.9 ml·kg^{-1}·min^{-1}), the proportion of Xhosa and Caucasian athletes within the top group are equivalent (53% vs. 47%), but the proportion of Xhosas in the 'lower' group is far greater (82% vs. 18%). This can be interpreted to mean that for Caucasians to perform well in endurance running they need to have a very high $\dot{V}O_2$ max, whereas a large proportion of Xhosa athletes are able to compensate for a relatively 'lower' $\dot{V}O_2$ max. Are there biological factors that compensate for the 'lower' $\dot{V}O_2$ max? Are there biological factors that contribute to the high $\dot{V}O_2$ max? Are these factors mutually exclusive (as might be implied by such categorization), or are the world champion athletes those who have the high $\dot{V}O_2$ max as well as the factors that others, less-well endowed for $\dot{V}O_2$ max, use to compensate for their misfortune? Two candidates for difference are the fractional utilization of $\dot{V}O_2$ max used during a race and the submaximal running economy. The fractional utilization of $\dot{V}O_2$ max used during a race is comprehensively covered in another chapter (Chapter 10). Therefore, I will focus on aspects related to running economy for the remainder of this section.

Running economy is a factor that was shown a long time ago to correlate with performance in well-trained distance runners (Farrell et al. 1979; Conley and Krahenbuhl 1980). Saltin et al. (1995b) showed that Kenyan runners were more economical than Scandinavian runners and Weston et al. (2000) showed that black, Xhosa-speaking, South African runners were more economical than white South African runners matched for 10 km performance. Given the fact that economical running is actually defined by relatively low oxygen cost at a given running speed, this factor could indeed compensate for a relatively 'low' $\dot{V}O_2$ max. However, could it not also be considered as the factor that results in a relatively 'low' $\dot{V}O_2$ max? What are the factors underlying the expression of the 'economical running of African endurance runners'? Is it possible that this is an inherited trait?

Factors that could influence the economy of endurance running can be found at levels ranging from the whole body to skeletal muscle cells to gene polymorphisms influencing either the whole body or the specific protein phenotypes. Before discussing these underlying factors, I will also attempt to answer the question: How consistent is the finding that running economy influences performance? To address this question, I would like to highlight three recent articles (Abe et al. 1998; Grant et al. 1997; Maldonado et al. 2002).

Running economy and performance

First, it seems that in some study cohorts, running economy does not predict performance: Grant et al. (1997) tested 16 male middle-and long-distance runners who were all above the putative minimum $\dot{V}O_2$ max for elite and sub-elite endurance performance, but neither $\dot{V}O_2$ max nor running economy correlated well with performance determined from a 3 km time trial on an indoor track. Although up to this point, I have discussed road runners, this is not only because of the fact that these were track runners: Williams and Cavanaugh (1987) previously showed in 10 km runners that running economy did not predict performance. We also did steady state running economy tests in a sub-set (n = 16) of the cohort of subjects presented in Figure 9.2 (Panel A), all of whom also achieved the putative minimum max for elite and sub-elite endurance runners (Figure 9.2, Panel B). This time, using peak treadmill velocity as the measure of performance (according to Noakes et al. 1990, this is a better predictor of performance than $\dot{V}O_2$ max), we could demonstrate that neither $\dot{V}O_2$ max (r = 0.50), nor running economy (r = –0.40) were strongly associated with performance (see Figure 9.3, Panels A and B respectively).

However, the second article I would like to highlight indicates that $\dot{V}O_2$ max and running economy should not be considered separately: Abe et al. (1998) pointed out that although it is acknowledged that relatively poorer running economy can be offset by a high $\dot{V}O_2$ max, many authors have not really taken this into account when assessing the predictive value of running economy, or differences in running economy between groups. These authors investigated sub-elite middle distance track runners and found that the *ratio* of the energy cost of running at a fixed submaximal workload to the energy cost of running at the maximal workload could account for approximately 50% of variability in performance over 1500 m, 3,000 m and 5,000 m. Therefore, they proposed that these two variables should be considered as a single, combined variable. When we used this parameter, we found that the relationship to laboratory endurance performance was better (r = –0.61; p < 0.05) (Figure 9.3, Panel C). Also, Xhosa and Caucasian runners did not cluster differently, suggesting that better running economy in Xhosa athletes may become a less relevant variable for performance if accompanied by a lower max.

Third, the factors influencing running economy may differ depending on the preferred race distance. Maldonado et al. (2002) investigated anthropometric factors that could influence running economy: both body mass and height were inversely related to running economy in athletes who competed in 800 m and 1500 m events, but neither of these two anthropometric variables were related to economy in athletes participating in the longer middle-distance events (5,000 m to 10,000 m) or those participating in marathons. In our sub-cohort of 16 subjects, body mass was also not strongly associated with economy (r = –0.29), and even less so when economy was expressed as a ratio to max $\dot{V}O_2$ (r = 0.12). The finding was similar for height (height vs. economy: r = –0.17; height vs. economy relative to $\dot{V}O_2$ max: r = 0.14).

Maldonado et al. (2002) concluded that endurance runners are not a homogeneous group and their phenotypes may differ to a certain extent when taking into account their favoured racing distance. I suggest that this is another factor that may be complicating the search for endurance-related gene polymorphisms. Certainly it is a factor that complicates the interpretation of

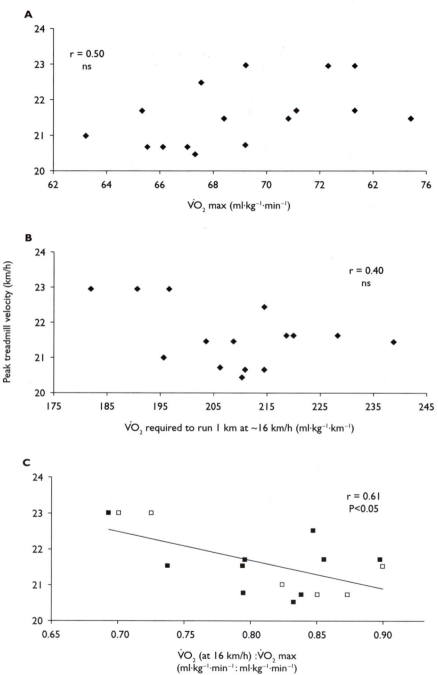

physiological literature on 'endurance runners' and comparisons between ethnic groups. For example, the subjects in the study by Coetzer *et al.* (1993), who did not differ in running economy, did not specialize in the same racing distances. This may, in part, explain why the findings do not coincide with others who did show better running economy in African endurance runners when they were matched for their favourite running distance (Weston *et al.* 2000). In their study of the demographic characteristics of elite Ethiopian endurance runners, Scott *et al.* (2003) divided their cohort of runners into those who favoured marathon running, those favouring 5–10 km races and those racing up to 1500 m, thus taking preference into account. However, it is important to note that athletes may participate in two or more of the endurance running sub-disciplines: track, road and cross-country, and athletes may favour different distances within each sub-discipline. This has not previously been taken into account. For our current studies (Kohn, unpublished), we are calculating an average preferred racing distance (PRD_A).

Running economy: methodological considerations

A question relating to running economy raised by the above discussion is: 'What running speed is the correct speed at which to test running economy?' One tradition is to test running economy at 16.1 km/h (equivalent to 10 miles/h or 268 m/min) (Grant *et al.* 1997), because early studies used this pace (e.g. Conley and Krahenbuhl 1980). However, not all subjects are equally comfortable at this speed. Larsen *et al.* (2004) tested their Nandi youth (athletes and non-athletes; I hesitate to use the terms 'runners and non-runners' for these cohorts, since the non-athletes ran a lot during daily life activities, but simply did not train consistently or compete) at between 8 and 12 km/h for town boys and between 9.5 and 14 km/h for village boys. Thus, economy was expressed as the oxygen cost to run 1 km. However, we have tested runners' economy at three different speeds: easy (64% of individual peak treadmill speed (PTS)), moderate (72% of PTS) and intense (80% of PTS). Plotting all these data revealed a trend for the oxygen cost to decrease as the running speed increased (see Figure 9.4a) for most individuals (see Figure 9.4b, and Figures 9.5a and b). It was also clear, that the improvement in running economy with increasing speed can be more clearly seen when comparing easy vs. intense running speeds (Figure 9.5b) than easy vs. moderate running speeds (Figure 9.5a). Middle-distance athletes have also been found to be more economical than marathon runners at higher running speeds (above 19 km/h) (Daniels and Daniels 1992).

Figure 9.3   *(opposite)* Neither $\dot{V}O_2$ max, nor running economy correlated significantly with performance (peak treadmill speed, PTS) achieved during an incremental test to exhaustion. However, there was a significant relationship between the ratio of running economy and $\dot{V}O_2$ max and PTS, indicating that the composite variable is a better predictor of treadmill performance.

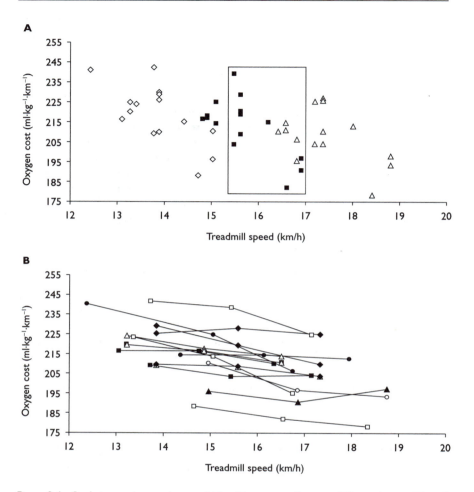

Figure 9.4 **A** plots running economy of 16 subjects tested at easy (◊), moderate (■) and intense (△) speeds corresponding to percentages of individual peak treadmill speed of 64, 72 and 80% respectively. The boxed data are those that were used to calculate economy in the previous figure. **B** indicates the relationship between each subject's 3 economy tests and overall indicates that in many cases the running economy expressed as ml·kg⁻¹·km⁻¹ is different depending on the running speed at which the subject was tested. It looks as if there is a tendency for running economy to improve in most subjects as the running speed increased. This is illustrated in a different way in Figure 9.5.

This brings us to yet another question! 'What are the best units with which to express running economy?' Expressing running economy in units of absolute V̇O₂/min takes into account the real oxygen cost of the work. Broadly speaking it is true that a larger person will require more oxygen since running is a weight-

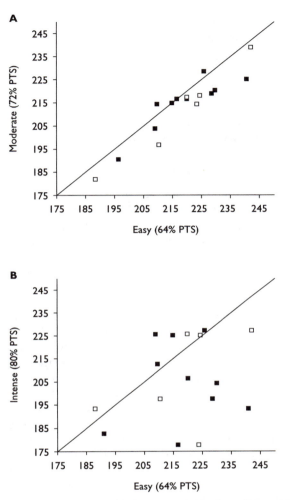

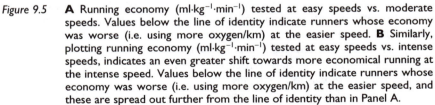

Figure 9.5   **A** Running economy (ml·kg^{-1}·min^{-1}) tested at easy speeds vs. moderate speeds. Values below the line of identity indicate runners whose economy was worse (i.e. using more oxygen/km) at the easier speed. **B** Similarly, plotting running economy (ml·kg^{-1}·min^{-1}) tested at easy speeds vs. intense speeds, indicates an even greater shift towards more economical running at the intense speed. Values below the line of identity indicate runners whose economy was worse (i.e. using more oxygen/km) at the easier speed, and these are spread out further from the line of identity than in Panel A.

bearing sport and there is therefore an influence of body mass on oxygen cost of locomotion. This is certainly true across the animal kingdom where body mass and oxygen cost of locomotion differs substantially between species (Taylor 1994). However, there is still controversy surrounding whether it is more appropriate to express oxygen cost as $ml\cdot kg^{-1}\cdot min^{-1}$, $ml\cdot kg^{-0.75}\cdot min^{-1}$ or $ml\cdot kg^{-0.66}\cdot min^{-1}$, or as in Larsen *et al.*'s (2004) study as $\dot{V}O_2/kg/km$ or $/kg^{0.75}/km$ (see Chapter 8). Most exercise physiologists know the arguments for using these various units (for review see Svedenhag 2000). Although scientists in other areas have the expertise to uncover some of the factors influencing running economy, if they do not express the variable correctly, this may influence the conclusions they draw.

Running economy: a multi-disciplinary approach

Physiology, genetics, biomechanics and anthropometry

If gene polymorphisms influencing running economy are to be found, it is necessary to understand what individual factors contribute to running economy, because it is most likely that several genes contribute to this complex phenotype (see Chapters 12–14 in this book). One fairly obvious factor influencing the oxygen cost of running at a specific speed is the athlete's running biomechanics. How would we begin to look for genes that may be influencing biomechanics? Or is this also a variable that is too complex and which needs to be broken down into components?

Anderson (1996) defined the influence of biomechanics on running as 'the efficiency with which power is converted to [forward] translocation'. This is influenced by factors such as limb morphology and other anthropometric dimensions, and the patterns of movement (including e.g. vertical oscillation vs. horizontal displacement; or stride length and frequency), as well as kinetics of movements (e.g. ground reaction forces in various directions). The data available for endurance runners were comprehensively reviewed by Anderson in 1996. Despite a high density of information in his review, which is an excellent document for uncovering and explaining the 'complex, multifactorial entity' of running economy, his final conclusion is interesting within the context of this book: 'At higher levels of competition, it is likely that "natural selection" tends to eliminate those athletes who failed to either inherit or develop characteristics which favour economy'. On the one hand this is an exciting statement for the geneticists who are intent on investigating whether there is a group of gene polymorphisms that are unique to elite endurance runners and on the other hand it is an exciting statement for the sport scientists who are intent on discovering the extent to which the characteristics that influence running economy can be 'developed' by intervention strategies.

As mentioned above, the absolute cost of running is affected by body mass. However, it may be more relevant to investigate the influences of leanness, muscle or fat mass. It may also be affected by other components of body size, such as height and lower limb length. Gene polymorphisms influencing various components of body size possibly relevant to endurance performance have been found in the broader population, for example fat free mass (Roth *et al.* 2003), adult height (Ellis et al. 2001) and leanness (Lavebratt et al. 2005). Although anthropometry of African athletes has not been comprehensively investigated in all the studies, the existing research on black endurance runners has shown that they differ from their white counterparts in terms of some measured body dimensions. South African runners of the Xhosa-speaking group, are shorter and lighter than their white counterparts (Bosch et al. 1990; Coetzer et al. 1993; Marino et al. 2004; Weston et al. 1999). Weston et al. (2000) showed that this difference affected running economy whether expressed per kg body mass or per $kg^{0.66}$, but this was not the case in Bosch et al.'s study (1990). Despite differences in height and body mass, the black marathon runners were not more efficient than their white counterparts at submaximal running speeds.

Other anthropometry variables determined by Bosch et al. (1990) included percentage body fat (derived from seven skinfold measurements) and lower limb length (trochanter height), neither of which differed significantly between groups. However, since there were significant differences in height between groups, these data together imply that if lower limb length had been expressed relative to stature, the African runners may have had relatively longer lower limbs. Early literature on anthropometry and endurance running performance pointed out that the ratios between different body size or body segment length variables may be more important than each variable alone (e.g. Burke and Brush 1979).

Certainly body size and shape are substantially influenced by inheritance, with different studies attributing different proportions of the observed variation to genetic effects. This is understandable since different descriptors of 'body size' or 'body shape', or both, were used as well as different study designs, for example large cohorts with a minimum of two parents and one offspring in each nuclear family, twin pairs, adoptees and their biological vs. adoptive families, and nuclear families from ethnically different groups (Katzmarzyk et al. 2000; Livshits et al. 2002; Sanchez-Andres 1995; Sharma et al. 1984; Vogler et al. 1995). Of importance here are the conclusions that up to 75% of inter-individual variation in some of the studied traits were calculated to be genetically influenced (Livshits et al. 2002), the maternal influence is higher (Sanchez-Andres 1995; Sharma et al. 1984), and when considering somatotype scores (endomorphy, mesomorphy and ectomorphy), there was a stronger genetic influence on mesomorphy, although all somatotypes were significantly influenced (Katzmarzyk et al. 2000; Sanchez-Andres 1995). Furthermore, dimensions including height or length measurements were more strongly influenced by genetics than breadth dimensions (Sharma et al. 1984). However, how genetics may affect, for example the lower limb length:height ratios is unknown.

Also, a more in-depth investigation of skinfold thicknesses at the various sites measured by Bosch et al. (1990) indicated that despite no significant differences in overall percentage body fat, the body fat was differently distributed in the African runners who exhibited significantly lower skinfold thicknesses in the limbs (triceps, front thigh and medial calf). Although not significantly different, only the abdominal skinfold thickness was higher in the African than the Caucasian runners. The authors hypothesized that the inertia of the legs would be lower. Although this had no statistically significant effect on running economy at 16 km·h^{-1}, the cumulative effect over race distance may be important, or the effect may become important at higher running speeds.

Composite descriptors of body composition, such as endomorphy and mesomorphy, have previously been shown to be good indicators of running performance (Bale et al. 1986). Whether this is also true for a cohort of elite runners (who may all fit into the optimal range) is not known. Saltin et al. (1995b) found that elite Kenyan runners had a lower body mass index (19.2 kg·m^{-2}) (lower BMI is an indicator of a linear body shape) than elite Scandinavian runners (20.6 kg·m^{-2}). In the same study, they found that running economy in their Kenyan cohort was similar to the Scandinavian cohort at lower speeds, but 5–15% better at higher speeds. The highest speed used to test running economy was 16 km·h^{-1} when running on a 2.8% gradient. Taking into account the fact that the Kenyan runners (and recently also the Ethiopian runners) excel at team cross-country (not only because of their top runner but because of the depth of runners amongst the top finishers in this team competition) it may be necessary for sport scientists to consider doing more testing on economy during gradient treadmill testing. We are currently analysing data on the speed with which the Kenyan runners train during various types of training sessions, including hill training (Jackson, Lyoka and Myburgh, unpublished data).

Although not a comparative study between populations, Larsen et al. (2004) found that 15–18 year-old Nandi (a sub-group particularly successful at running within the Kalenjin, who themselves are particularly successful) boys had a mean BMI of 18.5 kg·m^{-2}. These data, and the fact that town vs. village boys did not differ, suggest that the Nandi runners' body shape is inherent rather than a response to training. We are currently analysing anthropometry data collected in elite and sub-elite Kenyan runners derived from more than 30 different measurements on each individual (Jackson, Lyoka and Myburgh, unpublished data). Instead of comparing the Kenyan elite runners to elite runners from another race, we are comparing elite and sub-elite runners from the same Kenyan group (Kalenjin) to determine if the elite performers differ or not. It is possible that the traits that make the difference for world-class performance amongst elite runners are not the same as those that make the difference between average and elite endurance performance, which themselves differ from those that separate average endurance performers from poor performers.

Physiology, histology and cellular energy cost

Besides structural and biomechanical influences, there are also other biological factors that could influence running economy. Such parameters may include: (i) the work of breathing (which does not directly influence translocation); (ii) fibre type proportions; (iii) the ratio of concentric to eccentric muscle contraction; and (iv) efficiency of adenosine triphosphate (ATP) utilization. With regard to running economy, the influence of these factors is difficult to determine accurately, therefore they will be discussed with reference to the exercise physiology literature in general, as well as from the stand-point that they could theoretically influence running economy.

(i) The respiratory muscles require a substantial proportion of the cardiac output during maximal exercise, estimated to be ~15% (Harms et al. 1997), indicating that the oxygen cost of breathing will influence the overall oxygen cost of running. Within this context, it is interesting to note that oxygen cost of breathing increases non-linearly as the ventilatory volume increases with higher speeds of running in incremental exercise tests (Marks et al. 2005) so that breathing becomes relatively more expensive. Using a technique verified by Coast et al. (1993), Marks et al. (2005) determined that the oxygen cost of breathing at $\dot{V}O_2$ max was 18 ± 4% of $\dot{V}O_2$ max (assessed on a cycle ergometer). These data indicate that there is some variation between individuals regarding the relative proportion of max used for breathing.

Although the work of breathing itself is not frequently determined and has not been determined in any of the comparative studies so far, the relationship between minute ventilation ($\dot{V}E$) and running economy has been investigated in several studies. In trained subjects, running economy became worse and ventilation volume increased from the beginning to the end of a 5 km race (Thomas et al. 1999) and statistically there was a significant association between these variables. Some of the comparisons of black and white endurance athletes have indicated differences in submaximal oxygen consumption (Coetzer et al. 1993; Weston et al. 2000) and maximal or submaximal ventilation volume ($\dot{V}E$) (Bosch et al. 1990; Coetzer et al. 1993). In the study by Bosch et al. (1990), this was only apparent at $\dot{V}O_2$ max. Since respiratory exchange ratio (RER) at maximal exercise has been shown to be lower in African endurance runners in some studies (Coetzer et al. 1993), one might speculate that the efficiency of African endurance runners could be, in part, due to a better ability to control hyperventilation at high running intensities. However, such a hypothesis should be regarded with caution, since in the study by Coetzer et al. (1993), the difference in $\dot{V}E$ at $\dot{V}O_2$ was no longer apparent when corrected for body size differences (Coetzer et al. 1993) and because Weston et al. (1999) were able to relate the lower RER to higher oxidative enzyme capacities in their Xhosa cohort. Despite this caution, it might be worth noting that athletes have been shown to have a decreased ventilatory response to hypoxia and hypercapnia compared to sedentary controls (Byrne-Quinn et al. 1971). Since this response in some athletes has been associated with a similar response in non-athletic family members (Scoggin et al. 1978), there may even be a genetic influence.

(ii) An intramuscular parameter that influences whole body parameters is fibre type. Fibre type nomenclature is conferred in different ways, depending on the method used to assess the fibre characteristics, for example the proportions of the different fibre types determined from a histological assessment of the pH lability of the myosin ATPase enzyme (Brooke and Kaiser 1970) vs. the mobility of the myosin heavy chain (MHC) isoforms (the contractile protein that contains embedded within its structure, the myosin ATPase enzyme) do not completely correspond (Staron 1997). Nonetheless, in vitro assessments of individual fibres (He *et al.* 2000) as well as associations between fibre type and whole body exercise economy (Coyle *et al.* 1992) have both indicated that there is an influence of fibre type. He *et al.* (2000) determined the oxygen cost of contraction at single fibre level and showed that fibres containing mainly slow, MHC I are more efficient. Also at the level of whole muscle in rodent models, slow muscle is more efficient than fast (Barclay *et al.* 1993), especially under conditions of fatigue (Myburgh 2004). Coyle *et al.* (1992) determined the economy of cycling at three fixed workloads (~50, 60 and 70% of $\dot{V}O_2$ max) with a fixed pedalling cadence (80 rpm) and found that the percentage of slow twitch fibres correlated with efficiency. However, the fibre type in black South African runners tends to be faster than that of performance-matched white runners (Coetzer *et al.* 1993; Weston *et al.* 1999) and thus is probably not the variable contributing to their better running economy.

(iii) Although undergraduate textbooks teach that one cross-bridge cycle (= 'crossbridge formation-force transduction-actomyosin release) breaks down one molecule of ATP, this is a simplified version of our current understanding and it may only hold true for simple, moderately loaded, concentrically shortening contractions (Barclay 2003). In reality many other conditions may prevail, such as shortening contractions against a heavy load (during which the extent of shortening per ATP utlized is reduced) or shortening contractions at very low loads. More efficient cross-bridge cycling can only occur if the cross-bridge is able to attach, produce force and detach more than once per ATP molecule consumed. This may be the case during shortening contractions against low loads (e.g. less than 20% of maximum as suggested by Barclay (2003) or eccentric contractions). Eccentric contractions are known to be more economical per unit of force produced than concentric contractions (Ryschon *et al.* 1997). In human subjects *in vivo* this has been found for contractions of the tibialis anterior and extensor digitorum longus muscles and it has been confirmed in the more controlled environment of *in situ* stimulation of rat gastrocnemius muscle (Beltman *et al.* 2004). It is possible that the ratio of work done eccentrically vs. concentrically during a complex whole body task such as running, could influence the overall economy of the movement. Ryschon *et al.* (1997) also indicated that isometric contraction is even more efficient than concentric contraction. Even during such a dynamic movement as running, there are likely to be stabilizer muscles that are contracting isometrically. Some of the variations in running style, particularly pertaining to a) the movement of the upper body and b) the duration and extent of knee flexion vs. extension, may therefore influence running economy in ways we have not previously thought of.

(iv) At the level of whole muscle contraction, economy of force production can be defined as total energy consumed/unit of force produced by the whole muscle. This is influenced by, for example the efficiency of the cross-bridges (as explained above), the amount of energy used by the ion pumps relative to the myosin ATPase, the metabolic efficiency of the major substrate replenishing ATP, and the efficiency with which the force produced during the actomyosin interaction is transduced to the tendons and their boney attachments (the latter will be discussed later). The influence most of these factors have on muscle energy utilization has been investigated and debated in the context of adaptations that occur with chronic or acute exposure to altitude/hypoxia. These models assume that any adaptations in response to lower oxygen provision would prove to be useful for more economical movement (e.g. Hochachka et al. 1991). Although this assumption may be flawed, there is evidence that altitude or hypoxic training could improve running economy (recently reviewed by Saunders et al. 2004). Here I will concentrate on possible intramuscular mechanisms for such an improvement.

During the relaxation phase of cyclical contraction, the Na^+-K^+ATPase pumps restore the resting membrane potential and the sarcoplasmic reticulum ATPase pumps (SERCA) remove free ionic calcium from the muscle cytosol. Green et al. (2000) showed that a three-week exposure to altitude (~6,000 m) in mountaineers downregulated the Na^+-K^+ATPase pump number by ~14% without any change in muscle oxidative potential or fibre type, indicating a highly specific response. This response is likely to alter the 'set-point' of the resting membrane potential which could result in more efficient relaxation. Similar to the myosin heavy chains, the SERCA are expressed in different isoforms, including SERCA1 and SERCA2a in skeletal muscle (Green et al. 2003). The expression of the different isoforms is thought to be influenced mainly by fibre type, and this may therefore be one of the mechanisms explaining the influence of fibre type on economy. However, the influence of 10 weeks of endurance training was not a switch in isoforms (as might be seen for myosin heavy chain expression), but a downregulation of SERCA1, with no change in SERCA2a (Green et al. 2003). Interestingly, this change resulted in downregulation of the maximal Ca^{2+}ATPase activity indicating an energetic change in the process of muscle relaxation. Neither Na^+-K^+ATPase content, nor SERCA isoforms have been investigated in African endurance runners.

Biochemistry: metabolic

Muscle cell efficiency is not only determined by the efficiency of the processes using ATP, but also by the efficiency of the processes supplying ATP. The influence of metabolic supply on the oxygen cost of contraction is related to the fact that substrates oxidized for ATP provision are not equivalent in the amount of oxygen utilized per ATP provided (Holden et al. 1995). Carbohydrate oxidation is more efficient than fat oxidation. Andean natives, who have lived at altitude for generations, utilize more carbohydrate than fat as fuel during exercise (Hochachka et al. 1991) and non-athletes taken to altitude (4,300 m) for three weeks decreased their reliance on fat and increased their carbohydrate oxidation during easy exercise (Roberts *et al.* 1996). Improved capacity to fully oxidize carbohydrate as a substrate is likely to be the mechanism for these observations. This would be accompanied by decreased lactate accumulation which has been shown to be a result of altitude acclimatization (Grassi *et al.* 1996). Both Kenyan and South African black athletes accumulate lower blood lactate during exercise (Saltin *et al.* 1995b; Weston *et al.* 1999). One might expect lower lactate dehydrogenase (LDH) activities in these athletes. However, neither of the two studies investigating enzyme activities in African and Caucasian runners determined LDH activities (Saltin *et al.* 1995a; Weston *et al.* 1999). Saltin *et al.* (1995a) did investigate differences in LDH isozyme distribution and found that Kenyan runners had a higher ratio of $LDH_{1-2}:LDH_{4-5}$. But 14 days of altitude training by the Scandinavian runners was associated with an adaptation in their LDH ratios so that the difference between the two ethnic groups was no longer apparent. It is interesting to note that LDH activity was significantly upregulated in response to moderate altitude exposure in a study by Green *et al.* (2000). Further investigation of these issues is required.

Physiology and biochemistry: connective tissue

As mentioned earlier, muscle efficiency is also influenced by the elements that are required to transduce the force produced by the contractile proteins. These are the structural elements such as tendons and other components of connective tissue. The major relevant components of the extracellular matrix (ECM) are collagen fibrils and proteoglycans (for review see Kjaer 2004). They are situated distant from the cross-bridges but are linked to them via the intracellular cytoskeletal proteins and the integrins. The latter is a large protein that spans the sarcolemma and has both intracellular and extracellular domains. The roles of connective tissue in muscle are multiple, but include the strengthening of the tissue (Huijing 1999), the temporary storage of elastic energy during cyclical movement (Alexander and Bennet-Clark 1977) and the transmission of the cumulative force produced by cycling cross-bridges (Trotter 1993).

Intramuscular connective tissue is arranged in different structures such as the endomysium and perimysium, which in turn connect to the tendons. The former is more elastic whilst the latter is stiffer and hence important for force transmission (Trotter and Purslow 1992). The importance of the specific connective tissue proteins for muscle function is slowly being delineated. For example, knocking out the expression of a specific collagen sub-type (collagen XV, which is a minor collagen in terms of quantity expressed in comparison to other sub-types) will cause the development of skeletal muscle myopathy in mice (Eklund *et al.* 2001). Also, knocking out a specific sub-type of integrin (alpha7) causes muscle damage at the myotendinous junction particularly in response to contraction (Mayer *et al.* 1997). It is also conceivable that polymorphisms in some of these or other proteins exist that could affect the economy of movement. The context in which the effects of such polymorphisms are currently being investigated is not in relation to exercise performance, but in relation to, for example, skeletal muscle myopathies (e.g. Duggan *et al.* 1997).

In addition to the existence of inherent differences conferred by polymorphisms, it is also known that exercise training influences the turnover of connective tissue (e.g. Langberg *et al.* 1999). Since the early response to training intervention is to increase both synthesis and degradation of collagen (at least for the first 3–4 weeks), whereas by week 11 synthesis predominates (Langberg *et al.* 1999; Kjaer 2004), this suggests that the early response may be one of remodelling whereas the late response could increase the quantity of connective tissue. The next question is: 'How do such adaptations affect exercise performance?'

Adaptations of connective tissue in response to exercise training could affect any or all of its functions. Functional characteristics of connective tissue that have been tested include the load–strain relationship (a measure of elasticity or compliance) and stiffness. Different parts of the connective tissue network differ in their characteristics, for example, the bone–tendon attachment, the proportion of the tendon that is unattached to any other structure and the proportion of muscular connective tissue attaching to the tendon, the muscular connective tissue and the intramuscular cytoskeleton. The ability to distinguish these and evaluate the properties of each in human subject testing is not simple (and in some instances not possible). However, since the groundbreaking work of Komi *et al.* (1987), several groups are beginning to investigate the properties of connective tissue *in vivo*, during various activities, for example the tibialis anterior and its associated tendon with contraction in the isometric mode (Ito *et al.* 1998), the gastrocnemius muscle and associated musculo-tendinous junction and Achilles tendon during walking (Fukunaga *et al.* 2001), or even the vastus lateralis tendon-aponeurosis complex during isometric knee extensions (Bojsen-Møller *et al.* 2003). Although their technique of assessing connective tissue during contraction (ultrasonography) would be difficult to use during very dynamic movements, the force exerted during jumping tasks involving the same muscle-connective tissue complex was later shown to correlate with the stiffness of the connective tissue (Bojsen-Møller *et al.* 2005).

What is the relevance of all this information for running? Alexander (2002) sums it up well by stating that we 'exploit the elastic properties' of our tendons so that 'metabolic energy can be saved' during movement. However, more compliant connective tissue may be less able to control the direction of force application. It remains to be determined how these factors influence whole body running economy in African and white endurance athletes. In the past, more attention has been paid to the skeletal muscle proteins that are associated with high oxidative capacity (Saltin *et al.* 1995a; Weston *et al.* 1999). However, in the future it is likely that the expression of additional proteins, including those involved in transduction of force (rather than activation of contraction, force production or relaxation) will be assessed. Since it is very difficult to get muscle biopsies from world-class athletes and this is certainly not warranted for very hypothetical investigations ('fishing expeditions'), one approach would be to determine in sub-elite and then elite athletes if any of these factors are adaptable to training interventions.

Sport science

Training of elite athletes encompasses far more than dividing training up into endurance and high intensity training, or outdoor and indoor training. Hence it has become important for sport scientists to unravel the mysteries of 'optimal training' and for exercise biologists to determine the physiological and bio-chemical effects of different types of training, or different ratios of training to recovery.

Saunders et al. (2004) have reviewed the running economy literature comprehensively and have concluded that there is little research investigating the effects of various regimens of off-road training in elite runners. However, two studies done in sub-elite runners and orienteers respectively are worth considering. In sub-elite runners intensive, continuous distance training and high-intensity, moderate duration interval training both improved running economy, but short-duration, sprint-intervals did not (Franch et al. 1998). Also in well-trained endurance runners (cross-country orienteers), replacement of a substantial portion of the endurance training (~30%) with explosive training has been shown to improve running economy and endurance performance over 5 km (Paavolainen et al. 1999). In contrast to Franch et al. (1998), Paavolainen et al. (1999) intervened not only with explosive sprint training, but also with explosive training involving jumping exercises and low-load, high-speed weight training. Although this combination of training proved successful, it is difficult to distinguish which portion of the training was responsible or what tissues may have adapted.

Several other questions have not been adequately addressed: (i) Do external factors affect the economy of running to the same extent in all athletes? One thinks of windy conditions or the hilly conditions typical of cross-country races. A more specifically phrased question is: Are black runners more economical when running uphill (or downhill!) and, if so why? Certainly it is not always possible to test athletes using the most sophisticated equipment, particularly in remote locations. However, sport scientists are trained in the methodology of field testing and monitoring. Nonetheless, so far, only Billat et al. (2003) have investigated training habits of Kenyan athletes, but from written records rather than using any portable equipment. The current worldwide focus on nanotechnologies may give rise to new portable biomolecular sensors for non-invasive laboratory- and field-research. Although, it is of course crucial that such sensors should not hamper the athlete (Myburgh 2003).

(ii) Can an economical running style be learned? If so, do black runners consider this to be an important aspect of training? Hawley (2002) has suggested that there is a minimum duration of training required to increase mitochondrial capacity. Is there also a minimum amount of training required to achieve greater running economy?

(iii) Do psychological factors influence running economy? It is possible that competition stress may affect either running mechanics or energy cost, or both. Heart rate during racing is known to be higher than during training at similar speeds. Competition strategy could affect running economy since drafting during running is estimated to be able to save up to 3–6% of energy cost (Pugh 1970 and Kyle 1979). Would all endurance athletes benefit to the same extent from drafting? Or is this a strategy that should be employed specifically by athletes with a less than optimal body size or running style?

A multidisciplinary approach combining exercise biology and sport science

It is clear from the above discussion of running economy that, although this trait is measured as a physiological variable, it is impossible to discuss it comprehensively without accessing information gleaned via research in multiple different disciplines. What is more remarkable is that running economy is generally not considered to be particularly complex (athlete + treadmill + oxygen analyser = can measure running economy!). In a previous review (Myburgh 2003) I also discussed in some detail the aspects of optimal training and recovery and touched upon the 'newer' science of assessing competition strategies.

Conclusion

For those reading this book, we either have been, or will in future be fascinated both by our eminently capable research subjects' expertise, and by our own expanding research methodologies with which we aim to gain a better understanding of the mechanisms underlying their expert performances. So, while at this point there are still 'more questions than answers' to explain why east African endurance runners are so dominant, scientists are currently poised to provide more answers by moving toward a multidisciplinary, co-operative and integrative approach.

References

Abe, D., Yanagawa, K., Yamanobe, K. and Tamura, K. (1998) 'Assessment of middle-distance running performance in sub-elite young runners using energy cost of running', *European Journal of Applied Physiology and Occupational Physiology* 77, 320–5.

Alexander, R. M. (2002) 'Tendon elasticity and muscle function', *Comparative Biochemistry and Physiology – Part A: Molecular and Integrative Physiology* 133, 1001–11.

Alexander, R. M. and Bennet-Clark, H. C. (1977) 'Storage of elastic strain energy in muscle and other tissues', *Nature* 265, 114–17.

Anderson, T. (1996) 'Biomechanics and running economy', *Sports Medicine* 22, 76–89.

Bale, P., Bradbury, D. and Colley, E. (1986) 'Anthropometric and training variables related to 10km running performance', *British Journal of Sports Medicine* 20, 170–3.

Bangsbo, J. and Larsen, H. (eds) (2000) *Running and Science*, Copenhagen: Munksgaard.

Barclay, C. J. (2003) 'Models in which many cross-bridges attach simultaneously can explain the filament movement per ATP split during muscle contraction', *International Journal of Biological Macromolecules* 32, 139–47.

Barclay, C. J., Constable, J. K. and Gibbs, C. L. (1993) 'Energetics of fast- and slow-twitch muscles of the mouse', *Journal of Physiology* 472, 61–80.

Beltman, J. G., van der Vliet, M. R. Sargeant, A. J. and de Haan, A. (2004) 'Metabolic cost of lengthening, isometric and shortening contractions in maximally stimulated rat skeletal muscle', *Acta Physiologica Scandinavica* 182, 179–87.

Billat, L. V. (2001a) 'Interval training for performance: a scientific and empirical practice. Special recommendations for middle- and long-distance running. Part I: Aerobic interval training', *Sports Medicine* 31, 13–31.

Billat, L. V. (2001b) 'Interval training for performance: a scientific and empirical practice. Special recommendations for middle- and long-distance running. Part II: Anaerobic interval training', *Sports Medicine* 31, 75–90.

Billat, L. V., Lepretre, P.-M., Heugas, A.-M, Laurence, M.-H., Salim, D. and Koralsztein, J. P. (2003) 'Training and bioenergetic characteristics in elite male and female Kenyan runners', *Medicine and Science in Sports and Exercise* 35, 297–304.

Bojsen-Møller, J., Hansen, P., Aagaard, P., Kjæær, M. and Magnusson, S. P. (2003) 'Measuring mechanical properties of the *vastus lateralis* tendon-aponeurosis complex *in vivo* by ultrasound imaging', *Scandinavian Journal of Medicine and Science in Sports* 13, 259–65.

Bojsen-Møller, J., Magnusson, S. P., Rasmussen, L. R., Kjær, M. and Aagaard, P. (2005) 'Muscle performance during maximal isometric and dynamic contractions is influenced by the stiffness of the tendinous structures', *Journal of Applied Physiology* 99, 986–94.

Bosch, A. N., Goslin, B. R., Noakes, T. D. and Dennis, S. C. (1990) 'Physiological differences between black and white runners during a treadmill marathon', *European Journal of Applied Physiology and Occupational Physiology* 61, 68–72.

Brandon, L. J. (1995) 'Physiological factors associated with middle distance running performance', *Sports Medicine* 19, 268–77.

Brooke, M. H. and Kaiser, K. K. (1970) 'Muscle fiber types: how many and what kind?' *Archives of Neurology* 23, 369–79.

Burke, E. J. and Brush, F. C. (1979) 'Physiological and anthropometric assessment of successful teenage female distance runners', *Research Quarterly* 50, 180–6.

Byrne-Quinn, E., Weil, J. V., Sodal, E., Filley, G. F. and Grover, R. F. (1971) 'Ventilatory control in the athlete', *Journal of Applied Physiology* 30, 91–8.

Coast, J. R., Rasmussen, S. A., Krause, K. M., O'Kroy, J. A., Loy, R. A. and Rhodes, J. (1993) 'Ventilatory work and oxygen consumption during exercise and hyperventilation', *Journal of Applied Physiology* 74, 793–8.

Coetzer, P., Noakes, T. D., Sanders, B., Lambert, M. I., Bosch, A. N., Wiggins, T. and Dennis, S. C. (1993) 'Superior fatigue resistance of elite black South African distance runners', *Journal of Applied Physiology* 75, 1822–7.

Conley, D. L. and Krahenbuhl, G. S. (1980) 'Running economy and distance running performance of highly trained athletes', *Medicine and Science in Sports Exercise* 12, 357–60.

Costill, D. L. (1967) 'The relationship between selected physiological variables and distance running performance', *Journal of Sports Medicine and Physical Fitness* 7, 61–6.

Coyle, E. F. (1999) 'Physiological determinants of endurance exercise performance', *Journal of Science and Medicine in Sport* 2, 181–9.

Coyle, E., Sidossis, L., Horowitz, J. and Beltz, J. (1992) 'Cycling efficiency is related to the percentage of type I muscle fibers', *Medicine and Science in Sports and Exercise* 24, 782–8.

Daniels, J. and Daniels, N. (1992) 'Running economy of elite male and elite female runners', *Medicine and Science in Sports and Exercise* 24, 483–9.

Duggan, D. J., Gorospe, J. R., Fanin, M., Hoffman, E. P. and Angelini, C. (1997) 'Mutations in the sarcoglycan genes in patients with myopathy', *New England Journal of Medicine* 336, 618–24.

Eklund, L., Piuhola, J., Komulainen, J., Sormunen, R., Ongvarrasopone, C., Fässler, R., Muona, A., Ilves, M., Ruskoaho, H., Takala, T. E. S. and Pihlajaniemi, T. (2001) 'Lack of type XV collagen causes a skeletal myopathy and cardiovascular defects in mice', *Proceedings of the National Academy of Sciences* 98, 1194–9.

Ellis, J. A., Stebbing, M. and Harrap, S. B. (2001) 'Significant population variation in adult male height associated with the Y chromosome and the aromatase gene', *Journal of Clinical Endocrinology and Metabolism* 86, 4147–50.

Farrell, P. A., Wilmore, J. H., Coyle, E. F., Billing, J. E. and Costill, D. L. (1979) 'Plasma lactate accumulation and distance running performance', *Medicine and Science in Sports* 11, 338–44.

Foster, C., Costill, D. L., Daniels, J. T. and Fink, W. J. (1978) 'Skeletal muscle enzyme activity, fiber composition and VO_2 max in relation to distance running performance', *European Journal of Applied Physiology and Occupational Physiology* 39, 73–80.

Franch, J., Madsen, K., Djurhuus, M. S. and Pedersen, P. K. (1998) 'Improved running economy following intensified training correlates with reduced ventilatory demands', *Medicine and Science in Sports and Exercise* 30, 1250–6.

Fukunaga, T., Kubo, K., Kawakami, Y., Fukashiro, S., Kanehisa, H. and Maganaris C. N. (2001) '*In vivo* behaviour of human muscle tendon during walking', *Proceedings of the Royal Society of London, Series B, Biological Sciences* 268, 229–33.

Grant, S., Craig, I., Wilson, J. and Aitchison, T. (1997) The relationship between 3km running performance and selected physiological variables. *Journal of Sports Sciences* 15, 403–10.

Grassi, B., Marzorati, M., Kayser, B., Bordini, M., Colombini, A., Conti, M., Marconi, C. and Cerretelli, P. (1996) 'Peak blood lactate and blood lactate vs. workload during acclimatization to 5050m and in deacclimatization', *Journal of Applied Physiology* 80, 685–92.

Green, H. J., Ballantyne, C. S., MacDougall, J. D., Tarnopolsky, M. A. and Schertzer, J. D. (2003) 'Adaptations in human muscle sarcoplasmic reticulum to prolonged submaximal training', *Journal of Applied Physiology* 94, 2034–42.

Green, H., Roy, B., Grant, S., Burnett, M., Tupling, R., Otto, C., Pipe, A. and McKenzie, D. (2000) 'Downregulation in muscle Na^+-K^+-ATPase following a 21-day expedition to 6,194 m', *Journal of Applied Physiology* 88, 634–40.

Harms, C. A., Babcock, M. A., McClaran, S. R., Pegelow, D. F., Nickele, G. A., Nelson, W. B. and Dempsey, J. A. (1997) 'Respiratory muscle work compromises leg blood flow during maximal exercise', *Journal of Applied Physiology* 82, 1573–83.

Hawley, J. A. (2002) 'Adaptations of skeletal muscle to prolonged, intense endurance training', *Clinical and Experimental Pharmacology and Physiology* 29, 218–22.

He, Z. H., Bottinelli, R., Pellegrino, M. A., Ferenczi, M. A. and Reggiani, C. (2000) 'ATP consumption and efficiency of human single muscle fibers with different myosin isoform composition', *Biophysics Journal* 79, 945–61.

Hochachka, P. W., Stanley, C., Matheson, G. O., McKenzie, D. C., Allen, P. S. and Parkhouse, W. S. (1991) 'Metabolic and work efficiencies during exercise in Andean natives', *Journal of Applied Physiology* 70, 1720–30.

Holden, J. E., Stone, C. K., Clark, C. M., Brown, W. D., Nicles, J., Stanley, C. and Hochachka, P. W. (1995) 'Enhanced cardiac metabolism of plasma glucose in high altitude natives: adaptation against chronic hypoxia', *Journal of Applied Physiology* 79, 222–8.

Holloszy, J. O. and Coyle, E. F. (1984) 'Adaptations of skeletal muscle to endurance exercise and their metabolic consequences', *Journal of Applied Physiology* 56, 831–8.

Huijing, P. A. (1999) 'Muscle as a collagen fiber reinforced composite: a review of force transmission in muscle and whole limb', *Journal of Biomechanics* 32, 329–45.

Irrcher, I., Adhihetty, P. J., Joseph, A. M., Ljubicic, V. and Hood, D. A. (2003) 'Regulation of mitochondrial biogenesis in muscle by endurance exercise', *Sports Medicine* 33, 783–93.

Ito, M., Kawakami, Y., Ichinose, Y., Fukashiro, S. and Fukunaga, T. (1998) 'Nonisometric behaviour of fascicles during isometric contractions of a human muscle', *Journal of Applied Physiology* 85, 1230–5.

Katzmarzyk, P. T., Malina, R. M., Pérusse, L., Rice, T., Province, M. A., Rao, D. C. and Bouchard, C. (2000) 'Familial resemblance for physique: heritabilities for somatotype components', *Annals of Human Biology* 27, 467–77.

Kjæær, M. (2004) 'Role of extracellular matrix in adaptation of tendon and skeletal muscle to mechanical loading', *Physiological Review* 84, 649–98.

Kohn, T. A. (2005) 'Characteristics and adaptation of skeletal muscle to endurance training', unpublished Ph.D. thesis, Stellenbosch University.

Komi, P. V., Salonen, M., Jarvinen, M. and Kokko, O. (1987) 'In vivo registration of Achilles tendon forces in man. I. Methodological development', *International Journal of Sports Medicine* 8 Suppl. 1, 3–8.

Kyle, C. R. (1979) 'Reduction of wind resistance and power output of racing cyclists and runners traveling in groups', *Ergonomics* 22, 387–97.

Langberg, H., Skovgaard, D., Petersen, L. J., Bülow, J. and Kjær M. (1999) 'Type-1 collagen turnover in peritendinous connective tissue after exercise determined by microdialysis', *Journal of Physiology* 521, 299–306.

Larsen, H. B., Christensen, D. L., Nolan, T. and Sondergaard, H. (2004) 'Body dimensions, exercise capacity and physical activity level of adolescent Nandi boys in western Kenya', *Annals of Human Biology* 31, 159–73.

Lavebratt, C., Wahlqvist, S., Nordfors, L., Hoffstedt, J. and Arner, P. (2005) 'AHSG gene variant is associated with leanness among Swedish men', *Human Genetics* 117, 54–60.

Livshits, G., Roset, A., Yakovenko, K., Trofimov, S. and Kobyliansky, E. (2002) 'Genetics of human body size and shape: body proportions and indices', *Annals of Human Biology* 29, 271–89.

Maldonado, S., Mujika, I. and Padilla, S. (2002) 'Influence of body mass and height on the energy cost of running in highly trained middle- and long-distance runners', *International Journal of Sports Medicine* 23, 268–72.

Marino, F. E., Lambert, M. I. and Noakes, T. D. (2004) 'Superior performance of African runners in warm humid but not in cool environmental conditions', *Journal of Applied Physiology* 96, 124–30.

Marks, D. W., Robergs, R. A., Nelson, J., Vella, C., Bell-Wilson, J. and Apkarian, M. (2005) 'Oxygen cost of ventilation and its effect on the plateau', *Journal of Exercise Physiology Online* 8 (5), 1–13.

Mayer, U., Saher, G., Fässler, R., Bornemann, A., Echtermeyer, F., Von Der Mark, H., Miosge, N., Poschl, E. and Von Der Mark, K. (1997) 'Absence of integrin alpha7 causes a novel form of muscular dystrophy', *Nature Genetics* 17, 318–23.

Mujika, I. and Padilla, S. (2003) 'Scientific bases for precompetition tapering strategies', *Medicine and Science in Sports and Exercise* 35, 1182–7.

Myburgh, K. H. (2003) 'What makes an endurance athlete world-class? Not simply a physiological conundrum', *Comparative Biochemistry and Physiology – Part A: Molecular and Integrative Physiology* 136, 171–90.

Myburgh, K. H. (2004) 'Can any metabolites partially alleviate fatigue manifestations at the cross-bridge?' *Medicine and Science in Sports Exercise* 36, 20–7.

Noakes, T. D., Myburgh, K. H. and Schall, R. (1990) 'Peak treadmill running velocity during the max test predicts running performance', *Journal of Sports Sciences* 8, 35–45.

Paavolainen, L. M., Hakkinen, K., Hamalainen, I., Nummela, A. T. and Rusko, H. K. (1999) 'Explosive-strength training improves 5-km running time by improving running economy and muscle power', *Journal of Applied Physiology* 86, 1527–33.

Pugh, L. G. (1970) 'Oxygen intake in track and treadmill running with observations on the effect of air resistance', *Journal of Physiology* 207, 823–35.

Roberts, A. C., Butterfield, G. E., Cymerman, A., Reeves, J. T., Wolfel, E. E. and Brooks, G. A. (1996) 'Acclimatization to 4300m altitude decreases reliance on fat as a substrate', *Journal of Applied Physiology* 81, 1762–71.

Roth, S. M., Metter, E. J., Lee, M. R., Hurley, B. F. and Ferrell, R. E. (2003) 'C174T polymorphism in the CNTF receptor gene is associated with fat-free mass in men and women', *Journal of Applied Physiology* 95, 1425–30.

Rupert, J. L. (2003) 'The search for genotypes that underlie human performance phenotypes', *Comparative Biochemistry and Physiology – Part A: Molecular and Integrative Physiology* 136, 191–203.

Ryschon, T. W., Fowler, M. D., Wysong, R. E., Anthony, A. and Balaban, R. S. (1997) 'Efficiency of human skeletal muscle *in vivo*: comparison of isometric, concentric, and eccentric muscle action', *Journal of Applied Physiology* 83, 867–74.

Saltin, B., Kim, C. K., Terrados, N., Larsen, H., Svedenhag, J. and Rolf, C. J. (1995a) 'Morphology, enzyme activities and buffer capacity in leg muscles of Kenyan and Scandinavian runners', *Scandinavian Journal of Medicine and Science in Sports* 5, 222–30.

Saltin, B., Larsen, H., Terrados, N., Bangsbo, J., Bak, T., Kim, C. K., Svedenhag, J. and Rolf, C. J. (1995b) 'Aerobic exercise capacity at sea level and at altitude in Kenyan boys, junior and senior runners compared with Scandinavian runners', *Scandinavian Journal of Medicine and Science in Sports* 5, 209–21.

Sanchez-Andres, A. (1995) 'Genetic and environmental influences on somatotype components: family study in a Spanish population', *Human Biology* 67, 727–38.

Saunders, P. U., Pyne,D. B., Telford, R. D. and Hawley, J. A. (2004) 'Factors affecting running economy in trained distance runners', *Sports Medicine* 34, 465–85.

Scoggin, C. H., Doekel, R. D., Kryger, M. H., Zwillich, C. W. and Weil, J. V. (1978) 'Familial aspects of decreased hypoxic drive in endurance athletes', *Journal of Applied Physiology* 44, 464–8.

Scott, R. A., Georgiades, E., Wilson, R. H., Goodwin, W. H., Wolde, B. and Pitsiladis, Y. P. (2003) 'Demographic characteristics of elite Ethiopian endurance runners', *Medicine and Science in Sports and Exercise* 35, 1727–32.

Sharma, K., Byard, P. J., Russell, J. M. and Rao, D. C. (1984) 'A family study of anthropometric traits in a Punjabi community: I. Introduction and familial correlations', *American Journal of Physical Anthropology* 63, 389–95.

Sjödin, B. andSvedenhag, J. (1985) 'Applied physiology of marathon running', *Sports Medicine* 2, 83–99.

Staron, R. S. (1997) 'Human skeletal muscle fiber types: delineation, development, and distribution', *Canadian Journal of Applied Physiology* 22, 307–327.

Svedenhag, J. (2000) 'Running economy', in Bangsbo, J., Larsen, H. (eds) *Running and Science*, Copenhagen: Munksgaard, pp. 85–105.

Taylor, C. R. (1994) 'Relating energetics and mechanics during exercise', in Jones, J. (ed.) *Comparative Vertebrate Exercise Physiology: Unifying Physiological Principles*, San Diego, CA: Academic, pp. 181–215.

Thomas, D. Q., Fernhall, B. and Grant, H. (1999) 'Changes in running economy during a 5-km run in trained men and women runners', *Journal of Strength and Conditioning Research* 13, 162–7.

Trotter, J. A. (1993) 'Functional morphology of force transmission in skeletal muscle', *Acta Anatomica* 146, 205–22.

Trotter, J. A., Purslow, P. P. (1992) 'Functional morphology of the endomysium in series fibered muscles', *Journal of Morphology* 212, 109–22.

Vogler, G. P., Sorensen, T. I., Stunkard, A. J., Srinivasan, M. R. and Rao, D. C. (1995) 'Influences of genes and shared family environment on adult body mass index assessed in an adoption study by a comprehensive path model', *International Journal of Obesity Related Metabolic Disorders* 19, 40–5.

Weston, A. R., Karamizrak, O., Smith, A., Noakes, T. D. and Myburgh, K. H. (1999) 'African runners exhibit greater fatigue resistance, lower lactate accumulation, and higher oxidative enzyme activity', *Journal of Applied Physiology* 86, 915–23.

Weston, A. R., Mbambo, Z. and Myburgh, K. H. (2000) 'Running economy of African and Caucasian distance runners', *Medicine and Science in Sports and Exercise* 32, 1130–4.

Williams, K. R. and Cavanagh, P. R. (1987) 'Relationship between distance running mechanics, running economy, and performance', *Journal of Applied Physiology* 63, 1236–45.

Chapter 10

Studies of physiological and neuromuscular function of black South African distance runners

Yolande Harley and Timothy D. Noakes

Introduction

Black athletes of African origin display a distinct athletic superiority in international running events of varying distances. This phenomenon is also apparent in South Africa, where the performance of black long-distance runners dominates the performance of athletes from other ethnic backgrounds. As with the remarkable achievements of east and north African runners, the disproportionate success of black South African (SA) runners, compared to runners of other ethnicities, suggests that they could enjoy certain physiological advantages for endurance performance. However, the nature of any such advantages remains obscure. By investigating and describing performance-related traits specific to black SA runners, we can begin to identify the reasons for this African running phenomenon, both within South Africa and globally. In addition, identifying specific characteristics that are associated with distance running performance in these athletes may elucidate which physiological factors are central to endurance ability in general, ethnic considerations aside.

Scientists investigating athletic performance employ hypotheses, or models, when interpreting their collected data. By applying these models to our findings, we attempt to unravel the meanings hidden within the figures. However, the preconceptions inherent in these models can unduly influence the interpretation of the scientific results and will always bias the conclusions. World-renowned architect Frank Lloyd Wright held that 'The truth is more important than the facts'. Yet the truths we seek as scientists are always concealed. Hence we must objectively contend with the facts, and attempt not to betray the truth with biased assumptions. This acknowledged, hypothesis and speculation have an important role in science, when undertaken with a prudent and analytical approach.

A prevailing model or paradigm of the factors believed to determine long-distance running performance has been termed the A.V. Hill Cardiovascular/ Anaerobic/Catastrophic model (Noakes 2000; Noakes and St Clair 2004). This model posits that exercise performance is ultimately determined by the capacity of the athlete's heart to pump as large a volume of blood as is possible to the exercising muscles. The maximal functional capacity of the heart then establishes ('limits') the maximal amount of oxygen that the exercising muscles are able to consume. This value for the maximum rate at which oxygen can be taken up and used by the body during exercise is known as the maximum oxygen consumption ($\dot{V}O_2$ max) (Brooks et al. 2000). Since, according to this model, it is the rate of oxygen consumption by the exercising muscles that determines their capacity to produce force, so it must be that the best athletes will be those whose muscles receive and then consume the greatest volumes of oxygen during exercise. In this model, an inadequate supply of oxygen to the muscles during exercise causes an accumulation of metabolites, such as hydrogen ions, in the exercising muscle. This accumulation then causes localized muscle fatigue and ultimately the termination of exercise (Noakes and St Clair 2004).

Since the fatigue mechanisms described by this model are restricted to the muscle, they exclude the possibility that any non-muscular factors may influence or limit endurance performance. Yet, as there are a multitude of physiological, biomechanical, neural and psychological factors involved in any endurance activity, it follows that multiple factors may well be involved in determining or 'limiting' endurance performance. The candidate physiological variables that we wish to consider and which could play a role in limiting endurance performance are not only numerous, they are also diverse, ranging from mechanisms related to oxygen supply, metabolite accumulation and muscle contractility, to substrate availability and neural drive (Enoka and Stuart 1992; Fitts 1994; Brooks et al. 2000). In a similar manner to the Cardiovascular/Anaerobic/Catastrophic model, other fatigue models have been proposed and all adopt a reductionist approach in an attempt to isolate a single factor, or small number of related factors, as the sole limit to endurance performance. While there is undoubtedly some value in all of these reductionist models, the view that a solitary variable, or a few variables, can wholly account for inter-individual differences in athletic performance is questionable. For if individual physiological variables cannot account for the complex metabolic behaviour that occurs during physical activity (St Clair Gibson and Noakes 2004), it is unlikely that a single factor can account for fatigue or for variations in endurance performance (Bergh et al. 2000; Brooks et al. 2000). Indeed, although many studies have attempted to describe a single factor as the cause of fatigue (Enoka and Stuart 1992), this 'cardinal exercise stopper' has never been identified (Gandevia 2001) despite a century of study. In contrast, the remarkable feature of humans is their ability to maintain physiological and metabolic homeostasis without evidence of biological failure during exercise under diverse, demanding stresses (Noakes and St Clair 2004). Therefore, in all probability, inter-individual variations in performance are the product of many factors, involving multiple physiological processes and many different mechanisms, none of which is the exclusive 'limiting' factor (Enoka and Stuart 1992; Fitts 1994; Brooks et al. 2000).

If it is accepted that numerous interacting physiological and biomechanical variables are active during fatiguing exercise, then the integration and control of these mechanisms will be central to endurance performance. Fatigue during exercise involves both descending signals from the central nervous system (CNS) to the periphery, as well as ascending signals to the CNS from the periphery. In addition to any local effects in initiating fatigue, tissue-specific and circulating metabolic variables can act as signallers of physiological change, stimulating feedback from the tissues or the circulation to the CNS (Lambert *et al.* 2005; St Clair Gibson and Noakes 2004). While the metabolic and neural variables from the different physiological systems may interact directly with each other, the information they convey may also be integrated in the CNS. This would allow a role for the brain in the regulation of endurance performance, as postulated in the recently described Central Governor Model of Exercise Physiology.

The Central Governor Model posits that the brain regulates exercise performance by quantitatively and qualitatively altering motor unit recruitment in order to insure an optimum performance without risking the health of either the brain or the body (Noakes 2000; Noakes and St Clair 2004; Noakes *et al.* 2004a; St Clair Gibson and Noakes 2004). For example, this model proposes that the brains of elite long-distance runners will drive their muscles to contract in such a way that they will run as fast as possible for the given distance, without causing any permanent physical harm. By receiving physiological information from the rest of the body and integrating it with other information from within the CNS, as well as information from the environment and from memories of prior activity, the brain can subconsciously and consciously alter neural drive to the muscles, and hence alter exercise performance. This model can explain a range of observed phenomena in endurance exercise, such as the classical 'end spurt' (Catalano 1974; Kay *et al.* 2001) in which athletes speed-up near the end of races of distances from 1–42 km or longer (Noakes and St Clair 2004). This phenomenon cannot, however, be explained by the traditional A.V. Hill Cardiovascular/Anaerobic/Catastrophic model (Noakes and St Clair 2004), or indeed by any other model which posits that fatigue is due to progressive failure of peripheral, skeletal muscle function.

The data from SA runners presented here will therefore be discussed with these models in mind. As described earlier, our belief is that multiple physiological and biomechanical systems work in concert to regulate the functioning of the body during exercise. We have examined certain factors from some of these systems in our studies of SA runners. These will be discussed in the appropriate sections of this review, with each section summarizing the findings relevant to the different physiological systems. The number of physiological factors that could be involved in determining any possible ethnic differences in running ability is potentially vast, hence the research described will be incomplete. Consequently, this review will not comprehensively examine each of the physiological systems potentially involved in any ethnic differences in endurance performance, but will rather highlight aspects from each system that have been studied. The goal will be to illustrate how various factors may all play a role in explaining this African running phenomenon and how these factors are likely to function in an integrated manner during fatiguing endurance activity. Potentially relevant anthropometric, cardiorespiratory, biomechanical, metabolic, neuro-muscular and central nervous system factors have been examined and the inte-gration of these factors will be discussed. The potential importance of genetic, nutritional, psychological, social and environmental factors in determining ethnic differences in running ability is acknowledged but are beyond the scope of either our expertise or our current research findings.

Our studies of black SA runners have used white SA runners of nearly similar performance levels as the comparison group. It is acknowledged that the classification of the ethnic groups or races on genetic or physiological grounds is a hotly disputed concept and beyond the focus of this article. We are however partial to the belief that the concept of race is an unfortunate socio-political construct that should be abandoned as a matter of global priority. We recognize, however, that prolonged exposure over centuries to unique environmental influ-ences in specific geological areas might produce unusual biological adaptations that could favour performance in one area of human endeavour, for example long-distance running. However, individuals with such an adaptation do not necessarily belong to a separate human 'race'.

Thus for the purposes of this chapter, the 'black South African' runners in our studies were males living in the Western Cape of South Africa, of Southern African descent, with the majority being descended from the Xhosa tribe. The 'white South African' runners were Caucasian males living in the Western Cape of South Africa, of European descent (including English, Scottish, Irish, German and Dutch). The terms 'black' and 'white' will be used for the sake of brevity during the rest of this review.

The 'ethnic' studies that will be discussed include those of Bosch et al. (1990) (n = 19), Coetzer et al. (1993) (n = 20), Weston et al. (1999, 2000) (n = 17 and n = 16, respectively), Marino et al. (2004) (n = 12) and Harley et al. (unpublished data; n = 32). While all of these studies compared black to white SA runners, they matched them differently. Coetzer et al. (1993) examined elite black and white runners. As a result, they selected runners who were matched for their race times over distances of 1 to 5 km, but whose performances were very different over longer distances. This was necessary because it is impossible to match the fastest black runners over longer distances to white runners as there are currently few, if any, white SA runners who can perform at an equiva-lent level. The other studies instead compared sub-elite black and white runners (Bosch et al. 1990; Weston et al. 1999; Weston et al. 2000; Marino et al. 2004; Harley et al. unpublished data). Bosch et al. (1990) matched runners for their best marathon times, while Weston et al. (1999, 2000) and Harley et al. (unpublished data) matched runners for best 10 km times. It has been suggested that any differences between groups should be apparent at the sub-elite, as well as the elite level, as black runners also dominate white runners at this level of performance (Bosch et al. 1990). The findings of these studies will be discussed in the context of the physiological system with which these findings are associated.

Body composition and heat loss

The body composition, or anthropometrical make-up of a runner can influence his or her distance-running ability (Tanaka and Matsuura 1982; Berg *et al.* 1998). The phenotype considered to be advantageous for performance in endurance running is one with low body mass, small stature and low body fat content, as well as low endomorphy and high ectomorphy (Bale *et al.* 1986; Noakes 1998). Anthropometrical differences occur between ethnic groups (Schutte *et al.* 1984; Hortobagyi *et al.* 1992; Nindl *et al.* 1998). However, the anthropometrical phenotype of individuals of any ethnicity depends on their ancestral geographical origin. The ancestry of black north (African) Americans, for example, is likely to stem from west Africa. In general west African athletes perform well in power sports and have a different anthropometrical phenotype to black east Africans or South Africans, who are smaller, lighter and more ectomorphic and who generally perform well in endurance sports (Noakes 1998).

The various research studies that have examined anthropometrical differences between sub-elite and elite black and white SA runners show fairly consistent findings. The most striking, and perhaps most obvious, discovery is that the black runners are always shorter (by approximately 10–15 cm) and lighter (by approximately 10–15 kg) than the white runners (Bosch *et al.* 1990; Coetzer *et al.* 1993; Weston *et al.* 1999; Harley *et al.* unpublished data). This also appears to be the case for sedentary black and white South Africans (Durandt 1995), and hence is likely to be an ethnic disparity that occurs in South African men, ranging from those who are inactive to those of elite athlete status. This phenotypic difference can be detected from an early age. Whether or not this difference is determined genetically or by early environmental influences, in particular by nutrition during infancy and adolescence, is presently unknown.

A smaller body mass may be advantageous during endurance activity as lighter runners have a lower metabolic rate (Dennis and Noakes 1999), and hence produce less heat when running at the same speed than do heavier runners. As a result they can more easily maintain a lower body temperature during exercise. This is advantageous since the rise in body temperature can be a limiting factor during exercise (Dennis and Noakes 1999; Kay and Marino 2000; Marino 2002). The benefits of a smaller body size appear to be important mainly when endurance exercise is performed in a hot, wet environment (Marino *et al.* 2000). Indeed, Marino *et al.* (2000) found that the extent of heat storage was positively correlated with body mass in athletes when running at 35 °C, only moderately correlated at 25 °C, and was unrelated at 15 °C. They suggested that, compared to heavier runners, lighter runners produce and store less heat at the same running speed and hence can run faster or further before reaching a limiting rectal temperature. In agreement with this, Dennis and Noakes (Dennis and Noakes 1999) calculated that an athlete of 50 kg would be able to maintain thermal homeostasis when running at 20 km·hr^{-1} in hot, humid conditions whereas an athlete of 65 kg would be able to maintain the same thermal balance only when running at about 16 km·hr^{-1}. Therefore, runners with a lower body mass appear to have a thermal advantage when running in conditions in which heat-dissipation mechanisms are unable to optimize heat loss in adverse environmental conditions.

However, what is the case in cooler conditions, in which thermoregulatory mechanisms are not as challenged? Marino et al. (2004) studied highly trained black and white runners exercising in hot and cool environments. They found that the black athletes ran faster than the white runners during an 8 km time trial in the heated condition (35°C). The black runners had lower relative rates of heat production and lower sweat rates compared to the white runners during this trial, but rectal temperatures were not different between groups. In contrast, performances were the same when the time trial was run in the cool condition (15°C). This suggests that the thermal advantages resulting from the smaller body mass of the black runners is unlikely to account for 'ethnic' differences in running performances in cool conditions.

Bosch et al. (1990) measured changes in skin and rectal temperature in black and white SA runners during a 42 km simulated marathon run on a laboratory treadmill in a thermoneutral environment. They found that the black runners had significantly higher pectoral skin temperatures than the white runners and were able to run at a higher percentage of $\dot{V}O_2$ max, and hence a higher exercise intensity, for the duration of the simulated marathon. Rectal temperatures were insignificantly lower in the black athletes throughout the run. Therefore, the black runners had the capacity to maintain higher skin temperatures and lower rectal temperatures, despite running at a higher relative exercise intensity (Figure 10.1). Maintaining a higher skin temperature would increase the potential for convective (skin to circulating air) heat losses, reducing the necessity to sweat as much when running in the heat. This would be advantageous during very prolonged exercise in the heat if no fluid is available to replace those sweat losses.

It is notable, for example, that the Khoi-San peoples of Southern Africa still hunt large antelope to their exhaustion by chasing the antelope for four or more hours in the midday heat whilst ingesting little if any fluid. Some believe that the ability to sweat and therefore to regulate the body temperature homoeostatically below some 'critical' value (Gonzalez-Alonso et al. 1999; Nielsen et al. 1997; Nybo and Nielsen 2001; Nybo and Secher 2004) provided humans with a significant biological advantage since they became able to chase non-sweating mammals in the heat until those mammals became incapacitated as a result of overheating (Heinrich 2001). Indeed, the ability to perform prolonged exercise in a waterless environment whilst sweating just enough to maintain a sub-critical body temperature would clearly be of substantial survival value since it

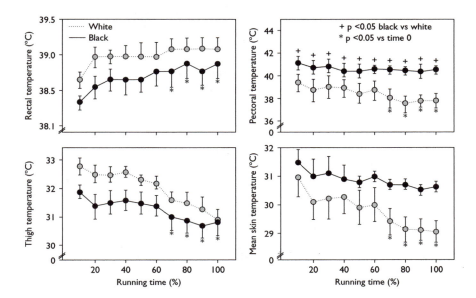

Figure 10.1   Bosch *et al.* (1990) found that black athletes maintained lower rectal (upper left panel) and thigh (bottom left panel) but higher pectoral and mean skin temperatures than did matched white runners when running at the same % of their best marathon pace in a simulated 42 km marathon on a laboratory treadmill. Since the rectal temperature is a variable that influences exercise performance, this ability of black runners to maintain a lower rectal temperature when running at the same running speed may provide a biological advantage.

would allow more exercise to be performed without developing a critical water deficit (Schmidt-Nielsen 1964; Schmidt-Nielsen 1972) (see Chapter 6). If the black runners in the study of Bosch *et al.* (1990) were indeed able to maintain higher skin temperatures and lower rectal temperatures than white athletes, this could provide a performance advantage by allowing a faster running speed to be maintained in self-paced activity in the heat (Marino *et al.* 2004), since it is known that exercise terminates when a particular rectal temperature (>40–41°C) is achieved (Gonzalez-Alonso *et al.* 1999; Nielsen *et al.* 1997; Nybo and Nielsen 2001; Nybo and Secher 2004).

Differences other than height and body mass have been observed between black and white SA runners. While percentage body fat measurements do not differ greatly between elite athletes of either ethnic group (Weston *et al.* 1999; Harley *et al.* unpublished data), black SA runners were found to have a significantly lower sum of skinfolds value than white runners (Coetzer *et al.* 1993; Harley *et al.* unpublished data). Other measures of body fat content could differ between groups as a result of possible variations in the density of the fat-free mass between ethnic groups since that density will affect body fat equations (Nindl et al. 1998). In addition, Bosch et al. (1990) noted a difference in fat patterning between black and white SA runners, which could also have affected these fat calculations. Whatever the cause of this discrepancy, however, the lesser subcutaneous body fat, as measured by the sum of skinfolds in the black athletes, could confer an advantage since any excess fat weight is an encumbrance that will hamper performance in a weight-bearing activity like long-distance running.

Although body fat content may be lower in black athletes, mesomorphy and the percentage of body muscle were greater in black compared to white SA runners (Harley et al. unpublished data). In addition, the black runners also had a significantly higher ratio of lean thigh volume to lean body mass than did the white runners, suggesting that the thighs of the black runners were larger or more muscular relative to the rest of their bodies compared to those of the white runners. This could be advantageous during high intensity running in which the prime muscle group involved in running is unusually large, relative to the athletes' body mass.

In summary, the anthropometrical phenotype of a distance runner can influence his or her performance. Differences in anthropometrical characteristics exist between black and white SA runners, which could well be related to differences in their distance running ability. Ethnic differences in body composition are therefore likely to play a role in the exceptional international running achievements of black African runners.

Cardiorespiratory factors

During exercise, an increase in oxygen and fuel consumption is necessary to meet the demands of the increased metabolic rate. The cardiovascular and respiratory systems must therefore operate and be regulated in an integrated manner during physical activity in order to meet the oxygen and substrate needs of the active tissue, while removing CO_2, metabolic waste products and heat. There are multiple cardiorespiratory regulatory mechanisms to control these metabolic changes, and efficient functioning of the cardiorespiratory system during exercise could, together with other factors, result in superior endurance performance (Coyle 1999).

Cardiorespiratory research in the exercise sciences has grown exponentially since the early experiments of A.V. Hill and colleagues in the 1920s. The potential role of cardiorespiratory factors in determining endurance performance has been more intensively studied than any other physiological factors. As a result of this research, various cardiorespiratory factors have been linked to endurance performance. In addition, reports of ethnic differences in cardiorespiratory-related variables suggest that cardiorespiratory factors could play a pivotal role in the observed differences in distance-running performance between ethnic groups (Bosch et al. 1990; Coetzer et al. 1993; Saltin et al. 1995b; Noakes 1998; Weston et al. 2000; Harley et al. unpublished data).

Oxygen consumption ($\dot{V}O_2$) increases with increasing workload during exercise. Maximal oxygen consumption, or $\dot{V}O_2$ max as described earlier, is generally considered to be an index of cardiorespiratory, circulatory and muscular fitness (Noakes et al. 2001). Indeed, $\dot{V}O_2$ max has been shown to have a significant association with endurance performance, and can be improved with training (Foster et al. 1978; Noakes et al. 1990; Morgan et al. 1995; Foster et al. 2001). The determinants of $\dot{V}O_2$ max are still debated, with the pump capacity of the heart, oxygen uptake by the lungs, blood oxygen transport and skeletal muscle factors all considered to play a role (di Prampero 1985; di Prampero and Ferretti 1990; Saltin and Strange 1992). Superior running economy, defined as a low $\dot{V}O_2$ max at any particular exercise intensity, may also be beneficial to endurance running (Noakes et al. 1990; Morgan et al. 1995). Thus it has been proposed that running success may, to a large part, be determined by $\dot{V}O_2$ max, running economy, and the ability to utilize a large fraction of $\dot{V}O_2$ max during competition (Costill et al. 1971).

Cardiovascular 'fitness' can be affected by ethnicity (Farrell et al. 1987; Pivarnik et al. 1995). In a study of elite Kenyan and Scandinavian endurance runners, Saltin et al. (1995b) reported that group $\dot{V}O_2$ max values were not significantly different. However, running economy was different between the two groups, with the oxygen cost at a given running speed being lower in the Kenyans than the Scandinavians, particularly at higher running speeds. The explanation for the superior Kenyan running economy, however, was not clear. Similarly, several studies have compared oxygen consumption in elite and sub-elite black and white SA runners (Bosch et al. 1990; Coetzer et al. 1993; Weston et al. 1999; Weston et al. 2000; Harley et al. unpublished data). The cardiorespiratory differences found between black and white SA runners in those studies are summarized in Table 10.1.

Bosch et al. (1990), Coetzer et al. (1993), Weston et al. (1999), Marino et al. (2004) and Harley et al. (unpublished data) all reported no difference in $\dot{V}O_2$ max between black and white SA runners. Most of those studies also found no inter-group differences for peak treadmill running velocity (Coetzer et al. 1993; Weston et al. 1999; Marino et al. 2004; Harley et al. unpublished data). Therefore, while $\dot{V}O_2$ max has been described as one of the main determinants of endurance performance (Costill 1967; Saltin and Åstrand 1967; Wyndham et al. 1969; Foster et al. 1978), disparities in $\dot{V}O_2$ max are unlikely to account for differences in performance between black and white SA runners. Similarly, although peak treadmill running velocity (PTRV) is a good predictor of field-based running performance (Noakes et al. 1990; Scott and Houmard 1994; Weston et al. 1999), there were no inter-group differences in this test even though there were inter-group differences in competitive running performance.

In the studies described above, the two ethnic groups were not usually matched for body mass due to natural size differences that occur between the groups. Weston et al. (2000), however, matched black and white SA runners for 10 km race time and for body mass and found lower $\dot{V}O_2$ max values in the black

Table 10.1 Cardiorespiratory comparison of black and white South African runners: summary of the data from Bosch et al. 1990, Coetzer et al. 1993, Weston et al. 1999, Weston et al. 2000, Marino et al. 2004 and Harley et al. (unpublished data)

Measurement	Bosch (1990)	Coetzer (1993)	Weston (1999)	Weston (2000)	Marino (2004)	Harley (unpub)
PTV	B < W	B = W	B = W	B = W	B = W	B = W
$\dot{V}O_2$max	B = W	B = W	B = W	B < W	B = W	B = W
Fractional $\dot{V}O_2$ utilisation	B > W	B > W	ND	B > W	ND	ND
Running economy	ND	B = W	ND	B > W	ND	B ≥ W
Fatigue resistance	ND	B > W	B > W	ND	B ≥ W	B > W
Peak RER	B = W	B < W	B = W	B = W	ND	B = W
Submax RER	B > W	B = W	B = W	B = W	ND	B = W
Peak HR	B = W	ND	B = W	B > W	ND	B = W
Submax HR	ND	ND	B = W	B ≥ W	B < W	B ≤ W

Note: ≤ and ≥ indicate that more than one similar measurement was made (e.g. at different exercise intensities) and only one/some were significantly different between groups. ND: not determined; $\dot{V}O_2$max: maximal oxygen consumption; PTV: peak treadmill velocity; RER: respiratory exchange ratio; HR: heart rate. Fatigue resistance: time to fatigue during running (Weston et al. 1999) and isometric quadriceps contraction (Coetzer et al. 1993; Harley unpublished data).

athletes. This finding that the black athletes were able to achieve the same performance in 10 km races as their white counterparts despite having a lower maximal oxygen uptake, suggests that $\dot{V}O_2$ max is not the only determinant of running performance, at least over 10 km. This finding also suggests that the similarity in $\dot{V}O_2$ max between black and white runners found in the other studies could be due to the subjects not being matched for body mass. As the study by Weston et al. (2000) is the only one to have matched for body mass, however, further research including an ethnic comparison with black and white runners matched for body mass is recommended before final conclusions regarding the relationship between $\dot{V}O_2$ max and ethnicity are drawn. But whether this finding of a lower $\dot{V}O_2$ max in black African athletes is real or not, it is unlikely to account for the observed superior performance of black African athletes (Noakes 1998), considering that a relatively low $\dot{V}O_2$max is considered disadvantageous for endurance performance.

The finding that the superiority of black African athletes is not primarily due to a greater capacity to consume oxygen is perhaps predictable for other reasons. Athletes can sustain exercise intensities eliciting 100% of their $\dot{V}O_2$ max values only over racing distances of 1–2 km (Noakes et al. 2004b). Yet it is not at these distances that the superiority of African runners in international competition is most evident. Rather, if the Africans' success were to be due solely to unusually high $\dot{V}O_2$ max values, one would expect these runners to be substantially better than runners of other ethnic origins also at 1500 m (or the mile). This is not the case; historically, the mile was dominated by Caucasians, especially runners from Scandanavia, Great Britain and the Commonwealth. More recently, north African runners from Algeria and Morocco have shown superior ability at this distance.

As mentioned earlier, superior running economy is beneficial to performance in endurance running (Costill et al. 1971; Noakes et al. 1990; Morgan et al. 1995). The level of oxygen utilized at a certain exercise intensity indicates the metabolic cost to the individual performing that exercise. If one athlete has a lower metabolic cost than another athlete at a particular workload, he/she is exercising more economically than the other athlete. Black SA runners consume less oxygen, and hence have a superior running economy, at higher running speeds (14–16 km·hr^{-1}) than white SA runners (Weston et al. 2000; Harley et al. unpublished data) (Figure 10.2). There may be many causes for this superior running economy in the black runners, including biomechanical differences, stride parameter differences, variations in neuromuscular recruitment or elastic energy utilization, and differences in muscle metabolism, including different uses of fuels or metabolic pathways.

In addition to a superior running economy, black SA runners are able to run at a higher percentage of max, that is, they can sustain a higher fractional utilization of their $\dot{V}O_2$ max than can white runners over racing distances greater than 5 km (Bosch et al. 1990) (Figure 10.3) (Coetzer et al. 1993; Weston et al. 2000). This would partly explain why black African runners can outperform white runners despite having a similar $\dot{V}O_2$ max.

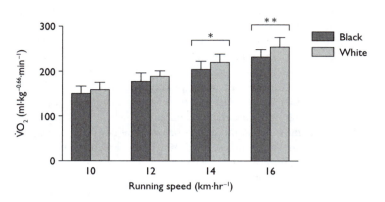

Figure 10.2 Harley *et al.* (unpublished data) found that oxygen consumption was lower in black compared to white SA runners at higher submaximal running speeds (14–16 km·hr⁻¹), demonstrating a greater running economy in the black runners. *p<0.05; **p<0.01.

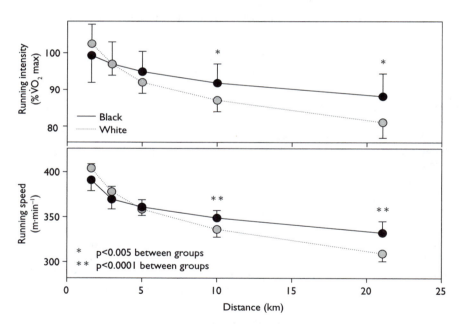

Figure 10.3 The study of Coetzer *et al.* (1993) found that elite black athletes were able to sustain a significantly higher percentage of their V̇O2 max than were white runners when running races longer than 5 km. This indicates that these athletes have superior fatigue resistance. Figure reprinted from Coetzer *et al.* (1993). Reprinted with permission.

Ethnic differences in fractional $\dot{V}O_2$ utilization and running economy may also help explain the observed differences in 'fatigue resistance' observed between the groups. For example, Weston *et al.* (1999) found that the time to fatigue during a submaximal running test was different between black and white SA runners, with the black runners continuing to exercise for 21% longer than the white runners. Fatigue resistance has been described as a 'crucial' element of distance running (Noakes 1998). Interestingly, this greater fatigue resistance in the black runners has also been observed during isometric activity of isolated muscle groups (Coetzer *et al.* 1993; Harley *et al.* unpublished data), and this will be discussed further in the section reviewing 'Neuromuscular factors'.

In order to sustain the increase in muscle oxygen consumption during exercise, there must be an equivalent increase in oxygen delivery to the exercising muscles. Ventilation and cardiac output therefore increase to meet the additional oxygen needs of the exercising muscles. The increase in heart rate (HR) is the major determinant of the increase in cardiac output during moderate to maximal exercise. Stroke volume increases with increasing exercise intensity to enhance blood flow and therefore oxygen transport to the tissues where it is needed (Brooks *et al.* 2000). The respiratory exchange ratio (RER), or the ratio of the volume of CO_2 produced to the volume of O_2 consumed per unit of time, provides a guide for estimating the nutrient mixture catabolized for energy, particularly the relative quantities of carbohydrate and fat. The RER increases with increasing exercise intensity (McArdle *et al.* 2002) indicating an increasing reliance on carbohydrate metabolism. Research comparing HR and RER values between black and white SA runners has not established any significant differences (see Table 10.1).

Thus most studies have reported no difference for peak HR or peak RER between black and white SA runners (Bosch *et al.* 1990; Weston *et al.* 1999; Weston *et al.* 2000; Harley *et al.* unpublished data). This suggests that there are also no inter-group differences in the maximal attainable HR or in fuel utilization when exercising maximally. Interestingly, Weston *et al.* (2000) found a higher peak HR in the black athletes despite a lower $\dot{V}O_2$ max. The black SA runners in that study also had a higher HR than the white runners when running at their 10 km race pace, suggesting that the black runners were running at a higher relative intensity than were the white runners (Weston *et al.* 2000). This may be related to the higher fractional utilization of $\dot{V}O_2$ reported in black SA runners, as discussed earlier (Bosch *et al.* 1990; Coetzer *et al.* 1993; Weston *et al.* 2000). Similarly, black runners have lower relative HR when running at high submaximal exercise intensities, which reflects their lower oxygen consumption (greater running economy) at these speeds (Marino *et al.* 2004; Harley *et al.* unpublished data). In contrast, most studies have not reported differences in RER between black and white SA runners at submaximal exercise intensities (Coetzer *et al.* 1993; Weston *et al.* 1999; Weston *et al.* 2000; Harley *et al.* unpublished data). This suggests that the fuel metabolism of the two ethnic groups is similar during exercise.

It is interesting to note that the ethnic differences in running economy and submaximal HR were apparent at the higher (14 km·hr^{-1} and above), but not always at the lower exercise intensities (Weston et al. 2000) (Marino et al. 2004; Harley et al. unpublished data). These physiological differences between the ethnic groups therefore seem to be operating at the high running intensities, similar to those achieved in competition. This phenomenon of ethnic physiological differences at high exercise intensities may not be restricted to South African runners. Saltin et al. (1995b) also found that elite Kenyan runners had a superior running economy than Scandinavian runners at high, but not at low running speeds.

In summary, measures of $\dot{V}O_2$ max, maximal HR and maximal RER showed no differences between black and white SA runners. In contrast, there were significant differences in fractional utilization of $\dot{V}O_2$ max, running economy and HR at higher (competitive) submaximal exercise intensities, with the black runners demonstrating a greater economy, or efficiency, than the white runners.

It therefore appears that, with respect to cardiorespiratory factors, it is their running economy, rather than their maximal capacity, that distinguishes black from white SA runners. This suggests that the Cardiovascular/Anaerobic/Catastrophic model cannot explain the exceptional performance of black African distance runners. Instead, further sources for the superior running economy of the black runners should be sought. It is not presently clear where the physiological or biomechanical origins of this greater running economy lie. This will be discussed subsequently.

Intramuscular factors

Technological advances over the course of the latter half of the twentieth century have allowed the study of intramuscular factors such as muscle protein contents, substrate levels and fibre composition, using biochemical and histochemical techniques (Bergstrom 1962; Bergstrom and Hultman 1966; Evans et al. 1982; Hamilton and Booth 2000). Although relatively little muscle biochemistry research has been conducted on African distance runners until now, this knowledge can be increased with recent developments and knowledge in muscle physiology.

During prolonged exercise, fatigue is evident in the muscle as a reduced contractile ability, associated with decreases in muscle tension, power and shortening velocity (Fitts 1996). Endurance training allows athletes to slow the effects of fatigue via altering various factors in the muscle. For example, muscle fibre composition alters with training (Howald et al. 1985) and the concentrations of muscle proteins, such as muscle monocarboxylate transporter proteins (Dubouchaud et al. 2000), also alter. These training-induced alterations can increase the oxidative capacity of the muscle, allowing for a greater aerobic energy metabolism (Howald et al. 1985) and potentially a performance advantage. In a similar way, differences in muscle fibre composition between ethnic groups could yield a variation in performance ability.

With the fatigue that occurs during prolonged exercise, there are changes in the concentrations of metabolites associated with muscle contraction (Masuda et al. 1999). These changes can affect the fatigue process either directly within the muscle or via sensory afferent feedback to the spinal cord and brain. Changes in the muscular concentrations of metabolites such as calcium, hydrogen, lactate, sodium and potassium can influence the contractile process (Fitts 1996; Masuda et al. 1999). Lactate is involved in whole body metabolism and the metabolic communication between tissues (Halestrap and Price 1999), and functions also as a metabolic intermediate that provides a means for distributing carbohydrate potential energy for oxidation and gluconeogenesis (Stainsby and Brooks 1990; Brooks 1991; Brooks 1998). Lactate flux in the muscle and blood may affect the development of fatigue, hence performance during endurance exercise, by influencing the rate of glycolysis, by altering the supply of lactate as a respiratory fuel and by altering the muscle pH.

Consistently it has been found that black SA distance runners have lower exercising blood or plasma lactate concentrations than white SA runners (Bosch et al. 1990; Coetzer et al. 1993; Weston et al. 1999; Harley et al. unpublished data), as shown in Table 10.2. Similarly, Saltin et al. (1995b) found that blood lactate concentrations were lower in elite Kenyan than Scandinavian runners at a given submaximal exercise intensity. This persistent finding remains unexplained, but with many possible causes.

The ethnic difference in exercising plasma lactate concentration could result from a difference in glycolytic pathway activity. This in turn may be due to the ethnic groups exercising at different relative intensities or metabolizing different relative proportions of carbohydrates and fats as fuels. The latter is perhaps unlikely, as RER during submaximal exercise is not consistently different between black and white runners (see Table 10.1). In addition, the ethnic differences in plasma lactate concentrations during exercise could result from differences between the groups in oxidative pathway activity involving the citric acid cycle or the electron transport chain. In support of this, Weston et al. (1999) found that the lower plasma lactate concentration in black compared to white SA runners after running at a high submaximal intensity was associated with a higher citrate synthase activity in the muscles of the black runners. This could result in ethnic differences in mitochondrial or cytosolic levels of pyruvate and, via the action of lactate dehydrogenase (LDH), different intramuscular lactate concentrations.

One of the most important factors determining skeletal muscle lactate production, uptake and consumption is the predominant muscle fibre type (Stallknecht et al. 1998; Gladden 2000). Individuals with a higher proportion of type IIB (fast glycolytic) fibres are likely to produce lactate at higher rates during exercise than are individuals with a high proportion of type I (slow oxidative) fibres (Karlsson et al. 1981), since type I fibres are metabolically more suited for lactate oxidation (Gladden 2000). Distance runners tend to have either equal numbers of type I and type II fibres or a predominance of type I fibres (Noakes

Table 10.2 Comparison of plasma lactate concentrations, fibre composition and muscle MCT concentrations in black and white South African runners: summary of the data from Bosch et al. 1990, Coetzer et al. 1993, Weston et al. 1999, Weston et al. 2000, Marino et al. 2004 and Harley et al. (unpublished data)

Measurement	Bosch (1990)	Coetzer (1993)	Weston (1999)	Weston (2000)	Marino (2004)	Harley (unpub)
Peak $_{pl}$[lac]	ND	B < W	B = W	B = W	ND	B < W
Submax $_{pl}$[lac]	B < W	B ≤ W	B ≤ W	B ▽ W	ND	B ≤ W
% Type I fibres	ND	B = W	B = W	ND	ND	B = W
Muscle [MCT1]	ND	ND	ND	ND	ND	B = W
Muscle [MCT4]	ND	ND	ND	ND	ND	B = W

Note: ≤ and ≥ indicate that more than one similar measurement was made (e.g. at different exercise intensities) and only one/some were significantly different between groups. ND: not determined; $_{pl}$[lac]: plasma lactate concentration; MCT: muscle monocarboxylate transporters.

1998), and individuals with a high proportion of type I fibres are generally less susceptible to fatigue than are those with a high proportion of type II fibres (Thorstensson and Karlsson 1976; Komi and Tesch 1979; Lorentzon *et al.* 1988; Li *et al.* 2002). A greater proportion of type I fibres is therefore advantageous for endurance activities (Noakes 1998), and muscle fibre composition is often considered one of the main determinants of endurance capacity (Caffier *et al.* 1992).

Skeletal muscle fibre type distribution has been investigated in elite and sub-elite black and white SA runners in three studies (Coetzer *et al.* 1993; Weston *et al.* 1999; Harley *et al.* unpublished data) (see Table 10.2). All found no significant difference in the proportion of the different muscle fibre types in the two groups, with the runners' type I fibre proportion falling roughly between 50 and 65%. Similarly, Saltin *et al.* (1995a) also reported no difference in muscle fibre proportions between Kenyan and Scandinavian runners. This lack of difference in fibre type proportions suggests that fibre composition does not account for the superior performance of black African runners, it also suggests that fibre composition is not the reason for the difference in exercising plasma lactate concentrations.

Another physiological variable that could be associated with both the ethnic performance difference and the ethnic difference in blood lactate concentrations during exercise is the concentration of monocarboxylate transporters (MCTs) in skeletal muscle. MCTs are integral membrane proteins that facilitate the transport of monocarboxylates, including lactate, across physiological membranes (Brooks *et al.* 1999). Variations in the activity or expression of these proteins in the muscle could therefore be associated with the ethnic differences in plasma lactate concentrations during exercise. In addition, training studies suggest that a greater skeletal muscle MCT content may be related to superior athletic capability (Dubouchaud *et al.* 2000), as a greater MCT content may delay the development of muscular acidosis, thereby potentially enhancing performance.

Only one study has investigated skeletal muscle MCT content in black African runners. This study (Harley *et al.* unpublished data) compared the vastus lateralis muscle concentrations of MCT1 and MCT4, the primary MCTs in skeletal muscle, in sub-elite black and white SA runners. The MCT1 and MCT4 contents in the vastus lateralis muscle were similar in the black and white runners (see Table 10.2). This suggests that the total cellular MCT1 or MCT4 contents in their muscles do not account for the superior performance of black SA runners. This finding also suggests that the total skeletal muscle MCT1 or MCT4 contents are unlikely to be responsible for the lower exercising plasma lactate concentrations measured in the black runners. This finding does not, however, preclude the involvement of MCTs in this ethnic difference in exercising plasma lactate concentrations. As MCTs are found in subcellular fractions within the muscle cell (Bonen *et al.* 2000; Butz *et al.* 2004), there could be a difference between the black and white athletes in the subcellular contents of MCTs. For example, MCT1 is found in the mitochondria, and is thought to facilitate lactate uptake into the mitochondria for oxidation (Brooks et al. 1999; Dubouchaud et al. 2000; Butz et al. 2004). If one ethnic group had a greater mitochondrial MCT1 content than another, they could theoretically have a metabolic advantage during exercise via enhanced cytosolic lactate clearance, more efficient fuel oxidation and greater cellular redox balance. Further investigation of the subcellular concentrations of skeletal muscle MCTs in black and white athletes is therefore recommended. In addition, variations in the efficiency of lactate transport across membranes may result not only from differences in MCT content, but also from differences in MCT activity (Tonouchi et al. 2002). It is also possible that the regulation of MCT activity could differ between black and white runners.

The plasma concentrations of sodium and potassium also change during exercise. These changes result from various mechanisms, one of which is muscle contraction, as muscle action potentials result in an influx of sodium into, and an efflux of potassium out of, muscle cells (Lindinger and Sjogaard 1991). These fluctuations have a multitude of effects in the exercising body, some of which aid performance and some of which may contribute to the development of fatigue (McKenna 1995; Lindinger and Sjogaard 1991; McKenna 1992; Sjogaard 1990). Sodium and potassium changes associated with the development of fatigue may occur via metabolic mechanisms (McKenna 1992), via neuromuscular mechanisms involving decreases in muscle membrane excitability (Juel et al. 1999; Masuda et al. 1999), as well as via indirect mechanisms involving ascending afferent sensory information to the brain (Lindinger and Sjogaard 1991).

Peak plasma potassium concentrations on completion of a maximal running test were significantly higher in black compared to white SA runners (5.53 ± 0.31 vs. 4.84 ± 0.49 mmol·L^{-1}) (Harley et al. unpublished data). In addition, plasma potassium concentrations were significantly higher (4.07 ± 0.33 vs. 3.63 ± 0.20 mmol·L^{-1}) and plasma sodium concentrations significantly lower (136.0 ± 1.9 vs. 138.3 ± 1.5 mmol·L^{-1}) in the black runners during recovery, three minutes after completion of the maximal running test (Harley et al. unpublished data). It is not clear whether the higher plasma potassium and lower plasma sodium concentrations in the black runners would be an advantage or a disadvantage to endurance performance. The implications of these findings are thus not clear. However further investigation of sodium and potassium flux during exercise in runners is recommended. In particular, an examination of the muscle concentrations of Na$^+$/K$^+$ pumps in the two ethnic groups is suggested, as a difference in the expression or activity of the Na$^+$/K$^+$ pumps could result in differences in muscle excitability (Clausen and Nielsen 1994) and hence muscle force output and performance.

In summary, while black African runners repeatedly display lower blood lactate concentrations during exercise, the basis for this physiological phenomenon has not been explained. Muscle fibre distributions and muscle MCT content are not different between the groups and do not, therefore, appear to account for differences in performance. Possible ethnic differences in muscle and plasma sodium and potassium flux during exercise need to be investigated further, and the source of these variations and the variations in exercising plasma lactate concentrations should be examined.

Neuromuscular factors

In the previous section, it was argued that differences in skeletal muscle fibre characteristics are one of the potential sources of ethnic differences in athletic performance. Similarly, neuromuscular characteristics could be a distinguishing determinant of this difference (Ama et al. 1990; Coetzer et al. 1993; Fukashiro et al. 2002). Together with cardiorespiratory and intramuscular factors, performance in distance running may be limited by characteristics of the neuromuscular system (Noakes 1988; Paavolainen et al. 1999b). Endurance performance and the mechanisms involved in fatigue include many components of this system (Paavolainen et al. 1999a), from central neural command to the muscle through to muscle protein activity (Enoka and Stuart 1992). Therefore, peripheral sites in the muscle as well as central nervous sites are potentially implicated in the fatigue process (Gandevia 2001). Modern electrophysiology has contributed greatly to recent advances in the knowledge of neuromuscular mechanisms related to fatigue and endurance performance (Enoka and Stuart 1992). Despite this, very little research using these techniques has been applied specifically to black African distance runners.

Two of the previously described findings relating to black African distance runners that are worthy of neuromuscular investigation are the enhanced fatigue resistance and the superior running economy of these athletes. Neuromuscular research that has addressed fatigue resistance will be discussed in this section, while neuromuscular research that has addressed running economy and its relationship to stretch-shortening cycle activity (SSCA) will be discussed in the following section.

The greater fatigue resistance of black compared to white SA runners has been noted during submaximal running (Weston et al. 1999), during repetitive isometric knee extensions (Coetzer et al. 1993) and during sustained submaximal isometric knee extensions (Harley et al. unpublished data). The latter two findings suggest that the black runners' superior fatigue resistance may involve more than advantages in cardiorespiratory variables or in running biomechanics. The finding by Harley et al. (unpublished data) that black runners could sustain static quadriceps muscle contractions for substantially longer than could white runners also suggests that black SA runners may have a greater fatigue resistance than white runners during endurance activity that is not restricted to running, or even to dynamic or intermittent isometric exercise. It is therefore possible that black SA athletes may have the potential to outperform white athletes during endurance sports other than running.

The black runners' superior performance in the sustained isometric contraction also suggests that the reason they generally out-perform white runners in

South Africa might not be due, or at least not exclusively due, to size differences (Marino *et al.* 2000; Marino *et al.* 2004) or muscle elasticity differences between these populations, as these factors should not affect performance in a static isometric fatigue test. The potential physiological differences that could account for the ethnic disparity in isometric performance are numerous, and may include peripheral factors within the muscle, as well as central factors associated with the neural control of the fatiguing contraction.

In order to determine the relative levels of fatigue-associated physiological changes in neuromuscular structures for the two groups, Harley *et al.* (unpublished data) included two electrical muscle stimulations, which were applied to the rectus femoris muscle at the beginning and end of the sustained muscle contraction. The first stimulation increased the force output from the sustained submaximal level by a similar amount in the black and the white runners. The second stimulation applied at the end of exercise, however, had a different effect in the two groups. The reduction in the additional force output produced by the first compared to the second stimulation was significantly greater in the white than the black runners (Figure 10.4). This suggests that there were greater fatigue effects in the structures and mechanisms affected by muscle stimulation in the white runners, when both were at their endurance limit. This occurred even though the time to fatigue for the sustained contraction was significantly longer in the black runners.

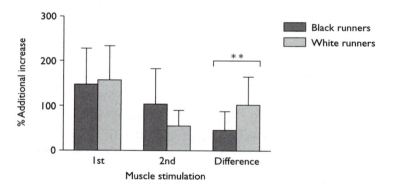

Figure 10.4 Harley *et al.* (unpublished data) examined the percentage increase in force output from a sustained submaximal level with electrical muscle stimulation during an isometric fatigue test in black and white SA runners. 'Difference' indicates the difference in the percentage increase in force output between the first and second stimulation. The reduction in additional force output from the first to the second stimulation was significantly greater for the white runners than the black runners. This suggests that there were greater fatigue effects in the structures and mechanisms affected by muscle stimulation for the white runners compared to the black runners, at their endurance limit.

Note: *'s indicate a significant difference between black and white groups. **$p < 0.01$.

Electrical stimulation to muscle produces force directly via motor neuron activation and indirectly by reflex spinal motor neuron activation (Collins *et al.* 2002). The better performance and hence greater fatigue resistance of the black athletes in the sustained contraction, therefore, appears to have been at least partly the result of a lesser degree of fatigue-related stress at the level of the muscle, the neuromuscular junction, the motor neuron or the spinal reflex loop.

Harley *et al.* (unpublished data) also noted additional neuromuscular differences between black and white SA runners upon examination of electromyographic (EMG) recordings from the rectus femoris during the sustained contraction. During this test the EMG amplitude increased significantly more over time in the white than the black runners, while the left shift in the EMG frequency spectrum was also greater for the white runners (Figure 10.5). These distinct neuromuscular profiles suggest a different central efferent (brain) response over time during the fatiguing contraction for the two ethnic groups. Efferent signals during a fatiguing task are modulated in response to afferent information from the periphery (Enoka and Stuart 1992). The differing efferent responses between the groups during the contraction may therefore reflect ethnic differences in exercise-induced physiological changes that originate either centrally or peripherally at the level of the muscle.

Similar to the ethnic comparison of sustained submaximal isometric activity, Harley *et al.* (unpublished data) also compared the performance of black and white SA runners during a sustained maximal isometric knee extension. Interestingly, although the black runners' time to fatigue during the maximal contraction was 40 s longer than that of the white runners, upon statistical analysis the times for the two groups were not significantly different. There were also no significant differences between the groups for the neuromuscular changes accompanying fatigue during the contraction. This may relate to the finding that black SA runners perform better than white SA runners during a submaximal running test, but not during a maximal running test (Weston *et al.* 1999). The ethnic difference in the physiological processes associated with fatigue during submaximal activity is therefore not apparent, or not as apparent, during maximal activity. Why this is the case is not clear. However, it may be related to differing neuromuscular recruitment strategies employed during submaximal and maximal exercise.

Investigation of non-fatiguing maximal knee extension exercise has revealed that black SA runners develop lower peak isometric and concentric peak torques than white SA runners (Coetzer *et al.* 1993; Harley *et al.* unpublished data). However, peak eccentric torque output was not significantly different between the ethnic groups (Harley *et al.* unpublished data). Correction of torque output for body mass resulted in no significant difference between the black and white runners for peak isometric or isokinetic torque output, while correction for lean thigh volume yielded similar results to the absolute, uncorrected torque output values (Coetzer *et al.* 1993; Harley *et al.* unpublished data).

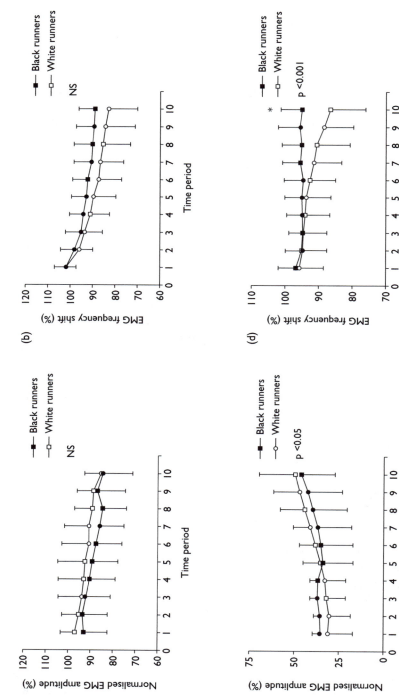

It is interesting that, while the two ethnic groups differed in strength iso-metrically and concentrically, this difference was not evident during maximal eccentric contractions. The neural commands that produce eccentric contrac-tions are different from those producing concentric and isometric contractions, and appear to involve the selective recruitment of certain types of motor units, as well as greater inhibition of the maximal number of motor units recruited, possibly for protective reasons (Enoka 1997; Spurway *et al.* 2000). This differ-ence between the contraction types could be related to the ethnic strength differences being apparent for maximal isometric and concentric, but not for eccentric contractions. The force output from a muscle appears to be related to the compliance or stiffness of the musculotendinous tissue (Michaut *et al.* 2001), and a difference in musculotendinous stiffness between individuals can affect their ability to produce eccentric force (Walshe and Wilson 1997). Musculo-tendinous stiffness factors could therefore also be associated with the different results for the eccentric compared to the isometric and concentric contractions. Further work is required to identify the reasons for this finding and whether or not it could have relevance to ethnic performance differences. It is perhaps unlikely that the lower isometric and concentric quadriceps strength in black SA runners could be directly related to their superior running performance when compared to their white counterparts. If a difference in muscle function were to be related to the ethnic performance difference, therefore, it is probably more likely to originate from a discrepancy in efficiency of submaximal contractions rather than in maximal capacity.

In summary, the superior fatigue resistance of black SA runners is not restricted to running, or even to dynamic or repetitive isometric exercise, but also occurs during sustained, static isometric exercise. Black and white SA run-ners have distinct neuromuscular profiles during fatiguing submaximal isometric activity, suggesting different efferent responses during fatigue for the two ethnic groups. These efferent adaptations to fatigue may differ quantitatively or quali-tatively, and could reflect ethnic differences in exercise-induced physiological changes that may originate either centrally or peripherally. These neuromuscular

Figure 10.5 (opposite) Harley *et al.* (unpublished data) examined electromyographic changes with time during quadriceps isometric fatigue tests in black and white SA runners, namely: EMG amplitude (a) and frequency shift (b) during a maximal fatigue test, and EMG amplitude (c) and frequency shift (d) during a submaximal fatigue test. During the submaximal test the EMG amplitude increased significantly more over time in the white runners than it did in the black runners, while the left shift in the EMG frequency spectrum was also greater for the white than for the black runners. These distinct neuro-muscular profiles suggest a different central efferent response over time during the fatiguing contraction for the two ethnic groups. The given p value indicates a significantly different interaction effect (EMG change over time) between black and white groups.

Note: *'s indicate a significant difference at a particular time point between black and white groups. *p<0.05.

differences may be related to the superior distance-running performance of black SA runners, and possibly runners from eastern and northern Africa. Further research is required to understand how the various neuromuscular mechanisms that operate during endurance activity function differently between the ethnic groups.

Biomechanical factors

Efficient 'running biomechanics' involve anthropometrical and neuromuscular aspects. The force output required to propel a runner forward is affected by mechanical and elastic factors, and a key tenet of the biomechanical model of endurance exercise is that an enhanced capacity to store and utilize elastic energy is advantageous to distance-running performance (Noakes 2000; Lambert and Noakes 2000). It is not surprising therefore, that some propose that elastic factors may be involved in the superior performance of black African runners (Noakes 1998).

The use of elastic energy during activities such as running is often discussed in the context of the stretch-shortening cycle. The stretch-shortening cycle (SSC) is a naturally occurring pattern of movement involving the lengthening or stretching of a muscle as part of an eccentric contraction, followed by the shortening of that muscle during a concentric contraction (Blanpied *et al.* 1995). For example, in running, the quadriceps muscles contract eccentrically during the initial loading and early midstance phase of the stride and then contract concentrically during the push-off phase. During a SSC movement, elastic energy is stored in the activated muscle during the stretching phase, and used in the subsequent shortening phase, resulting in a potentiation of performance (Hakkinen *et al.* 1986). Optimizing the force augmentation of the SSC would be desirable in sports that make common use of the SSC (Blanpied *et al.* 1995), such as running, where the locomotory muscles repeatedly perform the SSC action during alternating step cycles (Johnston 1991). The storage and recovery of elastic energy in the muscle-tendon complex is therefore pertinent to running performance (Farley *et al.* 1991), as the use of elastic energy will reduce the metabolic demands of the activity (Aura and Komi 1986) and delay the progression of fatigue.

The SSC is thought to work both through the use of elastic energy stored in the series elastic components of the muscle during the stretch phase, as well as through reflex potentiation (Bosco *et al.* 1982). A number of factors contribute to the storage and utilization of elastic energy, including the degree and velocity of pre-stretch (Aura and Komi 1986; Bosco *et al.* 1981), the transition time between the stretching and shortening phases (Bosco *et al.* 1981), the composition of the musculotendinous tissue (Kubo *et al.* 1999) and the level of pre-activation (Kyrolainen *et al.* 2003). Any of these factors may therefore contribute to ethnic differences in endurance performance. Variations in SSC performance in African distance runners have not, however, been investigated until recently.

Harley *et al.* (unpublished data) investigated SSC functioning in sub-elite black and white SA runners, by measuring force output and quadriceps EMG activity during three types of maximal jump: a squat jump (SJ) from a semi-squatting position with no countermovement; a countermovement jump (CJ) from a standing position with a preliminary countermovement; and a drop jump (DJ) from an elevated position onto the force plate with a subsequent jump off it. Neuromuscular efficiency, measured as mean force output per normalized EMG amplitude, was not significantly different between the black and the white runners during the push-off phase of any of the SSC jumps. If jump performance had been more efficient in one group than the other it could be proposed that this group made greater use of elastic energy than the other during SSC activity. However, this was not the case and it is therefore likely that elastic energy utilization is similar between trained black and white SA runners.

SSC delta values for the difference in the neuromuscular efficiency of the concentric phase between the three jump types gives an indication of the mechanical effect of SSC elastic energy on jumping performance. The black and white runners in the study by Harley *et al.* (unpublished data) had similar results for the difference in neuromuscular efficiency between the SJ and the CJ, the SJ and the DJ, and the DJ and the CJ. The 'difference in efficiency' values were all positive, indicating that the SSC is functioning as would be predicted in both ethnic groups, with elastic energy enhancing the efficiency of jumps that involve a prestretch (CJ and DJ). The lack of difference between ethnic groups, however, suggests that neither ethnic group benefited more from the prestretch than did the other. This again suggests that there is no difference in the efficiency of SCC functioning between black and white SA runners, at least during maximal jumping manoeuvres. It is recommended that in future research, SSC activity should be compared in black African and white runners during running, rather than jumping, so that a sport-specific comparison can be made.

The present data therefore suggest that elastic energy utilization is the same in black and white SA runners so that this performance component is not likely to contribute to the superiority of black SA runners. This is consistent with the previously described finding that black SA runners demonstrate a greater fatigue resistance than white runners during sustained submaximal isometric knee extension (Harley *et al.* unpublished data), which does not involve elastic energy utilization. These findings imply that the superior endurance of black compared to white SA runners is not the result of elastic factors.

The running stride is one of the endurance running factors that reflects the contributions of both muscle power and muscle elasticity. The time a runner takes to cover a certain distance is determined by stride length and stride frequency. These parameters can affect the economy of distance running (Cavanagh and Williams 1982), as the primary determinants of the cost of running are the energy cost of supporting body mass and the time course of generating the force (Kram and Taylor 1990). Distance runners will choose to run at a stride length that minimizes their oxygen uptake, suggesting that the stride parameters adopted by a runner are those that incur the lowest metabolic cost (Cavanagh and Williams 1982). Although stride parameters are repeatable, day-to-day measures in well-trained runners (Brisswalter and Legros 1994), they are affected by fatigue. Both stride frequency and stride length decrease, and ground contact time for each stride increases as a runner fatigues, resulting in a slower running speed (Sharwood 2003).

As stride parameters are associated with running economy, it follows that they may be related to distance running performance. Indeed, Harley et al. (unpublished data) found that stride length was significantly correlated with 10 km running time, while Brandon and Boileau (1992) reported that stride length contributed significantly to 1500 and 3,000 m running performance. In addition, the correlation discovered by Harley et al. (unpublished data) reached a higher level of significance when stride length was expressed relative to height, indicating that the further a runner travels with each stride for his height, the faster he runs a 10 km race. It is therefore of considerable interest that it has recently been found that, despite the significant difference in height between black and white SA runners, their mean stride lengths when running at 12 $km\cdot hr^{-1}$ were not significantly different (Harley et al. unpublished data). As a result, the ratio of stride length to height was significantly different between groups, with the black runners covering more distance per stride for their height. Therefore, as the ratio of stride length to height correlates positively with running performance, it is possible that this difference between the two ethnic groups could be a significant determinant of the superior performance of black SA runners compared to their white counterparts.

The reason for the difference in the ratio of stride length to height between the two ethnic groups is not known, although it could be related to differences between the groups in the power output of the muscles (due to contractile components of the muscle itself, biomechanical properties or neuromuscular recruitment differences) or to the elastic capacity of the muscles and tendons. However, there was no difference between these two ethnic groups in the efficiency of SSC functioning, as discussed earlier. This suggests that this stride difference is probably not the result of a difference in elastic energy utilization. It is therefore more likely to be the result of a greater relative power generation per stride in the black runners, although it could also possibly result from better integration or coordination of the recruitment of the multiple muscles involved in running. Regardless of the cause, this ethnic stride difference may well be related to the greater running economy of the black African athletes, and hence to their superior distance-running performance.

Central nervous factors

Of all the different physiological systems in the body that contribute to endurance activity, the role of the central nervous system (CNS) is probably the least understood. Certainly it is the least studied. Similarly, the part played by central nervous factors in ethnic variations in performance have not been investigated. Yet it is clear that the CNS plays a fundamental role in fatigue during physical activity, partly via the generation of the sensation of fatigue. It has been speculated that physiological factors set the outermost limits to performance, while psychological factors determine the more proximate ones (Ikai and Steinhaus 1961). As psychology is essentially the cognitive representation of brain physiology, this implies that an individual's physical capacity is determined by their physiological limits, while the limits to their physical performance are set by their brain.

Indeed, motor drive from the central nervous system can decrease if the individual performing the fatiguing task lacks motivation or does not want to continue to tolerate the increasing sensations of discomfort (Bigland-Ritchie 1984). Supraspinal fatigue, a subset of central fatigue, refers to the fatigue that results from a failure to generate output from the motor cortex (Gandevia 2001). Fatigue at the supraspinal level is demonstrated by the fact that transcranial magnetic stimulation of the motor cortex during a sustained maximal voluntary contraction can result in additional force output from the contracting muscle (Gandevia et al. 1996). This suggests that there is suboptimal output from the motor cortex, and that central fatigue may include not only a decreased neural drive from the motor cortex, but also a decreased drive to the motor cortex (Taylor and Gandevia 2001). As these 'drives' will influence a runner's motor output and hence his or her running speed, ethnic variations in neural drive could result in ethnic variations in running performance.

Numerous peripheral signals are relayed to the CNS during fatiguing activity, acting at multiple levels in the nervous system (Gandevia 2001). As the fatigue-related peripheral and central physiological mechanisms interact continually during physical activity, the distinction between the two is blurred. The Central Governor model, however, contends that the integration of the numerous peripheral and central physiological variables occurs in the central nervous system (Noakes et al. 2004c), such that the termination of an exercise bout, or a reduction in exercise intensity, results from a decrease in neural drive originating in the brain. The decrease in voluntary activation resulting from this mechanism of central regulation (as opposed to central fatigue) may serve to protect the various physiological systems from the harm potentially caused by excessive physical stress, by maintaining relative homeostasis in the body (Gandevia 2001; Noakes et al. 2004c).

The Central Governor model can explain many of the thorny physiological problems in exercise physiology, most especially the 'lactate and cardiac output paradoxes' of exercise in hypoxia (Noakes et al. 2004a), as well as the more obviously observable phenomena in sport such as the 'end-spurt' phenomenon (Catalano 1974) and the anticipatory nature of the pacing strategy during exercise (St Clair et al. 2001; St Clair Gibson et al. 2001; St Clair et al. 2003; Ansley et al. 2004; St Clair Gibson and Noakes 2004). This anticipatory behaviour is evident during self-paced exercise in the heat, where muscle recruitment and power output decrease before there is any abnormal increase in rectal temperature, HR or perception of effort (Tucker *et al.* 2004). This anticipatory response would reduce heat production, thereby ensuring that thermal homeostasis is maintained during exercise in hot conditions.

Interestingly, this anticipatory response during exercise in the heat was different between black and white SA runners. As described in the section on heat retention, Marino *et al.* (2004) found that white SA runners ran slower than black SA runners during a time trial in hot conditions (35°C; 60% relative humidity), but not in cool conditions. The fascinating discovery, however, was that the slower running speeds of white runners in the heat occurred from the outset of the exercise bout. Thus they did not wait to overheat before they slowed down; rather they began the time trial at a slower running speed. This indicates that the white runners ran slower in anticipation, presumably to insure that they did not overheat, as they were heavier and therefore less able to maintain the same body temperature in the heat if they chose to run at the same speed as the black runners. As this ethnic difference involved a feed-forward control of motor unit recruitment, this suggests that central nervous factors must be involved in the superior running performance of black compared to white SA runners, at least in hot conditions.

Whatever the physiological differences between SA black and white runners, the CNS has 'knowledge' of this, that is of the body's capacity for exercise in certain conditions, and alters the intensity of exercise early during the exercise bout to take this into account to ensure that a serious deviation from homeostasis is not allowed to occur.

Thus the Central Governor model would predict that the central governor in the brain of black African distance runners integrates the knowledge of prior exercise experience with the physiological signals it is receiving at any particular time, and regulates motor unit recruitment according to this information and according to the requirements of the present activity. While the same prediction would hold for white runners and runners from some other ethnic groups, physiological differences perhaps on an ethnic basis, would ultimately manifest in a lower final CNS motor output in white runners causing them to maintain a lower mean running speed over the course of a race than the black African runners.

Integration of factors

The previous sections have, like much of exercise physiology research, used a reductionist approach to discussing endurance performance and its relationship to ethnicity, by examining individual variables or bodily systems. This physiological compartmentalization, however, ignores the true complexity of how the human body actually functions. Individual physiological variables cannot account for the complex metabolic behaviour that occurs during physical activity (St Clair Gibson and Noakes 2004). Similarly, there is no single factor that can account for fatigue or for variations in endurance performance (Bergh et al. 2000; Brooks et al. 2000). The importance and redundancy of these multiple mechanisms involved in endurance performance will vary. Hence, it is possible that the relative value of various physiological factors to endurance performance may differ between ethnic groups.

The many different processes involved in fatigue during endurance performance are integrated and affect each other continuously (Enoka and Stuart 1992). Fatigue during exercise involves both descending signals from the CNS to the periphery, as well as ascending signals to the CNS from the periphery. As well as having local fatigue effects, tissue-specific and circulating metabolic variables can act as signallers of physiological change, stimulating feedback from the tissues or the circulation to the CNS. The various physiological variables may therefore affect each other directly or via indirect feedforward or feedback mechanisms (St Clair Gibson and Noakes 2004). Thus, aside from the roles of individual physiological factors in endurance performance, the integrated functioning of the different systems and the elements within each, can affect endurance ability. An athlete may perform well as a result of the interaction of many variables from different physiological systems in the body. The combined effect of multiple physiological factors may therefore result in the enhanced fatigue resistance and distance running ability of black African runners. This is precisely what this review has demonstrated. Multiple physiological and performance variables are significantly different between black and white SA runners, suggesting that the difference in distance running ability between these ethnic groups is likely to result from many physiological factors, rather than a single one.

This leads to the question of what the differing interrelated variables are. Table 10.3 summarises the various physiological and performance variables that have been found to differ significantly between black and white SA distance runners. The table shows that the factors that are different between the two ethnic groups are varied in nature, suggesting that an integration of many quite different factors may explain the superior endurance running ability of black African runners. Many of these factors will also, however, be linked. For example, the more efficient stride parameters of the black SA runners compared to their white counterparts may be reflected in their greater running economy. It should also be noted that, as only a small percentage of the many physiological factors that are likely to be involved in endurance performance have been compared in SA ethnic groups, there are probably many others that have not been discussed which are likely to contribute to the ethnic variation in performance.

It is likely that the purpose of this multiple-structure involvement in fatiguing activity is that physiological homeostasis is maintained, and no single metabolic system progresses to failure during fatiguing activity (Lambert et al. 2005). Having a large number of different variables involved in feedforward and feedback control could increase the gain of this homeostatic system, making it more robust (Lambert et al. 2005). It is possible that the black African

Table 10.3 Physiological and performance variables that differ between black and white South African distance runners: summary of the data from Bosch *et al.* 1990, Coetzer *et al.* 1993, Weston *et al.* 1999, Weston *et al.* 2000, Marino *et al.* 2004 and Harley *et al.* (unpublished data)

Variable	Reference
Body size	Bosch; Coetzer; Marino; Harley; Weston1999
Body fat content and patterning	Bosch; Coetzer; Harley
Body musculature	Harley (unpublished data)
Running performance in the heat	Marino
Running economy (high intensity)	Harley; Weston 2000
Fractional $\dot{V}O_2$ utilisation	Bosch; Coetzer; Weston 2000
Exercising plasma lactate	Bosch; Coetzer; Harley; Weston 1999
Exercising plasma sodium	Harley
Exercising plasma potassium	Harley
Citrate synthase activity	Weston 1999
Fatigue resistance	Coetzer; Harley; Marino; Weston 1999
Neuromuscular fatigue profile (EMG)	Harley
Peripheral fatigue during knee extension (muscle stimulation)	Harley
Stride biomechanics (stride length / height)	Harley
Isometric quadriceps strength	Coetzer; Harley
Concentric quadriceps strength	Harley

populations that excel in distance running have developed over time in a manner that would most efficiently maintain physiological homeostasis based on their environmental exposures, which were different from those to which other ethnic groups were exposed. While the maintenance of homeostasis would remain of crucial importance to all populations, it may be achieved slightly differently, and with different levels of efficiency, in people of different ethnicities.

Last of all, when discussing the integration of multiple factors, it is necessary to once again mention that physiological factors are by no means the only variables of importance to endurance performance. A host of factors, including genetic, nutritional, psychological, social and environmental factors will influence the superiority of black African distance runners.

In summary, it is likely that ethnic variations in distance running ability result from the integrated functioning of multiple interrelated physiological factors. Consequently research examining the biological basis of black African distance running performance must adopt an integrated approach, considering the contribution of multiple biological systems.

Future research

The recurrent finding of low blood lactate concentrations in black African distance runners during exercise is still not completely explained. Thus it is suggested that an ethnic comparison of the expression of skeletal muscle MCTs in the subcellular mitochondrial and sarcolemmal fractions should be conducted. In addition, investigation of potential ethnic differences in other proteins and pathways involved in lactate metabolism, such as the muscle concentration and activities of lactate dehydrogenase and citrate synthase, is also recommended. The differences found between black and white SA runners in the exercising concentrations of plasma sodium and potassium warrant further investigation. It is recommended that the sarcolemmal concentrations of the Na^+/K^+ pump be studied in these groups. The finding that black SA runners had a greater stride length relative to their height compared to their white counterparts should also be investigated further, considering that this variable is associated with distance running performance. If this greater stride length is related to a more efficient use of muscle power or biomechanics, then it could potentially explain the better running economy noted in the black runners. In this respect, it may be useful to record stride parameters in association with force and EMG measurements during running. While force output and EMG activity during SSC activity have been studied in black and white SA runners using jumping techniques, a more task-specific investigation would involve their measurement during running. In addition, based on the findings of Bosch et al. (1990) and Marino et al. (2000), the distribution and regulation of body temperature during exercise needs to be compared in black and white African runners.

Summary

The body of research investigating black and white SA distance runners has revealed that multiple physiological and performance variables differ significantly between these two ethnic groups. This suggests that the superior endurance performance of black SA runners, and possibly east and north African runners, may originate from many physiological factors, rather than a single factor. In addition, the factors that were different between the two ethnic groups were varied in nature, suggesting that an integration of many, considerably differing factors may explain the superior endurance running ability of black African runners.

Black SA runners are substantially smaller than white SA runners, with a lower body fat content and higher relative muscle content. This phenotype provides endurance performance advantages, particularly during exercise in hot conditions. Hence ethnic differences in body composition are likely to play a role in the superior international running achievements of black African runners. Maximal oxygen consumption values do not differ between black and white SA runners. Thus the ability to transport and consume larger maximal volumes of oxygen cannot explain the athletic superiority of the black runners. In contrast, there were significant ethnic differences in fractional utilization of oxygen and running economy at higher exercise intensities, with black runners demonstrating a greater economy, or efficiency, than white runners. It therefore appears that, with regard to cardiorespiratory factors, it is the economy of movement, rather than the maximum capacity of these systems, that determines the superiority of black SA runners. The superior running economy of the black athletes may be associated with their larger ratio of stride length to height. While the origin of this ethnic difference in stride length is not known, it could be related to the superior power output of the muscles or to the superior elasticity of the muscles and tendons of black SA runners. However, no difference was observed between ethnic groups for the efficiency of SSC functioning. The greater running economy of black SA runners may also be linked to their lower exercising blood lactate concentrations, although this relationship may not be causal. Although the source of this physiological phenomenon is also not yet fully explained, muscle fibre composition and total muscle MCT content do not appear to provide the explanation. As these factors do not differ between the two ethnic groups, they are also unlikely to account for performance differences between black African and white runners.

One of the key advantages enjoyed by black African distance runners appears to be their superior fatigue resistance during submaximal running. Interestingly, however, the enhanced fatigue resistance of black SA runners is not restricted to running, or even to dynamic or repetitive isometric exercise, but also occurs during sustained, static exercise. It is therefore possible that black African athletes may have the potential to outperform athletes of other ethnicities during endurance sports other than running. Black and white SA runners display distinct neuromuscular profiles during fatiguing activity, suggesting different efferent responses during fatigue in the two ethnic groups. These neuromuscular recruitment differences may be related to the superior fatigue resistance and, in turn, the superior distance running performance of black SA runners and possibly runners from eastern and northern Africa.

The Central Governor model posits that the brain regulates motor unit recruitment during exercise in order to insure an optimum performance while protecting physiological homeostasis. It is therefore possible that black African distance runners are better able to maintain homeostasis at higher levels of skeletal muscle recruitment than are white runners, allowing the black athletes to resist fatigue and perform better. This could result from a true metabolic difference between ethnic groups that makes the regulation of homeostasis easier in black African distance runners when running at higher exercise intensities. It is not yet clear which would be the most important 'homeostats' that regulate this response during exercise, but many of the factors discussed in this chapter may be involved. Indeed, the data suggest that multiple homeostats are functioning, such that ethnic variations in distance-running ability stem from the integrated functioning of multiple interrelated physiological factors.

Alternatively, there could exist a neurological difference that allows black African runners to recruit a larger skeletal muscle mass even though the threat to homeostasis is greater than in white athletes, who are unable to sustain equally high rates of energy expenditure (and as high levels of skeletal muscle recruitment) for as long during prolonged exercise. This explanation would require that black African athletes conquer the symptoms of distress more effectively during exercise than do white runners. That is, their higher running speeds are won at the cost of greater feelings of discomfort. On the other hand, it is also possible that black African athletes might feel less discomfort at the same level of homeostatic distress as do white athletes. All of these different possibilities invite scientific evaluation.

Perhaps the point to emphasize is that the human body acts as a complex system during exercise (St Clair Gibson and Noakes 2004) so that any attempt to explain superior athletic performance on the basis of a single organ system such as the heart, lungs or muscles will not be correct. Rather we argue that the superior biological functioning of black SA athletes is likely to be related to the centrally integrated control of whole body homeostasis during exercise.

In this case, any explanation for the superior success of African distance runners will be found in the way in which their innate physiology, training, environment, expectations and genes influence the integrated functioning of their bodies to yield an optimal balance between successful athletic performance and homeostatic safety.

Acknowledgements

The research undertaken in the MRC/UCT Research Unit For Exercise Science and Sports Medicine is funded by the Harry Crossley and Nellie Atkinson Staff Research Funds of the University of Cape Town, the Medical Research Council of South Africa, Discovery Health and the National Research Foundation of South Africa through the THRIP initiative.

References

Ama, P. F., Lagasse, P., Bouchard, C. and Simoneau, J. A. (1990) 'Anaerobic performances in black and white subjects', *Medicine and Science in Sports and Exercise* 22, 508–11.

Ansley, L., Robson, P. J., St Clair, G. A. and Noakes, T. D. (2004) 'Anticipatory pacing strategies during supramaximal exercise lasting longer than 30 s', *Medicine and Science in Sports and Exercise* 36, 309–14.

Aura, O. and Komi, P. V. (1986) 'Effects of prestretch intensity on mechanical efficiency of positive work and on elastic behavior of skeletal muscle in stretch-shortening cycle exercise', *International Journal of Sports Medicine*, 7, 137–43.

Bale, P., Bradbury, D. and Colley, E. (1986) 'Anthropometric and training variables related to 10km running performance', *British Journal of Sports Medicine* 20, 170–3.

Berg, K., Latin, R. W. and Coffey, C. (1998) 'Relationship of somatotype and physical characteristics to distance running performance in middle age runners', *Journal of Sports Medicine and Physical Fitness* 38, 253–7.

Bergh, U., Ekblom, B. and Åstrand, P. O. (2000) 'Maximal oxygen uptake "classical" versus "contemporary" viewpoints', *Medicine and Science in Sports and Exercise* 32, 85–8.

Bergström, J. (1962) 'Muscle electrolytes in man', *Scandinavian Journal of Clinical and Laboratory Investigation* 14 Suppl. 68, 511–13.

Bergström, J. and Hultman, E. (1966) 'The effect of exercise on muscle glycogen and electrolytes in normals', *Scandinavian Journal of Clinical and Laboratory Investigation* 18, 16–20.

Bigland-Ritchie, B. (1984) 'Muscle fatigue and the influence of changing neural drive', *Clinics in Chest Medicine* 5, 21–34.

Blanpied, P., Levins, J. A. and Murphy, E. (1995) 'The effects of different stretch velocities on average force of the shortening phase in the stretch-shorten cycle', *Journal of Orthopaedic and Sports Physical Therapy* 21, 345–53.

Bonen, A., Miskovic, D., Tonouchi, M., Lemieux, K., Wilson, M. C., Marette, A. and Halestrap, A. P. (2000) 'Abundance and subcellular distribution of MCT1 and MCT4 in heart and fast-twitch skeletal muscles', *American Journal of Physiology: Endocrinology and Metabolism* 278, E1067–E1077.

Bosch, A. N., Goslin, B. R., Noakes, T. D. and Dennis, S. C. (1990) 'Physiological differences between black and white runners during a treadmill marathon', *European Journal of Applied Physiology: Occupational Physiology* 61, 68–72.

Bosco, C., Komi, P. V. and Ito, A. (1981) 'Prestretch potentiation of human skeletal muscle during ballistic movement', *Acta Physiologica Scandinavica* 111, 135–40.

Bosco, C., Tarkka, I. and Komi, P. V. (1982) 'Effect of elastic energy and myoelectrical potentiation of triceps surae during stretch-shortening cycle exercise', *International Journal of Sports Medicine* 3, 137–40.

Brandon, L. J. and Boileau, R. A. (1992) 'Influence of metabolic, mechanical and physique variables on middle distance running', *Journal of Sports Medicine and Physical Fitness* 32, 1–9.

Brisswalter, J. and Legros, P. (1994) 'Daily stability in energy cost of running, respiratory parameters and stride rate among well-trained middle distance runners', *International Journal of Sports Medicine* 15, 238–41.

Brooks, G. A. (1991) 'Current concepts in lactate exchange', *Medicine and Science in Sports and Exercise* 23, 895–906.

Brooks, G. A. (1998) 'Mammalian fuel utilization during sustained exercise', *Comparative Biochemistry and Physiology. Part B, Biochemistry and Molecular Biology* 120, 89–107.

Brooks, G. A., Brown, M. A., Butz, C. E., Sicurello, J. P. and Dubouchaud, H. (1999) 'Cardiac and skeletal muscle mitochondria have a monocarboxylate transporter MCT1', *Journal of Applied Physiology* 87, 1713–18.

Brooks, G. A., Fahey, T. D., White, T. P. and Baldwin, K. M. (2000) *Exercise Physiology. Human Bioenergetics and Its Applications*, 3rd edn, Mountain View, CA: Mayfield Publishing Company.

Butz, C. E., McClelland, G. B. and Brooks, G. A. (2004) 'MCT1 confirmed in rat striated muscle mitochondria', *Journal of Applied Physiology* 97, 1059–66.

Caffier, G., Rehfeldt, H., Kramer, H. and Mucke, R. (1992) 'Fatigue during sustained maximal voluntary contraction of different muscles in humans: dependence on fibre type and body posture', *European Journal of Applied Physiology: Occupational Physiology* 64, 237–43.

Catalano, J. F. (1974) 'End-spurt following simple repetitive muscular movement', *Perceptual and Motor Skills* 39, 763–6.

Cavanagh, P. R. and Williams, K. R. (1982) 'The effect of stride length variation on oxygen uptake during distance running', *Medicine and Science in Sports and Exercise* 14, 30–5.

Clausen, T. and Nielsen, O. B. (1994) 'The Na+, K (+)-pump and muscle contractility', *Acta Physiologica Scandinavica* 152, 365–73.

Coetzer, P., Noakes, T. D., Sanders, B., Lambert, M. I., Bosch, A. N., Wiggins, T. and Dennis, S. C. (1993) 'Superior fatigue resistance of elite black South African distance runners', *Journal of Applied Physiology* 75, 1822–27.

Collins, D. F., Burke, D. and Gandevia, S. C. (2002) 'Sustained contractions produced by plateau-like behaviour in human motoneurones', *Journal of Physiology* 538, 289–301.

Costill, D. L. (1967) 'The relationship between selected physiological variables and distance running performance', *Journal of Sports Medicine and Physical Fitness* 7, 61–6.

Costill, D. L., Branam, G., Eddy, D. and Sparks, K. (1971) 'Determinants of Marathon running success', *Internationale Zeitschrift füür angewandte Physiologie* 29, 249–54.

Coyle, E. F. (1999) 'Physiological determinants of endurance exercise performance', *Journal of Science and Medicine in Sport* 2, 181–9.

Dennis, S. C. and Noakes, T. D. (1999) 'Advantages of a smaller bodymass in humans when distance-running in warm, humid conditions', *European Journal of Applied Physiology: Occupational Physiology* 79, 280–4.

di Prampero, P. E. (1985) 'Metabolic and circulatory limitations to VO2 max at the whole animal level', *Journal of Experimental Biology* 115, 319–31.

di Prampero, P. E. and Ferretti, G. (1990) 'Factors limiting maximal oxygen consumption in humans', *Respiration Physiology* 80, 113–27.

Dubouchaud, H., Butterfield, G. E., Wolfel, E. E., Bergman, B. C. and Brooks, G. A. (2000) 'Endurance training, expression, and physiology of LDH, MCT1, and MCT4 in human skeletal muscle', *American Journal of Physiology: Endocrinology and Metabolism* 278, E571–E579.

Durandt, J. J. (1995) 'The aerobic exercise capacity of sedentary black and white young adults', Honours thesis, unpublished work.

Enoka, R. M. (1997) 'Neural adaptations with chronic physical activity', *Journal of Biomechanics* 30, 447–55.

Enoka, R. M. and Stuart, D. G. (1992) 'Neurobiology of muscle fatigue', *Journal of Applied Physiology* 72, 1631–48.

Evans, W. J., Phinney, S. D. and Young, V. R. (1982) 'Suction applied to a muscle biopsy maximizes sample size', *Medicine and Science in Sports and Exercise* 14, 101–2.

Farley, C. T., Blickhan, R., Saito, J. and Taylor, C. R. (1991) 'Hopping frequency in humans: a test of how springs set stride frequency in bouncing gaits', *Journal of Applied Physiology* 71, 2127–32.

Farrell, S. W., Kohl, H. W. and Rogers, T. (1987) 'The independent effect of ethnicity on cardiovascular fitness', *Human Biology* 59, 657–66.

Fitts, R. H. (1994) 'Cellular mechanisms of muscle fatigue', *Physiological Reviews* 74, 49–94.

Fitts, R. H. (1996) 'Muscle fatigue: the cellular aspects', *American Journal of Sports Medicine* 24, S9–13.

Foster, C., Cadwell, K., Crenshaw, B., Dehart-Beverley, M., Hatcher, S., Karlsdottir, A. E., Shafer, N. N., Theusch, C. and Porcari, J. P. (2001) 'Physical activity and exercise training prescriptions for patients', *Cardiology Clinics* 19, 447–57.

Foster, C., Costill, D. L., Daniels, J. T. and Fink, W. J. (1978) 'Skeletal muscle enzyme activity, fiber composition and $\dot{V}O_2$ max in relation to distance running performance', *European Journal of Applied Physiology: Occupational Physiology* 39, 73–80.

Fukashiro, S., Abe, T., Shibayama, A. and Brechue, W. F. (2002) 'Comparison of viscoelastic characteristics in triceps surae between Black and White athletes', *Acta Physiologica Scandinavica* 175, 183–7.

Gandevia, S. C. (2001) 'Spinal and supraspinal factors in human muscle fatigue', *Physiological Reviews* 81, 1725–89.

Gandevia, S. C., Allen, G. M., Butler, J. E. and Taylor, J. L. (1996) 'Supraspinal factors in human muscle fatigue: evidence for suboptimal output from the motor cortex', *Journal of Physiology* 490 (Pt 2), 529–36.

Gladden, L. B. (2000) 'Muscle as a consumer of lactate', *Medicine and Science in Sports and Exercise* 32, 764–71.

Gonzalez-Alonso, J., Teller, C., Andersen, S. L., Jensen, F. B., Hyldig, T. and Nielsen, B. (1999) 'Influence of body temperature on the development of fatigue during prolonged exercise in the heat', *Journal of Applied Physiology* 86, 1032–9.

Hakkinen, K., Komi, P. V. and Kauhanen, H. (1986) 'Electromyographic and force production characteristics of leg extensor muscles of elite weight lifters during isometric, concentric, and various stretch-shortening cycle exercises', *International Journal of Sports Medicine* 7, 144–51.

Halestrap, A. P. and Price, N. T. (1999) 'The proton-linked monocarboxylate transporter (MCT) family: structure, function and regulation', *Biochemical Journal* 343 Pt 2, 281–99.

Hamilton, M. T. and Booth, F. W. (2000) 'Skeletal muscle adaptation to exercise: a century of progress', *Journal of Applied Physiology* 88, 327–31.

Heinrich, B. (2001) *Racing the Antelope*, New York: HarperCollins, pp. 1–292.

Hortobagyi, T., Israel, R. G., Houmard, J. A., O'Brien, K. F., Johns, R. A. and Wells, J. M. (1992) 'Comparison of four methods to assess body composition in black and white athletes', *International Journal of Sport Nutrition* 2, 60–74.

Howald, H., Hoppeler, H., Claassen, H., Mathieu, O. and Straub, R. (1985) 'Influences of endurance training on the ultrastructural composition of the different muscle fiber types in humans', *Pflüügers Archiv European Journal of Physiology* 403, 369–76.

Ikai, M. and Steinhaus, A. H. (1961) 'Some factors modifying the expression of human strength', *Journal of Applied Physiology* 16, 157–63.

Johnston, I. A. (1991) 'Muscle action during locomotion: a comparative perspective', *Journal of Experimental Biology* 160, 167–85.

Juel, C., Hellsten, Y., Saltin, B. and Bangsbo, J. (1999) 'Potassium fluxes in contracting human skeletal muscle and red blood cells', *American Journal of Physiology* 276, R184–R188.

Karlsson, J., Sjodin, B., Jacobs, I. and Kaiser, P. (1981) 'Relevance of muscle fibre type to fatigue in short intense and prolonged exercise in man', *Ciba Foundation Symposium* 82, 59–74.

Kay, D. and Marino, F. E. (2000) 'Fluid ingestion and exercise hyperthermia: implications for performance, thermoregulation, metabolism and the development of fatigue', *Journal of Sports Sciences* 18, 71–82.

Kay, D., Marino, F. E., Cannon, J., St Clair, G. A., Lambert, M. I. and Noakes, T. D. (2001) 'Evidence for neuromuscular fatigue during high-intensity cycling in warm, humid conditions', *European Journal of Applied Physiology* 84, 115–21.

Komi, P. V. and Tesch, P. (1979) 'EMG frequency spectrum, muscle structure, and fatigue during dynamic contractions in man', *European Journal of Applied Physiology: Occupational Physiology* 42, 41–50.

Kram, R. and Taylor, C. R. (1990) 'Energetics of running: a new perspective', *Nature* 346, 265–7.

Kubo, K., Kawakami, Y. and Fukunaga, T. (1999) 'Influence of elastic properties of tendon structures on jump performance in humans', *Journal of Applied Physiology* 87, 2090–6.

Kyrolainen, H., Finni, T., Avela, J. and Komi, P. V. (2003) 'Neuromuscular behaviour of the triceps surae muscle-tendon complex during running and jumping', *International Journal of Sports Medicine* 24, 153–5.

Lambert, E. V., St Clair Gibson, A. and Noakes, T. D. (2005) 'Complex systems model of fatigue: integrative homoeostatic control of peripheral physiological systems during exercise in humans', *British Journal of Sports Medicine* 39, 52–62.

Lambert, M. I. and Noakes, T. D. (2000) 'Dominance of the Africans in distance running', in *Marathon Medicine*, ed. Tunstall Pedoe, D., London: Royal Society of Medicine Press Ltd, pp. 50–62.

Li, J. L., Wang, X. N., Fraser, S. F., Carey, M. F., Wrigley, T. V. and McKenna, M. J. (2002) 'Effects of fatigue and training on sarcoplasmic reticulum Ca (2+) regulation in human skeletal muscle', *Journal of Applied Physiology* 92, 912–22.

Lindinger, M. I. and Sjogaard, G. (1991) 'Potassium regulation during exercise and recovery', *Sports Medicine* 11, 382–401.

Lorentzon, R., Johansson, C., Sjostrom, M., Fagerlund, M. and Fugl-Meyer, A. R. (1988) 'Fatigue during dynamic muscle contractions in male sprinters and marathon runners: relationships between performance, electromyographic activity, muscle cross-sectional area and morphology', *Acta Physiologica Scandinavica* 132, 531–6.

McArdle, W. D., Katch, F. I. and Katch, V. L. (2002) 'Measurement of human energy expenditure', in *Exercise Physiology*, Baltimore, MD: Lippincott Williams and Wilkins.

McKenna, M. J. (1992) 'The roles of ionic processes in muscular fatigue during intense exercise', *Sports Medicine* 13, 134–45.

McKenna, M. J. (1995) 'Effects of training on potassium homeostasis during exercise', *Journal of Molecular and Cellular Cardiology* 27, 941–9.

Marino, F. E. (2002) 'Methods, advantages, and limitations of body cooling for exercise performance', *British Journal of Sports Medicine* 36, 89–94.

Marino, F. E., Lambert, M. I. and Noakes, T. D. (2004) 'Superior performance of African runners in warm humid but not in cool environmental conditions', *Journal of Applied Physiology* 96, 124–30.

Marino, F. E., Mbambo, Z., Kortekaas, E., Wilson, G., Lambert, M. I., Noakes, T. D. and Dennis, S. C. (2000) 'Advantages of smaller body mass during distance running in warm, humid environments', *Pflüügers Archiv European Journal of Physiology* 441, 359–67.

Masuda, K., Masuda, T., Sadoyama, T., Inaki, M. and Katsuta, S. (1999) 'Changes in surface EMG parameters during static and dynamic fatiguing contractions', *Journal of Electromyography and Kinesiology* 9, 39–46.

Michaut, A., Pousson, M., Ballay, Y. and Van Hoecke, J. (2001) 'Short-term changes in the series elastic component after an acute eccentric exercise of the elbow flexors', *European Journal of Applied Physiology* 84, 569–74.

Morgan, D. W., Bransford, D. R., Costill, D. L., Daniels, J. T., Howley, E. T. and Krahenbuhl, G. S. (1995) 'Variation in the aerobic demand of running among trained and untrained subjects', *Medicine and Science in Sports and Exercise* 27, 404–9.

Nielsen, B., Strange, S., Christensen, N. J., Warberg, J. and Saltin, B. (1997) 'Acute and adaptive responses in humans to exercise in a warm, humid environment', *Pflüügers Archiv European Journal of Physiology* 434, 49–56.

Nindl, B. C., Kraemer, W. J., Emmert, W. H., Mazzetti, S. A., Gotshalk, L. A., Putukian, M., Sebastianelli, W. J. and Patton, J. F. (1998) 'Comparison of body composition assessment among lean black and white male collegiate athletes', *Medicine and Science in Sports and Exercise* 30, 769–76.

Noakes, T. D. (1988) 'Implications of exercise testing for prediction of athletic performance: a contemporary perspective', *Medicine and Science in Sports and Exercise* 20, 319–30.

Noakes, T. D. (1998) 'Why do Africans run so swiftly? A research challenge for African scientists', *South African Journal of Science* 94, 531–5.

Noakes, T. D. (2000) 'Physiological models to understand exercise fatigue and the adaptations that predict or enhance athletic performance', *Scandinavian Journal of Medicine and Science in Sports* 10, 123–45.

Noakes, T. D., Calbet, J. A., Boushel, R., Sondergaard, H., Radegran, G., Wagner, P. D. and Saltin, B. (2004a) 'Central regulation of skeletal muscle recruitment explains the reduced maximal cardiac output during exercise in hypoxia', *American Journal of Physiology: Regulatory, Integrative and Comparative Physiology* 287, R996–R999.

Noakes, T. D., Harley, Y. X. R., Bosch, A. N., Marino, F. E., St Clair Gibson, A. and Lambert, M. I. (2004b) 'Physiological function and neuromuscular recruitment in elite South African distance runners', *Equine and Comparative Exercise Physiology* 1, 261–71.

Noakes, T. D., Myburgh, K. H. and Schall, R. (1990) 'Peak treadmill running velocity during the VO2 max test predicts running performance', *Journal of Sports Sciences* 8, 35–45.

Noakes, T. D., Peltonen, J. E. and Rusko, H. K. (2001) 'Evidence that a central governor regulates exercise performance during acute hypoxia and hyperoxia', *Journal of Experimental Biology* 204, 3225–34.

Noakes, T. D. and St Clair, G. A. (2004) 'Logical limitations to the "catastrophe" models of fatigue during exercise in humans', *British Journal of Sports Medicine* 38, 648–9.

Noakes, T. D., St Clair, G. A. and Lambert, E. V. (2004c) 'From catastrophe to complexity: a novel model of integrative central neural regulation of effort and fatigue during exercise in humans', *British Journal of Sports Medicine* 38, 511–14.

Nybo, L. and Nielsen, B. (2001) 'Hyperthermia and central fatigue during prolonged exercise in humans', *Journal of Applied Physiology* 91, 1055–60.

Nybo, L. and Secher, N. H. (2004) 'Cerebral perturbations provoked by prolonged exercise', *Progress in Neurobiology* 72, 223–61.

Paavolainen, L., Nummela, A., Rusko, H. and Hakkinen, K. (1999a) 'Neuromuscular characteristics and fatigue during 10 km running', *International Journal of Sports Medicine* 20, 516–21.

Paavolainen, L. M., Nummela, A. T. and Rusko, H. K. (1999b) 'Neuromuscular characteristics and muscle power as determinants of 5-km running performance', *Medicine and Science in Sports and Exercise* 31, 124–30.

Pivarnik, J. M., Bray, M. S., Hergenroeder, A. C., Hill, R. B. and Wong, W. W. (1995) 'Ethnicity affects aerobic fitness in US adolescent girls', *Medicine and Science in Sports and Exercise* 27, 1635–8.

Saltin, B. and Åstrand, P. O. (1967) 'Maximal oxygen uptake in athletes', *Journal of Applied Physiology* 23, 353–8.

Saltin, B. and Strange, S. (1992) 'Maximal oxygen uptake: "old" and "new" arguments for a cardiovascular limitation', *Medicine and Science in Sports and Exercise* 24, 30–7.

Saltin, B., Kim, C. K., Terrados, N., Larsen, H., Svedenhag, J. and Rolf, C. J. (1995a) 'Morphology, enzyme activities and buffer capacity in leg muscles of Kenyan and Scandinavian runners', *Scandinavian Journal of Medicine and Science in Sports* 5, 222–30.

Saltin, B., Larsen, H., Terrados, N., Bangsbo, J., Bak, T., Kim, C. K., Svedenhag, J. and Rolf, C. J. (1995b) 'Aerobic exercise capacity at sea level and at altitude in Kenyan boys, junior and senior runners compared with Scandinavian runners', *Scandinavian Journal of Medicine and Science in Sports* 5, 209–21.

Schmidt-Nielsen, K. (1964) *Desert Animals*, London: Oxford University Press, pp. 1–270.

Schmidt-Nielsen, K. (1972) *How Animals Work*, Cambridge: Cambridge University Press, pp. 1–114.

Schutte, J. E., Townsend, E. J., Hugg, J., Shoup, R. F., Malina, R. M. and Blomqvist, C. G. (1984) 'Density of lean body mass is greater in blacks than in whites', *Journal of Applied Physiology* 56, 1647–9.

Scott, B. K. and Houmard, J. A. (1994) 'Peak running velocity is highly related to distance running performance', *International Journal of Sports Medicine* 15, 504–7.

Sharwood, K. A. (2003) 'The effects of endurance training on neuromuscular characteristics in masters runners', University of Cape Town: Thesis/Dissertation.

Sjogaard, G. (1990) 'Exercise-induced muscle fatigue: the significance of potassium', *Acta Physiologica Scandinavica Supplement* 593, 1–63.

Spurway, N. C., Watson, H., McMillan, K. and Connolly, G. (2000) 'The effect of strength training on the apparent inhibition of eccentric force production in voluntarily activated human quadriceps', *European Journal of Applied Physiology* 82, 374–80.

St Clair Gibson, A. and Noakes, T. D. (2004) 'Evidence for complex system integration and dynamic neural regulation of skeletal muscle recruitment during exercise in humans', *British Journal of Sports Medicine* 38, 797–806.

St Clair Gibson, A., Schabort, E. J. and Noakes, T. D. (2001) 'Reduced neuromuscular activity and force generation during prolonged cycling', *American Journal of Physiology. Regulatory, Integrative and Comparative Physiology* 281, R187–R196.

St Clair, G. A., Baden, D. A., Lambert, M. I., Lambert, E. V., Harley, Y. X., Hampson, D., Russell, V. A. and Noakes, T. D. (2003) 'The conscious perception of the sensation of fatigue', *Sports Medicine* 33, 167–76.

St Clair, G. A., Lambert, M. L. and Noakes, T. D. (2001) 'Neural control of force output during maximal and submaximal exercise', *Sports Medicine* 31, 637–50.

Stainsby, W. N. and Brooks, G. A. (1990) 'Control of lactic acid metabolism in contracting muscles and during exercise', *Exercise and Sport Sciences Reviews* 18, 29–63.

Stallknecht, B., Vissing, J. and Galbo, H. (1998) 'Lactate production and clearance in exercise. Effects of training. A mini-review', *Scandinavian Journal of Medicine and Science in Sports* 8, 127–31.

Tanaka, K. and Matsuura, Y. (1982) 'A multivariate analysis of the role of certain anthropometric and physiological attributes in distance running', *Annals of Human Biology* 9, 473–82.

Taylor, J. L. and Gandevia, S. C. (2001) 'Transcranial magnetic stimulation and human muscle fatigue', *Muscle Nerve* 24, 18–29.

Thorstensson, A. and Karlsson, J. (1976) 'Fatiguability and fibre composition of human skeletal muscle', *Acta Physiologica Scandinavica* 98, 318–22.

Tonouchi, M., Hatta, H. and Bonen, A. (2002) 'Muscle contraction increases lactate transport while reducing sarcolemmal MCT4, but not MCT1', *American Journal of Physiology. Endocrinology and Metabolism* 282, E1062–E1069.

Tucker, R., Rauch, L., Harley, Y. X. and Noakes, T. D. (2004) 'Impaired exercise performance in the heat is associated with an anticipatory reduction in skeletal muscle recruitment', *Pflügers Archiv European Journal of Physiology* 448, 422–30.

Walshe, A. D. and Wilson, G. J. (1997) 'The influence of musculotendinous stiffness on drop jump performance', *Canadian Journal of Applied Physiology* 22, 117–32.

Weston, A. R., Karamizrak, O., Smith, A., Noakes, T. D. and Myburgh, K. H. (1999) 'African runners exhibit greater fatigue resistance, lower lactate accumulation, and higher oxidative enzyme activity', *Journal of Applied Physiology* 86, 915–23.

Weston, A. R., Mbambo, Z. and Myburgh, K. H. (2000) 'Running economy of African and Caucasian distance runners', *Medicine and Science in Sports and Exercise* 32, 1130–4.

Wyndham, C. H., Strydom, N. B., van Rensburg, A. J. and Benade, A. J. (1969) 'Physiological requirements for world-class performances in endurance running', *South African Medical Journal* 43, 996–1002.

Chapter 11

Erythropoietic indices in elite Kenyan runners training at altitude

Effects of descent to sea level

Brian Moore, Robin Parisotto, Craig Sharp, Yannis Pitsiladis and Bengt Kayser

Introduction

The eastern Rift Valley is a geological depression that divides Kenya from north to south and is the homeland of the Kalenjin people. Between the valley floor and the lining mountains the altitude ranges between 1,700 to 4,100 m above sea level (a.s.l.). Here the red murram paths have served as a training ground for the many endurance athletes who have dominated running at Olympic and world record level at distances ranging from 800 m to the marathon for the past 40 years. Athletes bearing the names Keino, Kiptanui, Tergat, Tanui and Barsosio and indeed Kenyan running per se, are synonymous with indefatigability, athletic excellence and world records. A question often asked, and the focus of this book, is why this extraordinary level of success? As discussed in detail throughout the different chapters, the possible explanations offered for the global athletic dominance of athletes from this small corner of the world are numerous and range from physiological considerations including the capacity for endurance running at higher fractions of maximal oxygen consumption ($\dot{V}O_2$ max) (see Chapter 8), superior running economy (see Chapter 6), altitude adaptation and genetic advantage (see Chapter 14) and social and economic considerations (see Chapters 1–4). None, however, has been shown to provide a definitive and 'exclusive' explanation for the remarkable achievements of east African endurance athletes. What is often termed a 'Kenyan' running phenomenon may more accurately be described as an 'eastern Rift Valley' or 'Kalenjin' running phenomenon as this area and tribal group, respectively, typically account for the majority of the national endurance teams (see Chapter 14). The running 'sub-tribes' amongst the Kalenjin demography include the Nandi, Marakwet, Tugen, Kipsigis, Keiyo, Pogoi and Kisii. As mentioned in Chapter 14, the birthplaces of most of the best east African endurance athletes are not evenly distributed throughout east Africa, rather, they are concentrated in distinct regions of Kenya and Ethiopia, named Arsi and Nandi, respectively; these east African regions are at high altitude (see Figure 14.1 and 14.2 in Chapter 14). Therein lies a commonly proposed explanation for the success of east African endurance athletes: that their altitudinous habitat may be at least partially responsible for their dominance of endurance running.

In his seminal work on adaptation to hypoxia, the late Peter Hochachka advanced the idea that early phases of hominid evolution in the east African Rift area occurred under conditions of altitude hypoxia aggravated by drier and colder climates (Hochachka et al. 1998). An exposure over many generations to hypoxia and conditions of survival requiring an endurance capacity for a hunter-gatherer type life (Bramble and Lieberman 2004; see also Chapter 6) could have induced in our species an ancestral physiological phenotype genetically adapted for hypoxia tolerance and for endurance performance. This hypothesis led Hochachka to raise the following intriguing question: If an evolutionary early common hypoxic response is our species 'solution' to problems/requirements of hypoxia and/or endurance performance, could this hypoxia-defence mechanism be expressed in a down-regulated low capacity in indigenous high-altitude groups (e.g. Tibetans and Sherpas), and in an up-regulated high-capacity in groups selected for endurance performance, e.g. east Africans (Hochachka et al. 1998)? Cynthia Beall advanced an alternative view arguing that later evolutionary forces may have induced different, possibly independent patterns of altitude adaptation among the three main long-term altitude exposed human lineages, namely south Amerindians from the Andean plateau (i.e. Quechuas and Aymara), Tibetans and Sherpas of the Himalayan plateau and east Africans from the altitude plateaux in Ethiopia and Kenya (Beall 2003). Beall based her contention on the finding that there are differences in oxygen transport determinants between these populations. For example, Andeans show higher haemoglobin (Hb) concentrations than Tibetans, who have Hb concentrations similar to those of sea-level residents (Beall et al. 1998). Like Tibetans, east Africans have Hb concentrations in the normal (i.e. Ethiopians) to high (i.e. Kenyans) sea-level range, but for a given level of hypoxia, have a higher arterial oxygen saturation as compared to Andeans and Tibetans (Beall et al. 2002). Lowlanders acutely exposed to altitude increase their ventilation and cardiac output, at a given metabolic cost, to allow oxygen transport to be maintained. Within hours of exposure to altitude, Hb concentration and haematocrit (Hct) increase thus enhancing the oxygen transport capacity of blood. There is also a decrease in plasma volume resulting from a shift of water from the extracellular to the intracellular compartments. Over the course of a few days, plasma volume may decrease by up to 20%. Upon descent to low altitude, however, a rapid fall in Hct and Hb is observed, explained by an expansion of the plasma compartment (see Ward et al. 2000; Grover and Bärtsch 2001; Robach et al. 2002; Gamboa et al. 2006) even though neocytolysis targeting red cells also plays a role (Rice et al. 2001). Thus, these rapid changes in 'apparent' red cell mass are not a good indicator of de novo synthesis of red cells. Typically, when exposing lowlanders to high altitude, a 'true' increase in red cell mass may take up to several weeks to become apparent. This increase is due to new red cell synthesis in the bone marrow controlled by erythropoietin

(EPO). Upon acute exposure to altitude, a transient increase in EPO occurs, peaking on the third day and normalizing after one to two weeks, while the turnover of EPO remains increased, thus explaining the observed increase in red cell mass with longer-term hypoxia (Grover and Bärtsch 2001). It is this natural increase in red cell mass which is sought by endurance athletes and coaches using various modes of altitude training, of which the 'live high: train low' regimen has lately become increasingly popular (see Hahn et al. 2001 and Levine and Stray-Gundersen 2001 for reviews). The rationale for this training strategy is based on the traditional 'cardiovascular model' of fatigue which contends that exercise performance will be improved by increasing oxygen delivery (Stray-Gundersen et al. 2001; Stray-Gundersen and Levine 1999). This topic is currently under much debate (see 'Point to Counterpoint' discussion by Levine and Stray-Gundersen (2005) debating with Gore and Hopkins (2005) in Journal of Applied Physiology). Apart from increases in red cell mass, other explanations for the increased exercise performance with altitude training paradigms now include improved running economy and muscle buffer capacity (Saunders et al. 2004; Hahn and Gore 2001). Since east African athletes live and thrive at high altitude ('high' in the context of the current chapter denoting altitudes between 1,950 and 2,450 m a.s.l.; see below), research into the regulation of oxygen transport in these athletes is of interest in the quest to understand the effect of altitude exposure on endurance exercise performance. Indeed, in Chapter 1 of this book, John Bale reminds the reader that Kenyan track athletes won 11 medals in 6 events at the 1968 Olympic Games in Mexico City, ranging from the 4×400 m and the 800 m to the steeplechase and the 10,000 m. When 'explaining' this Kenyan running success in Mexico City, many of the most experienced journalists in world track and field labelled altitude as the key factor. Kenyan runners were seen as aberrations and it was implied that things would return to 'normal' with the next Olympics being at sea level; but they did not! Data on erythropoietic regulation in Kenyan runners are scant and little is known about what happens to their haematological status when these athletes visit lower altitudes for competition (Ashenden et al. 2003). This chapter provides new data on the haematological status of elite Kenyan runners upon descent to sea level following chronic altitude exposure. In addition, because of the potentially confounding effects of altitude exposure on indices of blood doping (Ashenden et al. 2001, 2003; Ashenden 2004), the haematological data of these athletes are contrasted with current standards of blood doping screening practices.

Study design and methodology

Athletes

Forty-one elite male Kenyan endurance runners with a mean (± SD) age of 25.8 ± 1.6 y were invited to participate in this study. All athletes gave their informed consent for blood samples to be obtained and their blood profiles reviewed within the context of an anti-doping protocol, in addition to haematological parameter tracking. This athlete cohort had collectively won five Olympic medals, 11 world championship medals and held world records in the 3,000 m, 3,000 m steeplechase and 5,000 m, and world bests over 5,000 m and 10,000 m on the road (Figure 11.1). These athletes were selected by their management agencies to compete on the Golden League/Grand Prix circuit based upon performances in both the Kenyan domestic season and national trials. Athletes specializing in the longer distances 5 km, 10 km, 21 km, or preparing for an autumn marathon, travelling to the lucrative and highly competitive US road-racing circuit, were also included.

All athletes participating in this study lived and trained in Eldoret (2,100 m a.s.l.), Nyahururu (2,350 m a.s.l.) or Thomson's falls (2,303 m a.s.l.). Other local training camps to which athletes migrated in the Rift Valley included: Iten (2,450 m a.s.l.), Kapsabet (1,950 m a.s.l.) and the Nandi Hills (2,000 m a.s.l.). This investigation was undertaken in the month of April 2001 while athletes were preparing for the World Athletic Championships in Edmonton, Canada.

Figure 11.1 Train hard win easy! Athletes in full flight in preparation for the Seville world championships in 1999.

Procedures

Blood samples were collected from all athletes (n = 41) while living and training at altitude. A subgroup of 10 of these elite runners was re-sampled seven days following descent to sea level and prior to competition. Each athlete completed an ad hoc questionnaire in order to ascertain training level in terms of duration and intensity. The extent of any illnesses, medication or nutritional supplementation was also noted, as was the known incidence of familial haemo-globinopathies (e.g. sickle cell trait) that could have had substantial effect on the measured haematological parameters.

Haematological analyses

Standardized phlebotomy procedures were applied in order to minimize the effects of diurnal variation and posture. Briefly, blood samples were drawn by a trained phlebotomist from an ante-cubital vein utilizing a closed vacuette system (i.e. two 3ml K_3 EDTA tubes and two 3 ml serum tubes, Greiner Bio-One Ltd., Stonehouse, UK) while the athletes were in a supine position in an unfasted state. The tubes were initially stored at 4°C for 18 hours (i.e. the time required for transportation from Eldoret to London) and subsequently aliquoted into cryotubes stored at –80°C prior to freighting on dry ice to the Department of Sports Haematology at the Australian Institute of Sport (AIS) in Canberra, Australia for analysis (Parisotto et al. 2000).

Flow cytometric erythrocyte analysis was performed on the Bayer Diagnostics ADVIA™ 120 utilizing the principles of flow cytometry, iso-volumetric sphering and hydrodynamic focusing (to reduce co-incidence). Direct erythrocyte measurements included red cell count (RBC), Hb, haematocrit (Hct) and mean cell volume (MCV). Simultaneous reticulocyte measurement (% retic) was undertaken for each sample. The analyser was calibrated against Bayer ADVIA™ diagnostics reference materials before samples were processed. Serum erythropoietin (EPO) determinations were made utilizing solid-phase, sequential chemilluminescent immulite assay (Diagnostic Products Corporation, Los Angeles, CA, USA) and controlled with three EPO levels (mean 15.2, 30.4 and 62.3 mU.mL^{-1}). Soluble transferrin concentrations (sTfr) were quantified using an automated immunonephelometric assay (Dade Behring, GmbH, Marburg, Germany) and controlled by two sTfr controls (mean 0.63 and 1.45 mg.L^{-1}).

ON-he and OFF-hr model scores

ON-he and OFF-hr scores were calculated as previously described (Gore et al. 2003), utilizing the following equations:

$$ON\text{-}he = Hb + 9.74\ln(EPO)$$
$$OFF\text{-}hr = Hb - 60 \div (Ret)$$

Table 11.1 A 'typical' training programme followed by elite Kenyan 1500 m and 5,000 m athletes training at high altitude training camps in Edoret, Kenya. This information was presented by Moses Kiptanui and Paul Koech at the Global Endurance Running Conference, Bristol 2001. This information is included as both training intensity and volume affect key haematological variables (see El-Sayed *et al.* 2005)

	6am Morning run	10am Main workout	4pm Individual
Monday	60mins at own pace	50mins steady	40mins easy
Tuesday	50mins at own pace	Hill session 20 × 150m	40 mins easy
Wednesday	60mins own pace	50 mins steady	30mins floats stretching
Thursday	50mins own pace	**Interval session***	20 mins easy
Friday	60mins own pace	50mins steady	Rest
Saturday	50mins own pace	**Interval session***	Rest
Sunday	**Long Run** : 60–80mins own pace		

Note: *16 × 400m/8 × 800m off 30 secs.

Where ln is the natural logarithm, Hb is haemoglobin concentration ($g.L^{-1}$), Ret is % reticulocytes and EPO is erythropoietin concentration ($mU.mL^{-1}$). The ON-he model was designed to detect the recent use of blood or blood-boosting agents and utilises the Hb and erythropoietin levels. This model can detect the recent administration of blood and/or blood boosting agents. The objective of the OFF-hr model (utilizing Hb and the reticulocyte count) is to detect the previous use of any blood-boosting agents within the period performance benefits remain.

Training

The training 'typically' undertaken by Kenyan 1500 m and 5,000 m athletes is described in Table 11.1. The main workout usually changes in focus as the track season approaches. The morning run is completed in a group beginning with an 'easy' eight-minute mile pace, accelerating to finish in sub-five-minute mile pace. High intensity track sessions are completed three times a week (i.e. on Tuesday, Thursday and Saturday). The evening training sessions are gentle and serve primarily as a regeneration workout and key component of the recovery programme.

Data analysis

Data were expressed as the mean ± SD or median (range). Statistical analysis was carried out using paired t-tests. Statistical significance was declared at $P < 0.05$.

Results

Changes in haematological parameters

The haematological variables of the elite Kenyan athletes at altitude (n = 41) and upon descent to sea level (n = 10) are presented in Table 11.2. The mean Hb and Hct for the group while living and training at an altitude of about 2,300 m was 164 g.L^{-1} and 49%, respectively, while the highest individual values were 185 g.L^{-1} and 56%, respectively (Figure 11.2). Of the 41 elite athletes, 10 (or 24%) had a Hct level above 50% and a Hb concentration above 170 g.L^{-1} (Figure 11.2). Significant reductions in Hb and Hct were found upon descent to sea level after a continuous stay at altitude (152 ± 7 g.L^{-1}, P<0.001; 45 ± 2%, P<0.001; Table 11.2). The serum EPO concentration at altitude was 8.4 ± 3.2 mU.mL^{-1} and was also significantly reduced following descent to sea level (6.1 ± 3.1 mU.mL^{-1}, P = 0.035; Table 11.2). The reticulocyte percentage, which reflects the rate of erythropoietic activity, was relatively high at altitude (1.7 ± 0.3%, with four athletes having reticulocyte counts greater than 2%; Figure 11.2) and was reduced, although non-significantly, following descent to sea level (1.5 ± 0.4%, P = 0.213; Table 11.2). Similarly, the average serum sTfr concentration at

Table 11.2 Haematological parameters (mean ± SD and range) for elite Kenyan athletes at altitude (baseline) and seven days following descent to sea level and prior to competition

Variable	Baseline (=41)	Baseline (n=10)	7 days after descent
Hb gL^{-1}	164 (9) 138–185	167 (7) 154–179	152 (7)* 140–164
Hct %	49 (3) 43–56	50 (2) 46–52	45 (2)* 42–48
Retic %	1.7 (0.3) 1.1–2.6	1.7 (0.3) 1.3–2.2	1.5 (0.4) 0.9–2.0
EPO MU·ml^{-1}	– –	8.4 (3.2) 4.0–13.4	6.1 (3.1)* 2.8–9.0
sTfr mg·L^{-1}	– –	0.95 (0.17) 0.63–1.36	0.87 (0.13)* 0.68–1.05
OFF-hr	88 (13) 54–119	91 (12) 69–105	82 (9)* 66–94
ON-he	–	185 (9) 169–192	166 (8)* 150–171

Note: * indicates significant difference from baseline.

altitude was 0.95 ± 0.17 mg.L^{-1} which was also non-significantly reduced following descent to sea level (0.87 ± 0.13 mg.L^{-1}, P = 0.323; Table 11.2).

ON-he and OFF-hr doping model scores

A graphical illustration of individual OFF-hr scores relative to false positive cut-off intervals for the 41 elite Kenyan athletes at altitude is presented in Figure 11.2. As indicated above, 10 out of the 41 athletes would have been required to undertake further testing including urine analysis given that their Hct was in excess of 50% or their haemoglobin levels greater than 170 g.L^{-1}, while four athletes with reticulocyte counts greater than 2% would also have been placed under further scrutiny (Figure 11.2). As shown, none of the elite Kenyan athletes would have been required to undertake further testing when using the OFF-hr model score limit of 133 imposed by the International Amateur Athletic Federation (IAAF). As expected, the values for ON-he (P<0.001) and OFF-hr (P = 0.016) were significantly reduced upon descent to sea level compared with values initially obtained at altitude (Table 11. 2).

Discussion

The main findings of the present investigation were first that elite Kenyan athletes training and living at high altitude have normal to high Hb values, second that several parameters of erythropoietic activity in these athletes, namely Hb, % reticulocyte count, serum EPO concentration and sTfr, change rapidly (i.e. within one week) upon descent to low altitude, and third that 'second-generation' blood doping tests, screening for illicit manipulation of erythropoiesis, must consider the effects of exposure to altitude hypoxia on red cell synthesis and turnover. These data corroborate earlier preliminary findings on six Kenyan athletes (Ashenden *et al.* 2003).

Performance and haemoglobin

The rapid 9% reduction in Hb concentration found one week after descent to low altitude indicates that blood volume and Hct are regulated differently at high altitude as compared to low altitude in Kenyan life-time altitude dwellers. At altitude a certain level of haemoconcentration seems typical and is rapidly reversible upon descent. These findings add to the disparity of published data on the changes of haemoglobin concentration and blood volume upon descent from real or simulated altitude and indicate the need for more data on the time course of changes in blood volume and erythropoiesis in the weeks after descent (Rice *et al.* 2001; Wilber 2001; Levine and Stray-Gundersen 2005; Gore and Hopkins 2005; Gamboa *et al.* 2006).

Maximum performance is determined by many factors. Simply utilizing recorded times for a given distance belies a host of variables and causal factors

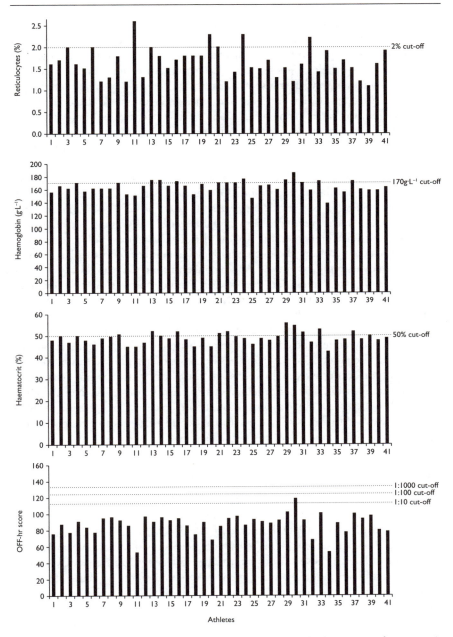

Figure 11.2 Graphical representation of the individual OFF-hr scores, haematocrit, haemoglobin and percent reticulocytes for the elite Kenyan athletes whilst at altitude (n=41).

Note: The respective cut-offs for the different haematological parameters are also shown.

that are implicated in the final performance. Race pace and tactics, weather, effects of recent training sessions, travel, proximity to national championships and to world championship selection events can all affect times recorded for each event. Nevertheless, since endurance performance relies on high aerobic capacity, changes in oxygen transport capacity are certainly of great importance. Mass oxygen transport depends, *inter alia*, on cardiac output and blood oxygen concentration, the latter being a function of Hb concentration and saturation. Increasing blood oxygen concentration increases $\dot{V}O_2$ max and is the rationale behind the illicit practice of blood doping (Ekblom et al. 1972; Turner et al. 1993).

The rapid changes in Hb and Hct upon descent are likely to be due to two mechanisms: rapid plasma expansion (Grover and Bärtsch 2001; Robach et al. 2002) and somewhat slower neocytolysis (Rice et al. 2001). While at high altitude the Kenyan athletes probably had a lower blood volume but higher Hb concentration since on descending to low altitude their blood volume increased by 10% as calculated from the decreased Hct (assuming no neocytolysis, which clearly is an oversimplification) while Hb concentration decreased by 9%. These findings corroborate similar data reported in altitude natives in Peru (Gamboa et al. 2006). With or without neocytolysis, it can be expected that such large changes in these haematological parameters would impact on oxygen transport capacity, although it is possible that an increased circulating blood volume may have partly counteracted these changes through a higher cardiac output. However, in the absence of specific measurements of arterial Hb saturation and cardiac output during maximal exercise in these athletes, it is not possible to assess the implications for performance of the changes observed. Nevertheless, despite the decreased Hb concentration upon descent, the present athletes competed well, with times very close to the world best times of that year and inside the Olympic standards of the previous year.

Altitude and anti-doping screening

While questions regarding the efficacy of altitude training persist (Gore and Hopkins 2005; Levine and Stray-Gundersen 2005), a regimen of blood (Ekblom et al. 1972; Buick et al. 1980; Turner et al. 1993) and/or EPO doping (Ekblom et al. 1991; Russell et al. 2002) has repeatedly been shown to improve endurance performance. Hence these various approaches, allegedly, are frequently subject to abuse by athletes and the development of tests to detect the abuse of recombinant human EPO, other erythropoietic accelerants or blood transfusions is thus highly relevant in the current context of global anti-doping efforts in elite sport (Malcovati et al. 2003; Ashenden 2004). Chronic altitude exposure has the potential to influence the indices of blood doping and the results of the anti-doping tests implemented by the International Olympic Committee (IOC) and World Anti-Doping Agency (WADA) (Ashenden et al. 2001, 2003; Ashenden 2004). There is therefore an urgent need to further understand how chronic altitude exposure and descent to sea-level altitude can influence erythropoiesis and blood doping screening tests.

While the reduction in Hb concentration upon descent and the diminished erythropoietic activity indexed through the percentage reticulocyte count may not have corresponded with equivalent reductions in performance, these parameters did have a marked effect on blood model scores currently utilized in the detection of EPO abuse. Given the significant contribution of Hb to the detection models and the corresponding unexpected substantial reduction in model scores, our data confirm that altitude exposure must be taken into account in detection paradigms, but to a greater extent than previously thought, as these athlete's scores were outside the lower range (95% confidence interval) previously applied to the detection models. This again implies that further research is required to assess the time course of Hb concentration changes in the weeks following altitude exposure among elite athletes, particularly those of east African origin upon descent from high altitude. While this research does not provide any further explanations for the dominance of east African runners, it does highlight a trend not previously reported (i.e. a rapid reduction in Hb concentration upon descent to sea level amongst long-term altitude dwelling athletes). It also confirms that elite Kenyan athletes, presenting without known or identified haemoglobinopathies will not trigger the second generation 'OFF' model EPO abuse detection tests. These second generation tests are cheap and effective and can distinguish athletes who are competing fairly from those who are not.

Even though many east African athletes choose to live and train elsewhere, most live and train in their native east African regions. For competition purposes, they frequently travel to sea-level to race. Therefore, for reasons of haematological tracking and anti-doping practices, it is paramount that the natural changes in erythropoietic indices from altitude exposure are considered. Applying the simple blood test thresholds (Hb > 170g.L^{-1} and Hct > 50%) to Kenyan or other chronically to altitude adapted athletes would produce a high proportion of false positive cases, with athletes being potentially incorrectly banned from competition.

Because of the limitations of the earlier tests, Gore *et al.* (2003) designed the second-generation 'ON' and 'OFF' scores and introduced these after the Sydney Olympic Games in 2000 to improve anti-doping screening and for reasons of economy (i.e. EPO detection is expensive). The chosen 'second-generation' parameters are: Hb, EPO, percentage reticulocyte count (Ret) and sTfr. In the case of endurance running and therefore this cohort, the relevant blood testing protocol most recently implemented by the IAAF is the Reticulocyte (OFF-hr) model (Gore *et al.* 2003). This blood test involves the measurement of Hb and reticulocytes. Its strength and specificity are based on the tenet that, following a sustained period of accelerated erythropoiesis, such as synthetic EPO administration, Hb levels stabilize for a period of weeks while at the same time the blood's physiological capacity, being saturated, results in the decreased, perhaps even halted production of red blood cells so that normal haemostatic balance may be regained. Consequently, the potential for the paradoxical phenomena of high Hb with low reticulocytes becomes possible. Ordinarily a high Hb concentration would be accompanied by a high reticulocyte count.

A high Hb and low reticulocyte count in an athlete could be explained by: (1) *Aplastic anaemia*, an acquired but rare blood disorder affecting all blood cell lines (e.g. red cells, white cells, and platelets) and therefore easily excluded; (2) red cell *neocytolysis* which is the selective destruction of young red cells, as observed in astronauts on re-entry after space travel (Trial and Rice 2004) and in high-altitude dwellers upon descent to sea level (Rice *et al.* 2001); or (3) evidence of erythropoietic withdrawal (Rice and Alfrey 2000) or previous blood doping using any agent. Only the latter possibility represents undeniable evidence of blood doping. There are no known medical abnormalities that mimic a concomitant increase in Hb concentration and decrease in reticulocytes with the exception of blood transfusions (Piron *et al.* 2001) and EPO administration (Parisotto *et al.* 2001), both leading to the quantitative changes that would elicit a positive blood doping test result (Parisotto *et al.* 2000; Sharpe *et al.* 2002).

The potential for altitude to compromise the OFF-hr model was recognized by its developers (Gore *et al.* 2003) when they designed specific cut-off scores for athletes at sea level and at altitude applying four levels of false positive rates (i.e. 1:10, 1:100, 1:1000 and 1:10000) for each location. For altitude testing specifically, the worst case scenario scores at the respective false positive rates were: 114, 125, 134 and 141 respectively. Amongst our present Kenyan cohort, the athlete with an extremely high Hb value (185) gave a score of 119 which is below the 1:100 false positive cut-off of 125 (and the IAAF cut-off of 133). This reasonably 'normal' score was due to a normal reticulocyte count of 1.2%. If on the other hand the reticulocyte count was depressed to 0.2%, consistent with decelerated erythropoiesis, the resultant score would be 173, well above the 1:10000 false positive cut-off. The combined strength of increased Hb and depressed reticulocytes to detect previous blood doping is clear.

The IAAF has now adopted the OFF-hr model test and used an adapted protocol for the first time at the 2005 World Championships in Helsinki. The cut-off levels are a Hb threshold of 170 $g.L^{-1}$, a Hct threshold of 50%, a reticulocyte threshold of >2.0% (indicative of accelerated erythropoiesis), a reticulocyte threshold of <0.2% (indicative of decelerated erythropoiesis) and an OFF-hr score of 133 (equivalent to a cut-off of 1:1000 at altitude or 1:10000 at sea level). Aside from the OFF-hr test the IAAF also has the discretion of conducting further blood tests including natural EPO levels which can be used in an extension of the OFF-hr model known as the OFF-hre model which has a greater discriminatory power (see Ashenden *et al.* 2003 and Gore *et al.* 2003 for further details). The objective of the OFF-hr model is to detect the previous use of blood doping whilst performance benefits remain; possibly for as long as four weeks following EPO administration (Russell *et al.* 2002). However, none of the Kenyan athletes would have been required to undergo further testing using the OFF-hr model score limit of 133 set by the IAAF. In general, it would appear that Kenyan athletes either residing, and/or sojourning to altitude and then descending or returning to sea level are at low risk of registering a false positive result using the current IAAF adopted OFF-hr test to detect previous blood doping (i.e. decelerated erythropoiesis). However the fact that a relatively high risk exists that a false positive may occur if Hb, Hct and percentage reticulocytes criteria are solely applied highlights the ineffectiveness of such a policy, with its potential for severe injustice.

In our cohort of 10 athletes descending from altitude to sea level, seven had normal EPO levels measured from samples taken at altitude. The mean ON-he score at altitude was 185 (highest score was 192), well below that of the 1:10 cut-off score allowing for altitude, i.e. 209. At sea-level the mean ON-he score was 166 (highest score was 171) well below the 1:10 cut-off score of 185. Despite the shortcomings of the ON-he model (e.g. amenability to manipulation by saline dilution), the evidence presented here from this small but select cohort is encouraging and would suggest that the ON-he model is capable of indirectly detecting blood doping whether by blood transfusion or by recombinant EPO doping (including Aranesp).

Conclusions

Elite Kenyan athletes intensely training at high altitude have a Hb concentration and Hct in the normal to high range as compared to lowlanders. When these athletes descend to low altitude for competition, these indices are reduced to a similar extent as the increases seen in lowlanders who engaged in high altitude training. If Hct and Hb alone are considered for blood doping control, many of these great athletes would be beyond the accepted higher limits. However, this serious problem can be overcome by using 'second-generation' tests which incorporate several haematological parameters in calculated scores and make allowances for the effects of altitude. The significance, if any, in terms of performance benefit/detriment of the rapid drop in Hb concentration upon descent to low altitude remains to be determined even though the extraordinary continuous global dominance of east African endurance runners seems indirect proof that any negative effect on performance is not of significance at world championship level. The question asked in the Introduction as to why this remarkable level of performance of east African athletes occurs therefore remains to be answered in terms of haematology.

Acknowledgements

The authors acknowledge the support of Professor Allan Hahn and technical assistance of Sally Wright at the Australian Institute of Sport (Canberra, Australia) and the following biomedical scientists/phlebotomists at Pathology Services (Ashford Hospital, Middlesex, England): Tony Newman-Smith, Shan

Adlam, Tony Newcombe and Jacqui Hough. The cooperation of the elite athletes who participated as subjects in the study is greatly appreciated. Their efforts have helped inform and change anti-doping testing practice in a way that greatly reduces the chances of such athletes being incorrectly banned from competition (i.e. through false positives), thus providing the means to distinguish athletes who are competing fairly from those who are not.

Bibliography

Ashenden, M. J. (2004) 'Contemporary issues in the fight against blood doping in sport', *Haematologica* 89 (8), 901–3.

Ashenden, M. J., Hahn, A. G., Martin, D. T., Logan, P., Parisotto, R. and Gore, C. J. (2001) 'A comparison of the physiological response to simulated altitude exposure and r-HuEPO administration', *Journal of Sports Sciences* 11 (19), 831–7.

Ashenden, M. J., Gore, C. J., Parisotto, R., Sharpe, K., Hopkins, W. G. and Hahn, A. G. (2003) 'Effect of altitude on second-generation blood tests to detect erythropoietin abuse by athletes', *Haematologica* 88, 1053–62.

Beall, C. M. (2003) 'High-altitude adaptations', *Lancet* 362, S14–15.

Beall, C. M., Brittenham, G. M., Strohl, K. P., Blangero, J., Williams-Blangero, S., Goldstein, M. C., Decker, M. J., Vargas, E., Villena, M., Soria, R., Alarcon, A. M. and Gonzales, C. (1998) 'Hemoglobin concentration of high-altitude Tibetans and Bolivian Aymara', *American Journal of Physical Anthropology* July 106 (3), 385–400. Erratum in *American Journal of Physical Anthropology* Dec. 107 (4), 421.

Beall, C. M., Decker, M. J., Brittenham, G. M., Kushner, I., Gebremedhin, A. and Strohl, K. P. (2002) 'An Ethiopian pattern of human adaptation to high-altitude hypoxia', *Proceedings of the National Academy of Sciences USA* 24 Dec. 99 (26), 17215–8.

Bramble, D. M. and Lieberman, D. E. (2004) 'Endurance running and the evolution of Homo', *Nature* 432, 345–52.

Buick, F. J., Gledhill, N., Froese, A. B., Spiet, L. and Myers, E. C. (1980) 'Effect of induced erythrocythaemia on aerobic work capacity', *Journal of Applied Physiology* 48 (4), 636–42.

Ekblom, B. and Berglund, B. (1991) 'Effect of erythropoietin administration on maximal aerobic power in man', *Scandinavian Journal of Medicine and Science in Sports* 1, 88–93.

Ekblom, B., Goldbarg, A. N. and Gullbring, B. (1972) 'Response to exercise after blood loss and reinfusion', *Journal of Applied Physiology* 83 (2), 175–80.

El-Sayed, M. S., Ali, N. and El-Sayed, Ali, Z. (2005) 'Haemorheology in exercise and training', *Sports Medicine* 35 (8), 649–70.

Gamboa, A., Gamboa, J. L., Holmes, C., Sharabi, Y., Leon-Velarde, F., Fischman, G. J., Appenzeller, O. and Goldstein, D. S. (2006) 'Plasma catecholamines and blood volume in native Andeans during hypoxia and normoxia', *Clinical Autonomic Research* 16 (1), 40–5.

Gore, C. J. and Hopkins, W. G. (2005) 'Counterpoint: Positive effects of intermittent hypoxia (live high: train low) on exercise performance are not mediated primarily by augmented red cell volume', *Journal of Applied Physiology* 99, 2055–7.

Gore, C. J., Parisotto, R., Ashenden, M. J., Stray-Gundersen, J., Sharpe, K., Hopkins, W., Emslie, K. R., Howe, C., Trout, G. J., Kazlauskas, R. and Hahn, A. G. (2003) 'Second-generation blood tests to detect erythropoietin abuse by athletes', *Haematologica* 88 (3), 333–44.

Grover, R. F. and Bärtsch, P. (2001) 'Blood', in *High Altitude: An Exploration of Human Adaptation*, ed. Hornbein, T. F. and Schoene, R. B., New York: Marcel Dekker Inc.

Hahn, A. G., Gore, C. J., Martin, D. T., Ashenden, M. J., Roberts, A. D. and Logan, PA. (2001) 'An evaluation of the concept of living at moderate altitude and training at sea level', *Comparative Biochemistry and Physiology – Part A, Molecular and Integrative Physiology* 128 (4), 777–89.

Hochachka, P. W., Gunga, H. C. and Kirsch, K. (1998) 'Our ancestral physiological phenotype: an adaptation for hypoxia tolerance and for endurance performance?' *Proceedings of the National Academy of Sciences* 95 (4), 1915–20.

Levine, B. D. and Stray-Gundersen, J. (2001) 'The effects of altitude training are mediated primarily by acclimatization, rather than by hypoxic exercise', *Advances in Experimental Medicine and Biology* 502, 75–88.

Levine, B. D. and Stray-Gundersen, J. (2005) 'Point: positive effects of intermittent hypoxia (live high: train low) on exercise performance are mediated primarily by augmented red cell volume', *Journal of Applied Physiology* 99 (5), 2053–5.

Malcovati, L., Pascutto, C. and Cazzola, M. (2003) 'Hematologic passport for athletes competing in endurance sports: a feasibility study', *Haematologica* 88 (5), 570–81.

Parisotto, R., Gore, C. J., Emslie, K. R., Ashenden, M. J., Brunara, C., Howe, C., Martin, D. T., Trout, G. J. and Hahn, A. G. (2000) 'A novel method utilizing markers of altered erythropoiesis for the detection of recombinant human erythropoietin abuse in athletes', *Haematologica* 85 (6), 564–72.

Parisotto, R., Wu, M., Ashenden, M. J., Emslie, K. R., Gore, C. J., Howe, C., Kazlauskas, R., Sharpe, K., Trout, G. J. and Xie, M. (2001) 'Detection of recombinant human erythropoietin abuse in athletes utilizing markers of altered erythropoiesis', *Haematologica* 86 (2), 128–37.

Parisotto, R., Ashenden, M. J., Gore, C. J., Sharpe, K., Hopkins, W., and Hahn, A. G. (2003) 'The effect of common hematologic abnormalities on the ability of blood models to detect erythropoietin abuse by athletes', *Haematologica* 88 (8), 931–40.

Piron, M., Loo, M., Gothot, A., Tassin, F., Fillet, G., and Beguin, Y. (2001) 'Cessation of intensive treatment with recombinant human erythropoietin is followed by secondary anemia', *Blood* 97 (2), 442–8.

Rice, L. and Alfrey, C. P. (2000) 'Modulation of red cell mass by neocytolysis in space and on Earth', *Pflügers Archiv* 441, S2–3, R91–4.

Rice, L., Ruiz, W., Driscoll, T., Whitley, C. E., Tapia, R., Hachey, D. L., Gonzales, G. F. and Alfrey, C. P. (2001) 'Neocytolysis on descent from altitude: a newly recognized mechanism for the control of red cell mass', *Annals of Internal Medicine* 134 (8), 652–6.

Robach, P., Lafforgue, E., Olsen, N. V., Dechaux, M., Fouqueray, B., Westerterp-Plantenga, M., Westerterp, K. and Richalet, J. P. (2002) 'Recovery of plasma volume after 1 week of exposure at 4.350 m', *Pflüügers Archiv* 444, 821–8.

Russell, G., Gore, C. J., Ashenden, M. J., Parisotto, R. and Hahn, A. G. (2002) 'Effects of prolonged low doses of recombinant human erythropoietin during submaximal and maximal exercise', *European Journal of Applied Physiology* 86 (5), 442–9. Erratum in: *European Journal of Applied Physiology* 86 (6), 548.

Saunders, P. U., Telford, R. D., Pyne, D. B., Cunningham, R. B., Gore, C. J., Hahn, A. G. and Hawley, J. A. (2004) 'Improved running economy in elite runners after 20 days of simulated moderate-altitude exposure', *Journal of Applied Physiology* 96 (3), 931–7.

Sharpe, K., Hopkins, W., Emslie, K. R., Howe, C., Trout, G. J., Kazlauskas, R., Ashenden, M. J., Gore, C. J., Parisotto, R. and Hahn, A. G. (2002) 'Development of reference ranges in elite athletes for markers of altered erythropoiesis', *Haematologica* 87 (12), 1248–57.

Stray-Gundersen, J. and Levine, B. D. (1999) '"Living high and training low" can improve sea level performance in endurance athletes', *British Journal of Sports Medicine* 33 (3), 150–1.

Stray-Gundersen, J., Chapman, R. F. and Levine, B. D. (2001) '"Living high-training low" altitude training improves sea level performance in male and female elite runners', *Journal of Applied Physiology* 91 (3), 1113–20.

Trial, J. and Rice, L. (2004) 'Erythropoietin withdrawal leads to the destruction of young red cells at the endothelial-macrophage interface', *Current Pharmaceutical Design* 10 (2), 183–90.

Turner, D. L., Hoppeler, H., Noti, C., Gutner, H. P., Gerber, H., Schena, F., Kayser, B. and Ferretti, G. (1993) 'Limitations to VO2max in humans after blood retransfusion', *Respiration Physiology* 92 (3), 329–41.

Ward, M. P., Milledge, J. S. and West, J. B. (2000) *High Altitude Medicine and Physiology*, 3rd edn, London: Arnold.

Wilber, R. L. (2001) 'Current trends in altitude training', *Sports Medicine* 31 (4), 249–65.

Part III

Athleticogenomic perspectives

Chapter 12

Genes and human elite athletic performance

Daniel G. MacArthur and Kathryn N. North

Introduction

Elite athletes – athletes who have competed at national or international level in their chosen sport – represent a rare convergence of genetic potential and environmental factors, resulting in an individual with the capacity to compete at the highest level in one or more physical activities (Myburgh 2003). There is no question that environmental factors such as training and nutrition are essential for the development of an elite athlete. However, these factors alone are not sufficient – most of us could never achieve elite athlete status, however hard we trained. Just as genetic predisposition plays a major role in determining one's susceptibility to multifactorial diseases such as diabetes and cancer, elite athletic performance is substantially determined by genetic potential.

Heritability of performance-related traits

The first strong evidence for a genetic influence on physical performance came from studies which compared closely related individuals (twin pairs and nuclear families) to unrelated subjects to estimate the heritable component of variation in a number of physical traits. Heritability estimates (a composite measure of genetic and shared environmental factors) for many fitness- and performance-related traits have been calculated by several research groups (Bouchard *et al.* 1997). We will restrict our discussion to heritability estimates for measures of cardiorespiratory and skeletal muscle function, both of which are essential for performance in a wide variety of sports (Bouchard *et al.* 1997).

Genetic influences on several aerobic fitness and cardiac performance traits, both in the sedentary state and in response to a standardized 20-week aerobic exercise training programme, have been analysed as part of the ambitious HERITAGE (HEalth, RIsk factors, exercise Training And GEnetics) Family Study of 130 two-generation families (Bouchard *et al.* 1995). Maximal heritability estimates were close to 50% for maximal oxygen uptake ($\dot{V}O_2$max) in the sedentary state (Bouchard *et al.* 1998) and in response to training (Bouchard *et al.* 1999). Submaximal aerobic performance oxygen consumption and power output had maximal heritability estimates of 48–74% before training and 23–57% in their response to training (Perusse et al. 2001). The maximal heritability of oxygen uptake at the ventilatory threshold was similar (54–8%) in the sedentary state for Caucasians and African-Americans, but was lower in Caucasians (22%) than in African-Americans (51%) for its response to training (Gaskill et al. 2001). Moderate genetic influences were also observed in measures of cardiac function; the maximal heritability estimates were between 41 and 46% for stroke volume and cardiac output during submaximal exercise in the sedentary state, 24–38% for their response to training (An et al. 2000), and 29–34% for the exercise heart rate response to training (An et al. 2003c).

Significant genetic influences have also been identified for measures of skeletal muscle strength and performance. An early focus for heritability studies was variation in the relative proportions of skeletal muscle fibre types, with one study of a small twin-pair cohort suggesting, remarkably, that heritable factors accounted for as much as 99.5% of the phenotypic variance in this trait (Komi et al. 1977). However, a later study of a larger twin cohort (Bouchard et al. 1986) found much lower estimates of heritability (6–66%, depending on the method used for calculation), and a combined review of results from humans and animal models suggests that the real contribution of genetic factors to variation in human fibre type proportions is between 40 and 50% (Simoneau and Bouchard 1995).

Other skeletal muscle traits have also been analysed. Early twin studies suggested that the response to training of oxoglutarate dehydrogenase activity (Thibault et al. 1986) and muscle adaptation to endurance exercise (Hamel et al. 1986) are substantially influenced by genotype. A much larger analysis of 105 twin pairs and their parents suggested that 47–78% of the variance in vertical jump height, a measure of explosive power, was explained by genetic factors (Maes et al. 1996). A study of muscle strength measures in 41 twin pairs before and after a 10-week resistance training programme reported high heritability (30–77%) for several pre-training traits and lower heritability (~20%) for response to training (Thomis et al. 1998). More recently, a study of 16 twin pairs reported heritability indices of 22–93% for measures of anaerobic capacity and explosive power (Calvo et al. 2002), and an analysis of 19 families from the HERITAGE cohort found significant familial aggregation for a number of skeletal muscle phenotypes, including average size of type I (slow oxidative) fibres in the sedentary state, and maximal activity of energy production enzymes both in the sedentary state and in response to training (Rico-Sanz et al. 2003b).

The nature of genetic influences on some performance-related traits has been studied using segregation analysis, which involves following the inheritance pattern of specific phenotypes in nuclear families. One such analysis provided evidence for a single major gene accounting for more than 40% of the variance in oxygen uptake at the ventilatory threshold (Feitosa et al. 2002). A similar analysis of exercise heart rate and its response to training suggested that a major recessive gene accounted for 30% of baseline exercise heart rate, while a major dominant gene accounted for 27% of the variance in the exercise heart rate response to training (An *et al.* 2003a). While these findings do not provide information about the actual identity of the genes in question, they suggest that single major genes contribute to a substantial fraction of phenotypic variance in at least some performance-related traits. This finding has encouraged attempts to identify genetic loci and specific polymorphisms that impact on human physical performance.

Cardiorespiratory and skeletal muscle performance genes

Genome-wide linkage analyses

Genome-wide linkage analysis has proved invaluable in the identification of causative genes in a vast array of human diseases and other traits (Baron 2001). This technique involves correlating a specific phenotype with genotyping data from large numbers of genetic markers spread throughout the genome to identify regions in which a genetic variation co-segregates with variation in the examined trait(s). While this approach is relatively straightforward for Mendelian monogenic traits, the analysis of complex quantitative phenotypes, determined by variation at multiple genetic loci as well as by multiple environmental influences, is more problematic. Nevertheless segregation analysis has suggested that a large proportion of the underlying genetic variance for some performance-related traits is due to single major genes (An *et al.* 2003a; Feitosa *et al.* 2002), making linkage approaches more feasible. Indeed linkage studies have already identified a number of genetic regions showing significant associations with variation in human physical performance traits.

The majority of these genome-wide linkage studies have utilized the HERITAGE family cohort (Bouchard *et al.* 1995). Suggestive linkage peaks have been identified associated with variation in $\dot{V}O_2$ max (Bouchard *et al.* 2000; Rico-Sanz *et al.* 2004), maximal power output (Rico-Sanz *et al.* 2004), exercise stroke volume and cardiac output (Rankinen *et al.* 2002a), and blood pressure both in resting subjects (Rice *et al.* 2002b) and following exercise (Rankinen *et al.* 2001a). A genome-wide screen for loci linked to fat-free body mass, an indicator of skeletal muscle bulk, has been performed in another cohort (Chagnon *et al.* 2000). Several important fitness traits that may have an influence on athletic performance, such as body composition and fat distribution (Chagnon *et al.* 2001; Rice *et al.* 2002a), and glucose and insulin metabolism-related traits (An *et al.* 2003b), have also been analysed by genome-wide screens. The linkage peaks identified by each of these studies provide candidate genes for performance-related traits which can now be investigated using genetic association studies and other related approaches.

Genetic associations with performance-related traits

Genetic association studies are commonly used to test the influence of variation at a candidate locus on specific performance traits. Candidate genes are selected based on *a priori* information, such as localization to a linkage peak from genome-wide scans in humans or animal models and/or experimental data suggesting some functional involvement in the biological trait of interest (Allen *et al.* 2002). Polymorphic sites within the candidate gene are identified and genotyped in a large cohort of individuals for whom phenotypic data are available, and the possibility of correlations between genotype and phenotype is assessed using a variety of statistical approaches (Romero *et al.* 2002). Association studies examining performance-related genes fall into two major categories: case-control studies involving comparisons of genotype frequencies in cohorts of sedentary controls and elite athletes (discussed in the next section), and cross-sectional association studies which examine differences in performance-related phenotypic measurements between individuals with different genotypes.

Genetic association studies, while an extremely useful tool for examining potential effects of a specific genetic variant, must always be interpreted with caution (Lewis 2002; Romero *et al.* 2002). As with any statistical analysis, there is a non-trivial probability of a false positive result due to chance, particularly in studies involving multiple gene-trait analyses or the splitting of cohorts into separately analysed sub-groups (Ioannidis 2003). In addition, studies which have not been carefully controlled for ethnic background and other potential confounding factors carry an additional risk of false positive results due to population stratification (Lewis 2002). Finally, it is important to note that even if a genetic association is solid, there is a substantial possibility that the actual causative variant is not the genotyped polymorphism but some other variant in strong linkage disequilibrium. While each of these potential sources of error can be addressed in any individual study, all reported genetic associations should be regarded as tentative until there is (i) a biologically plausible and well-supported mechanism by which the variant could influence the trait in question, and (ii) replication of the association in other independent cohorts.

In this section we will focus on studies examining the genetic associations with measures of cardiorespiratory function and skeletal muscle strength in healthy (non-diseased) subjects. Associations between muscle strength and the *ACTN3* gene will be discussed later, in the context of results from elite athlete case-control studies while association studies on the *ACE I/D* polymorphism are discussed in the next chapter of this book. For a comprehensive list of candidate genes associated with a variety of fitness- and performance-related traits see the latest release of the human gene map for performance and health-related fitness phenotypes (Wolfarth *et al.* 2005) and subsequent updates.

Candidate genes for cardiorespiratory function

Cardiorespiratory performance traits are among the most heavily studied phenotypes in analyses of human variation. Cardiorespiratory disease is a major contributing factor to morbidity and mortality in all industrialized nations. The understanding of genetic variation in cardiorespiratory function may help to predict an individual's risk of disease long before the onset of symptoms (Higgins 2000), as well as an individual's potential athletic performance, particularly with respect to endurance events (Bouchard et al. 1997).

Several genes have been associated with cardiorespiratory performance traits. The CKMM gene encodes the cytosolic muscle isoform of creatine kinase, an enzyme responsible for the rapid regeneration of ATP during intensive muscle contraction (Echegaray and Rivera 2001). Five carriers of a rare muscle creatine kinase variant identified by isoelectric focusing exhibited significantly better scores for exercise performance indicators than five carriers of the common CKMM allele (Bouchard et al. 1989). The same group demonstrated a highly significant association between a restriction fragment length polymorphism (RFLP) in CKMM and the response of $\dot{V}O_2$ max to a 20-week endurance training programme in 240 unrelated members of the HERITAGE family cohort (Rivera et al. 1997a), and subsequently showed strong evidence of genetic linkage between CKMM and the training response of $\dot{V}O_2$ max in 495 individuals from 98 nuclear families (Rivera et al. 1999). While these studies provide solid evidence for the association of variations in CKMM with $\dot{V}O_2$ max, it is interesting to note that no association was found between the same variations and elite endurance athlete status in another study by the same group (Rivera et al. 1997b).

The M235T missense polymorphism in the angiotensinogen gene (AGT) has also been the subject of several association studies. In a group of 61 healthy post-menopausal women, including 24 elite endurance athletes, the M235T polymorphism was associated with several measures of cardiorespiratory performance, including heart rate, systolic blood pressure and arteriovenous O_2 difference during exercise (McCole et al. 2002). Two separate studies on elite endurance athletes found an association between the TT genotype and greater left ventricular mass: in a cohort of 50 male and 30 female athletes the association was highly significant (Karjalainen et al. 1999), whereas in 83 male athletes the association was only significant in a combined analysis with genotype at the ACE I/D polymorphism (Diet et al. 2001). This association may be present only in trained athletes, as no evidence for the association was identified in a study of 110 healthy males (Linhart et al. 2000) or 426 controls randomly selected from the Finnish population (Kauma et al. 1998). Similarly to CKMM, the AGT M235T variant was not found to be significantly associated with elite endurance athlete status in a case-control study of 60 elite endurance athletes and 400 healthy controls (Alvarez et al. 2000).

Three recent studies have identified associations between missense polymorphisms in the *ADRB2* gene, which encodes the β_2-adrenergic receptor, and cardiorespiratory performance traits. Analysis of a cohort of 19 sedentary, 20 active and 24 elite endurance athletic postmenopausal women demonstrated significantly lower $\dot{V}O_2$ max in women homozygous for the Glu27 allele than carriers of the Gln27 allele (Moore *et al.* 2001). Two later studies examined the phenotypic effects of another polymorphism, Arg16Gly: in a study of 267 normotensive adults, Gly16 homozygotes demonstrated higher performance than Arg16 carriers in a number of measures of cardiac left ventricular function (Grundberg *et al.* 2004), whereas in a group of 31 healthy adults Gly16 homozygotes had a significantly greater heart rate response to exercise than Arg16 homozygotes (Eisenach *et al.* 2004).

Several other polymorphisms have been associated with variation in $\dot{V}O_2$ max. An early study examining RFLPs in several mitochondrial genes showed significant associations between several variants and both $\dot{V}O_2$ max in the untrained state and the change in $\dot{V}O_2$ max in response to training ($\Delta\dot{V}O_2$ max) in 46 sedentary young adult males (Dionne *et al.* 1991). A later study demonstrated a highly significant association between specific alleles at the *HLA-A* locus and $\dot{V}O_2$ max in 16 pairs of male twin sportsmen (Rodas *et al.* 1997). More recently, RFLP haplotypes of the Na^+-K^+-ATPase $\alpha2$ gene *ATP1A2* showed a marginal association ($P = 0.054$) with $\Delta\dot{V}O_2$ max and highly significant associations with the response of maximal power output to training (ΔW_{max}) in 472 sedentary Caucasian members of the HERITAGE cohort following a 20-week training programme (Rankinen *et al.* 2000). Common missense variants of the apolipoprotein E gene, *APOE*, showed significant associations with $\Delta\dot{V}O_2$ max in 120 healthy volunteers subjected to six months of supervised exercise training (Thompson *et al.* 2004). Finally, the common Gly482Ser missense polymorphism in the peroxisome proliferator-activated receptor γ coactivator 1 (PGC-1α) gene *PPARGC1* was found to be significantly associated with the influence of physical activity energy expenditure on predicted max in 599 healthy middle-aged subjects (Franks *et al.* 2003).

Several studies have examined potential genetic influences on cardiac performance traits. Highly significant associations were demonstrated between an intronic polymorphism in the peroxisome proliferator-activated receptor α gene, *PPARA*, and left ventricular growth response to a 10-week physical training programme in 144 young male army recruits, as well as various measures of cardiac size in a 1148-member randomly selected German cohort (Jamshidi *et al.* 2002). More recently, six homozygotes for a common nonsense polymorphism in the adenosine monophosphate deaminase 1 gene *AMPD1* were shown to have significantly lower values for many cardiorespiratory function parameters, including cardiac stroke volume, power output, systolic blood pressure, and heart rate during exercise, compared to 497 carriers of the functional allele (Rico-Sanz *et al.* 2003a).

Candidate genes for skeletal muscle function

Skeletal muscle function traits have also been the subject of genetic association studies. Unfortunately for the study of the genetic basis of athletic performance – which is almost exclusively a youthful pursuit – many of these studies have been performed in elderly individuals, where loss of muscle strength represents a major quality of life issue, and it is unclear how readily their results can be extrapolated to variation in muscle function in younger individuals.

The CNTF and CNTFR genes, which encode ciliary neurotrophic factor (CNTF) and the CNTF-specific α-receptor subunit (CNTFR), have been analysed in two separate studies on subjects aged from 20 to 90 years as part of the Baltimore Longitudinal Study of Aging (Roth et al. 2001; Roth et al. 2003). Individuals heterozygous for a common polymorphism in the CNTF gene, which is predicted to generate a null allele due to abnormal splicing (Takahashi et al. 1994), demonstrated significantly greater muscle contractile function than did homozygotes for the functional allele (Roth et al. 2001). Similarly, individuals heterozygous for a single nucleotide polymorphism (SNP) in the 3' untranslated region of the CNTFR gene displayed significantly higher quadriceps strength than did homozygotes for the more common allele (Roth et al. 2003).

Polymorphisms in the vitamin D receptor gene, VDR, have also been associated with muscle strength phenotypes. A BsmI RFLP corresponding to a SNP in the final intron of the VDR gene was significantly associated with quadriceps and grip strength in 307 non-obese women aged over 70 years (Geusens et al. 1997). The same RFLP and a closely linked length polymorphism in a poly-A repeat were analysed in a cohort of 175 healthy women aged 20–39 years, and identified a weakly significant association with hamstring strength (Grundberg et al. 2004). However, this study failed to replicate the association of the BsmI RFLP with quadriceps and grip strength reported by Geusens et al. (1997), suggesting that there may be an age-dependent component to these associations.

Several other genetic variations linked to skeletal muscle function have been identified in cohorts of elderly individuals. These variations include an ApaI RFLP in the IGF2 gene, encoding insulin-like growth factor II, which was a significant predictor of grip strength in 693 elderly males (Sayer et al. 2002); the K153R amino acid polymorphism in the myostatin gene, GDF-8, which was associated with overall strength in 286 women aged 70–79 years (Seibert et al. 2001); and a SNP in the promoter region of the COL1A1 gene, which encodes the type I collagen α_1 chain, which showed a weak association with lower grip and biceps strength of the dominant arm in 352 males aged between 71 and 86 years (van Pottelbergh et al. 2001).

The applicability of association studies performed in cohorts of elderly individuals to phenotypic effects in younger humans is uncertain, but it is possible that some of these polymorphisms influence muscle strength throughout life. As such they represent plausible candidate genes for muscle performance traits in athletes.

Case-control studies of candidate genes in elite athletes

The best-characterized polymorphism associated with human performance is the ACE I/D polymorphism, which has been the subject of a large number of case-control studies in elite athletes, as well as association studies on a number of performance-related phenotypes in non-athlete cohorts. Studies on the ACE gene in the context of human performance are discussed in depth in the next two chapters of this book (Chapters 13 and 14), so we will reserve our attention here for other polymorphisms that have been linked to elite athlete status.

The ACTN3 R577X polymorphism

The ACTN3 gene encodes the protein α-actinin-3, a member of an evolutionarily ancient and highly conserved family of actin-binding proteins which function in the dynamic cross-linking of actin filaments in a variety of cellular contexts (MacArthur and North 2004). α-Actinin-3 has the most restricted expression pattern of the four human α-actinins, localizing almost exclusively to fast glycolytic skeletal mucle fibres, where it tethers the actin-containing thin filaments of the muscle contractile apparatus in the dense region known as the Z line (Mills et al. 2001). Several lines of evidence suggest that α-actinin-3 performs a variety of structural and signalling functions in fast skeletal muscle fibres in humans (MacArthur and North 2004).

A common nonsense polymorphism (R577X) in the ACTN3 gene results in complete deficiency of α-actinin-3 in homozygotes (North et al. 1999) and is found at frequencies of between 10 and 54% in a variety of human populations (Mills et al. 2001). As a consequence, almost 20% of the global human population do not express detectable levels of α-actinin-3 in their fast skeletal muscle fibres. If α-actinin-3 does perform unique and non-redundant roles in fast fibres, as seems likely based on its strong evolutionary conservation and similar expression patterns in mammals (Mills et al. 2001), then its absence would be expected to have a detrimental effect on performance in activities which rely on rapid, forceful muscle contraction, such as sprinting and weight-lifting. This possibility was explored in an investigation of ACTN3 R577X genotype frequencies in 436 healthy controls compared to two cohorts of elite Australian athletes: 107 sprint/power athletes and 194 endurance athletes (Yang et al. 2003).

This study identified a strong association between the R577X polymorphism and elite athlete status. In sprint/power athletes the frequency of the XX (α-actinin-3 deficient) genotype was approximately three-fold lower than the frequency in controls for both males ($P < 0.001$) and females ($P < 0.01$), supporting the hypothesis that deficiency of α-actinin-3 is deleterious for fast muscle fibre function. The opposite trend was seen in endurance athletes, which had significantly *higher* frequencies of the XX genotype than controls in females

($P < 0.05$) but not in males, suggesting that the absence of α-actinin-3 may be beneficial for endurance performance and that this effect may be gender-specific.

The association between R577X and human performance has since been supported by a number of more recent studies. Direct replication of this association in a case-control analysis of a cohort of Finnish elite sprint and endurance athletes demonstrated a lower frequency of XX in 68 sprinters and a higher frequency in 40 endurance athletes than in 120 controls (Niemi and Majamaa 2005). Several other studies have found associations between R577X and muscle performance phenotypes in non-athlete cohorts, the largest of which was an analysis of elbow flexor strength measurements in 247 men and 355 women before and after a standardized 12-week resistance training protocol (Clarkson *et al.* 2005). This study found that in females, but not males, the XX genotype was associated with lower baseline isometric strength and – surprisingly – with *higher* gains in dynamic strength following training. The baseline strength findings of Clarkson *et al.* (2005) suggest that α-actinin-3 deficiency reduces muscle power in non-athlete females, a finding that has since been supported by an analysis of knee extensor strength in 193 females (Walsh *et al.* 2005). Reduced muscle strength in α-actinin-3 deficient individuals would explain the lower frequency of the XX genotype in athletes competing in sprint events, which require tremendous muscle power. The increased response to training seen in XX individuals by Clarkson *et al.* (2005) is intriguing, but at this stage has not been replicated in other cohorts.

The influence of the R577X polymorphism on muscle function has biological plausibility, as the 577X allele has been shown to completely eliminate expression of a structural and signalling protein expressed in fast skeletal muscle fibres. The independent replication of lower XX genotype frequency in elite sprinters in two separate cohorts, in conjunction with a growing number of studies suggesting decreased muscle strength and sprint performance in XX non-athletes, support the notion that the R577X polymorphism is one of the genetic factors underlying variation in muscle performance in both athletes and the general population. However, the precise biochemical and physiological mechanisms by which α-actinin-3 deficiency alters human muscle function are not yet known (MacArthur and North 2004), and are the subject of ongoing investigation by our group and others.

Other variants linked to elite athlete status

Associations with elite athlete status have been reported for a number of other human genetic polymorphisms. A weak association ($0.05 > P > 0.01$) between an RFLP in the $α_{2a}$-adrenoceptor gene (*ADRA2A*) and elite endurance athlete status was identified in a cohort of 148 Caucasian male elite endurance athletes and 148 Caucasian sedentary male controls (Wolfarth *et al.* 2000). The same study found no evidence for an association between athlete status and an RFLP in the $β_2$-adrenoceptor gene *ADRB2*, but a later study of a missense polymorphism (Gln27Glu) in the *ADRB2* gene showed slightly different geno-type frequencies between a cohort of 39 sedentary and active postmenopausal women and a group of 24 postmenopausal female elite endurance athletes (Moore *et al.* 2001). Although the authors did not explicitly compare genotype frequencies between the two groups, the data in the article demonstrate a small but significant difference (exact Pearson's χ^2 test, P = 0.036). The Glu/Glu genotype was less common in the athlete group, and was weakly associated with lower $\dot{V}O_2$ max and higher body mass index (Moore *et al.* 2001).

More recently, a correlation was demonstrated between a 9 base pair inser-tion/deletion polymorphism (denoted +9/–9) in exon 1 of the bradykinin β_2 receptor gene *BDKBR2* and running distance in 81 Olympic-standard track athletes (Williams *et al.* 2004). The study showed a weakly significant linear trend of increasing frequency of the –9 allele with running distance in the athletes (P = 0.04 for comparison of ≤5,000 m vs. ≥5,000 m), and a more highly significant trend in combination with *ACE* I/D-allele frequencies (P = 0.001). *BDKBR2* genotype alone, and in combination with *ACE* genotype, also showed highly significant associations with a measure of the efficiency of skeletal muscle contraction in 115 healthy controls (Williams *et al.* 2004). There was no difference in *BDKBR2* genotype or allele frequencies between Olympic athlete and control groups, possibly due to the presence of individuals from multiple different sporting groups in the athlete cohort. The –9 allele of *BDKBR2* had previously been associated with higher transcriptional activity of the *BDKBR2* gene (Braun *et al.* 1996) and with a reduced left-ventricular growth response to a 10-week exercise programme (Brull *et al.* 2001). Since the bradykinin β_2 receptor is a downstream effector of ACE, the finding of similar phenotypic support to the reported associations of *ACE* I/D with elite athlete status and other performance-related phenotypes (reviewed in Chapter 13), and suggests that at least some of the effects of *ACE* genotype on performance may be related to downstream effects on the bradykinin pathway (Williams *et al.* 2004).

Finally, the common Gly482Ser polymorphism in the *PPARGC1A* gene, which encodes peroxisome proliferator-activated receptor-γ coactivator 1α, has been reported to be associated with elite endurance athlete status, with the 482Ser allele found to be at a significantly lower frequency in a cohort of 104 elite Spanish male endurance athletes than in 100 unfit male controls from the UK (Lucia *et al.* 2005).

Conclusions

The process of identifying and genotyping candidate genetic variations for performance-related traits has accelerated over the last five years, due to two major advances: first, a massive increase in publically available data on the loca-tion of many human genes and common genetic polymorphisms; and second, an increasing understanding of the biochemical and physiological functions of many human genes. The results of these advances have been catalogued since

2001 in releases of the human gene map for performance and health-related fitness phenotypes (Rankinen *et al.* 2001b; Pérusse *et al.* 2003; Rankinen *et al.* 2002b; Rankinen *et al.* 2004; Wolfarth *et al.* 2005), an annual publication which catalogues all of the genetic variants reported to be associated with elite athlete status or with specific physical fitness, health or performance traits. The number of new genes associated with fitness and performance traits has grown steadily over the last five years: between 2000 and 2004, the number of loci reported to be associated with endurance phenotypes increased from 22 to 37, while the number of loci linked with strength and anaerobic fitness grew from 2 to 13 (Wolfarth *et al.* 2005).

The majority of these association studies have been performed in Caucasian populations, however, and it is still unclear whether their results can be extrapolated to non-Caucasian groups such as east Africans. Although this question has not yet been addressed systematically, there are some lines of evidence suggesting that the genetic factors influencing human physical performance may actually differ substantially between ethnic groups. First, at least two of the polymorphisms that have been convincingly associated with elite athlete status in Caucasian cohorts have failed to show an association with athlete status in east African cohorts: the *ACE* I/D polymorphism (Scott *et al.* 2005) and the *ACTN3* R577X polymorphism (Yang *et al.* 2005). In addition, there have been two genome-wide linkage analyses in the HERITAGE cohort, one for cardiac output and stroke volume (Rankinen *et al.* 2002a) and another for maximal exercise capacity phenotypes (Rico-Sanz *et al.* 2004), in which Caucasian and African-American families were analysed. In both of these studies, there was no obvious overlap between the linked chromosomal regions in the two groups. These results suggest that quite different genetic loci may underlie variation in performance-related traits in different ethnic groups; however, much larger linkage analyses and further, more carefully targeted association studies will be required to confirm this possibility.

Bibliography

Allen, D. L., Harrison, B. C. and Leinwand, L. A. (2002) 'Molecular and genetic approaches to studying exercise performance and adaptation', *Exercise and Sport Sciences Reviews* 30, 99–105.

Alvarez, R., Terrados, N., Ortolano, R., Iglesias-Cubero, G., Reguero, J. R., Batalla, A., Cortina, A., Fernandez-Garcia, B., Rodriguez, C., Braga, S., Alvarez, V. and Coto, E. (2000) 'Genetic variation in the renin-angiotensin system and athletic performance', *European Journal of Applied Physiology* 82, 117–20.

An, P., Borecki, I. B., Rankinen, T., Pérusse, L., Leon, A. S., Skinner, J. S., Wilmore, J. H., Bouchard, C. and Rao, D. C. (2003a) 'Evidence of major genes for exercise heart rate and blood pressure at baseline and in response to 20 weeks of endurance training: the HERITAGE family study', *International Journal of Sports Medicine* 24, 492–8.

An, P., Hong, Y., Weisnagel, S. J., Rice, T., Rankinen, T., Leon, A. S., Skinner, J. S., Wilmore, J. H., Chagnon, Y. C., Bergman, R. N., Bouchard, C. and Rao, D. C.

(2003b) 'Genomic scan of glucose and insulin metabolism phenotypes: the HERITAGE family study', *Metabolism* 52, 246–53.

An, P., Pérusse, L., Rankinen, T., Borecki, I. B., Gagnon, J., Leon, A. S., Skinner, J. S., Wilmore, J. H., Bouchard, C. and Rao, D. C. (2003c) 'Familial aggregation of exercise heart rate and blood pressure in response to 20 weeks of endurance training: the HERITAGE family study', *International Journal of Sports Medicine* 24, 57–62.

An, P., Rice, T., Gagnon, J., Leon, A. S., Skinner, J. S., Bouchard, C., Rao, D. C. and Wilmore, J. H. (2000) 'Familial aggregation of stroke volume and cardiac output during submaximal exercise: the HERITAGE Family Study', *International Journal of Sports Medicine* 21, 566–72.

Baron, M. (2001) 'The search for complex disease genes: fault by linkage or fault by association?', *Molecular Psychiatry* 6, 143–9.

Bouchard, C., An, P., Rice, T., Skinner, J. S., Wilmore, J. H., Gagnon, J., Pérusse, L., Leon, A. S. and Rao, D. C. (1999) 'Familial aggregation of $\dot{V}O_2$ max response to exercise training: results from the HERITAGE Family Study', *Journal of Applied Physiology* 87, 1003–8.

Bouchard, C., Chagnon, M., Thibault, M. C., Boulay, M. R., Marcotte, M., Cote, C. and Simoneau, J. A. (1989) 'Muscle genetic variants and relationship with performance and trainability', *Medicine and Science in Sports and Exercise* 21, 71–7.

Bouchard, C., Daw, E. W., Rice, T., Pérusse, L., Gagnon, J., Province, M. A., Leon, A. S., Rao, D. C., Skinner, J. S. and Wilmore, J. H. (1998) 'Familial resemblance for $\dot{V}O_2$ max in the sedentary state: the HERITAGE Family Study', *Medicine and Science in Sports and Exercise* 30, 252–8.

Bouchard, C., Leon, A. S., Rao, D. C., Skinner, J. S., Wilmore, J. H. and Gagnon, J. (1995) 'The HERITAGE Family Study. Aims, design, and measurement protocol', *Medicine and Science in Sports and Exercise* 27, 721–9.

Bouchard, C., Malina, R. M. and Pérusse, L. (1997) *Genetics of Fitness and Physical Performance*, Champaign, IL: Human Kinetics.

Bouchard, C., Rankinen, T., Chagnon, Y. C., Rice, T., Pérusse, L., Gagnon, J., Borecki, I., An, P., Leon, A. S., Skinner, J. S., Wilmore, J. H., Province, M. and Rao, D. C. (2000) 'Genomic scan for maximal oxygen uptake and its response to training in the HERITAGE Family Study', *Journal of Applied Physiology* 88, 551–9.

Bouchard, C., Simoneau, J. A., Lortie, G., Boulay, M. R., Marcotte, M. and Thibault, M. C. (1986) 'Genetic effects in human skeletal muscle fiber type distribution and enzyme activities', *Canadian Journal of Physiology and Pharmacology* 64, 1245–51.

Braun, A., Kammerer, S., Maier, E., Bohme, E. and Roscher, A. A. (1996) 'Polymorphisms in the gene for the human B2-bradykinin receptor. New tools in assessing a genetic risk for bradykinin-associated diseases', *Immunopharmacology* 33, 32–5.

Brull, D., Dhamrait, S., Myerson, S., Erdmann, J., Woods, D., World, M., Pennell, D., Humphries, S., Regitz-Zagrosek, V. and Montgomery, H. (2001) 'Bradykinin B2BKR receptor polymorphism and left-ventricular growth response', *Lancet* 358, 1155–6.

Calvo, M., Rodas, G., Vallejo, M., Estruch, A., Arcas, A., Javierre, C., Viscor, G. and Ventura, J. L. (2002) 'Heritability of explosive power and anaerobic capacity in humans', *European Journal of Applied Physiology* 86, 218–25.

Chagnon, Y. C., Borecki, I. B., Pérusse, L., Roy, S., Lacaille, M., Chagnon, M., Ho-Kim, M. A., Rice, T., Province, M. A., Rao, D. C. and Bouchard, C. (2000) 'Genome-wide search for genes related to the fat-free body mass in the Quebec family study', *Metabolism: Clinical and Experimental* 49, 203–7.

Chagnon, Y. C., Rice, T., Pérusse, L., Borecki, I. B., Ho-Kim, M.-A., Lacaille, M., Paré, C., Bouchard, L., Gagnon, J., Leon, A. S., Skinner, J. S., Wilmore, J. H., Rao, D. C. and Bouchard, C. (2001) 'Genomic scan for genes affecting body composition before and after training in Caucasians from HERITAGE', *Journal of Applied Physiology* 90, 1777–87.

Clarkson, P. M., Devaney, J. M., Gordish-Dressman, H., Thompson, P. D., Hubal, M. J., Urso, M., Price, T. B., Angelopoulos, T. J., Gordon, P. M., Moyna, N. M., Pescatello, L. S., Visich, P. S., Zoeller, R. F., Seip, R. L. and Hoffman, E. P. (2005) 'ACTN3 genotype is associated with increases in muscle strength in response to resistance training in women', *Journal of Applied Physiology* 99, 154–63.

Crisan, D. and Carr, J. (2000) 'Angiotensin I-converting enzyme: genotype and disease associations', *Journal of Molecular Diagnostics* 2, 105–15.

Diet, F., Graf, C., Mahnke, N., Wassmer, G., Predel, H. G., Palma-Hohmann, I., Rost, R. and Bohm, M. (2001) 'ACE and angiotensinogen gene genotypes and left ventricular mass in athletes', *European Journal of Clinical Investigation* 31, 836–42.

Dionne, F. T., Turcotte, L., Thibault, M. C., Boulay, M. R., Skinner, J. S. and Bouchard, C. (1991) 'Mitochondrial DNA sequence polymorphism, $\dot{V}O_2$ max, and response to endurance training', *Medicine and Science in Sports and Exercise* 23, 177–85.

Echegaray, M. and Rivera, M. A. (2001) 'Role of creatine kinase isoenzymes on muscular and cardiorespiratory endurance: genetic and molecular evidence', *Sports Medicine* 31, 919–34.

Eisenach, J. H., McGuire, A. M., Schwingler, R. M., Turner, S. T. and Joyner, M. J. (2004) 'The Arg16/Gly β2-adrenergic receptor polymorphism is associated with altered cardiovascular responses to isometric exercise', *Physiological Genomics* 16, 323–8.

Feitosa, M. F., Gaskill, S. E., Rice, T., Rankinen, T., Bouchard, C., Rao, D. C., Wilmore, J. H., Skinner, J. S. and Leon, A. S. (2002) 'Major gene effects on exercise ventilatory threshold: the HERITAGE Family Study', *Journal of Applied Physiology* 93, 1000–6.

Franks, P. W., Barroso, I., Luan, J., Ekelund, U., Crowley, V. E., Brage, S., Sandhu, M. S., Jakes, R. W., Middelberg, R. P., Harding, A. H., Schafer, A. J., O'Rahilly, S. and Wareham, N. J. (2003) 'PGC–1α genotype modifies the association of volitional energy expenditure with $\dot{V}O_2$max', *Medicine and Science in Sports and Exercise* 35, 1998–2004.

Gaskill, S. E., Rice, T., Bouchard, C., Gagnon, J., Rao, D. C., Skinner, J. S., Wilmore, J. H. and Leon, A. S. (2001) 'Familial resemblance in ventilatory threshold: the HERITAGE Family Study', *Medicine and Science in Sports and Exercise* 33, 1832–40.

Geusens, P., Vandevyver, C., Vanhoof, J., Cassiman, J. J., Boonen, S. and Raus, J. (1997) 'Quadriceps and grip strength are related to vitamin D receptor genotype in elderly nonobese women', *Journal of Bone and Mineral Research* 12, 2082–8.

Grundberg, E., Brandstrom, H., Ribom, E. L., Ljunggren, O., Mallmin, H. and Kindmark, A. (2004) 'Genetic variation in the human vitamin D receptor is associated with muscle strength, fat mass and body weight in Swedish women', *European Journal of Endocrinology* 150, 323–8.

Hamel, P., Simoneau, J. A., Lortie, G., Boulay, M. R. and Bouchard, C. (1986) 'Heredity and muscle adaptation to endurance training', *Medicine and Science in Sports and Exercise* 18, 690–6.

Higgins, M. (2000) 'Epidemiology and prevention of coronary heart disease in families', *American Journal of Medicine* 108, 387–95.

Ioannidis, J. P. (2003) 'Genetic associations: false or true'?. *Trends in Molecular Medicine* 9, 135–8.

Jamshidi, Y., Montgomery, H. E., Hense, H. W., Myerson, S. G., Torra, I. P., Staels, B., World, M. J., Doering, A., Erdmann, J., Hengstenberg, C., Humphries, S. E., Schunkert, H. and Flavell, D. M. (2002) 'Peroxisome proliferator-activated receptor α gene regulates left ventricular growth in response to exercise and hypertension', *Circulation* 105, 950–5.

Jordan, B. D., Relkin, N. R., Ravdin, L. D., Jacobs, A. R., Bennett, A. and Gandy, S. (1997) 'Apolipoprotein E ε4 associated with chronic traumatic brain injury in boxing', *JAMA* 278, 136–40.

Karjalainen, J., Kujala, U. M., Stolt, A., Mantysaari, M., Viitasalo, M., Kainulainen, K. and Kontula, K. (1999) 'Angiotensinogen gene M235T polymorphism predicts left ventricular hypertrophy in endurance athletes', *Journal of the American College of Cardiology* 34, 494–9.

Kauma, H., Ikaheimo, M., Savolainen, M. J., Kiema, T. R., Rantala, A. O., Lilja, M., Reunanen, A. and Kesaniemi, Y. A. (1998) 'Variants of renin-angiotensin system genes and echocardiographic left ventricular mass', *European Heart Journal* 19, 1109–17.

Komi, P. V., Viitasalo, J. H., Havu, M., Thorstensson, A., Sjodin, B. and Karlsson, J. (1977) 'Skeletal muscle fibres and muscle enzyme activities in monozygous and dizygous twins of both sexes', *Acta Physiologica Scandinavica* 100, 385–92.

Lewis, C. M. (2002) 'Genetic association studies: design, analysis and interpretation', *Briefings in Bioinformatics* 3, 146–53.

Linhart, A., Sedlácek, K., Jáchymová, M., Jindra, A., Beran, S., Vondrácek, V., Heller, S. and Hork?, K. (2000) 'Lack of association of angiotensin-converting enzyme and angiotensinogen genes polymorphisms with left ventricular structure in young normotensive men', *Blood Pressure* 9, 47–51.

Lucia, A., Gómez-Gallego, F., Barroso, I., Rabadán, M., Bandrés, F., San Juan, A. F., Chicharro, J. L., Ekelund, U., Brage, S., Earnest, C. P., Wareham, N. J. and Franks, P. W. (2005) 'PPARGC1A genotype (Gly482Ser) predicts exceptional endurance capacity in European men', *Journal of Applied Physiology* 99, 344–8.

MacArthur, D. G. and North, K. N. (2004) 'A gene for speed? The function and evolution of α-actinin-3', *Bioessays* 26, 786–95.

McCole, S. D., Brown, M. D., Moore, G. E., Ferrell, R. E., Wilund, K. R., Huberty, A., Douglass, L. W. and Hagberg, J. M. (2002) 'Angiotensinogen M235T polymorphism associates with exercise hemodynamics in postmenopausal women', *Physiological Genomics* 10, 63–9.

Maes, H. H., Beunen, G. P., Vlietinck, R. F., Neale, M. C., Thomis, M., Vanden Eynde, B., Lysens, R., Simons, J., Derom, C. and Derom, R. (1996) 'Inheritance of physical fitness in 10-yr-old twins and their parents', *Medicine and Science in Sports and Exercise* 28, 1479–91.

Mills, M., Yang, N., Weinberger, R., Vander Woude, D. L., Beggs, A. H., Easteal, S. and North, K. (2001) 'Differential expression of the actin-binding proteins, α-actinin-2 and -3, in different species: implications for the evolution of functional redundancy', *Human Molecular Genetics* 10, 1335–46.

Moore, G. E., Shuldiner, A. R., Zmuda, J. M., Ferrell, R. E., McCole, S. D. and Hagberg, J. M. (2001) 'Obesity gene variant and elite endurance performance', *Metabolism* 50, 1391–2.

Myburgh, K. H. (2003) 'What makes an endurance athlete world-class? Not simply a physiological conundrum', *Comparative Biochemistry and Physiology* 136, 171–90.

Niemi, A. K. and Majamaa, K. (2005) 'Mitochondrial DNA and ACTN3 genotypes in Finnish elite endurance and sprint athletes', *European Journal of Human Genetics*, advance online publication.

North, K. N., Yang, N., Wattanasirichaigoon, D., Mills, M., Easteal, S. and Beggs, A. H. (1999) A common nonsense mutation results in α-actinin-3 deficiency in the general population. *Nature Genetics* 21, 353–4.

Pérusse, L., Gagnon, J., Province, M. A., Rao, D. C., Wilmore, J. H., Leon, A. S., Bouchard, C. and Skinner, J. S. (2001) 'Familial aggregation of submaximal aerobic performance in the HERITAGE Family Study', *Medicine and Science in Sports and Exercise* 33, 597–604.

Pérusse, L., Rankinen, T., Rauramaa, R., Rivera, M. A., Wolfarth, B. and Bouchard, C. (2003) 'The human gene map for performance and health-related fitness phenotypes: The 2002 update', *Medicine and Science in Sports and Exercise* 35, 1248–64.

Rankinen, T., An, P., Pérusse, L., Rice, T., Chagnon, Y. C., Gagnon, J., Leon, A. S., Skinner, J. S., Wilmore, J. H., Rao, D. C. and Bouchard, C. (2002a) 'Genome-wide linkage scan for exercise stroke volume and cardiac output in the HERITAGE Family Study', *Physiological Genomics* 10, 57–62.

Rankinen, T., An, P., Rice, T., Sun, G., Chagnon, Y. C., Gagnon, J., Leon, A. S., Skinner, J. S., Wilmore, J. H., Rao, D. C. and Bouchard, C. (2001a) 'Genomic scan for exercise blood pressure in the Health, Risk Factors, Exercise Training and Genetics (HERITAGE) Family Study', *Hypertension* 38, 30–7.

Rankinen, T., Pérusse, L., Rauramaa, R., Rivera, M. A., Wolfarth, B. and Bouchard, C. (2001b) 'The human gene map for performance and health-related fitness phenotypes', *Medicine and Science in Sports and Exercise* 33, 855–67.

Rankinen, T., Pérusse, L., Rauramaa, R., Rivera, M. A., Wolfarth, B. and Bouchard, C. (2004) 'The human gene map for performance and health-related fitness phenotypes: the 2003 update', *Medicine and Science in Sports and Exercise* 36, 1451–69.

Rankinen, T., Pérusse, L., Borecki, I., Chagnon, Y. C., Gagnon, J., Leon, A. S., Skinner, J. S., Wilmore, J. H., Rao, D. C. and Bouchard, C. (2000) 'The Na^+-K^+-ATPase α2 gene and trainability of cardiorespiratory endurance: the HERITAGE Family Study', *Journal of Applied Physiology* 88, 346–51.

Rankinen, T., Pérusse, L., Rauramaa, R., Rivera, M. A., Wolfarth, B. and Bouchard, C. (2002b) 'The human gene map for performance and health-related fitness phenotypes: the 2001 update', *Medicine and Science in Sports and Exercise* 34, 1219–33.

Rice, T., Chagnon, Y. C., Pérusse, L., Borecki, I. B., Ukkola, O., Rankinen, T., Gagnon, J., Leon, A. S., Skinner, J. S., Wilmore, J. H., Bouchard, C. and Rao, D. C. (2002a) 'A genomewide linkage scan for abdominal subcutaneous and visceral fat in black and white families', *Diabetes* 51, 848–55.

Rice, T., Rankinen, T., Chagnon, Y. C., Province, M. A., Pérusse, L., Leon, A. S., Skinner, J. S., Wilmore, J. H., Bouchard, C. and Rao, D. C. (2002b) 'Genomewide linkage scan of resting blood pressure', *Hypertension* 39, 1037–43.

Rico-Sanz, J., Rankinen, T., Joanisse, D. R., Leon, A. S., Skinner, J. S., Wilmore, J. H., Rao, D. C. and Bouchard, C. (2003a) 'Associations between cardiorespiratory responses to exercise and the C34T AMPD1 gene polymorphism in the HERITAGE Family Study', *Physiological Genomics* 14, 161–6.

Rico-Sanz, J., Rankinen, T., Joanisse, D. R., Leon, A. S., Skinner, J. S., Wilmore, J. H.,

Rao, D. C., Bouchard, C. and HERITAGE Family (2003b) 'Familial resemblance for muscle phenotypes in the HERITAGE Family Study', *Medicine and Science in Sports and Exercise* 35, 1360–6.

Rico-Sanz, J., Rankinen, T., Rice, T., Leon, A. S., Skinner, J. S., Wilmore, J. H., Rao, D. C. and Bouchard, C. (2004) 'Quantitative trait loci for maximal exercise capacity phenotypes and their responses to training in the HERITAGE Family Study', *Physiological Genomics* 16, 256–60.

Rivera, M. A., Dionne, F. T., Simoneau, J. A., Pérusse, L., Chagnon, M., Chagnon, Y., Gagnon, J., Leon, A. S., Rao, D. C., Skinner, J. S., Wilmore, J. H. and Bouchard, C. (1997a) 'Muscle-specific creatine kinase gene polymorphism and $\dot{V}O_2$ max in the HERITAGE Family Study', *Medicine and Science in Sports and Exercise* 29, 1311–17.

Rivera, M. A., Dionne, F. T., Wolfarth, B., Chagnon, M., Simoneau, J. A., Pérusse, L., Boulay, M. R., Gagnon, J., Song, T. M., Keul, J. and Bouchard, C. (1997b) 'Muscle-specific creatine kinase gene polymorphisms in elite endurance athletes and sedentary controls', *Medicine and Science in Sports and Exercise* 29, 1444–7.

Rivera, M. A., Pérusse, L., Simoneau, J. A., Gagnon, J., Dionne, F. T., Leon, A. S., Skinner, J. S., Wilmore, J. H., Province, M., Rao, D. C. and Bouchard, C. (1999) 'Linkage between a muscle-specific CK gene marker and $\dot{V}O_2$ max in the HERITAGE Family Study', *Medicine and Science in Sports and Exercise* 31, 698–701.

Rodas, G., Ercilla, G., Javierre, C., Garrido, E., Calvo, M., Segura, R. and Ventura, J. L. (1997) 'Could the A2A11 human leucocyte antigen locus correlate with maximal aerobic power?', *Clinical Science* 92, 331–3.

Romero, R., Kuivaniemi, H., Tromp, G. and Olson, J. (2002) 'The design, execution, and interpretation of genetic association studies to decipher complex diseases', *American Journal of Obstetrics and Gynecology* 187, 1299–312.

Roth, S. M., Metter, E. J., Lee, M. R., Hurley, B. F. and Ferrell, R. E. (2003) 'C174T polymorphism in the CNTF receptor gene is associated with fat-free mass in men and women', *Journal of Applied Physiology* 95, 1425–30.

Roth, S. M., Schrager, M. A., Ferrell, R. E., Riechman, S. E., Metter, E. J., Lynch, N. A., Lindle, R. S. and Hurley, B. F. (2001) 'CNTF genotype is associated with muscular strength and quality in humans across the adult age span', *Journal of Applied Physiology* 90, 1205–10.

Sagnella, G. A., Rothwell, M. J., Onipinla, A. K., Wicks, P. D., Cook, D. G. and Cappuccio, F. P. (1999) 'A population study of ethnic variations in the angiotensin-converting enzyme I/D polymorphism: relationships with gender, hypertension and impaired glucose metabolism', *Journal of Hypertension* 17, 657–64.

Sayer, A. A., Syddall, H., O'Dell, S. D., Chen, X. H., Briggs, P. J., Briggs, R., Day, I. N. and Cooper, C. (2002) 'Polymorphism of the *IGF2* gene, birth weight and grip strength in adult men', *Age and Ageing* 31, 468–70.

Scott, R. A., Moran, C., Wilson, R. H., Onywera, V., Boit, M. K., Goodwin, W. H., Gohlke, P., Payne, J., Montgomery, H. and Pitsiladis, Y. P. (2005) 'No association between Angiotensin Converting Enzyme (ACE) gene variation and endurance athlete status in Kenyans', *Comparative Biochemistry and Physiology – Part A: Molecular and Integrative Physiology* 141, 169–75.

Seibert, M. J., Xue, Q. L., Fried, L. P. and Walston, J. D. (2001) 'Polymorphic variation in the human myostatin (GDF–8) gene and association with strength measures in the Women's Health and Aging Study II cohort', *Journal of the American Geriatrics Society* 49, 1093–6.

Simoneau, J. A. and Bouchard, C. (1995) 'Genetic determinism of fiber type proportion in human skeletal muscle', *FASEB Journal* 9, 1091–5.

Takahashi, R., Yokoji, H., Misawa, H., Hayashi, M., Hu, J. and Deguchi, T. (1994) 'A null mutation in the human *CNTF* gene is not causally related to neurological diseases', *Nature Genetics* 7, 79–84.

Thibault, M. C., Simoneau, J. A., Cote, C., Boulay, M. R., Lagasse, P., Marcotte, M. and Bouchard, C. (1986) 'Inheritance of human muscle enzyme adaptation to isokinetic strength training', *Human Heredity* 36, 341–7.

Thomis, M. A., Beunen, G. P., Maes, H. H., Blimkie, C. J., Van Leemputte, M., Claessens, A. L., Marchal, G., Willems, E. and Vlietinck, R. F. (1998) 'Strength training: importance of genetic factors', *Medicine and Science in Sports and Exercise* 30, 724–31.

Thompson, P. D., Tsongalis, G. J., Seip, R. L., Bilbie, C., Miles, M., Zoeller, R., Visich, P., Gordon, P., Angelopoulos, T. J., Pescatello, L., Bausserman, L. and Moyna, N. (2004) 'Apolipoprotein E genotype and changes in serum lipids and maximal oxygen uptake with exercise training', *Metabolism* 53, 193–202.

van Berlo, J. H. and Pinto, Y. M. (2003) 'Polymorphisms in the RAS and cardiac function', *International Journal of Biochemistry and Cell Biology* 35, 932–43.

van Damme, R., Wilson, R. S., Vanhooydonck, B. and Aerts, P. (2002) 'Performance constraints in decathletes', *Nature* 415, 755–6.

van Pottelbergh, I., Goemaere, S., Nuytinck, L., De Paepe, A. and Kaufman, J. M. (2001) 'Association of the type I collagen alpha1 Sp1 polymorphism, bone density and upper limb muscle strength in community-dwelling elderly men', *Osteoporosis International* 12, 895–901.

Walsh, S., Metter, J., Hurley, B. F., Ferrucci, L. and Roth, S. M. (2005) 'The R577X polymorphism in the Actn3 gene is associated with muscle strength in women', *Medicine and Science in Sports and Exercise* 37, S164.

Williams, A. G., Dhamrait, S. S., Wootton, P. T. E., Day, S. H., Hawe, E., Payne, J. R., Myerson, S. G., World, M., Budgett, R., Humphries, S. E. and Montgomery, H. E. (2004) 'Bradykinin receptor gene variant and human physical performance', *Journal of Applied Physiology* 96, 938–42.

Wolfarth, B., Bray, M. S., Hagberg, J. M., Pérusse, L., Rauramaa, R., Rivera, M. A., Roth, S. M., Rankinen, T. and Bouchard, C. (2005) 'The human gene map for performance and health-related fitness phenotypes: the 2004 update', *Medicine and Science in Sports and Exercise* 37, 881–903.

Wolfarth, B., Rivera, M. A., Oppert, J. M., Boulay, M. R., Dionne, F. T., Chagnon, M., Gagnon, J., Chagnon, Y., Pérusse, L., Keul, J. and Bouchard, C. (2000) 'A polymorphism in the alpha$_{2a}$-adrenoceptor gene and endurance athlete status', *Medicine and Science in Sports and Exercise* 32, 1709–12.

Yang, N., MacArthur, D. G., Gulbin, J. P., Hahn, A. G., Beggs, A. H., Easteal, S. and North, K. (2003) *ACTN3* genotype is associated with human elite athletic performance. *American Journal of Human Genetics* 73, 627–31.

Yang, N., MacArthur, D. G., Wolde, B., Onywera, V. O., Boit, M. K., Wilson, R. K., Scott, R. A., Pitsiladis, Y. P. and North, K. N. (2005) 'α-actinin-3 genotype is not associated with endurance performance in elite east-African runners', *Medicine and Science in Sports and Exercise* 37, S472.

Chapter 13

Genetics and endurance performance

Helen M. Luery, Kyriacos I. Eleftheriou and Hugh E. Montgomery

Introduction

Endurance athletic performance (defined as distances from 800 m to marathon) was until recently, dominated by European athletes: in 1986, 48.3% of the top 20 performances were by European athletes while 26.6% were by African athletes. By 2003 the proportion of European achievement reduced to 11.7% while the proportion of African achievement increased to 85% (IAAF all time outdoor lists 2003, see <http://www.iaaf.org>). Most of the success of African athletes in international distance running has been amongst those of east African descent and in particular Kenyan athletes. This is in contrast to the dominance of west African runners in sprint events. The success of African athletes across all events has led to the belief that 'black' runners are somehow superior. So what, then, underpins this dramatic association of elite performance with race?

Physical performance is determined by the interaction of extensive and diverse physiological mechanisms. The predominance of one racial group over another in any athletic discipline suggests superior functional capacity in one or many of these. While many such signature characteristics have yet to be identified and elucidated, some progress has been made. Unique body proportions, relating specifically to lower limb length and mass, have been speculated to enhance running economy (Saltin *et al.* 1995b) and may help explain the unusual ability of east African endurance runners to maintain high intensity endurance exercise (Coetzer *et al.* 1993; Weston *et al.* 1999). So, too, may specific differences in skeletal muscle metabolism, such as increased citrate synthase activity and higher concentrations of 3-hydroxyacyl-CoA-dehydrogenase activity (Coetzer *et al.* 1993; Saltin *et al.* 1995a; Weston *et al.* 1999).

The origin of such physiological differences may lie with genetic predisposition, environmental selection/conditioning, or (more likely) an interaction of genes with environment. The fact that there is a genetic contribution, however, is not in doubt. While it is the common inheritance of some 27,000 genes that makes us all human, the presence of multiple small common variations within each gene offers the propensity for us all to be different from one another.

In general, at least 30% of the variance in any human characteristic can be accounted for by genetic factors. This is also true of sporting prowess where the entire range of physiological processes (alluded to above) that underpin athletic prowess will themselves all be influenced by a vast array of genetic elements. The impact of each genetic element in determining ultimate phenotype will also be heavily influenced by environmental influences (ranging from diet and climate to training regimen). Despite the methodological difficulties inherent in the identification of genetic elements of influence, in excess of 100 gene variants of putative or established influence have already been identified (Rankinen et al. 2004). Just as such genetic variation may help explain inter-individual differences in performance characteristics, so too may it contribute extensively to inter-*racial* differences of this type. To date, no such specific loci have been identified which have been shown to contribute to the pre-eminence of east African runners. Any discussion must therefore, *ipso facto*, centre upon those identified mechanisms and the elements identified elsewhere, which might be of influence.

Genetic markers associated with maximal oxygen consumption

There is likely to be a variety of genetic variants that might influence predisposition to elite endurance performance through changes in aerobic capacity/oxygen delivery and utilization. Maximal oxygen uptake ($\dot{V}O_2$ max) is a measure of the integrated working of the cardiopulmonary, circulatory, and muscle units in delivering and utilizing oxygen for aerobic work. Genetic factors are likely to influence each of these components, thus a substantial genetic contribution to variance $\dot{V}O_2$ max is to be expected. Indeed, early familial studies suggested that there was a strong genetic influence upon $\dot{V}O_2$ max (Lesage et al. 1985; Fagard et al. 1991), with up to 40% of the inter-individual variance in $\dot{V}O_2$ max seemingly due to genetic factors (Bouchard et al. 1986).

What genetic elements, then, might be of influence? Bouchard and colleagues used genome-wide scanning to find loci of association with training-related changes in $\dot{V}O_2$ max in two-generation white families (Bouchard et al. 2000). In the study, 289 markers covering the 22 autosomal chromosomes were used. After adjustments for a number of covariates, baseline $\dot{V}O_2$ max was 'suggestively linked' with chromosomal locations 4q12, 8q24.12, 11p15.1, and 14q21.3 with 'potentially useful linkages' seen in a further 18 loci. A number of genes have been identified and mapped to these regions and include the β and γ sarcoglycans, the sulfonylurea receptor (involved in regulating the secretion of insulin), syntrophin β-1 and dystrophin-glycoprotein complex, and lamin A/C. The dystrophin-glycoprotein complex is thought to be involved in providing stability to the myofibre membrane and to link the intracellular actin cytoskeleton with the extracellular basement membrane. A further five chromosomal loci found to be 'suggestively linked' with the increase in $\dot{V}O_2$ max after training

(1p11.2, 2p16.1, 4q26, 6p21.33 and 11p14.1) with another locus showing 'potentially useful linkages' ($0.01 > p < 0.05$). Genes mapped in these areas include the voltage gates K^+-channel, the long QT syndrome locus, fatty acid binding protein 2, pancreatic co-lipase, calmodulin 2, calcineurin B, cardiac calsequestrin and 3-β-hydroxysteroid dehydrogenase. The genes are involved in cardiac contractility, long chain fatty acid absorption, calcium signalling in cardiac and skeletal muscle, and steroid hormone synthesis, which are all biologically plausible mechanisms that could influence $\dot{V}O_2$ max changes through exercise training (Bouchard *et al.* 2000).

Beyond such mapping, some specific candidate-gene association studies have been performed. Sarcolemmal sodium potassium ATPase plays an important role in maintaining electrolyte gradients across the cell membrane (Gambert and Duthie 1983), and its activity increases during high intensity activity. Surpassing its capacity during high intensity exercise may limit maximum muscle activity (Clausen *et al.* 1998). In support, Rankinen reported an association between the increase in $\dot{V}O_2$ max with endurance training and the α subunit isoform 2 exon 21–22 marker of the Na^+-K^+-ATPase gene (Rankinen *et al.* 2000a) Meanwhile, the skeletal muscle isozyme of creatine kinase (CKMM) is involved in generating ATP, and the CKMM *NcoI* polymorphism may account for as much as 9% of the training-related change in $\dot{V}O_2$ max (Rivera *et al.* 1997). Much as with the ACE I/D polymorphism, the *NcoI* polymorphism occurs in a non-coding region of the gene, and may thus be in linkage disequilibrium with another locus or gene in the region yet to be identified. Polymorphic variation in mitochondrial DNA has been associated with baseline $\dot{V}O_2$ max in sedentary young males, and also with its response to training (Dionne *et al.* 1991). Finally, the Gln variant of the adrenergic receptor $\beta 2$ (ADRB2) Gln27Glug polymorphism has been associated with higher values of $\dot{V}O_2$ max in post-menopausal women (McCole *et al.* 2004). The Trp64Arg polymorphism of the adrenergic receptor $\beta 3$ (ADRB3) gene was also investigated, with Trp/Trp homozygotes exhibiting lower $\dot{V}O_2$ max (McCole *et al.* 2004).

As components of the circulating (endocrine) renin-angiotensin system (RAS), the renally-derived aspartyl protease renin cleaves the liver-synthesized $\alpha 2$ globulin angiotensinogen to produce decapeptide angiotensin I. This is acted upon by the peptidyl dipeptidase angiotensin converting enzyme (ACE), to generate the octapeptide angiotensin II (Ang II) which acts through two receptors (AT_1 and AT_2) (Timmermans and Smith 1994). A third receptor (AT_4) is more sensitive to the degradation product angiotensin IV. The exact roles of the AT_2 and AT_4 receptors are still unclear: the AT_1 receptor is known to induce vasoconstriction and adrenal aldosterone release when stimulated by Ang II. Tissue kallikreins cleave kininogen to form decapeptide bradykinin. ACE is a potent kininase, and bradykinin levels are thus inversely related to ACE activity. Bradykinin activates two main receptor classes – BK1 and BK2. Action on the latter leads to vasodilation. Increasing ACE activity therefore promotes hypertension (increased AT_1 receptor activation) and reduces hypotensive responses (reduced BK2 receptor activation). As a result, ACE plays a central role in the regulation of blood pressure, and electrolyte and fluid balance (Kem and Brown 1990). However, local paracrine RAS are now also well described in diverse human tissues. These include the vasculature, heart, kidney, brain, uterus, ovary, testis, adipose tissue and skeletal muscle (Dzau 1988; Lee *et al.* 1992; Hagemann *et al.* 1994; Jonsson *et al.* 1994; Harris and Cheng 1996; Buikema *et al.* 1997; Jones and Woods 2003). Here they serve a variety of functions in the regulation of tissue growth, and metabolic and injury responses. A polymorphism of the ACE gene has been identified in which the absence (deletion 'D' allele) rather than the presence (insertion 'I' allele) of a 287-bp marker in intron 16 is associated with raised circulating ACE activity (Rigat *et al.* 1990) as well as tissue (Costerousse *et al.* 1993; Danser *et al.* 1995). A small study of 60 post-menopausal women reported an association of the ACE I-allele with $\dot{V}O_2$ max (Hagberg *et al.* 1998), with similar findings reported by Abraham and colleagues in patients with heart failure (Abraham *et al.* 2002). However, in contrast, Bouchard found no evidence of linkage on chromosome 17 (which includes the ACE locus on 17q23) for either baseline $\dot{V}O_2$ max or its increase after 20 weeks of endurance training (Bouchard *et al.* 1995). Similarly, studies of army recruits found no association (Sonna *et al.* 2001; Woods *et al.* 2002).

Once again, few studies have investigated the genetic contribution to $\dot{V}O_2$ max performance in African athletes. However, it appears from work conducted comparing $\dot{V}O_2$ max in Caucasian populations and African populations that there are no substantial differences in maximum aerobic capacity between these groups. Saltin has shown that Kenyan elite long-distance runners have a high $\dot{V}O_2$ max, but that this is not substantially higher than that observed in Scandinavian athletes. In fact, when scaling for body dimension, there was a trend for the Scandinavian runners to have a higher $\dot{V}O_2$ max (Saltin *et al.* 1995b). Indeed, Weston *et al.* (2000) showed that South African runners with similar 10 km race times to their Caucasian counterparts had the lowest $\dot{V}O_2$ max values. Further studies have investigated whether African athletes may respond better (in terms of $\dot{V}O_2$ max) to a given training stimulus (Andersen 1994; Saltin *et al.* 1995b; Skinner *et al.* 2001; Larsen 2003). These studies have found no difference between those of African descent and Caucasian controls. In fact when normalized by body mass or dimension it appears that the control groups often have an advantage.

Interestingly, however, African runners do seem to run at a higher proportion of $\dot{V}O_2$ max (Coetzer *et al.* 1993; Weston *et al.* 1999) (see Chapter 10 in this book), and African endurance runners seem to have a lower blood lactate accumulation for the same relative work rate when expressed as a proportion of $\dot{V}O_2$ max (Coetzer *et al.* 1993; Weston *et al.* 1999). Together this suggests that endurance athletes of African descent may have a higher anaerobic or lactate threshold when expressed as a proportion of $\dot{V}O_2$ max. However, In the 2004 update of the human gene-map for performance there were no polymorphisms identified that were associated with anaerobic or lactate threshold, onset of blood lactate or lactate accumulation (Wolfarth *et al.* 2005).

Genetic markers associated with oxygen delivery and utilization

Ventilation

In normal subjects, maximum exertional ventilatory capacity should not be a limiting factor for exercise capacity. However, in elite endurance athletes, maximum ventilation may represent an important limiting factor.

During intense exercise, accumulating adenosine monophosphate (AMP) activates adenosine monophosphate deaminase (AMPD) and AMP activated protein kinase, enhancing fat oxidation and glucose transport. AMPD displaces the equilibrium of the myokinase reaction towards ATP production. Thus AMPD may be an important regulator of muscle energy metabolism during exercise. The skeletal muscle-specific isoform (M) of AMPD is encoded by the AMPD1 gene, which accounts for more than 95% of total muscle AMPD (Fishbein *et al.* 1993). AMPD deficiency may result in a higher oxidative metabolism during exercise (Norman *et al.* 2001) and therefore may result in altered ventilation during exercise. In keeping with this hypothesis, Rico-Sanz *et al.* (2003) demonstrated that the presence of nonsense mutation (C to T transition) in this gene was associated with relative AMPD deficiency. The T homozygotes showed smaller increases in ventilation following a 20-week endurance training programme.

Meanwhile, the ACE I/D polymorphism has also been associated with hypoxic ventilatory response (Patel *et al.* 2003). Subjects exercised at 50% of workload at ventilatory threshold whilst breathing 12.5% oxygen. Minute ventilation was significantly higher in those of II genotype (39.6 ± 4.1% vs. 27.9 ± 2.0% vs. 28.4 ± 2.2% for II vs. ID vs. DD, respectively) (Patel *et al.* 2003).

Once again, data relating to the dominant east African runners are lacking. However, in a study comparing physiological characteristics of black athletes of African descent and white athletes of African descent, maximal ventilation was not a differentiating feature of the ability to sustain a higher percentage of $\dot{V}O_2$ max (Coetzer *et al.* 1993).

Cardiac output

Cardiac size (and possibly contractile performance) may influence physical performance, at least in race horses (Buhl *et al.* 2005; Young *et al.* 2005). An increase in the utilization of glucose and a corresponding decrease in fatty acid oxidation is an important metabolic adaptation of the physiologically hypertrophied heart. Sack and Rader suggested that this results from the down-regulation of fatty acid oxidation enzyme mRNA levels (Sack *et al.* 1996).

Animal models have confirmed that inhibition of fatty acid oxidation is associated with cardiac hypertrophy (Binas *et al.* 1999; Chiu *et al.* 2001). Childhood mitochondrial cardiomyopathy has been found to be related to disorders of cardiac energy metabolism (Kelly and Strauss 1994). Peroxisome proliferator-activated receptor α (PPARα) regulates mitochondrial free fatty acid ptake and free fatty acid oxidation (Fruchart *et al.* 1999). PPARα is downregulated in cardiac hypertrophy (Barger *et al.* 2000). The relationship between a novel polymorphism in intron 7 of the human PPARα and left ventricular hypertrophy was studied in 144 healthy male military recruits undergoing basic army training (Jamshidi *et al.* 2002). Left ventricular mass was increased in homozygotes for the G-allele but was significantly greater in those heterozygous for the C-allele and in the CC homozygotes. Amongst 578 men and 564 women participating in the third MONICA Augsburg survey, left ventricular mass (as measured by echocardiography) was significantly higher in homozygotes for the C-allele – an effect amplified amongst the hypertensive (Jamshidi *et al.* 2002).

The relationship between left ventricular mass and other genotypes (e.g. Adducin, Interleukin-6, and Endothelial Nitric Oxide Synthase) (Winnicki *et al.* 2002; Karvonen *et al.* 2002; Losito *et al.* 2003) has been investigated with mixed success. However, these studies have focused on hypertrophic responses to pathological stimuli. Whether there is a relationship between these genotypes and exercise-related or physiological hypertrophy has yet to be determined.

Myocardial RAS may play an important role in the regulation of left ventricular growth responses. RAS components including ACE are expressed in myocardium (Danser *et al.* 1999) and such expression increases with cardiac growth (Lievre *et al.* 1995). In addition, the administration of ACE inhibitors to humans may lead to greater regression in left ventricular mass than is seen with other similarly hypotensive agents (Cruickshank *et al.* 1992; Schmieder *et al.* 1996; Schmieder *et al.* 1998). The ACE D-allele is associated with greater left ventricular ACE activity (Danser *et al.* 1995) and, in Caucasian military recruits, with the increase in left ventricular mass associated with a 10-week training programme (Montgomery *et al.* 1997). This increase in growth response has since been confirmed using cardiac magnetic resonance imaging (Myerson *et al.* 2001). Such studies have also suggested that these effects are not mediated through polymorphic variation in the angiotensin II type 1 receptor. However, kinins may inhibit myocardial growth (Linz and Scholkens 1992) and increased ACE activity may therefore promote cardiac growth through increased kinin degradation (Murphey *et al.* 2000; Brull *et al.* 2001). Murphey *et al.* (2000) found that the ACE D-allele has a significant effect on the *in vivo* degradation of bradykinins in humans. Lung *et al.* (1997) describe a polymorphic variant of the bradykinin 2 receptor (B2BKR) gene where the absence (−) rather than the presence (+) of a 9bp deletion in the gene is associated with greater gene expression. B2BKR and ACE were found to interact in an additive fashion in determining physiological left ventricular growth in 109 military recruits after 10 weeks of basic army training (Brull *et al.* 2001). This suggests that kinins have a role in the regulation of left ventricular growth and may mediate some of the effects of ACE. As yet, no studies have compared the cardiac growth (or functional) response to exercise between African and Caucasian athletic populations, nor the differential genetic influences on these.

Oxygen extraction

It has been suggested that there is between 24% and 47% hereditability of haemodynamic parameters (Bielen *et al.* 1991). In post-menopausal women, a Gln27Glu polymorphism of the β_2-adrenergic receptor is associated with submaximal ($P = 0.004$) and maximal ($P = 0.006$) exercise a-vDO$_2$ differences, with those homozygous for the β_2-AR Gln allele having the greatest a-vDO$_2$. The association with submaximal exercise was also found to interact with physical activity levels. In those homozygous for the Gln allele and the lowest physical activity levels, the differences in a-vDO$_2$ was greatest and in those with the highest physical activity levels there was no difference in a-vDO$_2$ (McCole *et al.* 2004). However, no studies have evaluated differences in oxygen extraction between African and Caucasian elite endurance athletes.

Skeletal muscle

Genetic factors influence both basal (untrained) skeletal mass and the hypertrophic response to training. In fact, among postmenopausal women, genetic factors may be responsible for up to half the variance of lean body mass (Arden and Spector 1997) and as much as 80% of the variance in human skeletal muscle mass in younger individuals (Seeman *et al.* 1996). Genetic influences also appear to for be stronger on mass-associated skeletal muscle function (such as static strength and power) when compared to muscular endurance, and stronger in males than females (Bouchard *et al.* 1997). Low body mass might confer a performance advantage to the endurance runner, as may a specific reduction in leg mass (see Chapter 6). However, increased muscle strength may also be associated with improved elastic recoil in the muscle-tendon unit resulting in improved running efficiency (see Chapter 10). For both of these reasons, genetic influences on muscle mass may play an important role in determining interracial differences in sporting phenotype.

The anabolic effect of growth hormone (GH) is mediated through insulin-like growth factor I (IGF-I) with *free* IGF-I being the major biologically active hormonal form (Janssen *et al.* 2003). At the same time, the growth of tissues such as muscle is reliant on normal thyroid function (Weiss and Refetoff 1996). Thyroid hormone promotes the secretion of growth hormone (GH) and is necessary for normal GH expression *in vitro* (Crew and Spindler 1986; Ceda *et al.* 1992) and *in vivo* (Shapiro *et al.* 1978). Not all the effects of thyroid hormone on the IGF-I system are mediated by GH: T$_4$ can stimulate IGF-I activity in the absence of GH (Gaspard *et al.* 1978; Burstein *et al.* 1979;

Chernausek *et al.* 1982). Serum iodothyrodine levels have been associated with two polymorphisms of the type 1 deiodinase (D1) gene (Peeters *et al.* 2003). More specifically, the D1 haplotype 2 allele (aT-bA) show slower activity, and haplotype 3 allele higher activity (aC-bG). Peeters has demonstrated that elderly male carriers of the D1a-T variant have a higher lean body mass (P = 0.03) and higher isometric grip strength (P = 0.047) and maximum leg extensor strength (P = 0.07). It was concluded that the D1a-T polymorphism may be associated with increased muscle mass through decreased D1 activity and increase of IGF-I levels (which were also demonstrated in the study) (Peeters *et al.* 2005).

Interleukin-15 (IL-15) is an anabolic cytokine produced in skeletal muscle and has been shown to have direct effects on muscle anabolism in both animal and *in vitro* models (Quinn *et al.* 1995; Quinn *et al.* 1997; Carbo *et al.* 2000). Muscle responses to 10 weeks of resistance training and the influence of variations in the IL-15 receptor alpha gene (IL15RA) were examined (Riechman *et al.* 2004). A polymorphism of IL15RA was strongly associated with muscle hypertrophy and accounted for 7.1% of the variation in responses. A further polymorphism at exon 4 was also independently associated with muscle hypertrophy and accounted for a further 3.5% of the variation. These results suggest that IL-15 may be an important mediator of muscle mass response to exercise training in humans (Riechman *et al.* 2004).

Myostatin is a member of a group of related molecules called transforming growth factors beta (TGF-β). The muscular breeds of Piedmontese cattle have inherent mutations of their myostatin gene (Kambadur *et al.* 1997; McPherron and Lee 1997). Interference with this gene in mice was related to a generalized increase in muscle mass, suggesting that myostatin has an inhibitory effect on skeletal muscle growth (McPherron *et al.* 1997; Szabo *et al.* 1998). In human studies polymorphisms of the myostatin gene have been associated with hip flexion strength in older women (Seibert *et al.* 2001) and the amount of muscle wasting in Human Immunodeficiency Virus (HIV) infection (Gonzalez-Cadavid *et al.* 1998).

Glucocorticoids are also known to play a significant role in determining body composition (Christy 1971). A polymorphism (ER22/23EK) of the glucocorticoid receptor gene 9in codons 22 and 23 has been shown to be associated with relative glucocorticoid resistance, low cholesterol levels and increased insulin sensitivity (van Rossum *et al.* 2002). Non-carriers and carriers of the ER22/23EK variant were compared for anthropometric parameters, body composition and muscle strength in a group of 350 subjects who were observed from age 13 to 36 years (van Rossum *et al.* 2004). At 36 years of age the male ER22/23EK carriers were taller, had greater lean body mass and thigh circumference and had greater muscle strength in both the upper and lower body. No differences in body mass index or fat mass were observed. The female carriers at age 36 had smaller waist and hip circumferences but also had no differences in body mass index. It was concluded by the investigators that the ER22/23EK polymorphism is associated with 'sex specific, beneficial body composition at young-adult age, as well as greater muscle strength in males' (van Rossum *et al.* 2004: 4008).

Genetic factors not only influence skeletal muscle mass, but function. Ciliary Neurotrophic Factor (CNTF) is a member of the IL-6 family (Siegel *et al.* 2000; Giehl 2001; English 2003) which may have trophic effects on skeletal muscle (Vergara and Ramirez 2004). CNTF administration affects the expression of several muscle proteins (Boudreau-Lariviere *et al.* 1996), increases cross-sectional area of innervated soleus muscle fibres (Guillet *et al.* 1999), and limits atrophy after denervation in rat models (Helgren *et al.* 1994). An association between the CNTF receptor gene (CNTFR) and fat-free mass has been reported (Roth *et al.* 2003), while the A (rather than G) allele of the G>A CNTF polymorphism is associated with higher peak torque of both knee extensors and flexors (Roth *et al.* 2001). Type I collagen contains two $\alpha 1$ polypeptide chains and one $\alpha 2$ chain encoded respectively by the collagen type I alpha 1 (COL11) and alpha 2 (COL1A2) genes (Jarvinen *et al.* 2002). They offer structural support, attach myocytes and muscle bundles to each other (Jarvinen *et al.* 2002), and contribute to the integrity and tensile strength of muscle (Han *et al.* 1999; Takala and Virtanen 2000). Slow muscle has more type 1 collagen and fast muscle more type III collagen (Miller *et al.* 2001). A polymorphism of the binding site of the Sp1 transcription factor in the gene encoding for the alpha 1 chain of type 1I collagen exists, in which the s (rather than S) allele has been associated with lower biceps and grip strength on the dominant side (van Pottelbergh *et al.* 2001).

Vitamin D receptors (VDR) are expressed in skeletal muscle (Costa *et al.* 1986) and may influence its function: vitamin D deficiency can lead to myopathy, while 1,25 dihydroxyvitamin D can have rapid effects on muscle through phosphorylation and activation of secondary messengers (Buitrago *et al.* 2001). Young VDR-null mice have smaller muscle fibres and high expression of markers of early muscle differentiation (Endo *et al.* 2003). A polymorphic variation of the VDR gene has been associated with skeletal muscle function in both post-menopausal (Geusens *et al.* 1997) and pre-menopausal women (Grundberg *et al.* 2004).

Renin-angiotensin systems also seem to profoundly influence skeletal muscle function. The primary requirement of skeletal muscle during sustained exercise is fatigue resistance. Skeletal muscle RAS might influence muscle function through Angiotensin II (Ang II) genesis or kinin degradation. Ang II is a trophic agent for vascular smooth muscle (Berk *et al.* 1989) and also in cardiac muscle (Liu *et al.* 1998; Wollert and Drexler 1999). Increased ACE expression, as marked by the ACE D-allele might be expected to be associated with skeletal muscle hypertrophy in response to exercise. Ang II infusion leads to cachexia in rodent models, which is not attributable to an anorexic effect (Brink *et al.* 2001) and loss of body mass (Brink *et al.* 1996) suggesting that Ang II also plays a metabolic role. RAS expression plays an important role in the regulation of fat storage in adipocytes (Shenoy and Cassis 1997; Ailhaud 1999). Meanwhile bradykinin influences glycogen levels, lactate concentration (Linz *et al.* 1996), the expression of the GLUT4 glucose transporter (Taguchi *et al.* 2000) and the availability of glucose-free fatty acid substrate (Wicklmayr *et al.* 1980). Whether through any of these mechanisms, ACE genotype is associated with differences in skeletal muscle form and function. Amongst military recruits a relative anabolic response was observed in those with the ACE I-allele, despite conditions of high calorie expenditure (Montgomery *et al.* 1999). Delta Efficiency (DE) (the ratio of external mechanical work to internal work performed by skeletal muscle) has been found to increase significantly over a period of training in Caucasian military recruits of II genotype, compared to those of DD genotype (Williams *et al.* 2000). In a standardized repetitive elbow flexion exercise pre training performance was independent of ACE genotype. However, exercise duration increased significantly for those heterozygous for the I-allele when compared the D-allele homozygotes (Montgomery *et al.* 1998). Meanwhile, quadriceps strength is D-allele associated in patients with chronic obstructive pulmonary disease (Hopkinson *et al.* 2004), and gains in quadriceps muscle strength in response to strength training seem to be associated with the ACE D-allele in young adult men (Folland *et al.* 2000).

Such effects may in part be related to genotype associations with skeletal muscle fibre type: the I-allele may be associated with a higher proportion of Type I fibres, and the D-allele with a lower proportion of Type IIb (Scott *et al.* 2001). However, both Kenyan and Scandinavian athletes have a high proportion of Type I fibres (Saltin *et al.* 1995a) and a study comparing untrained African boys and Danish boys revealed no difference in muscle fibre type distribution (Larsen 2003) (see Chapter 8). This implies that the factors relating to muscle hypertrophy and muscle fibre type distribution are not decisive in African elite endurance athlete performance.

The activity of citrate synthase has been related to performance in running (Evertsen *et al.* 1999) and as such as been scrutinized as a potential difference between African endurance athletes and their Caucasian counterparts. Studies of inter-racial differences in citrate synthase activity have generated equivocal results (Saltin *et al.* 1995a; Weston *et al.* 1999). An increased muscle mitochondrial capacity would explain a lower lactate level for a given work rate (Ivy *et al.* 1980) but no polymorphisms have been related to citrate synthase activity to date. However, levels of 3-hydroxyacyl-CoA-Dehydrogenase (HAD) differ between Kenyan and Scandinavian athletes (Saltin *et al.* 1995a) and between black and white African athletes (Weston *et al.* 1999), although no HAD gene polymorphisms have yet been related to performance, measures of aerobic capacity or HAD activity in elite athletes.

Running economy

Running economy is expressed as the steady state submaximal oxygen uptake at a given running velocity. The lower the oxygen consumption at any given velocity the better the economy. When compared to Caucasians, elite African endurance athletes have lower $\dot{V}O_2$ max values while still being able to achieve the same performance over a 10 km race (Weston *et al.* 1999). This difference is partly attributed to a 5% greater running economy ($P < 0.05$). When oxygen consumption for a given work rate was normalized for body mass, this difference was attenuated and running economy found to be 8% better in African runners, compared to Caucasian runners (Weston *et al.* 1999). Saltin *et al.* (1995b) also found that Kenyan runners are more economical than Scandinavian runners even when the data were normalized for differences in body size (reviewed in Chapters 8–10).

Running economy is a complex function of muscle fibre type (relating to contractility and metabolic profiles), body shape and size, and gait (which is a function of many physiological characteristics including lever length, muscle length, muscle fibre orientation, and flexibility). It is therefore not surprising that, to date, no polymorphisms have been related to running economy per se.

Genetic markers associated with elite long-distance running

Through various mechanisms, a number of genetic variants may be associated with elite endurance running status. An actin-binding protein found in skeletal muscle (see previous chapter), alpha-actinin 3 is involved in the regulation of myofibrillar architecture and contractile co-ordination. Humans have two alpha-actinin genes: ACTN-2 (expressed in all fibres) and ACTN-3 (specifically expressed in Type 2 or fast twitch myofibres). Alpha-actinin-3 may be absent in nearly one fifth of healthy Caucasians because of homozygosity for a common stop-codon polymorphism in the ACTN3 gene, R577X (North *et al.* 1999). While the presence of such allelic variation seems of little significance among the sedentary, probably due to adequate compensation through increased α-actinin-2 (North *et al.*1999), this would not seem to be the case among elite athletes. In a study by Yang *et al.* (2003) both male and female elite sprint athletes (n = 107) were shown to have significantly higher frequencies of the 577R allele than the 436 controls. The frequency of 577RX heterozygotes was also higher than anticipated in females among sprint athletes and lower in female endurance athletes, suggesting a sex-specific effect.

Studies to date suggest the ACE I-allele to be associated with fatigue resistance/enhanced endurance performance. Over a 10-week period of basic military training, the duration for which young Caucasian males could perform repetitive loaded biceps curls doubled for those of II genotype, but did not change for those of DD genotype (Montgomery *et al.* 1998). Subsequently, an increase in I-allele frequency was observed with event distance amongst UK Olympic-standard runners with I-allele frequency 0.35, 0.53 and 0.62 amongst runners in 200, 400–3,000 and 5,000 m distances respectively (Myerson *et al.* 1999). Nazarov and colleagues studied Russian athletes prospectively stratified by the duration of their event (SDA < 1 min, MDA 1 to 20 min). Compared to controls and short-distance athletes (exercise times of < 1 min), outstanding middle-distance athletes (exercise durations 1–20 min) demonstrated an excess of the I-allele (Nazarov *et al.* 2001). I-allele frequency was higher among long-distance swimmers than short-distance swimmers (Tsianos *et al.* 2005), and among elite high-altitude mountaineers than amongst controls (Montgomery *et al.* 1998). The I-allele is also associated with success in summitting Mont Blanc (the highest mountain in western Europe) (Tsianos *et al.* 2005). Meanwhile, in the South African Ironman Triathlon, the fastest 100 South African born finishers also exhibit a higher frequency of the I-allele compared with South African controls (Collins *et al.* 2004). The I-allele is also found in excess among elite long-distance cyclists (Alvarez *et al.* 2000), and Australian national rowers (Gayagay *et al.* 1998).

A variety of studies demonstrate that such associations do not depend merely on 'elite athlete status' per se (Karjalainen *et al.* 1999; Taylor *et al.* 1999; Rankinen *et al.* 2000b; Woods *et al.* 2000; Sonna *et al.* 2001; Montgomery and Dhamrait 2002) confirming the association instead with endurance performance. The mechanism underlying this association remains to be elucidated, but may depend in part on allele-specific changes in mechanical/metabolic efficiency with training or skeletal muscle fibre type (see above).

Could the I-allele influence thus extend to the east African populations? Care must be taken in such extrapolative studies, given that the functional association of one polymorphism may differ in scale (or indeed be absent) in one race when compared to another. Thus, recent studies have shown that other variants of the ACE gene are more closely associated with circulating ACE levels than the I/D polymorphism in African populations (Zhu *et al.* 2000; Cox *et al.* 2002). A transition at nucleotide 22982 in the sequence AF118569 (Zhu *et al.* 2000) or 31958 (Cox *et al.* 2002) has been found to show the largest phenotypic differences in ACE levels between genotypes. The greatest differences in ACE levels in Afro-Caribbean subjects between genotypes were found between genotypes at A22982G where the A-allele has been associated with lower circulating ACE levels than the G-allele (Cox *et al.* 2002; Soubrier *et al.* 2002). To date, only one study has attempted to identity an association of ACE I/D genotype with such endurance performance among east African runners (Scott *et al.* 2005). ACE I/D genotype was determined in 221 national Kenyan athletes, 70 international Kenyan athletes, and 85 members of the general Kenyan population. So too was ACE A22982G genotype, thought to be more closely associated with ACE activity (at least in the circulation) than the I/D polymorphism. ACE I/D and A22982G genotypes explained 13 and 24% of variation in circulating ACE activity. However, neither genotype seemed associated with elite endurance athlete status. Such results may in part relate to the small number of controls for comparison, to the more modest influence of ACE genotype on ACE activity when compared to Caucasians, or to an unidentified association of ACE genotype with expression of a neighbouring (but different) gene.

Conclusions

Human form and function are dictated by the interaction of genes with environmental stimuli. Thus variations in environmental exposures will strongly influence phenotype. However, although a core genetic inheritance is common to all humans, small functional variations exist in these genes, which dictate that individual (or racial) responses to environmental challenge will differ. Such genetic differences influence sporting performance through associated differences in anatomy and physiology and their response to training stimuli. There are now in excess of 100 gene variants related to human performance (Rankinen et al. 2004).

African endurance athletes have become increasingly successful over the last 20 years and different hypotheses have been made regarding such excess success in relation to population size. To date few physiological differences have been reliably identified between elite African endurance athletes and their Caucasian counterparts and even fewer genetic associations which may be able to explain these physiological differences have been found. Nonetheless, the search for such factors may bring value far beyond the simple explanation of inter-racial differences, helping to understand the fundamental physiology of exercise itself.

Bibliography

Abraham, M. R., Olson, L. J., Joyner, M. J., Turner, S. T., Beck, K. C. and Johnson, B. D. (2002) 'Angiotensin-converting enzyme genotype modulates pulmonary function and exercise capacity in treated patients with congestive stable heart failure', Circulation 106, 1794–9.

Ailhaud, G. (1999) 'Cross talk between adipocytes and their precursors: relationships with adipose tissue development and blood pressure', Annals of the New York Academy of Sciences 892, 127–33.

Alvarez, R., Terrados, N., Ortolano, R., Iglesias-Cubero, G., Reguero, J. R., Batalla, A., Cortina, A., Fernandez-Garcia, B., Rodriguez, C., Braga, S., Alvarez, V. and Coto, E. (2000) 'Genetic variation in the renin-angiotensin system and athletic performance', European Journal of Applied Physiology 82, 117–20.

Andersen, L. B. (1994) 'Blood pressure, physical fitness and physical activity in 17-year-old Danish adolescents', Journal of Internal Medicine 236, 323–9.

Arden, N. K. and Spector, T. D. (1997) 'Genetic influences on muscle strength, lean body mass, and bone mineral density: a twin study', Journal of Bone and Mineral Research 12, 2076–81.

Barger, P. M., Brandt, J. M., Leone, T. C., Weinheimer, C. J. and Kelly, D. P. (2000) 'Deactivation of peroxisome proliferator-activated receptor-alpha during cardiac hypertrophic growth', Journal of Clinical Investigation 105, 1723–30.

Berk, B. C., Vekshtein, V., Gordon, H. M. and Tsuda, T. (1989) 'Angiotensin II-stimulated protein synthesis in cultured vascular smooth muscle cells', Hypertension 13, 305–14.

Bielen, E., Fagard, R. and Amery, A. (1991) 'The inheritance of left ventricular structure and function assessed by imaging and Doppler echocardiography', American Heart Journal 121, 1743–9.

Binas, B., Danneberg, H., McWhir, J., Mullins, L. and Clark, A. J. (1999) 'Requirement for the heart-type fatty acid binding protein in cardiac fatty acid utilization', *FASEB Journal* 13, 805–12.

Bouchard, C., Leon, A. S., Rao, D. C., Skinner, J. S., Wilmore, J. H. and Gagnon, J. (1995) 'The HERITAGE family study. Aims, design, and measurement protocol', *Medicine and Science in Sports Exercise* 27, 721–9.

Bouchard, C., Lesage, R., Lortie, G., Simoneau, J. A., Hamel, P., Boulay, M R., Perusse, L., Theriault, G. and Leblanc, C. (1986) 'Aerobic performance in brothers, dizygotic and monozygotic twins', *Medicine and Science in Sports Exercise* 18, 639–46.

Bouchard, C., Malina, R. M. and Perusse, L. (1997) *Genetics of Fitness and Physical Performance*, Champaign, IL: Human Kinetics.

Bouchard, C., Rankinen, T., Chagnon, Y. C., Rice, T., Perusse, L., Gagnon, J., Borecki, I., An, P., Leon, A. S., Skinner, J. S., Wilmore, J. H., Province, M. and Rao, D. C. (2000) 'Genomic scan for maximal oxygen uptake and its response to training in the HERITAGE Family Study', *Journal of Applied Physiology* 88, 551–9.

Boudreau-Larivière, C., Sveistrup, H., Parry, D. J. and Jasmin, B. J. (1996) 'Ciliary neurotrophic factor: regulation of acetylcholinesterase in skeletal muscle and distribution of messenger RNA encoding its receptor in synaptic versus extrasynaptic compartments', *Neuroscience* 73, 613–22.

Brink, M., Price, S. R., Chrast, J., Bailey, J. L., Anwar, A., Mitch, W. E. and Delafontaine, P. (2001) 'Angiotensin II induces skeletal muscle wasting through enhanced protein degradation and down-regulates autocrine insulin-like growth factor I', *Endocrinology* 142, 1489–96.

Brink, M., Wellen, J. and Delafontaine, P. (1996) 'Angiotensin II causes weight loss and decreases circulating insulin-like growth factor I in rats through a pressor-independent mechanism', *Journal of Clinical Investigation* 97, 2509–16.

Brull, D., Dhamrait, S., Myerson, S., Erdmann, J., Woods, D., World, M., Pennell, D., Humphries, S., Regitz-Zagrosek, V. and Montgomery, H. (2001) 'Bradykinin B2BKR receptor polymorphism and left-ventricular growth response', *Lancet* 358, 1155–6.

Buhl, R., Ersboll, A. K., Eriksen, L. and Koch, J. (2005) 'Changes over time in echocardiographic measurements in young Standardbred racehorses undergoing training and racing and association with racing performance', *Journal of the American Veterinary Medical Association* 226, 1881–7.

Buikema, H., Pinto, Y. M., van Geel, P. P., Rooks, G., de Langen, C. D., de Graeff, P. A. and van Gilst, W. H. (1997) 'Differential inhibition of plasma versus tissue ACE by utibapril: biochemical and functional evidence for inhibition of vascular ACE activity', *Journal of Cardiovascular Pharmacology* 29, 684–91.

Buitrago, C., Vazquez, G., De Boland, A. R. and Boland, R. (2001) 'The vitamin D receptor mediates rapid changes in muscle protein tyrosine phosphorylation induced by 1, 25 (OH) (2)D (3)', *Biochemical and Biophysical Research Communications* 289, 1150–6.

Burstein, P. J., Draznin, B., Johnson, C. J. and Schalch, D. S. (1979) 'The effect of hypothyroidism on growth, serum growth hormone, the growth hormone-dependent somatomedin, insulin-like growth factor, and its carrier protein in rats', *Endocrinology* 104, 1107–11.

Carbo, N., Lopez-Soriano, J., Costelli, P., Busquets, S., Alvarez, B., Baccino, F. M., Quinn, L. S., Lopez-Soriano, F. J. and Argiles, J. M. (2000) 'Interleukin–15 antagonizes muscle protein waste in tumour-bearing rats', *British Journal of Cancer* 83, 526–31.

Ceda, G. P., Fielder, P. J., Donovan, S. M., Rosenfeld, R. G. and Hoffman, A. R. (1992) 'Regulation of insulin-like growth factor-binding protein expression by thyroid hormone in rat GH3 pituitary tumor cells', *Endocrinology* 130, 1483–9.

Chernausek, S. D., Underwood, L. E. and Van Wyk, J. J. (1982) 'Influence of hypothyroidism on growth hormone binding by rat liver', *Endocrinology* 111, 1534–8.

Chiu, H. C., Kovacs, A., Ford, D. A., Hsu, F. F., Garcia, R., Herrero, P., Saffitz, J. E. and Schaffer, J. E. (2001) 'A novel mouse model of lipotoxic cardiomyopathy', *Journal of Clinical Investigation* 107, 813–22.

Christy, N. P. (1971) *The Human Adrenal Cortex*, New York: Medical Dept, Harper & Row.

Clausen, T., Nielsen, O. B., Harrison, A. P., Flatman, J. A. and Overgaard, K. (1998) 'The Na^+, K^+ pump and muscle excitability', *Acta Physiologica Scandinavica* 162, 183–90.

Coetzer, P., Noakes, T. D., Sanders, B., Lambert, M. I., Bosch, A. N., Wiggins, T. and Dennis, S. C. (1993) 'Superior fatigue resistance of elite black South African distance runners', *Journal of Applied Physiology* 75, 1822–7.

Collins, M., Xenophontos, S. L., Cariolou, M. A., Mokone, G. G., Hudson, D. E., Anastasiades, L. and Noakes, T. D. (2004) 'The ACE gene and endurance performance during the South African Ironman Triathlons', *Medicine and Science in Sports Exercise* 36, 1314–20.

Costa, E. M., Blau, H. M. and Feldman, D. (1986) '1, 25-dihydroxyvitamin D3 receptors and hormonal responses in cloned human skeletal muscle cells', *Endocrinology* 119, 2214–20.

Costerousse, O., Allegrini, J., Lopez, M. and Alhenc-Gelas, F. (1993) 'Angiotensin I-converting enzyme in human circulating mononuclear cells: genetic polymorphism of expression in T-lymphocytes', *Biochemical Journal* 290 (Pt 1), 33–40.

Cox, R., Bouzekri, N., Martin, S., Southam, L., Hugill, A., Golamaully, M., Cooper, R., Adeyemo, A., Soubrier, F., Ward, R., Lathrop, G. M., Matsuda, F. and Farrall, M. (2002) 'Angiotensin-1-converting enzyme (ACE) plasma concentration is influenced by multiple ACE-linked quantitative trait nucleotides', *Human Molecular Genetics* 11, 2969–77.

Crew, M. D. and Spindler, S. R. (1986) 'Thyroid hormone regulation of the transfected rat growth hormone promoter', *Journal of Biological Chemistry* 261, 5018–22.

Cruickshank, J. M., Lewis, J., Moore, V. and Dodd, C. (1992) 'Reversibility of left ventricular hypertrophy by differing types of antihypertensive therapy', *Journal of Human Hypertension* 6, 85–90.

Danser, A. H. J., Schalekamp, M. A., Bax, W. A., van den Brink, A. M., Saxena, P. R., Riegger, G. A. and Schunkert, H. (1995) 'Angiotensin-converting enzyme in the human heart. Effect of the deletion/insertion polymorphism', *Circulation* 92, 1387–8.

Danser, A. H. J., Saris, J. J., Schuijt, M. P. and van Kats, J. P. (1999) 'Is there a local renin-angiotensin system in the heart?', *Cardiovascular Research* 44, 252–65.

DeMaria, A. N., Neumann, A., Lee, G., Fowler, W. and Mason, D. T. (1978) 'Alterations in ventricular mass and performance induced by exercise training in man evaluated by echocardiography', *Circulation* 57, 237–44.

Dionne, F. T., Turcotte, L., Thibault, M. C., Boulay, M. R., Skinner, J. S. and Bouchard, C. (1991) 'Mitochondrial DNA sequence polymorphism, VO2max, and response to endurance training', *Medicine and Science in Sports Exercise* 23, 177–85.

Djouadi, F., Weinheimer, C. J., Saffitz, J. E., Pitchford, C., Bastin, J., Gonzalez, F. J. and Kelly, D. P. (1998) 'A gender-related defect in lipid metabolism and glucose homeostasis in peroxisome proliferator-activated receptor alpha-deficient mice', *Journal of Clinical Investigation* 102, 1083–91.

Dzau, V. J. (1988) 'Tissue renin-angiotensin system: physiologic and pharmacologic implications. Introduction', *Circulation* 77, I1–3.

Endo, I., Inoue, D., Mitsui, T., Umaki, Y., Akaike, M., Yoshizawa, T., Kato, S. and Matsumoto, T. (2003) 'Deletion of vitamin D receptor gene in mice results in abnormal skeletal muscle development with deregulated expression of myoregulatory transcription factors', *Endocrinology* 144, 5138–44.

English, A. W. (2003) 'Cytokines, growth factors and sprouting at the neuromuscular junction', *Journal of Neurocytology* 32, 943–60.

Evertsen, F., Medbo, J. I., Jebens, E. and Gjovaag, T. F. (1999) 'Effect of training on the activity of five muscle enzymes studied on elite cross-country skiers', *Acta Physiologica Scandinavica* 167, 247–57.

Fagard, R., Bielen, E. and Amery, A. (1991) 'Heritability of aerobic power and anaerobic energy generation during exercise', *Journal of Applied Physiology* 70, 357–62.

Fishbein, W. N., Sabina, R. L., Ogasawara, N. and Holmes, E. W. (1993) 'Immunologic evidence for three isoforms of AMP deaminase (AMPD) in mature skeletal muscle', *Biochimica et Biophysica Acta* 1163, 97–104.

Folland, J., Leach, B., Little, T., Hawker, K., Myerson, S., Montgomery, H. and Jones, D. (2000) 'Angiotensin-converting enzyme genotype affects the response of human skeletal muscle to functional overload', *Experimental Physiology* 85, 575–9.

Fruchart, J. C., Duriez, P. and Staels, B. (1999) 'Peroxisome proliferator-activated receptor-alpha activators regulate genes governing lipoprotein metabolism, vascular inflammation and atherosclerosis', *Current Opinion in Lipidology* 10, 245–57.

Gambert, S. R. and Duthie, E. H., Jr (1983) 'Effect of age on red cell membrane sodium - potassium dependent adenosine triphosphatase (Na$^+$-K$^+$ ATPase) activity in healthy men', *Journal of Gerontology* 38, 23–5.

Gaspard, T., Wondergem, R., Hamamdzic, M. and Klitgaard, H. M. (1978) 'Serum somatomedin stimulation in thyroxine-treated hypophysectomized rats', *Endocrinology* 102, 606–11.

Gayagay, G., Yu, B., Hambly, B., Boston, T., Hahn, A., Celermajer, D. S. and Trent, R. J. (1998) 'Elite endurance athletes and the ACE I-allele–the role of genes in athletic performance', *Human Genetics* 103, 48–50.

Geusens, P., Vandevyver, C., Vanhoof, J., Cassiman, J. J., Boonen, S. and Raus, J. (1997) 'Quadriceps and grip strength are related to vitamin D receptor genotype in elderly nonobese women', *Journal of Bone and Mineral Research* 12, 2082–8.

Giehl, K. M. (2001) 'Trophic dependencies of rodent corticospinal neurons', *Reviews in the Neurosciences* 12, 79–94.

Gonzalez-Cadavid, N. F., Taylor, W. E., Yarasheski, K., Sinha-Hikim, I., Ma, K., Ezzat, S., Shen, R., Lalani, R., Asa, S., Mamita, M., Nair, G., Arver, S. and Bhasin, S. (1998) 'Organization of the human myostatin gene and expression in healthy men and HIV-infected men with muscle wasting', *Proceedings of the National Academy of Sciences USA* 95, 14938–43.

Grundberg, E., Brandstrom, H., Ribom, E. L., Ljunggren, O., Mallmin, H. and Kindmark, A. (2004) 'Genetic variation in the human vitamin D receptor is associated with muscle strength, fat mass and body weight in Swedish women', *European Journal of Endocrinology* 150, 323–8.

Guillet, C., Auguste, P., Mayo, W., Kreher, P. and Gascan, H. (1999) 'Ciliary neurotrophic factor is a regulator of muscular strength in aging', *Journal of Neuroscience* 19, 1257–62.

Hagberg, J. M., Ferrell, R. E., McCole, S. D., Wilund, K. R. and Moore, G. E. (1998) 'VO2 max is associated with ACE genotype in postmenopausal women', *Journal of Applied Physiology* 85, 1842–6.

Hagemann, A., Nielsen, A. H. and Poulsen, K. (1994) 'The uteroplacental renin-angiotensin system: a review', *Experimental and Clinical Endocrinology* 102, 252–61.

Han, X. Y., Wang, W., Myllyla, R., Virtanen, P., Karpakka, J. and Takala, T. E. (1999) 'mRNA levels for alpha-subunit of prolyl 4-hydroxylase and fibrillar collagens in immobilized rat skeletal muscle', *Journal of Applied Physiology* 87, 90–6.

Harris, R. C. and Cheng, H. F. (1996) 'The intrarenal renin-angiotensin system: a paracrine system for the local control of renal function separate from the systemic axis', *Experimental Nephrology* 4 Suppl. 1, 2–7.

Helgren, M. E., Squinto, S. P., Davis, H. L., Parry, D. J., Boulton, T. G., Heck, C. S., Zhu, Y., Yancopoulos, G. D., Lindsay, R. M. and DiStefano, P. S. (1994) 'Trophic effect of ciliary neurotrophic factor on denervated skeletal muscle', *Cell* 76, 493–504.

Hopkinson, N. S., Nickol, A. H., Payne, J., Hawe, E., Man, W. D., Moxham, J., Montgomery, H. E. and Polkey, M. I. (2004) 'Angiotensin converting enzyme genotype and strength in chronic obstructive pulmonary disease', *American Journal of Respiratory and Critical Care Medicine* 170, 395–9.

Ivy, J. L., Withers, R. T., Van Handel, P. J., Elger, D. H. and Costill, D. L. (1980) 'Muscle respiratory capacity and fiber type as determinants of the lactate threshold', *Journal of Applied Physiology* 48, 523–7.

Jamshidi, Y., Montgomery, H. E., Hense, H. W., Myerson, S. G., Torra, I. P., Staels, B., World, M. J., Doering, A., Erdmann, J., Hengstenberg, C., Humphries, S. E., Schunkert, H. and Flavell, D. M. (2002) 'Peroxisome proliferator-activated receptor alpha gene regulates left ventricular growth in response to exercise and hypertension', *Circulation* 105, 950–5.

Janssen, J. A., van der Lely, A. J. and Lamberts, S. W. (2003) 'Circulating free insulin-like growth-factor-I (IGF-I) levels should also be measured to estimate the IGF-I bioactivity', *Journal of Endocrinological Investigation* 26, 588–94.

Jarvinen, T. A., Jozsa, L., Kannus, P., Jarvinen, T. L. and Jarvinen, M. (2002) 'Organization and distribution of intramuscular connective tissue in normal and immobilized skeletal muscles. An immunohistochemical, polarization and scanning electron microscopic study', *Journal of Muscle Research and Cell Motility* 23, 245–54.

Jones, A. and Woods, D. R. (2003) 'Skeletal muscle RAS and exercise performance', *International Journal of Biochemistry and Cell Biology* 35, 855–66.

Jonsson, J. R., Game, P. A., Head, R. J. and Frewin, D. B. (1994) 'The expression and localisation of the angiotensin-converting enzyme mRNA in human adipose tissue', *Blood Pressure* 3, 72–5.

Kambadur, R., Sharma, M., Smith, T. P. and Bass, J. J. (1997) 'Mutations in myostatin (GDF8) in double-muscled Belgian Blue and Piedmontese cattle', *Genome Research* 7, 910–6.

Kanakis, C. and Hickson, R. C. (1980) 'Left ventricular responses to a program of lower-limb strength training', *Chest* 78, 618–21.

Karjalainen, J., Kujala, U. M., Stolt, A., Mantysaari, M., Viitasalo, M., Kainulainen, K. and Kontula, K. (1999) 'Angiotensinogen gene M235T polymorphism predicts left ventricular hypertrophy in endurance athletes', *Journal of the American College of Cardiology* 34, 494–9.

Karvonen, J., Kauma, H., Kervinen, K., Rantala, M., Ikaheimo, M., Paivansalo, M., Savolainen, M. J. and Kesaniemi, Y. A. (2002) 'Endothelial nitric oxide synthase gene Glu298Asp polymorphism and blood pressure, left ventricular mass and carotid artery atherosclerosis in a population-based cohort', *Journal of Internal Medicine* 251, 102–10.

Kelly, D. P. and Strauss, A. W. (1994) 'Inherited cardiomyopathies', *New England Journal of Medicine* 330, 913–9.

Kem, D. C. and Brown, R. D. (1990) 'Renin–from beginning to end', *New England Journal of Medicine* 323, 1136–7.

Koren, M. J., Devereux, R. B., Casale, P. N., Savage, D. D. and Laragh, J. H. (1991) 'Relation of left ventricular mass and geometry to morbidity and mortality in uncomplicated essential hypertension', *Annals of Internal Medicine* 114, 345–52.

Larsen, H. B. (2003) 'Kenyan dominance in distance running', *Comparative Biochemistry and Physiology – Part A, Molecular and Integrative Physiology* 136, 161–70.

Lee, M. A., Paul, M., Bohm, M. and Ganten, D. (1992) 'Effects of angiotensin-converting enzyme inhibitors on tissue renin-angiotensin systems', *American Journal of Cardiology* 70, 12C–19C.

Lesage, R., Simoneau, J. A., Jobin, J., Leblanc, J. and Bouchard, C. (1985) 'Familial resemblance in maximal heart rate, blood lactate and aerobic power', *Human Heredity* 35, 182–9.

Levy, D., Garrison, R. J., Savage, D. D., Kannel, W. B. and Castelli, W. P. (1990) 'Prognostic implications of echocardiographically determined left ventricular mass in the Framingham Heart Study', *New England Journal of Medicine* 322, 1561–6.

Lievre, M., Gueret, P., Gayet, C., Roudaut, R., Haugh, M. C., Delair, S. and Boissel, J. P. (1995) 'Ramipril-induced regression of left ventricular hypertrophy in treated hypertensive individuals. HYCAR Study Group', *Hypertension* 25, 92–7.

Linz, W. and Scholkens, B. A. (1992) 'A specific B2-bradykinin receptor antagonist HOE 140 abolishes the antihypertrophic effect of ramipril', *British Journal of Pharmacology* 105, 771–2.

Linz, W., Wiemer, G. and Scholkens, B. A. (1996) 'Role of kinins in the pathophysiology of myocardial ischemia, in vitro and in vivo studies', *Diabetes* 45 Suppl. 1, S51–8.

Liu, Y., Leri, A., Li, B., Wang, X., Cheng, W., Kajstura, J. and Anversa, P. (1998) 'Angiotensin II stimulation in vitro induces hypertrophy of normal and postinfarcted ventricular myocytes', *Circulation Research* 82, 1145–59.

Losito, A., Kalidas, K., Santoni, S. and Jeffery, S. (2003) 'Association of interleukin-6 - 174G/C promoter polymorphism with hypertension and left ventricular hypertrophy in dialysis patients', *Kidney International* 64, 616–22.

Lung, C. C., Chan, E. K. and Zuraw, B. L. (1997) 'Analysis of an exon 1 polymorphism of the B2 bradykinin receptor gene and its transcript in normal subjects and patients with C1 inhibitor deficiency', *Journal of Allergy and Clinical Immunology* 99, 134–46.

McCole, S. D., Shuldiner, A. R., Brown, M. D., Moore, G. E., Ferrell, R. E., Wilund, K. R., Huberty, A., Douglass, L. W. and Hagberg, J. M. (2004) 'Beta2- and beta3-adrenergic receptor polymorphisms and exercise hemodynamics in postmenopausal women', *Journal of Applied Physiology* 96, 526–30.

McPherron, A. C., Lawler, A. M. and Lee, S. J. (1997) 'Regulation of skeletal muscle mass in mice by a new TGF-beta superfamily member', *Nature* 387, 83–90.

McPherron, A. C. and Lee, S. J. (1997) 'Double muscling in cattle due to mutations in the myostatin gene', *Proceedings of the National Academy of Sciences USA* 94, 12457–61.

Miller, T. A., Lesniewski, L. A., Muller-Delp, J. M., Majors, A. K., Scalise, D. and Delp, M. D. (2001) 'Hindlimb unloading induces a collagen isoform shift in the soleus muscle of the rat', *American Journal of Physiology Regulatory, Integrative and Comparative Physiology* 281, R1710–7.

Montgomery, H., Clarkson, P., Barnard, M., Bell, J., Brynes, A., Dollery, C., Hajnal, J., Hemingway, H., Mercer, D., Jarman, P., Marshall, R., Prasad, K., Rayson, M., Saeed, N., Talmud, P., Thomas, L., Jubb, M., World, M. and Humphries, S. (1999) 'Angiotensin-converting-enzyme gene insertion/deletion polymorphism and response to physical training', *Lancet* 353, 541–5.

Montgomery, H. and Dhamrait, S. (2002) 'ACE genotype and performance', *Journal of Applied Physiology* 92, 1774–5; author reply 1776–7.

Montgomery, H. E., Clarkson, P., Dollery, C. M., Prasad, K., Losi, M. A., Hemingway, H., Statters, D., Jubb, M., Girvain, M., Varnava, A., World, M., Deanfield, J., Talmud, P., McEwan, J. R., McKenna, W. J. and Humphries, S. (1997) 'Association of angiotensin-converting enzyme gene I/D polymorphism with change in left ventricular mass in response to physical training', *Circulation* 96, 741–7.

Montgomery, H. E., Marshall, R., Hemingway, H., Myerson, S., Clarkson, P., Dollery, C., Hayward, M., Holliman, D. E., Jubb, M., World, M., Thomas, E. L., Brynes, A. E., Saeed, N., Barnard, M., Bell, J. D., Prasad, K., Rayson, M., Talmud, P. J. and Humphries, S. E. (1998) 'Human gene for physical performance', *Nature* 393, 221–2.

Murphey, L. J., Gainer, J. V., Vaughan, D. E. and Brown, N. J. (2000) 'Angiotensin-converting enzyme insertion/deletion polymorphism modulates the human in vivo metabolism of bradykinin', *Circulation* 102, 829–32.

Myerson, S., Hemingway, H., Budget, R., Martin, J., Humphries, S. and Montgomery, H. E. (1999) 'Human angiotensin I-converting enzyme gene and endurance performance', *Journal of Applied Physiology* 87, 1313–6.

Myerson, S. G., Montgomery, H. E., Whittingham, M., Jubb, M., World, M. J., Humphries, S. E. and Pennell, D. J. (2001) 'Left ventricular hypertrophy with exercise and ACE gene insertion/deletion polymorphism: a randomized controlled trial with losartan', *Circulation* 103, 226–30.

Nazarov, I. B., Woods, D. R., Montgomery, H. E., Shneider, O. V., Kazakov, V. I., Tomilin, N. V. and Rogozkin, V. A. (2001) 'The angiotensin converting enzyme I/D polymorphism in Russian athletes', *European Journal of Human Genetics* 9, 797–801.

Norman, B., Sabina, R. L. and Jansson, E. (2001) 'Regulation of skeletal muscle ATP catabolism by AMPD1 genotype during sprint exercise in asymptomatic subjects', *Journal of Applied Physiology* 91, 258–64.

North, K. N., Yang, N., Wattanasirichaigoon, D., Mills, M., Easteal, S. and Beggs, A. H. (1999) 'A common nonsense mutation results in alpha-actinin-3 deficiency in the general population', *Nature Genetics* 21, 353–4.

Patel, S., Woods, D. R., Macleod, N. J., Brown, A., Patel, K. R., Montgomery, H. E. and Peacock, A. J. (2003) 'Angiotensin-converting enzyme genotype and the ventilatory response to exertional hypoxia', *European Respiratory Journal* 22, 755–60.

Peeters, R. P., van den Beld, A. W., van Toor, H., Uitterlinden, A. G., Janssen, J. A., Lamberts, S. W. and Visser, T. J. (2005) 'A polymorphism in type I deiodinase is associated with circulating free insulin-like growth factor I levels and body composition in humans', *Journal of Clinical Endocrinology and Metabolism* 90, 256–63.

Peeters, R. P., van Toor, H., Klootwijk, W., de Rijke, Y. B., Kuiper, G. G., Uitterlinden, A. G. and Visser, T. J. (2003) 'Polymorphisms in thyroid hormone pathway genes are associated with plasma TSH and iodothyronine levels in healthy subjects', *Journal of Clinical Endocrinology and Metabolism* 88, 2880–8.

Quinn, L. S., Haugk, K. L. and Damon, S. E. (1997) 'Interleukin–15 stimulates C2 skeletal myoblast differentiation', *Biochemical and Biophysical Research Communications* 239, 6–10.

Quinn, L. S., Haugk, K. L. and Grabstein, K. H. (1995) 'Interleukin–15: a novel anabolic cytokine for skeletal muscle', *Endocrinology* 136, 3669–72.

Rankinen, T., Perusse, L., Borecki, I., Chagnon, Y. C., Gagnon, J., Leon, A. S., Skinner, J. S., Wilmore, J. H., Rao, D. C. and Bouchard, C. (2000a) 'The Na (+)-K (+)-ATPase alpha2 gene and trainability of cardiorespiratory endurance: the HERITAGE Family Study', *Journal of Applied Physiology* 88, 346–51.

Rankinen, T., Perusse, L., Rauramaa, R., Rivera, M. A., Wolfarth, B. and Bouchard, C. (2004) 'The human gene map for performance and health-related fitness phenotypes: the 2003 update', *Medicine and Science in Sports Exercise* 36, 1451–69.

Rankinen, T., Wolfarth, B., Simoneau, J. A., Maier-Lenz, D., Rauramaa, R., Rivera, M. A., Boulay, M. R., Chagnon, Y. C., Perusse, L., Keul, J. and Bouchard, C. (2000b) 'No association between the angiotensin-converting enzyme ID polymorphism and elite endurance athlete status', *Journal of Applied Physiology* 88, 1571–5.

Rico-Sanz, J., Rankinen, T., Joanisse, D. R., Leon, A. S., Skinner, J. S., Wilmore, J. H., Rao, D. C. and Bouchard, C. (2003) 'Associations between cardiorespiratory responses to exercise and the C34T AMPD1 gene polymorphism in the HERITAGE Family Study', *Physiological Genomics* 14, 161–6.

Riechman, S. E., Balasekaran, G., Roth, S. M. and Ferrell, R. E. (2004) 'Association of interleukin–15 protein and interleukin–15 receptor genetic variation with resistance exercise training responses', *Journal of Applied Physiology* 97, 2214–9.

Rigat, B., Hubert, C., Alhenc-Gelas, F., Cambien, F., Corvol, P. and Soubrier, F. (1990) 'An insertion/deletion polymorphism in the angiotensin I-converting enzyme gene accounting for half the variance of serum enzyme levels', *Journal of Clinical Investigation* 86, 1343–6.

Rivera, M. A., Dionne, F. T., Simoneau, J. A., Perusse, L., Chagnon, M., Chagnon, Y., Gagnon, J., Leon, A. S., Rao, D. C., Skinner, J. S., Wilmore, J. H. and Bouchard, C. (1997) 'Muscle-specific creatine kinase gene polymorphism and VO$_2$max in the HERITAGE Family Study', *Medicine and Science in Sports Exercise* 29, 1311–17.

Rivera, M. A., Wolfarth, B., Dionne, F. T., Chagnon, M., Simoneau, J. A., Boulay, M. R., Song, T. M., Perusse, L., Gagnon, J., Leon, A. S., Rao, D. C., Skinner, J. S., Wilmore, J. H., Keul, J. and Bouchard, C. (1998) 'Three mitochondrial DNA restriction polymorphisms in elite endurance athletes and sedentary controls', *Medicine and Science in Sports Exercise* 30, 687–90.

Roth, S. M., Metter, E. J., Lee, M. R., Hurley, B. F. and Ferrell, R. E. (2003) 'C174T polymorphism in the CNTF receptor gene is associated with fat-free mass in men and women', *Journal of Applied Physiology* 95, 1425–30.

Roth, S. M., Schrager, M. A., Ferrell, R. E., Riechman, S. E., Metter, E. J., Lynch, N. A., Lindle, R. S. and Hurley, B. F. (2001) 'CNTF genotype is associated with muscular strength and quality in humans across the adult age span', *Journal of Applied Physiology* 90, 1205–10.

Sack, M. N., Rader, T. A., Park, S., Bastin, J., McCune, S. A. and Kelly, D. P. (1996)

'Fatty acid oxidation enzyme gene expression is downregulated in the failing heart', *Circulation* 94, 2837–42.

Saltin, B., Kim, C. K., Terrados, N., Larsen, H., Svedenhag, J. and Rolf, C. J. (1995a) 'Morphology, enzyme activities and buffer capacity in leg muscles of Kenyan and Scandinavian runners', *Scandinavian Journal of Medicine and Science in Sports* 5, 222–30.

Saltin, B., Larsen, H., Terrados, N., Bangsbo, J., Bak, T., Kim, C. K., Svedenhag, J. and Rolf, C. J. (1995b) 'Aerobic exercise capacity at sea level and at altitude in Kenyan boys, junior and senior runners compared with Scandinavian runners', *Scandinavian Journal of Medicine and Science in Sports* 5, 209–21.

Schmieder, R. E., Martus, P. and Klingbeil, A. U. (1996) 'Reversal of left ventricular hypertrophy in essential hypertension. A meta-analysis of randomized double-blind studies', *JAMA* 275, 1507–13.

Schmieder, R. E., Schlaich, M. P., Klingbeil, A. U. and Martus, P. (1998) 'Update on reversal of left ventricular hypertrophy in essential hypertension (a meta-analysis of all randomized double-blind studies until December 1996)' *Nephrology, Dialysis, Transplantation* 13, 564–9.

Scott, R. A., Moran, C., Wilson, R. H., Onywera, V., Boit, M. K., Goodwin, W. H., Gohlke, P., Payne, J., Montgomery, H. and Pitsiladis, Y. P. (2005) 'No association between Angiotensin Converting Enzyme (ACE) gene variation and endurance athlete status in Kenyans', *Comparative Biochemistry and Physiology – Part A, Molecular and Integrative Physiology* 141, 169–75.

Scott, W., Stevens, J. and Binder-Macleod, S. A. (2001) 'Human skeletal muscle fiber type classifications', *Physical Therapy* 81, 1810–6.

Seeman, E., Hopper, J. L., Young, N. R., Formica, C., Goss, P. and Tsalamandris, C. (1996) 'Do genetic factors explain associations between muscle strength, lean mass, and bone density? A twin study', *American Journal of Physiology* 270, E320–7.

Seibert, M. J., Xue, Q. L., Fried, L. P. and Walston, J. D. (2001) 'Polymorphic variation in the human myostatin (GDF–8) gene and association with strength measures in the Women's Health and Aging Study II cohort', *Journal of the American Geriatrics Society* 49, 1093–6.

Shapiro, L. E., Samuels, H. H. and Yaffe, B. M. (1978) 'Thyroid and glucocorticoid hormones synergistically control growth hormone mRNA in cultured GH1 cells', *Proceedings of the National Academy of Sciences USA* 75, 45–9.

Shenoy, U. and Cassis, L. (1997) 'Characterization of renin activity in brown adipose tissue', *American Journal of Physiology* 272, C989–99.

Siegel, S. G., Patton, B. and English, A. W., (2000) 'Ciliary neurotrophic factor is required for motoneuron sprouting', *Experimental Neurology* 166, 205–12.

Skinner, J. S., Jaskolski, A., Jaskolska, A., Krasnoff, J., Gagnon, J., Leon, A. S., Rao, D. C., Wilmore, J. H. and Bouchard, C. (2001) 'Age, sex, race, initial fitness, and response to training: the HERITAGE Family Study', *Journal of Applied Physiology* 90, 1770–6.

Sonna, L. A., Sharp, M. A., Knapik, J. J., Cullivan, M., Angel, K. C., Patton, J. F. and Lilly, C. M. (2001) 'Angiotensin-converting enzyme genotype and physical performance during US Army basic training', *Journal of Applied Physiology* 91, 1355–63.

Soubrier, F., Martin, S., Alonso, A., Visvikis, S., Tiret, L., Matsuda, F., Lathrop, G. M. and Farrall, M. (2002) 'High-resolution genetic mapping of the ACE-linked QTL influencing circulating ACE activity', *European Journal of Human Genetics* 10, 553–61.

Szabo, G., Dallmann, G., Muller, G., Patthy, L., Soller, M. and Varga, L. (1998) 'A deletion in the myostatin gene causes the compact (Cmpt) hypermuscular mutation in mice', *Mammalian Genome* 9, 671–2.

Taguchi, T., Kishikawa, H., Motoshima, H., Sakai, K., Nishiyama, T., Yoshizato, K., Shirakami, A., Toyonaga, T., Shirontani, T., Araki, E. and Shichiri, M. (2000) 'Involvement of bradykinin in acute exercise-induced increase of glucose uptake and GLUT–4 translocation in skeletal muscle: studies in normal and diabetic humans and rats', *Metabolism* 49, 920–30.

Takala, T. E. and Virtanen, P. (2000) 'Biochemical composition of muscle extracellular matrix: the effect of loading', *Scandinavian Journal of Medicine and Science in Sports* 10, 321–5.

Taylor, R. R., Mamotte, C. D., Fallon, K. and van Bockxmeer, F. M. (1999) 'Elite athletes and the gene for angiotensin-converting enzyme', *Journal of Applied Physiology* 87, 1035–7.

Tsianos, G., Eleftheriou, K. I., Hawe, E., Woolrich, L., Watt, M., Watt, I, Peacock, A., Montgomery, H. E., Grant, S. (2005) 'Performance at altitude and angiotensin I-converting enzyme genotype', *European Journal of Applied Physiology* 93, 630–3.

Timmermans, P. B. and Smith, R. D., (1994) 'Angiotensin II receptor subtypes: selective antagonists and functional correlates', *European Heart Journal* 15 Suppl. D, 79–87.

Vakili, B. A., Okin, P. M. and Devereux, R. B. (2001) 'Prognostic implications of left ventricular hypertrophy', *American Heart Journal* 141, 334–41.

Van Pottelbergh, I., Goemaere, S., Nuytinck, L., De Paepe, A. and Kaufman, J. M. (2001) 'Association of the type I collagen alpha1 Sp1 polymorphism, bone density and upper limb muscle strength in community-dwelling elderly men', *Osteoporos International* 12, 895–901.

van Rossum, E. F., Koper, J. W., Huizenga, N. A., Uitterlinden, A. G., Janssen, J. A., Brinkmann, A. O., Grobbee, D. E., de Jong, F. H., van Duyn, C. M., Pols, H. A. and Lamberts, S. W. (2002) 'A polymorphism in the glucocorticoid receptor gene, which decreases sensitivity to glucocorticoids in vivo, is associated with low insulin and cholesterol levels', *Diabetes* 51, 3128–34.

van Rossum, E. F., Voorhoeve, P. G., te Velde, S. J., Koper, J. W., Delemarre-van de Waal, H. A., Kemper, H. C. and Lamberts, S. W. (2004) 'The ER22/23EK polymorphism in the glucocorticoid receptor gene is associated with a beneficial body composition and muscle strength in young adults', *Journal of Clinical Endocrinology and Metabolism* 89, 4004–9.

Vergara, C. and Ramirez, B. (2004) 'CNTF, a pleiotropic cytokine: emphasis on its myotrophic role', *Brain Research. Brain Research Reviews* 47, 161–73.

Watanabe, K., Fujii, H., Takahashi, T., Kodama, M., Aizawa, Y., Ohta, Y., Ono, T., Hasegawa, G., Naito, M., Nakajima, T., Kamijo, Y., Gonzalez, F. J. and Aoyama, T. (2000) 'Constitutive regulation of cardiac fatty acid metabolism through peroxisome proliferator-activated receptor alpha associated with age-dependent cardiac toxicity', *Journal of Biological Chemistry* 275, 22293–9.

Weiss, R. E. and Refetoff, S. (1996) 'Effect of thyroid hormone on growth. Lessons from the syndrome of resistance to thyroid hormone', *Endocrinology and Metabolism Clinics of North America* 25, 719–30.

Weston, A. R., Karamizrak, O., Smith, A., Noakes, T. D. and Myburgh, K. H. (1999) 'African runners exhibit greater fatigue resistance, lower lactate accumulation, and higher oxidative enzyme activity', *Journal of Applied Physiology* 86, 915–23.

Weston, A. R., Mbambo, Z. and Myburgh, K. H. (2000) 'Running economy of African and Caucasian distance runners', *Medicine and Science in Sports Exercise* 32, 1130–4.

Wicklmayr, M., Dietze, G., Gunther, B., Schifmann, R., Bottger, I., Geiger, R., Fritz, H. and Mehnert, H. (1980) 'The kallikrein-kinin system and muscle metabolism–clinical aspects', *Agents Actions* 10, 339–43.

Wieling, W., Borghols, E. A., Hollander, A. P., Danner, S. A. and Dunning, A. J. (1981) 'Echocardiographic dimensions and maximal oxygen uptake in oarsmen during training', *British Heart Journal* 46, 190–5.

Williams, A. G., Rayson, M. P., Jubb, M., World, M., Woods, D. R., Hayward, M., Martin, J., Humphries, S. E. and Montgomery, H. E. (2000) 'The ACE gene and muscle performance', *Nature* 403, 614.

Winnicki, M., Somers, V. K., Accurso, V., Hoffmann, M., Pawlowski, R., Frigo, G., Visentin, P. and Palatini, P. (2002) 'alpha-Adducin Gly460Trp polymorphism, left ventricular mass and plasma renin activity', *Journal of Hypertension* 20, 1771–7.

Wolfarth, B., Bray, M. S., Hagberg, J. M., Perusse, L., Rauramaa, R., Rivera, M. A., Roth, S. M., Rankinen, T. and Bouchard, C. (2005) 'The human gene map for performance and health-related fitness phenotypes: the 2004 update', *Medicine and Science in Sports Exercise* 37, 881–903.

Wollert, K. C. and Drexler, H. (1999) 'The renin-angiotensin system and experimental heart failure', *Cardiovascular Research* 43, 838–49.

Woods, D. R., Humphries, S. E. and Montgomery, H. E. (2000) 'The ACE I/D polymorphism and human physical performance', *Trends in Endocrinology and Metabolism* 11, 416–20.

Woods, D. R., World, M., Rayson, M. P., Williams, A. G., Jubb, M., Jamshidi, Y., Hayward, M., Mary, D. A., Humphries, S. E. and Montgomery, H. E. (2002) 'Endurance enhancement related to the human angiotensin I-converting enzyme I-D polymorphism is not due to differences in the cardiorespiratory response to training', *European Journal of Applied Physiology* 86, 240–4.

Yang, N., MacArthur, D. G., Gulbin, J. P., Hahn, A. G., Beggs, A. H., Easteal, S. and North, K. (2003) 'ACTN3 genotype is associated with human elite athletic performance', *American Journal of Human Genetics* 73, 627–31.

Young, L. E., Rogers, K. and Wood, J. L. (2005) 'Left ventricular size and systolic function in Thoroughbred racehorses and their relationships to race performance', *Journal of Applied Physiology* 99 (4), 1278–85.

Zeldis, S. M., Morganroth, J. and Rubler, S. (1978) 'Cardiac hypertrophy in response to dynamic conditioning in female athletes', *Journal of Applied Physiology* 44, 849–52.

Zhu, X., McKenzie, C. A., Forrester, T., Nickerson, D. A., Broeckel, U., Schunkert, H., Doering, A., Jacob, H. J., Cooper, R. S. and Rieder, M. J. (2000) 'Localization of a small genomic region associated with elevated ACE', *American Journal of Human Genetics* 67, 1144–53.

Chapter 14

Evidence for the 'natural' east African athlete

Robert A. Scott, William H. Goodwin,
Bezabeh Wolde, Vincent O. Onywera, Mike K. Boit,
William O'Connell and Yannis Pitsiladis

Introduction

When compared to our mammalian cousins, humans are fairly unremarkable in terms of physical performance. The very fastest humans are capable of top sprinting speeds of just over 10 metres per second, while other mammals can achieve speeds nearly three times as fast. However, our capabilities in endurance running (defined as the ability to sustain running for extended periods of time using primarily aerobic metabolism), although not comparable to other mammalian endurance specialists, are unique among the primates. This has led to the belief that our endurance abilities have been central to our evolutionary history (Bramble and Lieberman 2004). Our unique endurance ability relative to the other primates is due to a number of adaptations beneficial to endurance running in the genus *Homo*. Some of these adaptations, such as narrowing of the hips, are traceable in the fossil record to all members of the *Homo* genus. Others, however, such as lengthening of the legs relative to body mass are more recent adaptations, first identifiable in the more recent *Homo erectus*. Further skeletal adaptations such as shortening of the femoral neck to reduce stress during running are specific to *Homo sapiens* (modern humans). These adaptations and their importance in endurance running are reviewed in detail by Bramble and Lieberman (2004). Modern humans exhibit wide variation in every aspect of their physicality. Although the timescales are short (~150,000 years) relative to the age of the *Homo* genus (~2 million years), it is intriguing to consider that some of this human variation could contribute to the variation in endurance running potential between individuals and populations.

In sporting competition, there are many examples of individuals or populations who dominate their particular event. The vast majority of elite athletes will retire without an Olympic medal, yet others win many during illustrious careers. Likewise, some nations are ever-present on the medal podium in certain events at the expense of others. Some examples, such as that of the USA and their domination of basketball, are readily explained by participation rates, coaching, and training provision (Phillips 1976). Others, however, such as the domination of east Africans in distance running are not so readily explained.

Environmental factors appear to be influential in the success of east African runners. As discussed below, evidence that east Africans run long distances to school each day sustains the perception of east Africans as excellent endurance athletes. However, most discussions in the popular media on east African running will allude to the possibility that east Africans have a genetic advantage in distance running. This idea is augmented in the media by the concurrent success of athletes of west African ancestry in sprint-based events. Indeed, as can be seen from Table 14.1, the statistics surrounding the success of African athletes are compelling. Evidence that many of the world's best African runners originate from distinct regions of Ethiopia and Kenya, rather than being evenly distributed throughout (Scott et al. 2003; Onywera et al. 2006), appears to further sustain the notion that the success of east African runners is a genetically mediated phenomenon. It has been proposed that this may reflect a genetic similarity among such populations achieved through selection for an athletic phenotype (Manners 1997) (see Chapter 3 in this book). However, such beliefs are not without implications, not only in augmenting disparities in sport, but also in society. Hoberman (1997) gives a detailed discussion of the origin of the 'natural black athlete' stereotype and the detrimental effects on American society. Of course, history has shown that ideas of racial genetic superiority are dangerous. Despite this, there is a common perception that 'black' athletes have some form of genetic advantage in athletic competition (Entine 2001).

When stereotypes of black athletic superiority are held by fellow athletes, they ultimately give African athletes a psychological advantage which will serve to perpetuate their current domination (Hamilton 2000). This concept, known as 'stereotype threat' has been proposed to account for some of the inter-population differences in sporting performance (Baker and Horton 2003). Some studies

Table 14.1 Male world records from 100 m to marathon

Distance	Athlete	Time	Ancestral origin
100 m	Asafa Powell (JAM)	9.77s	West Africa
110 m Hurdles	Colin Jackson (GBR)	12.91s	West Africa
200 m	Michael Johnson (USA)	19.32s	West Africa
400 m	Michael Johnson (USA)	43.18s	West Africa
400 m Hurdles	Kevin Young (USA)	46.78s	West Africa
800 m	Wilson Kipketer (KEN)	1:41.11	East Africa
1,000 m	Noah Ngeny (KEN)	2:11.96	East Africa
1500 m	Hicham El Guerrouj (MOR)	3:26.00	North Africa
Mile	Hicham El Guerrouj (MOR)	3:43.13	North Africa
3,000 m	Daniel Komen(KEN)	7:20.67	East Africa
5,000 m	Kenenisa Bekele (ETH)	12:37.35	East Africa
10,000 m	Kenenisa Bekele (ETH)	26:20.31	East Africa
Marathon	Paul Tergat (KEN)	2:04.55	East Africa

Source: Scott et al. 2003.

have also suggested that success in a task is often based more on the perception of ability rather than actual ability (e.g. Stone *et al.* 1999). The expectation that east African athletes will win most major competitions may well be a self-fulfilling prophecy when it is strongly held by athletes competing to be the first non-African runner, rather than the gold medal winner.

Environmental determinants of east African success

As mentioned previously, and shown in Figures 14.1 and 14.2, east African athletes are not evenly distributed throughout east Africa. Rather, they are concentrated in distinct regions of Ethiopia and Kenya: Arsi and Nandi, respectively. This may appear to support the belief that genetic variation within east Africa influences this distribution; however, Saltin *et al.* (1995b), concluded that geographical and ethnic disparities in athlete production within Kenya

Figure 14.1 Map of Ethiopia showing elite athlete production of each region.

Note: The 14 regions of Ethiopia used in regional classification of Ethiopian athletes and controls are shown. Darkly shaded regions produce a high number of athletes, light shading shows otherwise. The line represents the Rift Valley, and the Central Ethiopian highlands are denoted by triangles.

Source: (Scott *et al.* 2003).

were more likely to be attributable to cultural and environmental rather than genetic differences. Our study of Ethiopian runners, while finding that the athletes were concentrated in certain regions of Ethiopia, concluded that this was likely to be due to environmental and cultural factors (Scott *et al.* 2003). The regions of Ethiopia that produced most athletes were at high altitude (Figure 14.1) and there was an increased prevalence of athletics relative to the other regions. Our findings in Kenya echo those in Ethiopia (Figure 14.2), where an excess of the Kenyan runners are from the Rift Valley Province: again an altitudinous area (Onywera *et al.* 2006). Therein lie other commonly proposed explanations for the success of east African athletes: that their altitudinous habitat is partially responsible for their superior endurance performance.

Many endurance athletes use altitude training to improve performance. The theory behind this is that the lower levels of oxygen at altitude elicit a larger training response and induce positive haematological adaptation to improve oxygen transport (see Wilber 2001 for review). It is presently unclear, however, what, if any, advantage those indigenous to altitude gain for endurance performance. Physiological indices of oxygen transport such as haemoglobin concentrations have been shown to be similar in elite Kenyan and Scandinavian runners (Saltin *et al.* 1995b). It has been suggested, however, that endurance training and altitude combine synergistically in those native to moderate altitude to induce positive haematological adaptation beneficial to endurance performance, and that this may partially account for the success of east African athletes (Schmidt *et al.* 2002). However, the potential benefit to endurance performance gained by those indigenous to altitude requires further research (see Chapter 11).

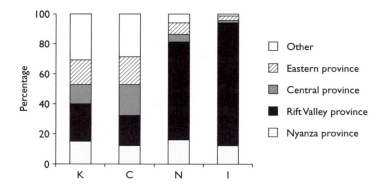

Figure 14.2 Regional distribution of subject groups and general Kenyan population (K).

Note: Regional distribution of controls (C) did not differ from the Kenyan population ($P = 0.23$), but differed from both national (N) ($P < 0.001$) and international athletes (I) ($P = 0.001$). National athletes also differed from international athletes ($P = 0.022$).

Source: Onywera *et al.* 2005.

An interesting finding from the study by Saltin *et al.* (1995b) was that Kenyan boys who were physically active during childhood, using running as a form of transport to and from school but not undertaking any structured training, had 30% higher maximal oxygen uptake ($\dot{V}O_2$ max) than sedentary Kenyan boys (see Chapter 8 for further information). These children were travelling around 90 km per week on foot. It seems therefore that the anecdotal explanation of east African children covering long distances to school, and thereby training for endurance performance may have some validity. The importance of childhood activity in the success of east African runners was echoed in our studies of elite Ethiopian (Scott *et al.* 2003) and Kenyan runners (Onywera *et al.* 2006). Both studies compared the distance and method of travel to school between elite Ethiopian and Kenyan runners and the general population of their respective country. It was found in both studies that the athletes had travelled further to school each day and more had travelled by running than was prevalent in the general population. Figure 14.3 shows the distance travelled to school by national standard athletes, international level athletes and a control group representative of the general Kenyan population. It can be seen that over 80% of the international athletes ran to school as children, compared to less than 20% of the control group (Onywera *et al.* 2006). The athlete groups also travelled further than the control group as shown in Figure 14.4, where it can be seen that half of the international athletes had travelled further than 5 km to school compared to a quarter of controls (Onywera *et al.* 2006). East African children often have to run home to eat during lunch breaks and by doing so can run well in excess of 20 km each day. Such distances are beyond children in western populations, and exceed those that some distance runners may cover as part of a structured training programme. It is likely that such physical activity levels, prevalent in rural east Africa, are influential in the production of so many successful runners. The conclusion by Saltin *et al.* (1995b) was that the success of Kenyan runners, and the Nandi tribe in particular, was probably due to cultural factors such as the success of previous Nandi runners and by the culture of organized training and competition instilled in Nandi schools. A further discussion of the cultural influences on the success of the Nandi can be found in the chapters by Bale and Manners (Chapter 1 and 3). In the quoted environmental studies of Ethiopian and Kenyan athletes, it was also found that the athletes were of a distinct ethnic origin, displaying an excess of athletes of Cushitic origin in Ethiopia and an excess of Bantu athletes in Kenya relative to their source populations (Scott *et al.* 2003; Onywera *et al.* 2006). This may be considered to reflect an underlying genetic phenomenon. However, ethnic groups are not evenly distributed throughout east Africa but are regionally clustered, which makes it difficult to establish which, if any, is the causal factor for the distinct ethnic characteristics of east African athletes relative to their source populations. It may simply be the case that the distinct ethnicity of the athletes relative to controls is a reflection of their geographical clustering in an area that is at altitude.

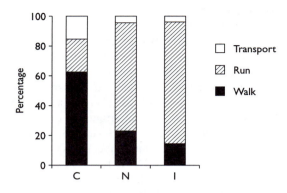

Figure 14.3 Method of travel to school of Kenyan control subjects (C), national athletes (N), and international athletes (I).

Note: The percentage of participants using each method of travel to school is shown. Controls (C) differed significantly from both national (N) and international (I) athlete groups in their distance travelled to school ($P < 0.001$).

Source: Onywera *et al.* 2005.

Physiological determinants of east African success

In attempts to understand the reasons behind the success of east African distance runners, or more generally, black African distance runners, a number of studies have compared physiological characteristics important to distance running between groups of black and white athletes. They have focused on comparing characteristics such as $\dot{V}O_2$ max, lactate accumulation and running economy between groups of black and white athletes. Although covered in greater detail in Chapter 10, black South African athletes were found to have lower lactate levels than white athletes for given exercise intensities (Bosch *et al.* 1990; Coetzer *et al.* 1993; Weston *et al.* 1999). It has also been shown that the black athletes had better running economy (Weston *et al.* 2000) and higher fractional utilization of $\dot{V}O_2$ max at race pace (Bosch *et al.* 1990; Coetzer *et al.* 1993; Weston *et al.* 2000). It has been suggested that if the physiological characteristics of subelite black African distance runners are present in elite African runners, this may help to explain the success of this racial group in distance running (Weston *et al.* 2000). However, this assertion is difficult to reconcile with earlier studies concluding that their findings were compatible with the concept that 'Black male individuals are well endowed to perform in sport events of short duration' (Ama *et al.* 1986: 1760). This conclusion was based on a study comparing skeletal muscle characteristics between 23 sedentary black males from five countries of west and central Africa and 23 Canadian Caucasian males. The finding that the sedentary black males had lower levels of type I muscle fibres (Ama *et al.* 1986) has been suggested to mean that they have a genetic advantage in their muscle fibre type distribution. This finding was not replicated in a further study comparing fibre type in untrained US black and white subjects (Duey *et al*. 1997), where it was concluded that racial differences in fibre type are small relative to the variability of the measure, yet the myth of the 'natural black athlete' pervades. Further studies comparing the performance of sedentary west and central African subjects with sedentary Canadian Caucasian subjects suggested that black subjects are less resistant to fatigue (Ama *et al*. 1990); in contrast to the quoted studies of black South African runners which showed that the black subjects had greater fatigue resistance than the Caucasian runners (Weston *et al*. 1999; Coetzer *et al*. 1993) (see Chapter 10 for further discussion). These contradictions highlight the problem associated with grouping athletes based simply on skin colour. Although these subjects originate from distinct regions of Africa, the results are often construed to reflect black athletes, regardless of their regional or ethnic origins. It is not clear, therefore, to what extent the findings in South African runners can be extrapolated to account for the success of east African runners.

The first study of elite Kenyan athletes was undertaken by Saltin *et al*. (1995b) and compared a number of physiological characteristics that could influenced exercise performance such as $\dot{V}O_2$ max and lactate accumulation between elite Scandinavian and Kenyan athletes. It was found that the Kenyan athletes had lower levels of lactate accumulation and markedly lower ammonia accumulation during graded exercise (see Chapter 8 in this book). A superior running economy was also found in the Kenyan runners, yet $\dot{V}O_2$ max was not different when compared to the Scandinavians. In another study published that

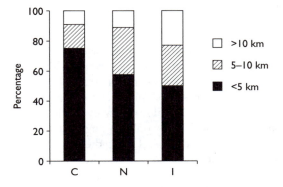

Figure 14.4 Distance travelled to school of Kenyan control subjects (C), national athletes (N), and international athletes (I).

Note: The percentage of participants travelling each distance to school is shown. All groups differed from each other in the distance that they travelled to school (C vs N: $P = 0.01$, C vs I: $P = 0.002$, N vs I: $P = 0.021$).

Source: Onywera *et al*. 2005.

same year by Saltin et al. (1995a), fibre type distribution was not different in elite Kenyan runners (senior and junior) from their Scandinavian counterparts, although the senior Kenyan runners had a statistically non-significant tendency toward higher muscle capillarity than their Scandinavian counterparts. However, the Kenyan junior runners had lower muscle capillarity than both the Scandinavian and Kenyan seniors (Saltin et al. 1995a), suggesting that training, and not genetic endowment, was more likely to be responsible for the higher capillarity of the Kenyan senior runners. These classic studies of elite Kenyan athletes by Saltin et al. (1995a, 1995b) demonstrated that factors such as increased childhood physical activity and hard training were probably the major contributors to the superior performances of these Kenyan runners. As many of the top Kenyan runners are from rural areas, rather than built-up towns and cities (Larsen 2003; Onywera et al. 2006), a recent study by Larsen et al. (2005) investigated the extent to which the $\dot{V}O_2$ max training response differed between Nandi town and village boys. This was designed to investigate if the trainability of $\dot{V}O_2$ max, which has been shown to be genetically influenced (Bouchard et al. 1999), was greater in the Nandi boys from rural areas compared to those from the town. Significantly, the study found that there was no difference between the increase in $\dot{V}O_2$ max of town and village boys. Even more interesting, perhaps, was the finding that the magnitude of the training response was similar to that previously found in Caucasian boys (Fournier et al. 1982), which perhaps demystifies some of the success of the Nandi runners, showing that they may not have an obvious genetic advantage in aerobic capacity.

Human genetic variation

Although physiological studies are required to better understand the factors influencing elite performance, the approach of comparing physiological characteristics between groups defined solely by skin colour does not offer insight into why some groups are more successful than others. Even within groups of similar skin colour, many ethnic and tribal groups exist, and even within these groups, there is considerable variation in physical characteristics. The inadequate classification of subjects into groups based on superficial characteristics such as skin colour will undoubtedly lead to equivocal results without identifying any underlying genetic mechanisms and will serve only to augment existing stereotypes of genetically advantaged black athletes. The studies listed above (Saltin et al. 1995a; Saltin et al. 1995b) offer some insight into the physiological determinants of elite performance and differences between the groups of African and Caucasian runners tested, but offer little insight into any genetic influences on the disproportionate success of east African runners. Despite the perpetuation of the idea that black athletes are genetically adapted for athletic performance (Hamilton and Weston 2000), there is no published evidence to date. The belief that genes are, in part at least, responsible for the success of Kenyan endurance athletes appears in the scientific literature. For example, in a recent review on Kenyan running (Larsen 2003), it is suggested that certain ethnic groups in Kenya have the 'proper genes' for distance running. However, until recently, no studies had attempted to assess this potential genetic effect (Moran et al. 2004; Scott et al. 2005a; Scott et al. 2005b). The concept of black athletic superiority is based on a preconception that each race constitutes a genetically homogeneous group, with race defined simply by skin colour. This belief is contrary to the assertion that there is more genetic variation among Africans than between African and Eurasian populations (Yu et al. 2002). The genetics of race is a controversial topic, which has produced a number of contrasting viewpoints. Some argue that there is a role for race, and that the potential benefits to be gained in terms of diagnosis, treatment and research of disease outweigh the potential social costs of linking race or ethnicity with genetics (Burchard et al. 2003). Others, however, advocate that race should be abandoned as a tool for assessing the prevalence of disease genotypes in certain populations, and that race is not an acceptable surrogate for genetics in assessing the risk of disease and efficacy of treatment in human populations (Cooper et al. 2003). Arguments for the inclusion of race in biomedical research often focus on the use of the term to identify single gene disorders and their medical outcome, and it is acknowledged that the genetic basis of complex phenotypes, such as athletic performance, are poorly understood and far more difficult to study. It is estimated that most human genetic variation is within all humans and that a marginal proportion (normally less than 10%) is confined to major continental groups (Cavalli-Sforza and Feldman 2003). Estimates from the human genome project and analysis of haplotype frequencies show that most haplotypes (linked segments of genetic variation, rarely subject to reassortment by recombination) are shared between two of the three major geographic populations: Europe, Asia and Africa (Gabriel et al. 2002). For example, it is currently estimated that the level of genetic diversity between human populations is not large enough to justify the use of the term race (see Jobling et al. 2004). Consequently, any differences in physiology, biochemistry and/or anatomy between groups defined solely by skin colour (e.g. comparing black with white) are not directly applicable to their source populations, even if the differences found are indeed genetically determined. This is not to say that genetics does not influence the success of east African athletes; it simply means that it is not as simple as black versus white. Studies of the distribution of mitochondrial and Y-Chromosome types in Ethiopia, as discussed below, highlight the fact that even one province of Ethiopia can display a very high level of genetic diversity relative to the entirety of Europe. In fact, based on the 'Out of Africa' hypothesis as discussed below, all non-African populations are composed of subsets of African genetic variation.

Potential genetic determinants of east African success

The capacity to become an elite athlete is not simply a result of physiological conditioning, but a rare, and advantageous, combination of factors: genetic, physiological, biochemical and environmental (Myburgh 2003) (also, see Chapter 9 in this book). Although no evidence exists for a genetic influence on the interpopulation differences in performance, MacArthur and North discuss, in their chapter (Chapter 12), the growing body of evidence to suggest that genetic variation does influence inter-individual variation in athletic performance. They describe the methodologies employed, and discuss the nuclear genome variants associated with physical performance to date. A number of genetic variants have been associated with the ability to sprint, jump high or run fast over long distances, to the extent that at least one company is now marketing a genetic test it claims can 'provide an insight into the best event in which to compete in the sport of your choice, so that the individual can obtain the best results for their effort' (<www.gtg.com.au>). A professional Australian Rugby team has also genotyped 18 of their 24 players for 11 exercise-related genes and are individualizing exercise training to suit the specific needs of their athletes on the basis of their observed genotype. However, research into genetics of performance is at a very early stage and, to date, has not shown any genetic variant to have a strong predictive effect on physical performance (Pitsiladis and Scott 2005). Gene associations may often show an excess of a particular variant in elite athletes relative to controls, but even among elite athletes genetic variation remains.

In addition to nuclear variants, polymorphisms in mitochondrial DNA (mtDNA) have also been suggested to influence the variation in human performance. mtDNA is a small (16,569 bp) genome (found in the mitochondria) which encodes 13 subunits of a number of enzyme complexes of oxidative phosphorylation, as well as components of the mitochondrial protein synthesis system (Anderson et al. 1981). It is subject to a matrilineal pattern of inheritance (mtDNA is inherited in its entirety from mother to child, only changing from mother to child as new mutations arise), which results in the accumulation of linked complexes of mutations down different branches of descent from a single ancestor. This linear pattern of inheritance can be used to trace the ancestral origins of individuals or populations (Richards et al. 2000). mtDNA is also a potential candidate gene for human performance, given that it codes for components of mitochondria, which provide aerobic energy, important in endurance exercise. It is therefore possible that variations in mtDNA could influence the capacity to produce energy. Family-based studies have often shown a strong maternal influence in the heritability of aerobic performance phenotypes such as $\dot{V}O_2$ max (Lesage et al. 1985; Bouchard et al. 1998; Bouchard et al. 1999), which, given its mode of inheritance, may suggest an influence of mtDNA. It has been suggested that polymorphisms in mtDNA are associated with $\dot{V}O_2$ max in the untrained state and with variation in the trainability of $\dot{V}O_2$ max (Dionne et al. 1991). It has also been suggested that polymorphisms in the non-coding region of mtDNA may account for some of the inter-individual variation in aerobic performance (Murakami et al. 2002).

We sought to study the mtDNA variation of elite Ethiopian athletes in order to establish whether mtDNA could be implicated in their success at distance running. This was of particular interest given the extent of mtDNA diversity in Ethiopia; there is a wide variety of mtDNA types present in the modern day Ethiopian population and many of these types are prevalent in east Africa and rarely found elsewhere. Equally, however, a number of mtDNA types are found in Ethiopia that are also found in Europe and Asia. The inheritance pattern of mtDNA allows phylogenetic trees of human evolution to be constructed. A simplified mtDNA tree is shown in Figure 14.5. At the root of this tree is 'Mitochondrial Eve' (mtEve), the common maternal ancestor of all modern humans, who lived in east Africa around 170,000 years ago (Ingman et al. 2000). Each of the descending branches of the tree is known as a haplogroup and is defined by the presence or absence of haplogroup specific polymorphisms. The earliest lineages are known as L1 types, which are almost exclusive to Africa, and are thought to have arisen in east Africa. In Ethiopia, there is a wide variety of mtDNA types belonging in almost equal proportions to all of the major African types (L1, L2 and L3) (Salas et al. 2002). These types are divergent and coalesce around 170,000 years ago in the time of 'mtEve'. Given that athletic success in east Africa is concentrated in particular subsets of the east African population (Scott et al. 2003) it was of interest to establish whether the elite athletes were genetically distinct as defined by their mtDNA types. Given that mtDNA haplogroups are defined by the presence of polymorphisms (as discussed below, some of which may have functional significance), combined with a lack of recombination, if mtDNA polymorphisms were important in the success of Ethiopian distance runners, selection for the mutations beneficial to exercise performance would have led to an increased frequency of the haplogroups which carry the polymorphism amongst elite athletes. Also, as some of the mtDNA haplogroups found commonly in Ethiopia are less frequent outside east Africa, if any of these haplogroups contain beneficial mutants, this would raise the question of whether this may partially account for the success of east African athletes in international distance running. The mtDNA haplogroup distribution of a control group (n = 109) representative of the general Ethiopian population was compared to that of 76 elite Ethiopian endurance athletes competing in distances from 5,000 m to marathon (Scott et al. 2005b). The haplogroup distribution of the control group was similar to data previously published (Passarino et al. 1998; Rando et al. 1998; Semino et al. 2002), with a divergent range of mtDNA haplogroups. Rather than the athletes being restricted to one branch of the tree, they were widespread throughout and did not differ from the control group (Figure 14.5). These findings do not support a role for mtDNA polymorphisms in the success of east Africans at distance running. Furthermore, the

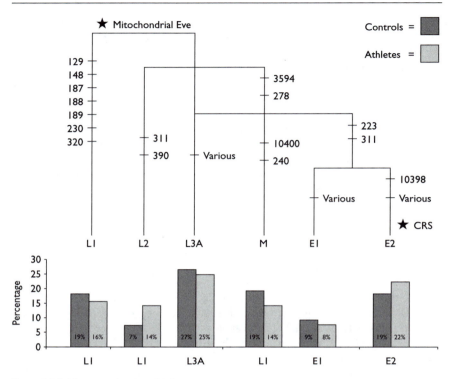

Figure 14.5 Human mitochondrial tree.

Note: Approximate positions of polymorphisms relative to the Cambridge Reference Sequence (CRS) (an arbitrary reference sequence used to compare mtDNA sequences) are shown. (Non-coding polymorphisms are shown minus 16,000.) Haplogroup topology is modelled upon more detailed human phylogenies (Maca-Meyer et al. 2001; Macaulay et al. 1999). Approximate positions of the ancestral mtDNA sequence to all modern humans: 'Mitochondrial Eve', are also shown. The percentage of each subject group belonging to each haplogroup is shown below.

diversity of mtDNA found in the athletes is in contrast to the concept that they are a genetically distinct group, as defined by mtDNA. Some of the athletes share a more recent common mtDNA ancestor with many Europeans than they do with other elite Ethiopian athletes. In addition, no difference in mtDNA haplogroup distribution was found between geographically or ethnically defined groups. When the mtDNA distribution of subjects from the Arsi region of Ethiopia, which produces a disproportionate number of elite athletes (Scott et al. 2003), was compared to that of other regions, it was found that the Arsi population had a mtDNA distribution as equally diverse as other regions. This finding does not support the hypothesis that such populations have remained genetically isolated for long periods of time.

The Y chromosome is the male equivalent of mtDNA, inherited solely from a single sex (i.e. males). Although often ignored in genetic association studies, the

Y chromosome is a potentially interesting candidate to study. While poor in genes and non-essential for survival (given the presence of XX females), it could in principle carry gene variants that might influence physical performance specifically in males, which may explain why the dominance of east African runners is primarily a male phenomenon (i.e. more than a sociological phenomenon linked to participation rates). The haploid nature of the chromosome means that it does not recombine, and thus haplotypes pass undisturbed from one generation to the next, with changes arising only due to new mutations. The availability of a highly resolved phylogeny (Ellis *et al.* 2002) allows Y chromosome haplogroups to be defined, and frequencies of particular haplogroups can then be compared between subject and control groups. Positive associations have previously been reported between specific haplogroups, a number of phenotypes (Jobling and Tyler-Smith 2003), and with ethnic origin (Passarino *et al.* 1998; Underhill *et al.* 2000; Semino *et al.* 2002). It is possible that there is something unique about the distribution of east African Y chromosome haplogroups that could have an influence on endurance performance. Although once thought to be devoid of genes, the male specific region (MSY) is now estimated to contain 156 genes (Skaletsky *et al.* 2003), some of which are expressed throughout the body. Despite this, there are as yet no clear candidates for genes directly affecting athletic ability, with no loci on the Y chromosome having been associated with physical performance (Wolfarth *et al.* 2005).

The association between Y chromosome and endurance athlete status in Ethiopians was studied in an attempt to examine whether elite Ethiopian runners are indeed a genetically distinct group, as defined by the Y chromosome, as may be inferred from the published Ethiopian demographic data (Scott *et al.* 2003). In addition to the control group used in the study of mtDNA, a second control group, comprised of individuals from the Arsi region (known to be the source of a disproportionate number of athletes (Figure 14.1) was used. The athlete cohort was the same as in the mtDNA study (Scott *et al.* 2005b), although confined to males in this instance. The distribution of the Y chromosome haplogroups of the Ethiopian subjects is shown in Figure 14.6. There were significant differences between the general Ethiopian control and the 5–10 km and combined endurance runners (5–10 km and marathon runners), and between the Arsi control and the 5–10 km runners, the marathon runners and the endurance athletes (Both athlete groups combined) as a whole. On deeper investigation, these associations appeared to have been produced by four Haplogroups E*, E3*, E3b1 and K* (xP). Haplogroups E*, E3* and K* (xP) were positively associated with elite performance in one or both endurance events, whilst haplogroup E3b1 was less common in the athletes than the general population. The finding that Y chromosome haplogroups are associated with elite athlete status in Ethiopians suggests that either an element of the Y chromosome genetics is influencing athletic performance, or that the Y chromosome haplogroup distributions were affected by previously unknown population stratification (i.e. the population from which the athletes originate

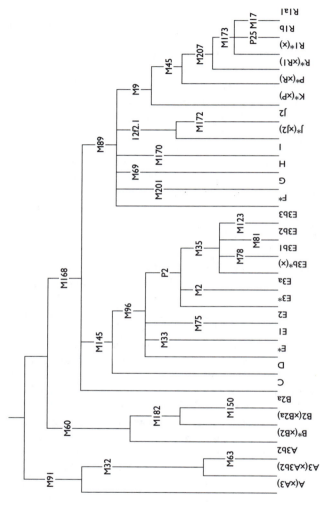

Figure 14.6 Y chromosome distribution of Ethiopian athletes and the general population.

Note: The percentage of each subject group belonging to each haplogroup is shown. The differences between athlete and control groups are shown in **bold**.

has a distinct Y chromosome distribution). However, the range of haplogroups in the athlete groups was similar to that of the two control groups, and haplogroups in both control and athlete groups were similar to those previously identified as being present in Ethiopian samples (Underhill *et al.* 2000; Semino *et al.* 2002). There was also no association found between the Y chromosome haplogroups of the subjects and their place of birth or language family. The observed associations could not, therefore, be readily explained by regional or cultural affiliation, and were less likely to be a result of simple population stratification. If there were something special about the genetics of the Arsi population that was predisposing them to endurance athletics, it may have been expected that the two control groups would be significantly different, and that the endurance athletes would be statistically different from the general control but very similar to the Arsi control. However, no difference was found between the control groups, and more differences were observed between the athletes and Arsi control than between the athletes and the general control (Figure 14.6) suggesting that the athletes were a distinct group. Currently, these haplogroup frequencies are being assessed in our Kenyan cohorts. If the same haplogroups are found to be under/over represented, this would provide strong evidence for a biological effect of the Y chromosome on elite athlete status.

The finding that populations such as those in the Arsi highlands are not arising from a long term, limited genetic isolate, as defined by mtDNA and Y chromosome, does not rule out an influence of genetics on their disproportionate success in distance running. In fact, recent reports on genetically modulated responses to altitude may offer some insight into ways in which genetics may influence their success. Evidence of different strategies to cope with hypobaric hypoxia (Beall 2003) used by geographically isolated indigenous populations may suggest that the unique adaptations of east Africans have some influence on their endurance success (see Chapter 11). Although no direct evidence is available, there are indications that genetic variation may influence the response to high altitude (Mortimer *et al.* 2004). The possibility exists, therefore, that environmental pressure in the form of hypobaric hypoxia has caused selection for variants conferring advantages in oxygen transport. In such high-altitude populations as Ethiopia, this may have the potential to concurrently influence the endurance phenotype. Although unlikely to be a genetic influence isolated to east Africans, it is entirely possible that subtle changes in the frequency of particular candidate genes for human performance in east Africans may have an influence on their disproportionate success. Alleles found in one population are usually common to all human populations, particularly when they occur at a frequency of over 20% in one population (Burchard *et al.* 2003). Alleles that occur at a lower frequency are more likely to be population specific. However, endurance performance is a very complex phenotype, and is reliant upon the successful integration of a number of physiological, biochemical, and biomechanical systems, which themselves are the product of the interaction of a multitude of factors. The success of east African runners is, therefore, unlikely to

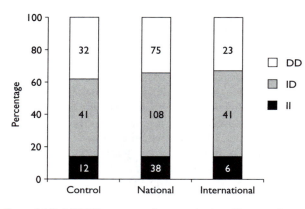

Figure 14.7 ACE I/D genotype frequencies in athletes and controls.

Note: The number of subjects for each genotype is indicated. No significant differences in genotype frequency were present between groups.

be the result of a single gene polymorphism, but it is probable that elite athletes rely on the presence of a combination of advantageous genotypes at a multitude of loci.

The ACE gene and east African Athletes

The chapters by Luery and colleagues (Chapter 12) and MacArthur and North (Chapter 13) summarise the current understanding of nuclear genes and their influence on athletic performance. One of the first, and the most studied, of the putative candidate genes for human performance is the Angiotensin converting enzyme (ACE) gene, where an insertion polymorphism (I) in intron 16 of the gene is associated with lower levels of circulating and tissue ACE than the deletion (D) (Rigat et al. 1990; Danser et al. 1995). Chapter 12 discusses the ACE gene and its functions in detail. In summary, the ACE I/D polymorphism has been associated with performance in mountaineers, where climbers were found to differ significantly from healthy controls in their genotype distribution (Montgomery et al. 1998). It was also shown that homozygotes for the I-allele had an 11-fold greater improvement in a bicep curl movement after training (Montgomery et al. 1998). The belief that the I-allele and, therefore, lower ACE levels improve endurance performance was sustained by the finding that the frequency of the I-allele increased linearly with event duration in a study of runners competing in < 200 m, 400–3,000 m, or > 5,000 m (Myerson et al. 1999). An excess of the I-allele has also been found in elite Australian rowers relative to Australian controls (Gayagay et al. 1998), and in elite Italian aerobic athletes relative to controls (Scanavini et al. 2002). However, these findings have not always been replicated (Rankinen et al. 2000a; Rankinen et al. 2000b). The I-allele of the ACE gene has been implicated as important in high altitude tolerance (Montgomery *et al.* 1998), shown by an increased frequency of Caucasian climbers with at least one I-allele being able to tolerate high altitude. It is plausible, therefore, in high altitude populations, such as those found in east Africa, that there has been a selective advantage for those carrying the I-allele. As discussed above, the I-allele has also been associated with endurance performance, which raises the possibility that the highland east Africans may have been adapted towards endurance performance indirectly. However, the lack of conclusive evidence in the role of the ACE I-allele in endurance performance further attests to the belief that a single gene effect is unlikely to be the final arbiter between success and failure in athletic performance, particularly not in differentiating success among populations, as evidenced by the number of other contributors discussed in other chapters.

ACE I/D genotype frequencies were tested in elite Kenyan athletes relative to the general population (Scott *et al.* 2005a). In east Africans, the association between the I-allele and endurance performance may be complicated further as the I-allele may not be associated with the ACE phenotype (circulating ACE levels) in the same way as in Caucasian populations (Rigat *et al.* 1990). Much of human DNA is non-coding, which is to say it does not code for a protein. The ACE I/D polymorphism is in one of these non-coding regions. ACE I/D is thought to be a genetic marker, which is inherited in concert with another polymorphism elsewhere in the ACE gene that is influencing ACE levels. The two alleles are said to be in complete 'linkage disequilibrium' when they are always inherited together on the same chromosome. The association between I/D and ACE levels has been described in Caucasians (Rigat *et al.* 1990), but

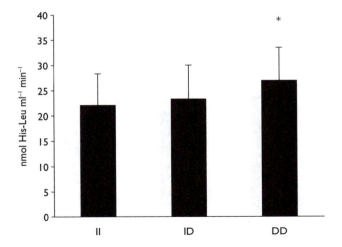

Figure 14.8 Circulating ACE activity levels (mean ± SD) according to I/D genotype.

Note: * indicates significant differences from II and ID groups.

more recent studies in African populations have shown that other variants elsewhere in the ACE gene are more closely associated with circulating ACE levels than the I/D polymorphism (Zhu et al. 2000; Zhu et al. 2001; Cox et al. 2002). A polymorphism elsewhere in the ACE gene (A22982G in the sequence AF118569 as in Rieder et al. (1999), or 31958 as in Cox et al. (2002)), has been found to show the largest phenotypic differences between genotypes (Zhu et al. 2000). Although all markers tested in Europeans showed significant differences in ACE levels between each genotype (probably due to linkage disequilibrium between genotypes), the most marked difference in ACE levels in both Afro-Caribbean and European subjects was found between genotypes at A22982G. The variant at 22982 has been suggested to be a potential functional variant in influencing ACE levels. Absolute linkage disequilibrium between I/D and 22982 has been shown for Caucasian populations (Soubrier et al. 2002) but not in Africans (Zhu et al. 2000; Cox et al. 2002). The I-allele at I/D has been shown to be in linkage disequilibrium with the A allele at A22982G and the D with the G, respectively (Soubrier et al. 2002). Consequently, the A allele has been associated with lower circulating ACE levels than the G allele (Cox et al. 2002; Soubrier et al. 2002). Given that the two variants are not in complete linkage disequilibrium in Africans, it was necessary to test for both variants in the athletes and controls.

For the study of elite Kenyan athletes and their ACE gene variation, 291 elite Kenyan endurance athletes (232 male, 59 female) and 85 control subjects (40 male, 45 female) were analysed for genotype at the I/D polymorphism and

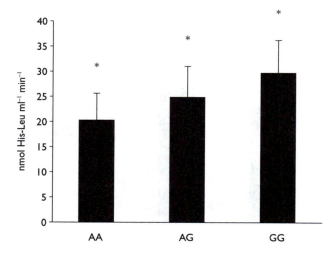

Figure 14.9 Circulating ACE activity levels (mean ± SD) according to 22982 genotype.

Note: * indicates significant differences between groups. All genotypes differed from each other.

A22982G. Seventy of the athletes (59 male, 11 female) had competed internationally representing Kenya (I, n = 70) and comprised many world-record holders, Olympic, World and Commonwealth champions. Of the 70 athletes, 42 have won Olympic, World or Commonwealth medals, have had a top three finish in an international marathon or equivalent road race, or have been ranked in the top 50 runners in the world at their event. Other athletes, classified as National (N), had competed at national level within Kenya (n = 221, 173 male, 48 female). All athletes had competed in distances from 3,000 m to marathon, where the energy source is predominantly aerobic. I/D genotype frequencies were similar in both athlete groups and controls (Figure 14.7). No significant differences were found in genotype frequencies between subject groups. As can be seen, the athletes showed no over-representation of II or AA genotypes as may have been expected from previous findings. However, the negative results may have been the result of a lack of linkage disequilibrium between the I/D polymorphism and the functional variant. It is known that the 22982 polymorphism shows the largest intergenotype difference in ACE levels, and it may be a functional polymorphism. This was supported when the ACE levels of controls was tested between I/D and 22982 genotypes. It can be seen from Figures 14.8 and 14.9 that 22982 genotype explains more of the variation in ACE levels and that there is a larger difference in ACE levels between genotypes at 22982. Genotype frequency at this polymorphism was then tested in athletes and controls to establish any frequency difference between them. Figure 14.10 shows that there was no significant difference in genotype frequency between athletes and controls. While the current controversy over the influence of ACE genotype on endurance performance persists, our study does not support a role for ACE gene variation in inter-individual or inter-population differences

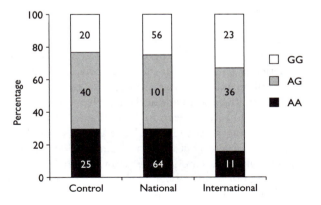

Figure 14.10 ACE 22982 genotype frequencies in athletes and controls.

Note: The number of subjects for each genotype is indicated. No significant differences in genotype frequency were present between groups.

in endurance performance. The absence of an association between the I/D polymorphism or genotype at A22982G with elite Kenyan athlete status also suggests that the ACE gene does not contribute significantly to the phenomenal success of Kenyan endurance runners in international distance running competition. Whether other nuclear genes are involved remains to be determined.

Conclusions

Previously identified performance genes do not appear to influence the success of east African athletes. Furthermore, the athletes, although arising from distinct geographic regions of east Africa, are not from a limited genetic isolate. It can be concluded, therefore, that at present there is no evidence that genetics plays a role in the determination of east African running success, and that any genetic effect is more likely to be as a result of an increased frequency of a particular candidate gene, not unique to east Africa, but conferring advantage in any population. Any allele that is having a major influence on the success of east Africans is likely to be present in other continental populations. For example, the E and K Y chromosome types found in excess in elite Ethiopian athletes are also found in parts of Europe and Asia. This highlights another important point surrounding the genetics of exercise performance. In most studies looking at the influence of genetic variation on performance, even in the most successful of athletes, genetic variation remains. It is normally the case that a particular genetic variant is more frequent in the elite athletes relative to a control population. Although this may satisfy the statistical requirement of $P < 0.05$, the biological importance remains to be elucidated. This highlights the fact that when any genetic influence on elite performance is considered, it is not a simple case of if you have the good gene variant, you will be successful, but if you do not you cannot achieve true success. It is likely that any single gene that offers advantage influences the fine-tuning of performance rather than simply conferring success or failure. The idea that genetics limits our performance is attractive, as most people remember school sports day where some children seemed innately more talented than others. Although there is likely to be some truth in the belief that genetics is partly responsible, currently, the genetic evidence is not sufficient to confirm it. Using the analogy of a car, it can be considered that all cars have an engine and four wheels, but that certain gene variants may offer a better tuned engine, fuel injection, lighter body, better tyres or any of a multitude of other advantages. Any of these 'gene variants' are likely to be found in excess amongst elite athletes, but the exact combinations needed for international success remain unknown. Another key factor, which is of paramount importance, is that the car must have a driver who is willing to push it to its limits. It is perhaps unlikely that east Africa is producing 'cars' that cannot be matched by those from other areas of the world. It is more likely that, in east Africa, those with a well-tuned engine realize their advantage through using it as children. Few other regions of the world have such high levels of childhood activity combined with such a cultural importance of distance running. This is in stark contrast to most western populations, where the prevalence of childhood obesity is reaching epidemic levels, with inactivity implicated as a major contributor.

The current research on the genetics of elite performance is at a very early stage and is hindered in a large part by technology and financing issues, but also by the difficulties associated with working with elite athletes. Having recently completed the largest collection of DNA samples from world-class athletes, we envisage significant advances leading to a better understanding of the genetic factors underlying the potential to succeed at the highest level of athletic competition. Concurrent to the domination of distance running by elite east African athletes, athletes of west African ancestry dominate sprint events (Table 14.1). Recently, a great number of DNA samples have also been collected from elite USA and west African sprinters in an attempt to better understand the genetics of elite sprint performance. The genetic comparison between elite sprinters (mainly of west African origin) and elite endurance athletes (mainly from east Africa) should reveal invaluable insight as these groups can be considered to be at the opposite extremes of human running performance.

In summary, it is unjustified at present to identify the phenomenon of east African running success as genetically mediated; to justify doing so one must identify the genes that are important. The unsubstantiated concept that east Africans are genetically adapted towards distance running leads to the perception amongst opponents that they are at a disadvantage, which will only serve to perpetuate the myth through stereotype threat. However, the domination of east African athletes is an exceptionally interesting phenomenon, which is likely to be the result of a number of components encompassing all areas of human variation. To this end, the International Centre for East African Running Science (ICEARS <www.icears.org>) has been formed. Those working within the centre aim to better understand the reasons for the success of east African runners, to add enlightenment to the phenomenon and also to better understand the extremes of human performance, by working with many of the finest athletes the world has ever seen.

Acknowledgements

The authors acknowledge the invaluable assistance of the Ethiopian Olympic Committee, the Ethiopian Athletics Federation, and Athletics Kenya. The cooperation of all subjects is greatly appreciated. This research was part funded and supported by The Royal Society, The Carnegie Trust for the Universities of Scotland, and the Wellcome Trust.

Bibliography

Ama, P. F., Lagasse, P., Bouchard, C. and Simoneau, J. A. (1990) 'Anaerobic performances in black and white subjects', *Medicine and Science in Sports and Exercise* 22, 508–11.

Ama, P. F., Simoneau, J. A., Boulay, M. R., Serresse, O., Theriault, G. and Bouchard, C. (1986) 'Skeletal muscle characteristics in sedentary black and Caucasian males', *Journal of Applied Physiology* 61, 1758–61.

Anderson, S., Bankier, A. T., Barrell, B. G., de Bruijn, M. H., Coulson, A. R., Drouin, J., Eperon, I. C., Nierlich, D. P., Roe, B. A., Sanger, F., Schreier, P. H., Smith, A. J., Staden, R. and Young, I. G. (1981) 'Sequence and organization of the human mitochondrial genome', *Nature* 290, 457–65.

Baker, J. and Horton, S. (2003) 'East African running dominance revisited: a role for stereotype threat?' *British Journal of Sports Medicine* 37, 553–5.

Beall, C. M. (2003) 'High-altitude adaptations', *Lancet* 362 Suppl., s14–s15.

Bosch, A. N., Goslin, B. R., Noakes, T. D. and Dennis, S. C. (1990) 'Physiological differences between black and white runners during a treadmill marathon', *European Journal of Applied Physiology: Occupational Physiology* 61, 68–72.

Bouchard, C., An, P., Rice, T., Skinner, J. S., Wilmore, J. H., Gagnon, J., Perusse, L., Leon, A. S. and Rao, D. C. (1999) 'Familial aggregation of $\dot{V}O_2$ max response to exercise training: results from the HERITAGE Family Study', *Journal of Applied Physiology* 87, 1003–8.

Bouchard, C., Daw, E. W., Rice, T., Perusse, L., Gagnon, J., Province, M. A., Leon, A. S., Rao, D. C., Skinner, J. S. and Wilmore, J. H. (1998) 'Familial resemblance for $\dot{V}O_2$ max in the sedentary state: the HERITAGE Family Study', *Medicine and Science in Sports and Exercise* 30, 252–8.

Bramble, D. M. and Lieberman, D. E. (2004) 'Endurance running and the evolution of Homo', *Nature* 432, 345–52.

Burchard, E. G., Ziv, E., Coyle, N., Gomez, S. L., Tang, H., Karter, A. J., Mountain, J. L., Perez-Stable, E. J., Sheppard, D. and Risch, N. (2003) 'The importance of race and ethnic background in biomedical research and clinical practice', *New England Journal of Medicine* 348, 1170–5.

Cavalli-Sforza, L. L. and Feldman, M. W. (2003) 'The application of molecular genetic approaches to the study of human evolution', *Nature Genetics* 33 Suppl, 266–75.

Coetzer, P., Noakes, T. D., Sanders, B., Lambert, M. I., Bosch, A. N., Wiggins, T. and Dennis, S. C. (1993) 'Superior fatigue resistance of elite black South African distance runners', *Journal of Applied Physiology* 75, 1822–7.

Cooper, R. S., Kaufman, J. S. and Ward, R. (2003) 'Race and genomics', *New England Journal of Medicine* 348, 1166–70.

Cox, R., Bouzekri, N., Martin, S., Southam, L., Hugill, A., Golamaully, M., Cooper, R., Adeyemo, A., Soubrier, F., Ward, R., Lathrop, G. M., Matsuda, F. and Farrall, M. (2002) 'Angiotensin–1-converting enzyme (ACE) plasma concentration is influenced by multiple ACE-linked quantitative trait nucleotides', *Human Molecular Genetics* 11, 2969–77.

Danser, A. H., Schalekamp, M. A., Bax, W. A., van den Brink, A. M., Saxena, P. R., Riegger, G. A. and Schunkert, H. (1995) 'Angiotensin-converting enzyme in the human heart. Effect of the deletion/insertion polymorphism', *Circulation* 92, 1387–8.

Dionne, F. T., Turcotte, L., Thibault, M. C., Boulay, M. R., Skinner, J. S. and Bouchard, C. (1991) 'Mitochondrial DNA sequence polymorphism, V̇O₂ max, and response to endurance training', *Medicine and Science in Sports and Exercise* 23, 177–85.

Duey, W. J., Bassett, D. R., Jr, Torok, D. J., Howley, E. T., Bond, V., Mancuso, P. and Trudell, R. (1997) 'Skeletal muscle fibre type and capillary density in college-aged blacks and whites', *Annals of Human Biology* 24, 323–31.

Ellis, N., Hammer, M., Hurles, M. E., Jobling, M. A., Karafet, T., King, T. E., de Knijff, P., Pandya, A., Redd, A., Santos, F. R., Tyler-Smith, C., Underhill, P. A., Wood, E., Thomas, M., Cavalli-Sforza, L., Jenkins, T., Kidd, J., Kidd, J., Forster, P., Zegura, P. and Kaplan, M. (2002) 'A nomenclature system for the tree of human Y-chromosomal binary haplogroups', *Genome Research* 12, 339–48.

Entine, J. (2001) *Taboo: Why Black Athletes Dominate Sports And Why We're Afraid To Talk About It*, New York: PublicAffairs.

Fournier, M., Ricci, J., Taylor, A. W., Ferguson, R. J., Montpetit, R. R. and Chaitman, B. R. (1982) 'Skeletal muscle adaptation in adolescent boys: sprint and endurance training and detraining', *Medicine and Science in Sports and Exercise* 14, 453–6.

Gabriel, S. B., Schaffner, S. F., Nguyen, H., Moore, J. M., Roy, J., Blumenstiel, B., Higgins, J., DeFelice, M., Lochner, A., Faggart, M., Liu-Cordero, S. N., Rotimi, C., Adeyemo, A., Cooper, R., Ward, R., Lander, E. S., Daly, M. J. and Altshuler, D. (2002) 'The structure of haplotype blocks in the human genome', *Science* 296, 2225–9.

Gayagay, G., Yu, B., Hambly, B., Boston, T., Hahn, A., Celermajer, D. S. and Trent, R. J. (1998) 'Elite endurance athletes and the ACE I-allele–the role of genes in athletic performance', *Human Genetics* 103, 48–50.

Hamilton, B. (2000) 'East African running dominance: what is behind it?' *British Journal of Sports Medicine* 34, 391–4.

Hamilton, B. and Weston, A. (2000) 'Perspectives on East African middle and long distance running', *Journal of Science and Medicine in Sport* 3, vi–viii.

Hoberman, J. (1997) *Darwin's Athletes. How Sport has Damaged Black America and Preserved the Myth of Race*, New York: Houghton Mifflin Company.

Ingman, M., Kaessmann, H., Paabo, S. and Gyllensten, U. (2000) 'Mitochondrial genome variation and the origin of modern humans', *Nature* 408, 708–13.

Jobling, M. A., Hurles, M. E. and Tyler-Smith, C. (2004) *Human Evolutionary Genetics*, New York: Garland Publishing.

Jobling, M. A. and Tyler-Smith, C. (2003) 'The human Y chromosome: an evolutionary marker comes of age', *Nature Reviews: Genetics* 4, 598–612.

Larsen, H. B. (2003) 'Kenyan dominance in distance running', *Comparative Biochemistry and Physiology: Part A, Molecular and Integrative Physiology* 136, 161–70.

Larsen, H. B., Nolan, T., Borch, C. and Sondergaard, H. (2005) Training response of adolescent Kenyan town and village boys to endurance running', *Scandinavian Journal of Medicine and Science in Sports* 15, 48–57.

Lesage, R., Simoneau, J. A., Jobin, J., Leblanc, J. and Bouchard, C. (1985) 'Familial resemblance in maximal heart rate, blood lactate and aerobic power', *Human Heredity* 35, 182–9.

Maca-Meyer, N., Gonzalez, A. M., Larruga, J. M., Flores, C. and Cabrera, V. M. (2001) 'Major genomic mitochondrial lineages delineate early human expansions', *BMC Genetics* 2, 13.

Macaulay, V., Richards, M., Hickey, E., Vega, E., Cruciani, F., Guida, V., Scozzari, R., Bonne-Tamir, B., Sykes, B. and Torroni, A. (1999) 'The emerging tree of West

Eurasian mtDNAs: a synthesis of control-region sequences and RFLPs', *American Journal of Human Genetics* 64, 232–9.

Manners, J. (1997) 'Kenya's Running Tribe', *The Sports Historian* 17, 14–27.

Montgomery, H. E., Marshall, R., Hemingway, H., Myerson, S., Clarkson, P., Dollery, C., Hayward, M., Holliman, D. E., Jubb, M., World, M., Thomas, E. L., Brynes, A. E., Saeed, N., Barnard, M., Bell, J. D., Prasad, K., Rayson, M., Talmud, P. J. and Humphries, S. E. (1998) 'Human gene for physical performance', *Nature* 393, 221–2.

Moran, C. N., Scott, R. A., Adams, S. M., Warrington, S. J., Jobling, M. A., Wilson, R. H., Goodwin, W. H., Georgiades, E., Wolde, B. and Pitsiladis, Y. P. (2004) 'Y chromosome haplogroups of elite Ethiopian endurance runners', *Human Genetics* 115, 492–7.

Mortimer, H., Patel, S. and Peacock, A. J. (2004) 'The genetic basis of high-altitude pulmonary oedema', *Pharmacology and Therapeutics* 101, 183–92.

Murakami, H., Ota, A., Simojo, H., Okada, M., Ajisaka, R. and Kuno, S. (2002) 'Polymorphisms in control region of mtDNA relates to individual differences in endurance capacity or trainability', *Japanese Journal of Physiology* 52, 247–56.

Myburgh, K. H. (2003) 'What makes an endurance athlete world-class? Not simply a physiological conundrum', *Comparative Biochemistry and Physiology: Part A, Molecular and Integrative Physiology* 136, 171–90.

Myerson, S., Hemingway, H., Budget, R., Martin, J., Humphries, S. and Montgomery, H. (1999) 'Human angiotensin I-converting enzyme gene and endurance performance', *Journal of Applied Physiology* 87, 1313–16.

Onywera, V. O., Scott, R. A., Boit, M. K. and Pitsiladis, Y. P. (2006) 'Demographic characteristics of elite Kenyan endurance runners', *Journal of Sports Sciences* 24 (4), 415–22.

Passarino, G., Semino, O., Quintana-Murci, L., Excoffier, L., Hammer, M. and Santachiara-Benerecetti, A. S. (1998) 'Different genetic components in the Ethiopian population, identified by mtDNA and Y-chromosome polymorphisms', *American Journal of Human Genetics* 62, 420–34.

Phillips, J. C. (1976) 'Racial variation in sports participation', *International Review of Sport Sociology* 3, 39–53.

Pitsiladis, Y. P. and Scott, R. (2005) 'Essay: The makings of the perfect athlete', *Lancet* 366 Suppl. 1, S16–S17.

Rando, J. C., Pinto, F., Gonzalez, A. M., Hernandez, M., Larruga, J. M., Cabrera, V. M. and Bandelt, H. J. (1998) 'Mitochondrial DNA analysis of northwest African populations reveals genetic exchanges with European, near-eastern, and sub-Saharan populations', *Annals of Human Genetics* 62 (Pt 6), 531–50.

Rankinen, T., Perusse, L., Gagnon, J., Chagnon, Y. C., Leon, A. S., Skinner, J. S., Wilmore, J. H., Rao, D. C. and Bouchard, C. (2000a) 'Angiotensin-converting enzyme ID polymorphism and fitness phenotype in the HERITAGE Family Study', *Journal of Applied Physiology* 88, 1029–35.

Rankinen, T., Wolfarth, B., Simoneau, J. A., Maier-Lenz, D., Rauramaa, R., Rivera, M. A., Boulay, M. R., Chagnon, Y. C., Perusse, L., Keul, J. and Bouchard, C. (2000b) 'No association between the angiotensin-converting enzyme ID polymorphism and elite endurance athlete status', *Journal of Applied Physiology* 88, 1571–5.

Richards, M., Macaulay, V., Hickey, E., Vega, E., Sykes, B., Guida, V., Rengo, C., Sellitto, D., Cruciani, F., Kivisild, T., Villems, R., Thomas, M., Rychkov, S., Rychkov, O., Rychkov, Y., Golge, M., Dimitrov, D., Hill, E., Bradley, D., Romano,

V., Cali, F., Vona, G., Demaine, A., Papiha, S., Triantaphyllidis, C., Stefanescu, G., Hatina, J., Belledi, M., Di Rienzo, A., Novelletto, A., Oppenheim, A., Norby, S., Al Zaheri, N., Santachiara-Benerecetti, S., Scozari, R., Torroni, A. and Bandelt, H. J. (2000) 'Tracing European founder lineages in the Near Eastern mtDNA pool', *American Journal of Human Genetics* 67, 1251–76.

Rieder, M. J., Taylor, S. L., Clark, A. G. and Nickerson, D. A. (1999) 'Sequence variation in the human angiotensin converting enzyme', *Nature Genetics* 22, 59–62.

Rigat, B., Hubert, C., Alhenc-Gelas, F., Cambien, F., Corvol, P. and Soubrier, F. (1990) 'An insertion/deletion polymorphism in the angiotensin I-converting enzyme gene accounting for half the variance of serum enzyme levels', *Journal of Clinical Investigation* 86, 1343–6.

Salas, A., Richards, M., De la, F. T., Lareu, M. V., Sobrino, B., Sanchez-Diz, P., Macaulay, V. and Carracedo, A. (2002) 'The making of the African mtDNA landscape', *American Journal of Human Genetics* 71, 1082–111.

Saltin, B., Kim, C. K., Terrados, N., Larsen, H., Svedenhag, J. and Rolf, C. J. (1995a) 'Morphology, enzyme activities and buffer capacity in leg muscles of Kenyan and Scandinavian runners', *Scandinavian Journal of Medicine and Science in Sports* 5, 222–30.

Saltin, B., Larsen, H., Terrados, N., Bangsbo, J., Bak, T., Kim, C. K., Svedenhag, J. and Rolf, C. J. (1995b) 'Aerobic exercise capacity at sea level and at altitude in Kenyan boys, junior and senior runners compared with Scandinavian runners', *Scandinavian Journal of Medicine and Science in Sports* 5, 209–21.

Scanavini, D., Bernardi, F., Castoldi, E., Conconi, F. and Mazzoni, G. (2002) 'Increased frequency of the homozygous II ACE genotype in Italian Olympic endurance athletes', *European Journal of Human Genetics* 10, 576–7.

Schmidt, W., Heinicke, K., Rojas, J., Manuel, G. J., Serrato, M., Mora, M., Wolfarth, B., Schmid, A. and Keul, J. (2002) 'Blood volume and hemoglobin mass in endurance athletes from moderate altitude', *Medicine and Science in Sports and Exercise* 34, 1934–40.

Scott, R. A., Georgiades, E., Wilson, R. H., Goodwin, W. H., Wolde, B. and Pitsiladis, Y. P. (2003) 'Demographic characteristics of elite Ethiopian endurance runners', *Medicine and Science in Sports and Exercise* 35, 1727–32.

Scott, R. A., Moran, C., Wilson, R. H., Onywera, V., Boit, M. K., Goodwin, W. H., Gohlke, P., Payne, J., Montgomery, H. and Pitsiladis, Y. P. (2005a) 'No association between Angiotensin Converting Enzyme (ACE) gene variation and endurance athlete status in Kenyans', *Comparative Biochemistry and Physiology: Part A, Molecular and Integrative Physiology* 141, 169–75.

Scott, R. A., Wilson, R. H., Goodwin, W. H., Moran, C. N., Georgiades, E., Wolde, B. and Pitsiladis, Y. P. (2005b) 'Mitochondrial DNA lineages of elite Ethiopian athletes', *Comparative Biochemistry and Physiology: Part B, Biochemistry and Molecular Biology* 140, 497–503.

Semino, O., Santachiara-Benerecetti, A. S., Falaschi, F., Cavalli-Sforza, L. L. and Underhill, P. A. (2002) 'Ethiopians and Khoisan share the deepest clades of the human Y-chromosome phylogeny', *American Journal of Human Genetics* 70, 265–8.

Skaletsky, H., Kuroda-Kawaguchi, T., Minx, P. J., Cordum, H. S., Hillier, L., Brown, L. G., Repping, S., Pyntikova, T., Ali, J., Bieri, T., Chinwalla, A., Delehaunty, A., Delehaunty, K., Du, H., Fewell, G., Fulton, L., Fulton, R., Graves, T., Hou, S. F., Latrielle, P., Leonard, S., Mardis, E., Maupin, R., McPherson, J., Miner, T., Nash, W.,

Nguyen, C., Ozersky, P., Pepin, K., Rock, S., Rohlfing, T., Scott, K., Schultz, B., Strong, C., Tin-Wollam, A., Yang, S. P., Waterston, R. H., Wilson, R. K., Rozen, S. and Page, D. C. (2003) 'The male-specific region of the human Y chromosome is a mosaic of discrete sequence classes', *Nature* 423, 825–37.

Soubrier, F., Martin, S., Alonso, A., Visvikis, S., Tiret, L., Matsuda, F., Lathrop, G. M. and Farrall, M. (2002) 'High-resolution genetic mapping of the ACE-linked QTL influencing circulating ACE activity', *European Journal of Human Genetics* 10, 553–61.

Stone, J., Lynch, C., Sjomeling, M. and Darley, J. M. (1999) 'Stereotype threat effects on black and white athletic performance', *Journal of Personality and Social Psychology* 77, 1213–27.

Underhill, P. A., Shen, P., Lin, A. A., Jin, L., Passarino, G., Yang, W. H., Kauffman, E., Bonne-Tamir, B., Bertranpetit, J., Francalacci, P., Ibrahim, M., Jenkins, T., Kidd, J. R., Mehdi, S. Q., Seielstad, M. T., Wells, R. S., Piazza, A., Davis, R. W., Feldman, M. W., Cavalli-Sforza, L. L. and Oefner, P. J. (2000) 'Y chromosome sequence variation and the history of human populations', *Nature Genetics* 26, 358–61.

Weston, A. R., Karamizrak, O., Smith, A., Noakes, T. D. and Myburgh, K. H. (1999) 'African runners exhibit greater fatigue resistance, lower lactate accumulation, and higher oxidative enzyme activity', *Journal of Applied Physiology* 86, 915–23.

Weston, A. R., Mbambo, Z. and Myburgh, K. H. (2000) 'Running economy of African and Caucasian distance runners', *Medicine and Science in Sports and Exercise* 32, 1130–4.

Wilber, R. L. (2001) 'Current trends in altitude training', *Sports Medicine* 31, 249–65.

Wolfarth, B., Bray, M. S., Hagberg, J. M., Perusse, L., Rauramaa, R., Rivera, M. A., Roth, S. M., Rankinen, T. and Bouchard, C. (2005) 'The human gene map for performance and health-related fitness phenotypes: the 2004 update', *Medicine and Science in Sports and Exercise* 37, 881–903.

Yu, N., Chen, F. C., Ota, S., Jorde, L. B., Pamilo, P., Patthy, L., Ramsay, M., Jenkins, T., Shyue, S. K. and Li, W. H. (2002) 'Larger genetic differences within Africans than between Africans and Eurasians', *Genetics* 161, 269–74.

Zhu, X., Bouzekri, N., Southam, L., Cooper, R. S., Adeyemo, A., McKenzie, C. A., Luke, A., Chen, G., Elston, R. C. and Ward, R. (2001) 'Linkage and association analysis of angiotensin I-converting enzyme (ACE)-gene polymorphisms with ACE concentration and blood pressure', *American Journal of Human Genetics* 68, 1139–48.

Zhu, X., McKenzie, C. A., Forrester, T., Nickerson, D. A., Broeckel, U., Schunkert, H., Doering, A., Jacob, H. J., Cooper, R. S. and Rieder, M. J. (2000) 'Localization of a small genomic region associated with elevated ACE', *American Journal of Human Genetics* 67, 1144–53.

Index

eBooks – at www.eBookstore.tandf.co.uk

A library at your fingertips!

eBooks are electronic versions of printed books. You can store them on your PC/laptop or browse them online.

They have advantages for anyone needing rapid access to a wide variety of published, copyright information.

eBooks can help your research by enabling you to bookmark chapters, annotate text and use instant searches to find specific words or phrases. Several eBook files would fit on even a small laptop or PDA.

NEW: Save money by eSubscribing: cheap, online access to any eBook for as long as you need it.

Annual subscription packages

We now offer special low-cost bulk subscriptions to packages of eBooks in certain subject areas. These are available to libraries or to individuals.

For more information please contact webmaster.ebooks@tandf.co.uk

We're continually developing the eBook concept, so keep up to date by visiting the website.

www.eBookstore.tandf.co.uk